RACE, PLACE, AND ENVIRONMENTAL JUSTICE AFTER HURRICANE KATRINA

RACE, PLACE, AND ENVIRONMENTAL JUSTICE AFTER HURRICANE KATRINA

STRUGGLES TO RECLAIM, REBUILD, AND REVITALIZE NEW ORLEANS AND THE GULF COAST

▼

EDITED BY

ROBERT D. BULLARD, PH.D.
CLARK ATLANTA UNIVERSITY

BEVERLY WRIGHT, PH.D.
DILLARD UNIVERSITY

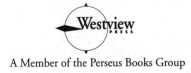

A Member of the Perseus Books Group

Designed by Trish Wilkinson
Set in 10 point Adobe Garamond

Library of Congress Cataloging-in-Publication Data
    Race, place, and environmental justice after Hurricane Katrina : struggles to reclaim, rebuild, and revitalize New Orleans and the Gulf Coast / edited by Robert D. Bullard, Beverly Wright.
        p.   cm.
    Includes bibliographical references and index.
    ISBN 978-0-8133-4424-9 (pbk. : alk. paper) 1. Emergency management—Louisiana—New Orleans. 2. Crisis management—Louisiana—New Orleans. 3. Disaster relief—Louisiana—New Orleans. 4. Hurricane Katrina, 2005. I. Bullard, Robert D. (Robert Doyle), 1946– II. Wright, Beverly, Ph.D.
    HV551.4.R34 2009
    976.3'35064—dc22   2008044517

10   9   8   7   6   5   4   3

CONTENTS

TABLES AND FIGURES

TABLES

FIGURES

ACRONYMS AND ABBREVIATIONS

AAA	African American Agenda
AALP	African-American Leadership Project
ACORN	Association of Community Organizations for Reform Now
AHC	ACORN Housing Corporation
ARNO	Animal Rescue New Orleans
ATSDR	Agency for Toxic Substances and Disease Registry
BFI	Browning Ferries Industries
BNOB	Bring New Orleans Back Commission
CBOR	The Citizens' Bill of Rights
C&D	Construction and Demolition
CDBG	Community Development Block Grant
CDC	Centers for Disease Control and Prevention
CERCLA or Superfund	Comprehensive Environmental Response, Compensation, and Liability Act
CIDA	Community In-Power Development Association
CPS	Current Population Survey
CSC	Churches Supporting Churches
CWA	Clean Water Act
DHS	U.S. Department of Homeland Security
DOJ	U.S. Department of Justice
DOT	U.S. Department of Transportation
DSCEJ	Deep South Center for Environmental Justice at Dillard University
EDS	Emergency Disaster Services
EJ	Environmental Justice
EPA	U.S. Environmental Protection Agency
ESI	Expanded Site Inspection
FEMA	Federal Emergency Management Agency
FHA	Federal Housing Administration
FTA	Federal Transit Administration
GAO	U.S. Government Accountability Office

GCM	Global Community Monitor
GIS	Geographic Information System
GNOFHAC	Greater New Orleans Fair Housing Action Center
GNOF	Greater New Orleans Foundation
GSA	General Services Administration
HANO	Housing Authority of New Orleans
HPC	Heterotrophic Plate Count
HRS	Hazard Ranking System
HUD	U.S. Department of Housing and Urban Development
IG	Inspector General
IHP	Individuals and Households Program
ISTEA	Intermodal Surface Transportation Efficiency Act of 1991
IWJ	Interfaith Worker Justice
LABB	Louisiana Bucket Brigade
LDEQ	Louisiana Department of Environmental Quality
LIHTC	Low-Income Housing Tax Credits
LMI	low-to-moderate income
LRA	Louisiana Recovery Authority
MPO	Metropolitan Planning Organization
NAACP	National Association for the Advancement of Colored People
NCBC	National Construction Battalion Center
NCC	National Council of Churches
NCP	National Contingency Plant
NEPA	National Environmental Policy Act
NFHA	National Fair Housing Alliance
NFIP	National Flood Insurance Program
NIMBY	Not In My Back Yard
NOPS	New Orleans Public Schools
NORA	New Orleans Redevelopment Agency
NORSD	New Orleans Recovery School District
NORTA	New Orleans Rapid Transit Authority
NPL	National Priorities List
NRC	National Research Council
NRCA	National Roofing Contractors Association
NRDC	Natural Resources Defense Council
OMB	Office of Management and Budget
OPA	Oil Pollution Act
OPSRRP	Orleans Parish Strategic Recovery and Revitalization Plan
ORDA	Office of Recovery and Development Administration
PAHs	Polyaromatic Hydrocarbons
PCIE	President's Council on Integrity and Efficiency
POGO	Project on Government Oversight
RCRA	Resource Conservation and Recovery Act

SAFETEA	Safe, Accountable, Flexible, Efficient Transportation Equity Act
SARA	Superfund Amendment and Reauthorization Act
SBA	U.S. Small Business Administration
SCI	Service Corporation International
SCLC	Southern Christian Leadership Conference
SDWA	Safe Drinking Water Act
SI	Site Inspection
S&WB	New Orleans Sewerage and Water Board
TCCI	Turkey Creek Community Initiatives
TCS	Taxpayers for Common Sense
TEA-21	Transportation Equity Act for the Twenty-First Century
TEJAS	Texas Environmental Justice Advocacy Services
TRB	Transportation Research Board
USEPA	U.S. Environmental Protection Agency
USGAO	U.S. Government Accountability Office
USW	United Steel Workers
VA	Veterans Administration

ACKNOWLEDGMENTS

This book grew out of the two "Race, Place, and Environment" symposia held at Dillard University in New Orleans in October 2006 and May 2008. Both events were convened to broaden and deepen our understanding of the environmental justice and health-equity implications of Hurricane Katrina and the efficacy of plans underway to reclaim, rebuild, and revitalize areas in New Orleans and the Gulf Coast ravaged by the 2005 storm.

We would like to thank all of the individuals who helped stimulate interest in post-Katrina New Orleans and the Gulf Coast through their participation in the symposia, including several members of our national planning committee, Cecil Corbin-Mark and Peggy Shepard, WE ACT, Inc., Vernice Miller-Travis, Environmental Support Center, and Donele Wilkins, Detroiters Working for Environmental Justice and the National Black Environmental Justice Network, and the contributors who endured the harassment and gentle nudges to keep us on track.

A special thanks to Michelle DePass at the Ford Foundation, Earthea Nance at the New Orleans Office of Recovery and Development Administration, Terri Wright at the W. K. Kellogg Foundation, Daria Neal, the Lawyer's Committee for Civil Rights Under the Law, Monique Harden and Nathalie Walker, Advocates for Environmental Human Rights, James Carr of the Fannie Mae Foundation, and Midge Taylor of the Public Welfare Foundation for their generous support in helping sponsor the symposia and the book project.

We also thank our able staff at the Deep South Center for Environmental Justice at Dillard University (Myra M. Lewis, Mary Williams, and Celeste Cooper) and the Environmental Justice Resource Center at Clark Atlanta University (Glenn S. Johnson and Angel O. Torres) for helping make this project successful.

FOREWORD

Marc H. Morial, President and CEO,
National Urban League

I remember exactly where I was, exactly what I was doing, and precisely who I was with when I first heard the dreadful news of the impending storm and when Hurricane Katrina finally hit the Gulf Coast of the United States. It pounded the shores in ravaging waves and viscerally pounded our collective psyche as we all witnessed with shock and horror a natural disaster, long anticipated and feared. The shock was followed by dismay as the man-made catastrophe dramatically played out, long after the cruel rains stopped and the waters began to slowly recede.

As a native son of New Orleans, my heart mourned the loss of life. I grieved for the people and the familiar places that were literally washed away forever, along with memorabilia that symbolized vast parts of our history and heritage never to be recovered again. I grieved for the people who unduly suffered waiting for food, drinking water, and rescue—people who literally waited for five days! For many, the rescue efforts came far too late, needless deaths that could have been prevented. I grieved for the loss of property and commerce in the Gulf Coast States: Louisiana, Mississippi, and Alabama. And I grieved for the mass exodus that amounted to the displacement of thousands of individuals and families now dispersed in cities across the nation. In truth, words cannot describe the utter disbelief and heartache that I still feel.

Hurricane Katrina was an insufferable tragedy that will never be forgotten. It destroyed not only lives but the illusion that some may have had that all is well on the policy-making level of preparing for disasters and catastrophes. It also exposed issues of inequity concerning race and class which painfully still exist in this country— issues that still need to be addressed and rectified.

Several years have passed since Hurricane Katrina struck and devastated New Orleans, but not a day goes by that I do not think of the awful tragedy that besieged the city that bore and raised me. As a native son of New Orleans, I feel deeply connected to the people there and those scattered across the country, all of whom I hold dear, and who continue to face the devastating and deadly economic and environmental aftershocks of Hurricane Katrina.

On a recent trip back to New Orleans, I spent some time surveying the damage to my mother's home. As I looked around at the house and surrounding land, I was overcome by a bitter mixture of nostalgia, sadness, anger, and the feeling that my native city had been abandoned by the government—doomed to become a modern-day Pompeii.

In my many conversations with family, friends, residents, and evacuees of New Orleans, I know that I am not alone in sometimes feeling a sense of utter hopelessness. Hopelessness is a natural human reaction to tragedy, and the magnitude of the tragedy of Katrina's wake guarantees profound and inexplicable despair impossible to deny. Yet, we must not succumb to despair. We must remember that hopelessness is the precursor to hope and that hope is the breeding ground for strength and courage.

The challenge of rebuilding, revitalizing, and restoring New Orleans and bringing people back home is a daunting mission but not an impossible one. Our rich heritage has taught us that nothing is impossible, as long as we remain steadfast, unified, and determined.

Hurricane Katrina has brought out our collective resilience. In the midst of tragedy we discovered and continue to discover the opportunity to learn, grow, and become stronger; to help our brothers and sisters in need; to strengthen our ties to our families and community; and to deepen our commitment and resolve to raise the funds necessary to help the most disadvantaged citizens get back on their feet.

But the work is far from over, homes need to be rebuilt and adequate, safe housing secured for the thousands of families still in FEMA trailers. Schools need to be rebuilt, and most importantly a master plan needs to be put securely in place to move evacuees back to New Orleans, into their rightful homes and into gainful employment.

As president and CEO of the National Urban League, I have staunchly advocated for the Katrina Bill of Rights, a National Urban League initiative that outlines policy recommendations to restore the city of New Orleans and Katrina survivors to full citizenship. The Katrina Bill of Rights consists of the following elements:

THE RIGHT TO RECOVER

The people of the Gulf Coast must be guaranteed the right to recover. To do that, they need immediate help to get back on their feet and rebuild their lives through extended unemployment assistance, a Katrina Victims Compensation Fund, and an independent nonpartisan commission to find out what went wrong.

THE RIGHT TO VOTE

We must secure the right to vote for the people of the Gulf Coast and assure that they have full voting rights in their home states. Katrina may have knocked over buildings, but we must not let it weaken the foundation of our democracy. The ballot is the best way to ensure that our displaced citizens have the voice they want—and deserve—in the rebuilding of their communities.

THE RIGHT TO RETURN

We must guarantee to every evacuee and every resident the right to return to their home. Every family should have the chance to come back to their hometown or neighborhood if they so choose. The Katrina Bill of Rights advocates that Congress institute a federal tax holiday for three years for returning Gulf residents making under $50,000 a year; provide a 50 percent tax holiday to businesses who pay their workers a living wage; and ensure homeowners have the right of first refusal to reclaim property. These are their homes—washed out or not.

THE RIGHT TO REBUILD

Every resident of the Gulf Coast has the right to rebuild and have a say in what the future of their home will be. Rebuilding the Gulf Coast around the principle of equal opportunity for all means that, as we rebuild, we must not tear down what has made us strong. We must not "pay for Katrina" by cutting Medicaid, education, and job training programs . . . increasing Medicare premiums . . . and gutting rural economic development efforts. Paying for the rebuilding on the backs of those whose lives are already ruined only adds insult to injury.

We must rebuild the Gulf in a way that doesn't benefit only the big contractors or big real estate developers . . . that doesn't divide us, but unites us . . . that doesn't turn New Orleans or Gulfport into gated communities, but that breaks down the barriers to success for all those who live there. We should institute a moratorium on collections and deficiency judgments on real and personal properties and prohibit negative credit reporting or the omission of negative events from credit scores when the incidents were a result of Katrina.

We need to encourage financial institutions to forbear on all loans and mortgages until people can move back and *live* in their homes. We must protect the people of the Gulf Coast from predatory lenders. And we should freeze all foreclosure proceedings against property in affected areas for a minimum of twelve months.

THE RIGHT TO WORK

Every Gulf Coast resident must be assured of the right to work—for there is no better antipoverty program than a good job. With reconstruction and rebuilding, there will be many new jobs created in the region—and it's our duty to ensure that they go to those from the Gulf region. We advocate that the government give local residents first choice on recovery and reconstruction jobs and contracts; and ensure that fair wages are paid and fairness in the workplace is upheld. Civil rights and equality of opportunity are not "red tape" to be cut when times are tough. Civil rights are who we are as a nation.

We need to commit to push for a Gulf Coast Economy that will sustain good-paying jobs for the people of the region. A vibrant economy and good-paying jobs will lift New Orleans out of the swamps of poverty. But the Katrina Bill of Rights cannot be fulfilled without a comprehensive plan and a coordinated effort that will transcend the region's political borders and direct the rebuilding.

Professors Robert D. Bullard and Beverly Wright have successfully taken on quite a responsibility in editing a book about the aftermath of Hurricane Katrina, New Orleans, and the Gulf Coast through the critical lens of environmental justice. The first of its kind, *Race, Place, and Environmental Justice After Hurricane Katrina: Struggles to Reclaim, Rebuild, and Revitalize New Orleans and the Gulf Coast,* offers civil rights activists, civil rights organizations and attorneys, students and citizens alike, a comprehensive guide of what needs to be done and what pitfalls need to be avoided to make sure that New Orleans does not wind up in the hands of greedy developers or a modern-day Pompeii at the dusty feet of a lame-duck government. Frederick Douglass said it best: "Power concedes to nothing without demand. It never has and never will."

PREFACE

August 29, 2005, is a day that will be remembered by people all over the world and is now a part of history in the United States to be remembered in the way we remember 9/11, or the days President Kennedy and Martin Luther King, Jr., were assassinated. This is the day that Hurricane Katrina hit the Gulf Coast of the United States. Its winds and water devastated parts of Louisiana, Mississippi, and Alabama, but it was the scenes in the mostly black city of New Orleans that have contributed significantly to giving this storm its infamous status.

The city of New Orleans lies below sea level and is located in what could be described as a bowl nearly surrounded by water. It is bordered by the Mississippi River on one end and Lake Pontchartrain on the other and is protected by a system of levees and canals designed to prevent storms from flooding it and neighboring parishes or counties.

Before Katrina, the city experienced a number of threatening storms, and intricate evacuation plans were executed for the protection of the public. For several years before Katrina analysts warned city and state officials of the weakened and substandard conditions of the city's levees and the impending disaster that would occur if hit by storm winds from a very powerful hurricane. Katrina, true to the predictions of the analysts, caused the levees to break and the pumps to fail to handle the amount of water inundating the city, resulting in the city being overrun by flood waters. This created a calamity and human crisis the magnitude of which had never before been seen in America, at least not in the age of television. In fact, the world was shown a facet of American society that had mostly been ignored and denied by the majority of American society.

As television cameras shot pictures of predominantly black New Orleans citizens stranded on rooftops and left in the New Orleans Superdome and Convention Center without food or water for days, the ugly truths relating to poverty and race in our government's response to its citizens became clear. The differential effects of this disaster were neither natural nor accidental. Moreover, race seems to be the most significant predictor of disparities that are tied to an existing system of privilege for some and discrimination against others.

There is another truth about the city of New Orleans that is probably known only by those of us who have lived here most of our lives and have experienced the almost strangling grip of racism that operates just under the radar, never detected by most visitors to our city. New Orleans was probably more racially polarized before Katrina, and remains so after Katrina, than it had been since the civil rights battles of the 1960s and 1970s. One gets the impression that all is not right in the city when CNN broadcasts the videotape of a beating by police officers of a 64-year-old retired black schoolteacher in the French Quarter. The fact that the incident was caught on tape showing extreme and unnecessary force—and that the police officers were found not guilty despite the taped evidence presented—may not surprise most: It looked so much like a replay of the Rodney King beating.

Before Katrina, the poverty in the city that was almost totally concentrated within the African-American community was taking its toll. Crime rates were higher than, or as high as, they had ever been. The school system was failing most of the city's children and the school board was embroiled in constant in-fighting, with battle after battle made public in the media. New Orleans was fighting state take-over of failing public schools, encroachment of charter schools at the expense of poor children in failing schools, special prosecutors investigating African-American politicians and businessmen who had contracts with the city, destruction of public housing as well as the imminent displacement of public housing residents, and change in the political structuring of the city largely due to the displacement of poor black former public housing residents. Additionally, New Orleans was fighting for the institution of a livable wage in a city where the number-one industry is tourism and was struggling to turn Louisiana toward being a right-to-work state.

This conundrum or complex web of social, cultural, historical, and economic factors sustained by the intractable consequences of a system of segregation, discrimination, and racism is the backdrop for Katrina. We could ask the question, "Why would anyone have expected this calamity called Katrina and its aftermath to have been different?" The answer of course is that we all expected more from our government. The whole is supposed to be greater than the sum of its parts, even when those parts are aberrant to society.

What Katrina uncovered was a truth that those of us fighting for environmental justice already knew. That truth is that minorities and the poor are more likely than all other groups to be underprepared and underserved, and to be living in unsafe, substandard housing. The impact is also cumulative. After a disaster, minorities and the poor suffer a much slower recovery because of the lethargic response by agencies whose participation is critical to their recovery. They often receive less information, are rejected more often for necessary loans, receive less government relief, and endure discrimination and rejection in their search for housing. Katrina victims experienced all of these calamities. Lower-income minority communities in New Orleans are disproportionately exposed to hazards and other disadvantages. Katrina exacerbated the risk and accelerated the pace of the injustice. The city displaced a large number of the poor and minority community by destroying public housing in a city with an extreme shortage of housing and affordable rental properties.

There is, however, reason for hope. Just before Katrina, many of us were beginning to feel that we could change the social and economic structure of the city. Moreover, we felt that we were finally breaking through many of the barriers that were keeping whites and blacks separate and apart, and our poor and working black citizens in poverty.

New Orleans had a very solid black middle-class community that loved the city and had become dedicated to the struggle of making New Orleans a better place for all of our children. This was probably best demonstrated by the organizations that had begun speaking out on behalf of all of our citizens.

One of the best examples and probably the most successful community collaboration efforts during this period was led by the Crescent City Chapter of the Links, Inc., in New Orleans. The Links organization is made up of highly educated, well-established African-American women often of means. This organization has chapters all over the United States and in Puerto Rico and Africa. Founded by Margaret Hawkins and Sarah Scott in Philadelphia, Pennsylvania, in 1946, the organization was envisioned as one that would respond to the needs and aspirations of black women in a way that other existing organizations had not at the time. It would implement progress in three areas defined as civic, educational, and cultural. Margaret Hawkins and Sarah Scott hoped that the organization would foster cultural appreciation through the arts, develop richer intergroup relationships, and help women who participated to understand and accept their social and civic responsibilities.

In the African-American community around the country, the Links organization is highly prestigious. Most people are familiar with its work in the arts, but we should also be aware of its many civic endeavors and charitable work in Africa and the Caribbean. It would be less than candid not to mention that in most African-American communities this group is seen as elitist. Thus, its activism of the New Orleans chapter is to many surprising.

The Crescent City Chapter of Links, Inc., in New Orleans made a stand on an unbelievably contentious issue, the police residency requirement. In every parish in the state of Louisiana, city employees, including police and firefighters, are required to live in the parish. The reason for this requirement has been bolstered by research that shows that a city is better served when police and firemen live where they work. Several police-connected organizations and some City Council persons representing the uptown, mostly white districts were lobbying for a waiver that would allow New Orleans police officers to live inside of Orleans parish.

The New Orleans chapter of the Links launched a campaign to uphold the residency requirement. They pulled together a collaborative of civil rights organizations, faith-based groups, black chambers of commerce, sororities, fraternities, and community-based organizations to defeat the waiver measure. Before the storm, the climate between blacks and whites, even white liberals, was tense. The fact that some issues had reached a boiling point was probably best symbolized by what we called Black Sunday during the Essence Music Festival on the July 4th, 2005, weekend. The Essence Festival, a musical extravaganza that includes seminars and lectures on every topic related to being black in America, has drawn black people from around the country to the city each year since 1995. To draw attention to the plight of African Americans in New Orleans and to bring to a national stage our many struggles, the 80,000 people attending the festival were asked not to shop or visit the French Quarter on that Sunday. It worked! The boycott was a success, and the phones began to ring from businesses around the city. We also heard Mayor Ray Nagin announce that he was in favor of a livable wage for workers in the city. In July of 2005, one month before Katrina, we as a people and a community of concerned activists garnered our biggest gains and logged the most progress in our political battles with the city.

The chapters of this book will attempt to fully analyze the Katrina phenomenon of environmental disparities as it reflects race and class. Environmental inequities not only exist by race, and often by income, but seem to be bolstered by our institutions that consistently underinvest in prevention and preparedness for certain groups, namely, minorities and the poor. It is the intent of this book to carefully unravel the threads woven into the patchwork of injustice that was uncovered by Katrina.

This "second disaster" of environmental and racial injustice has left its mark on residents in the low-income neighborhoods of the Ninth Ward and the mostly black middle-class neighborhoods of New Orleans East ravaged by Katrina, many of whom are convinced that federal, state, and local officials will not prioritize their communities for clean-up and rebuilding. They worry that their neighborhoods are slated for redevelopment that does not include them.

Some developers mistakenly looked at New Orleans as a clean slate for new development. What we know is that the slate is not clean, but the conversation on rebuilding a better community can begin. It is our hope that this book will lay the groundwork for a change in thinking that can guide policy, resulting in better lives for vulnerable populations exposed to chronic environmental risks worsened by Katrina.

Beverly Wright
Robert D. Bullard
October 2008

INTRODUCTION

Robert D. Bullard and Beverly Wright

In the real world, all communities are not created equal. If a community is poor, black, or on the wrong side of the tracks, it receives less protection than suburbs inhabited by affluent whites. Generally, rich people take land on higher elevations, leaving the poor and working class more vulnerable to flooding and environmental pestilence.

Race tracks closely with social vulnerability and the geography of environmental risks. We saw this pattern during Hurricane Katrina in 2005 and the levee breech that flooded New Orleans. These events shone the national spotlight on government ineptness, incompetence, and severe gaps in disaster preparedness, but for decades African Americans have been complaining about differential treatment, about being left behind, and about outright racial discrimination.

Katrina raised "a new class of problems that demand rigorous analysis, prudent planning, and courageous political leadership" (Daniels et al. 2006, 4). Our analysis uses an environmental justice frame to understand factors that support and impede post-disaster rebuilding, reconstruction, redevelopment, and recovery. We examine the role of race and place and how unequal protection and unequal treatment make some populations more vulnerable in the rebuilding and recovery process. We examine how physical location, socioeconomic status, race, and institutional constraints create and perpetuate racialized place. We also explore how environmental hazards develop into public health threats and how design factors mitigate or amplify their effects.

Racial disparities exist in natural-disaster preparedness, communication, physical impacts, psychological impacts, emergency response, clean-up, recovery, and reconstruction. Disaster mitigation and investments provide location-specific benefits, restricted to populations that live or own assets in the protected areas. Thus, "by virtue of where we live, work, or own property, some members of society are excluded from the benefits of these investments" (Boyce 2000).

1

The disaster in New Orleans after Katrina was unnatural and man-made. Flooding in the New Orleans metropolitan area largely resulted from breached levees and flood walls (Gabe, Falk, McCarthy, and Mason 2005). A May 2006 report from the Russell Sage Foundation, *In the Wake of the Storm: Environment, Disaster, and Race After Katrina,* found these same groups often experience a "second disaster" after the initial storm (Pastor, Bullard, Boyce, Fothergill, Morello-Frosch, and Wright 2006). Pre-storm vulnerabilities limit thousands of Gulf Coast low-income communities of color participation in the storm reconstruction, rebuilding, and recovery. In these communities, days of hurt and loss are likely to become years of grief, dislocation, and displacement.

Providing a political fix for social vulnerability (improvement in the overall quality of life for low-income people) and economic vulnerability (dismantling income and wealth gaps) has proved to be more daunting than providing an engineering fix for environmental vulnerability (shoring up levees, construction of disaster-resistant buildings, changes in land use, and restoration of wetlands and floodways). It is far easier for the Army Corps of Engineers to retrofit and rebuild levees than it is for other government agencies to root out racial injustice, dismantle centuries of mistrust, and rebuild "community."

Quite often the scale of a disaster's impact, as in the case of Hurricane Katrina, has more to do with the political economy of the country, region, and state than with the hurricane's category strength (Jackson 2005). Similarly, measures to prevent or contain the effects of disaster vulnerability are not equally provided to all. Typically, flood-control investments provide location-specific benefits—with the greatest benefits going to populations who live or own assets in the protected area.

Thus, by virtue of where people live, work, or own property, they may be excluded from the benefits of government-funded flood-control investments (Boyce 2000). New Orleans' new post-Katrina levee system will not provide the same level of protection for all of that city's residents. One need not be a rocket scientist to predict who is most likely to receive the least amount of protection or which communities are likely to be left behind and left vulnerable after the flood-proofing is completed—namely, the same groups who were deserted environmentally and economically before the devastating storm.

On August 29, 2005, Hurricane Katrina laid waste to New Orleans, a city founded in 1718 and later developed largely below sea level (Regional Planning Commission of Orleans 1969; Braumbach 1981). Katrina was complete in its devastation of homes, neighborhoods, institutions, and communities. Like most major urban centers, New Orleans was in crisis before Katrina (Pastor, Bullard, Boyce, Fothergill, Morello-Frosch, and Wright 2006). The city's coastal wetlands, which normally serve as a natural buffer against storm surge, had been destroyed by offshore drilling, Mississippi River levees, canals for navigation, pipelines, highway projects, agricultural and urban development.

Over the past century, more than 2,000 of the original 7,000 square miles of coastal marsh and swamp forests that formed the coastal delta of the Mississippi River have vanished. An average of 34 square miles of South Louisiana land, mostly marsh, has disappeared each year since the late 1950s. More than 80 percent of the nation's coastal wetland loss in this time occurred in Louisiana. From 1932 to 2000, the state lost 1,900 square miles of land to the Gulf of Mexico (Tibbetts 2006).

Hurricane Katrina pushed New Orleans closer to the coast because of extensive erosion at the coastal edge. This is a national problem. Researchers, policy makers, and environmentalists are calling for restoration of wetlands and barrier islands to help protect New Orleans the next time a hurricane strikes. Reversing this deadly trend will not be easy.

Katrina was likely the most destructive hurricane in U.S. history, costing over $70 billion in insured damage. It was also one of the deadliest storms, with a death toll of 1,325 and still counting, surpassed only by the 1928 hurricane in Florida (2,500 to 3,000 deaths) and the 1900 Galveston hurricane (8,000 deaths).

Although more than 80 percent of New Orleans was underwater in the aftermath of Katrina, the hurricane, in fact, did not make a direct hit on the city. Flooding was largely from breached levees and flood walls (Gabe, Falk, and McCarthy 2005). Katrina exposed the limitation of local, state, and federal government operations to implement an effective emergency preparedness and response plan. Post-Katrina reconstruction and rebuilding efforts point to challenges that have been forgotten or ignored for decades—social inequality and racial apartheid-type systems that have operated to create and maintain separate and unequal black and white populations (Bullard 2007a, Bullard 2007b). Ignoring and/or rebuilding on long-standing inequities will only complicate the recovery process of those families most in need of jobs at a livable wage, affordable housing, quality education, health care, accessible public transit, full-service supermarkets, banking and insurance, and safe parks.

The lethargic and inept emergency response after Katrina was a disaster that overshadowed the deadly storm itself. Yet, there is a second disaster-in-the-making—driven by racism, classism, elitism, paternalism, and old-fashioned greed. Several months after the storm, "A Twenty-Point Plan to Destroy Black New Orleans" was widely circulated based on trends and observations around policy decisions on re-entry, repopulation, environmental clean-up, flood control, coastal restoration, rebuilding, and reconstruction (Bullard 2006).

Three years after the storm, it is clear that much of this "unofficial" plan has been advanced by state and federal officials and powerful local opinion leaders. Loyola University law professor Bill Quigley delineated and expanded these trends in his "How to Destroy an African-American City in Thirty-three Steps—Lessons from Katrina" (Quigley 2007). Professor Quigley states that "if there is one word that sums up the way to destroy an African-American city after a disaster, that word is delay" (Quigley 2007, 1). The contributors to this volume understand that all communities are not created equal, and thus some get more than their fair share of the benefits or residential amenities while others receive more than their fair share of the costs or disamenities. Race, class, geography, and political power mitigate the distribution of benefits and costs. Some communities become opportunity rich while others become opportunity poor. At every income level, people-of-color communities often find themselves shortchanged on residential amenities, which many middle-income white communities take for granted, such as banking, shopping, supermarkets, parks and green space, bike lanes, nature trails, and sidewalks (Bullard 2007). The events in New Orleans and the Gulf Coast exposed institutional flaws, poor planning, and false assumptions that are built into the emergency response and homeland security plans and programs. Now after three years, questions still linger: What went wrong? Can it happen again? Is government equipped to plan for, mitigate against, respond to, and recover from natural and man-made disasters? Do race and class matter? Volumes of disaster research have found racial disparities in disaster clean-up, rebuilding, reconstruction, and recovery. Race also plays out in natural-disaster survivors' ability to rebuild, replace infrastructure, obtain loans, and locate temporary and permanent housing.

CLOSED DOORS AND BLOCKED OPPORTUNITY

Generally, compared with their middle-income and white counterparts, low-income and people-of-color disaster victims spend more time in temporary housing, shelters, trailers, mobile homes, and hotels—and are more vulnerable to permanent displacement. Some temporary trailer homes have not turned out to be all that temporary. Some disaster victims wonder if they can trust the government to protect them from harm. For example, some FEMA trailers provided to Hurricane Katrina and Rita evacuees proved to be contaminated with formaldehyde. Instead of providing decent and safe temporary housing, FEMA placed storm victims' health at risk in toxic travel trailers and took more than two years to correct this failure (Babington 2007).

In December 2005, the National Fair Housing Alliance (NFHA) released a report, *No Home for the Holidays: Report on Housing Discrimination Against Hurricane Katrina Survivors,* documenting high rates of housing discrimination against African Americans displaced by Katrina (National Fair Housing Alliance 2005). NFHA conducted tests over the telephone to determine what both African-American and white home seekers were told about unit availability, rent, discounts, and other terms and conditions of apartment leasing. In two-thirds of these tests, as we have seen, white callers were favored over African-American callers.

Generally, low-income and African-American disaster victims spend more time in temporary shelters and are more vulnerable to permanent displacement compared with their middle-income and white counterparts. More than a million Louisiana residents fled Katrina, and 100,000 to 300,000 of them could end up permanently displaced. The powerful storm ravaged an eight-parish labor market that supported 617,300 jobs (Randolph 2005). In September 2005, nearly 100,000 Katrina evacuees were still housed in 1,042 barrack-style shelters scattered across twenty-six states and the District of Columbia (Frank 2005).

FEMA contracted for 120,000 mobile homes for Louisiana, Mississippi, and Alabama storm victims until they could find more permanent housing in homes and apartments. However, the pace of getting evacuees out of shelters slowed because of infrastructure problems—water, sewer, and electricity—to accommodate trailers. Six weeks after the storm hit, FEMA had placed 4,662 Louisiana families in trailers, hotel rooms, or cruise ships docked in New Orleans (Maggi 2005).

To discourage housing evacuees, some Louisiana parishes near New Orleans adopted emergency ordinances limiting the density of mobile-home parks (Maggi 2005). Some small white rural towns adopted NIMBY-ism (Not in My Back Yard) to keep out temporary housing (Chang, Soundararajan, and Johnson 2005). No one, including FEMA (which provides the trailers and mobile homes), homeowners (who are trying to protect their property values), and storm victims (who must live in the tight quarters), is served well if temporary or permanent "Katrina ghettos" are created.

Some "temporary" homes have not proved to be that temporary. Thousands left homeless by the hurricane waited for months for new or repaired housing while living in hotels, temporary trailers, and mobile homes. Mobile homes are derisively known as storm magnets because of the endless reports over the years of trailer parks being demolished during bad weather. More than 9,000 families were living in temporary FEMA housing in Florida when Hurricane Dennis slammed into the Florida Panhandle in July 2005—down from a peak of about 15,000 after four hurricanes hit the state in 2004 (Becker 2005).

African Americans seeking housing in the Deep South are routinely met with discrimination. Disasters worsen this problem and intensify the competition for affordable housing. East Baton Rouge Parish population surged from 425,000 to 1.2 million as a result of Katrina (Naughton and Hosenball 2005, 36). Katrina made Baton Rouge one of the fastest-growing regions in the country (Mulligan and Fausset 2005). The influx of these new residents to the region created traffic gridlock and crowded the schools. Many of the mostly white suburban communities and small towns are not known for their hospitality toward blacks. Thousands of black hurricane evacuees faced the added burden of closed doors and housing discrimination, while their white counterparts were given preference.

THE IMPACT ON SMALL AND MINORITY-OWNED BUSINESSES

Disasters hit small and minority-owned businesses hardest because they are often undercapitalized, vulnerable, and sensitive to even small market shifts. Blacks are a large share of the three Gulf Coast states hardest hit by Katrina—Louisiana, Mississippi, and Alabama. Blacks make up 32.5 percent of the population in Louisiana, 36.3 percent in Mississippi, and 26 percent in Alabama.

The U.S. Census Bureau reports that in 1997 New Orleans had 9,747 black-owned firms, 4,202 Hispanic-owned firms, and 3,210 Asian-owned firms; Biloxi-Gulfport, Mississippi, had 1,305 black-owned firms, 273 Hispanic-owned firms, and 1,063 Asian-owned firms; and Mobile, Alabama, had 2,770 black-owned businesses, 478 Hispanic-owned businesses, and 549 Asian-owned firms (U.S. Bureau of the Census 2002).

Katrina affected over 2,000 black-owned businesses in Mississippi. These firms generated over $126 million in sales and receipts in 2004 (Hughes 2005, 149). Katrina adversely affected over 20,000 black-owned businesses in Louisiana. These firms generated sales and receipts of $886 million. Black-owned firms and black professionals, including doctors, dentists, and other service-related businesses, have been slow to return because many lost their core customers and clientele—mainly African Americans.

Katrina negatively impacted over 60,000 black-owned businesses in the Gulf Coast region that generate $3.3 billion a year (Hughes 2005, 150). This is not a small point since most black-owned firms employ blacks. Black-owned firms have met roadblocks and have been virtually frozen out of the clean-up and rebuilding of the Gulf Coast region. The matter was complicated by the U.S. Labor Department's decision to temporarily suspend the affirmative action rule and permit no-bid contracts. Billions of dollars were spent cleaning up the mess left by Katrina. Only 1.5 percent of the $1.6 billion awarded by FEMA went to minority businesses, less than a third of the 5 percent normally required by law (Yen 2005). The Army Corps of Engineers awarded about 16 percent of the $637 million in Katrina contracts to minority-owned firms.

After Katrina, President Bush suspended the Davis-Bacon Act, passed in 1931 during the Great Depression, that sets a minimum pay scale for workers on federal contracts by requiring contractors to pay the prevailing or average pay in the region (Edsall 2005, D3). Some leaders saw the suspension of the prevailing wage combined with the relaxation of federal rules requiring employees to hire only people with proper documents as spurring an influx of low-wage illegal immigrant workers (Pickel 2005).

This has heightened tension between African Americans and Latino immigrant workers. President Bush, after mounting pressure from Democrats, moderate Republicans, organized labor, and workers in the Gulf Coast region, reinstated the prevailing-wage rule (Witte 2005). The relaxation of documents rules was designed to assist Gulf Coast hurricane victims who lost their IDs, not to be a suspension of immigration laws.

Complaints about being shut out of the Gulf Coast reconstruction were not limited to minority-owned firms. Many white Gulf Coast workers and businesses also rail about being left out, while they see out-of-state companies receiving the lion's share of the contracts. The annual payroll alone in the metropolitan areas hardest hit by Katrina, New Orleans, Biloxi, and Mobile, exceeded $11.7 billion in 2002. About 75 percent of the businesses in the disaster area were non-employer firms such as sole proprietorships. And of the remaining small businesses, 80 percent had fewer than 20 employees. Small businesses employed 273,651 workers in the New Orleans area, 54,029 in Biloxi, and 107,586 in Mobile.

FEMA and the SBA were swamped with requests for disaster assistance. FEMA doesn't offer small business loans but does provide emergency cash grants up to $26,200 per person for housing, medical, and other disaster-related needs (Abrams

2005). Some Katrina victims claim they were unfairly denied emergency aid (Sullivan 2005). They accuse FEMA of leaving them behind a second time.

After Katrina, the staff at the SBA loan-processing center in Fort Worth tripled in size. SBA disaster loans serve as the only salvation for companies without insurance, or whose insurance didn't cover all the damage. SBA offers two types of loans to small businesses, that is, firms with fewer than 500 employees: The physical (property) disaster business loan—which provides businesses, of any size, with funds to repair or replace real estate, equipment, fixtures, machinery, and inventory—and the economic injury disaster loan are available to small businesses that have suffered substantial economic injury resulting from a disaster. Both types of disaster loans are available up to $1.5 million (Rosenberg 2005).

SBA disaster loans are not just for small businesses. Homeowners and renters who suffered damage from Hurricane Katrina are also eligible for low-interest disaster loans from the SBA (Willis 2005). SBA makes the majority of its disaster loans to homeowners and renters. The loans are for repairing or rebuilding disaster damage to private property owned by homeowners and renters. Homeowners may borrow up to $200,000 to repair or replace damaged or destroyed real estate. Homeowners and renters may borrow up to $40,000 to repair or replace damaged or destroyed personal property, including vehicles.

SBA's disaster home loans have low interest rates (less than 3 percent) and long terms (up to thirty years), helping to make recovery more affordable. The federal government is expected to provide financial assistance even as private insurance companies are withdrawing disaster coverage from homeowners in hurricane-prone regions. However, most rebuilding funds after disasters come from private insurance, not the government (Comerio 1998).

Before and after disasters strike, black business entrepreneurs are significantly more likely to be denied bank credit, and when successful, receive smaller loans relative to comparable non-minority businesses. A 2005 *New York Times* study discovered that the Small Business Administration had processed only a third of the 276,000 home loan applications it received (Eaton and Nixon 2005). During the same period, the SBA rejected 82 percent of the applications it received, a higher percentage than in most previous disasters. Well-off neighborhoods like Lakeview have received 47 percent of the loan approvals, while poverty-stricken neighborhoods have gotten 7 percent. The loan denial problem is not limited to poor black areas. Middle-class black neighborhoods in New Orleans East also had lower loan rates. This trend could spell doom for rebuilding black New Orleans neighborhoods.

Katrina hit black-owned banks especially hard. In 2005, *Black Enterprise Magazine* listed Liberty Bank as the third-largest African-American bank in the United States. Before Katrina, Liberty Bank and Dryades Bank had assets of $348.2 million and $102.9 million, respectively. Liberty operated nine branches in New Orleans, three in Baton Rouge, and one in Jackson. Katrina cost Liberty an estimated $40 million (Hughes 2005). In June 2008, it dropped to fifth place with assets of $320 million.

INSURANCE TUG-OF-WAR

Disasters often set the stage for a tug-of-war between insurers and disaster victims. The total economic losses from Katrina are expected to exceed $125 billion, with insurance companies paying an estimated $40 to $60 billion. How much financial responsibility the insurance companies end up bearing will depend on how insurers handle the claims—how they determine what is "wind" and what is "flood" damage.

FEMA estimates that the majority of households and businesses in the 12 Hurricane Katrina-affected counties in Alabama, Mississippi, and Louisiana do not have flood coverage. FEMA also estimates that 12.7 percent of the households in Alabama, 15 percent in Mississippi, and 46 percent in Louisiana have flood insurance, and only 8 percent of the businesses in hurricane-affected counties in Alabama, 15 percent in Mississippi, and 30 percent in Louisiana have flood coverage.

Disasters expose the unequal treatment of African Americans and intensify long-running disputes between insurance companies and consumers who live in redlined neighborhoods—disputes revolving around where standard homeowner's insurance coverage ends and flood insurance begins. For decades, consumers, black and white, have complained about insurance companies denying their claims on the basis that damage was not wind-related but flood-related. Damage from rising water is covered only by government-backed flood insurance.

African-American households are more likely than white households to lack health insurance. The uninsured rate for African Americans is more than 1.5 times the rate for white Americans. Nearly 16 percent of Americans did not have health insurance in 2003, up from 14.2 percent in 2000 (DeNavas-Walt, Proctor, and Mills 2004).

A 2001 Commonwealth Fund survey revealed that Hispanics and African Americans were most likely to be uninsured, as 46 percent and 33 percent of working-age Hispanics and African Americans, respectively, lacked insurance for all or part of the twelve months prior to the survey (Duchon et al. 2000). In comparison, 20 percent of both whites and Asian Americans ages 18–64 lacked health coverage for all or part of the previous twelve months (Duchon et al. 2000).

African-American households are also less likely to have homeowners' and rental insurance to cover storm losses and temporary living expenses (Bolin and Bolton 1986). African Americans are also less likely than whites to have insurance with major companies as a result of decades of insurance redlining (Peacock and Girard 1997). African Americans are more likely than whites to receive insufficient insurance settlement amounts. How insurance claims are settled can impact the ability of black households and neighborhoods to recover. Ultimately, this form of discrimination harms wealth creation of individual households and siphons off investments needed to rebuild the black community.

Many white insurance companies routinely redline black neighborhoods. Although insurance redlining is illegal, it is still practiced. It is not uncommon to find African Americans who live in majority-black zip codes paying twice the insurance premium that whites pay for comparable housing in mostly white suburban zip codes (Bullard, Johnson, and Torres 2000). Race does matter in urban credit and insurance markets (Dymski 1995; Squires 1996a).

The insurance industry, like its housing industry counterpart, "has long used race as a factor in appraising and underwriting property" (Squires 1996b). In general, black neighborhoods are left with check-cashing stations, pawnshops, storefront grocery stores, liquor stores, and fast-food operations, all well buttoned-up with wire mesh and bulletproof glass (Bullard, Grigsby, and Lee 1994).

A National Fair Housing Alliance (2005) report, *No Home for the Holidays: Report on Housing Discrimination Against Hurricane Katrina Survivors,* found housing discrimination against African Americans displaced by Hurricane Katrina. In NFHA telephone tests to determine what African American and white home seekers were told about housing availability, 66 percent of these tests, 43 of 65 instances, whites were favored over African Americans. NFHA also conducted five matched pair tests in which persons visited apartment complexes. In those five tests, Whites were favored over African Americans three times.

Because of the enormity of the damage from Katrina, insurance companies tried to categorize a lot of legitimate wind claims as flood-related. This problem of white-collar insurance "looting" has hit low-income, elderly, disabled, and people-of-color storm victims hardest because these groups are likely to have their insurance with small, less reputable companies due to racial redlining. Many, if not most, Katrina victims may not have resources to hire lawyers to fight the insurance companies. In an attempt to head off a floodgate of insurance disputes, Mississippi Attorney General Jim Hood filed suit to block insurance companies from denying flood claims in cases where those floods were caused by wind. He asserted that the insurance exclusion of water damage violates Mississippi's Consumer Protection Act and "deprives consumers of any real coverage choices" (Lee 2005). The lawsuit also accused some insurance companies of forcing storm victims into signing documents that stipulate their losses were flood-related, not wind-related, before they can receive payment or emergency expenses; the lawsuit would ban such practices (Paul 2005). Such a practice is tantamount to economic blackmail.

ORGANIZATION OF THIS BOOK

Dozens of books have been written on Hurricane Katrina, but none have focused on the environmental justice implications of the storm, flooding, clean-up, levee repair and "flood proofing," reconstruction, rebuilding, and recovery. This book uses an environmental justice and health-equity framework to examine the government response to what has been called the worst environmental disaster in U.S. history. It also focuses on environmental justice challenges in pre- and post-Katrina New Orleans and the Gulf Coast.

In exploring the geography of vulnerability, we ask why some populations and communities get left behind economically, spatially, and environmentally before and after disasters strike. Emergency transportation plans generally reflect the shortcomings of transportation planning in that most planners assume people have cars and drive. Transportation apartheid, a two-tiered system of people with cars and people without cars, is alive and well in most metropolitan regions—and was vividly portrayed in living color before, during, and after Hurricane Katrina.

The contributors to this book make clear the connection between race, class, and environmental vulnerability. We use an equity framework to analyze the economic recovery, housing, business opportunity, education, and access to basic services, including health care, supermarkets, banking, finance, and insurance. Equity issues revolve around which community needs are addressed first and which community residents are forced to wait.

In twelve chapters, the authors cover a wide range of topics and describe factors that continue to shape the rebuilding, reconstruction, revitalizations, and recovery of post-Katrina New Orleans. The authors examine the role government and nongovernmental organizations (NGOs) are playing in bringing some sense of normalcy back to the city. They examine the environmental and economic progress the city has made in the three years since the devastating storm and flood drowned 80 percent of New Orleans—forever changing one of the nation's oldest cities. From their analysis, it is clear that New Orleans and the Gulf Coast were far from achieving a race-neutral or color-blind status before the storm. Katrina exacerbated this racial and economic divide.

The introductory chapter, written by the co-editors, provides the sociological frame for the book. It places equity at the center of the analysis on a range of issues, including environmental, economic, health, and housing disparities. Our analysis also examines the role of race and class dynamics on quality of life and sustainability in pre- and post-Katrina New Orleans.

Chapter 1, also written by the co-editors, explores the challenges of racialized place in post-Katrina New Orleans. It explores the "politics" of pollution, clean-up, and waste disposal in pre- and post-Katrina New Orleans. Using an environmental justice frame, the authors explore factors that support and impede post-disaster rebuilding, reconstruction, redevelopment, and recovery. They also examine the connection of race and place and how unequal protection and unequal treatment make some New Orleans populations more vulnerable in the rebuilding and recovery process. The authors explore how physical location, socioeconomic status, race, and lingering institutional constraints create and perpetuate environmental disparities, how environmental hazards develop into public health threats, and how design factors mitigate or amplify their effects.

Chapter 2, written by Debra Lyn Bassett, explains the significance of place in law and policy. Hurricanes Katrina and Rita provided an opportunity for lawmakers, policy makers, and the public at large to take a closer look at the significance of race, place, and poverty and to recognize the broader structural considerations that often tend to favor the affluent while shifting risks onto the poor. People who are more economically and socially vulnerable—including the less educated, the low income, the elderly, and minorities—are the ones shunted into the places that are more geographically vulnerable.

Chapter 3, written by Robert D. Bullard, Glenn S. Johnson, and Angel O. Torres, examines how transportation provides access to opportunity and serves as a key component in addressing poverty, unemployment, and equal-opportunity goals while ensuring access to education, health care, and other public services. The analysis focuses on who is most likely to get left behind economically, especially individuals without cars—during economic recessions and boom times—and during natural and human-induced disasters—and why. Transportation, personal automobiles and public transportation, is a necessary and essential element in emergency preparedness, response, and evacuation from natural and human-induced disasters. The primary means of emergency evacuation in most disaster plans is the personal automobile.

Chapter 4, written by Mtangulizi Sanyika, details the struggle to ensure the right to return for all New Orleans' Katrina survivors. Despite the progress made in the rebuilding of New Orleans, the author reveals that many black New Orleanians are relegated to the status of the underclass, working poor, or marginalized upon returning to the city. He chronicles how major segments of black New Orleans are being left out of the recovery and how unofficial "separate and unequal" policies and practices have resulted in many of the city's residents living on the edge of social disaster. As they struggled to get their lives back together, black storm victims have had to organize against political disenfranchisement, housing discrimination, insurance redlining, unfair insurance settlements, land grabs, and permanent displacement from neighborhoods and public housing.

In Chapter 5, Robert Godsil, Albert Huang, and Gina Solomon examine environmental health threats and injustices that existed before and after the storm that have created an unparalleled challenge to clean up and rebuild devastated areas. The Environmental Protection Agency (EPA) has the legal authority necessary to clean up the environmental contamination caused by the hurricanes. Unfortunately, the EPA has waived its vast clean-up powers. The authors present findings to show how the federal government has largely ceded its leadership over the clean-up and rebuilding to state and local authorities. EPA has chosen to defer to poorly resourced local authorities that are under significant pressure to say that everything is "safe."

In Chapter 6, Shelia J. Webb describes health disparities and the disproportionate burden of disease, illness, and preventable deaths borne by African Americans. She notes that the most vulnerable population impacted by Hurricane Katrina received the greatest wounds and is still suffering from the hurricane. While literally hundreds of thousands of people were affected by this storm, the poor and underserved populations were disproportionately impacted and significantly bore the brunt of loss, devastation, and injustice. New Orleans, with its majority African-American population and large percentage of individuals living below the federal poverty line, became the embodiment of disproportional impact. The author argues for an overhaul in the city's health care delivery system, schools, businesses, transportation systems, infrastructure, and faith-based institutions in preparation for future disasters.

In Chapter 7, Earthea Nance discusses community-based environmental laboratories as a new paradigm for achieving environmental justice in post-Katrina New Orleans. Using the environmental justice framework of grassroots empowerment, the author presents community-based laboratories as an innovative way of bringing scientists and engineers into environmentally impacted communities to do environmental testing on a not-for-profit basis. Such laboratories increase people's access to knowledge by putting them in direct contact with scientists and engineers and by giving them affordable techniques for clean-up.

Rita J. King in Chapter 8 describes how the lack of a competitive bidding system in the earliest days and continuous chaos on the Gulf Coast hindered the effort to impose any meaningful accountability on those companies staking claim to the billions in federal recovery dollars. She examines how lucrative contracts to clean up New Orleans and the Gulf Coast states went to many of the same companies that have received contracts to clean up Afghanistan and Iraq—leading to profiteering, corruption, and waste. She chronicles how no-bid, cost-plus Katrina contracts created a crisis rife with opportunity for the well-placed corporation and how the revolving door between Capitol Hill and Wall Street created a cozy club for major contractors and politicians. The Department of Homeland Security (DHS) no-bid contracts were responsible for wasting almost a billion dollars on mobile homes and travel trailers, which included about 10,000 left sitting unused in a field in Arkansas.

In Chapter 9, Robert K. Whelan and Denise Strong provide insights on the choices and challenges of New Orleans' economic development and rebuilding efforts. Their analysis shows how competing economic development programs are not integrated into the workforce development initiatives in the region. Before Hurricane Katrina, the New Orleans economy suffered from fundamental problems—a large poverty population lacking basic skills, a lack of a diverse economic base, and a general lack of opportunity and dynamism. The government's focus in the region is on rebuilding the physical aspects of the city, more specifically homeowners' and neighborhood projects. The authors suggest that innovative and creative thinking is needed, due to New Orleans' pre-Katrina status, a slow economy, tourism decreasing after 9/11, businesses having difficulty reopening, office jobs having moved to Houston, Texas, the need for the workforce to upgrade its basic skills, and the lack of adequate housing and basic services.

In Chapter 10, Mafruza Khan focuses on innovative solutions that have emerged from the ground up, discusses important planning and policy issues that address structural barriers to opportunity for Hurricane Katrina survivors, and raises some questions about prevailing models of economic development and planning in relation to race. The author examines the historical and structural context that transformed New Orleans from a relatively poor but otherwise diverse and vibrant city to an impoverished black-majority one, and how race has driven and shaped exclusionary public policies that have created concentrated racialized poverty in New Orleans. She also provides an analysis of structural barriers to opportunity and demonstrates why race needs to be explicit and embedded in both the planning and policy frameworks for rebuilding. Race-conscious policies are critical for facilitating inclusion, participation, and accountability in rebuilding New Orleans, precisely because race-neutral polices may actually perpetuate structural barriers and historical inequities.

In Chapter 11, Lisa K. Bates and Rebekah A. Green present an empirical analysis of the reconstruction of residential housing in the Lower Ninth Ward and consider pre-storm problems, flood damage, and policy impediments to recovery. First, they present pre-Katrina data about racial disparities in housing security and affordability. Second, they examine the physical data forming the basis for depopulation plans, reporting the results of a survey of 3,211 residential units for structural damage, flood damage, and recovery activity. They then evaluate the Road Home program's effectiveness in assisting Ninth Ward homeowners' rebuilding. Finally, the authors present data on Road Home applications and funding receipt in the Ninth Ward compared to other New Orleans neighborhoods. Through this examination, they argue that due to pre-storm inequities in housing and program specifics, the post-Katrina Road Home program for housing recovery did not provide sufficient access or resources to meet the housing needs of large numbers of low- and moderate-income African-American families in New Orleans' Lower Ninth Ward after Katrina.

In Chapter 12, John R. Logan addresses four basic questions: (1) who was displaced by Hurricane Katrina, (2) how does the pattern of displacement affect people's chances of returning, (3) how are public policy decisions affecting the recovery process, and (4) what do shifts in local political influence portend for the future? His analysis indicates that policy choices for Hurricane Katrina will affect who can return to which neighborhoods and what forms of public and private assistance will significantly affect the future character of New Orleans. The new political geography of New Orleans will be a factor as policy decisions are made in the months and years to come. Some important questions—particularly whether city officials will encourage the rebuilding of the neighborhoods impacted the most—remain unanswered.

In the Afterword, the editors of the book, reflecting on the third anniversary of Hurricane Katrina, examine how race operates in explaining the uneven repopulation, rebuilding, recovery, and reclaiming of neighborhoods and institutions. Repopulation of New Orleans is tied more to who has resources, including financial settlements of housing and insurance claims, transportation, and employment. Thousands of native New Orleanians who were displaced by Katrina, most of whom are black and poor, still have a desire to return home but lack the resources.

Many Katrina evacuees may not be able to return to the city because of a severe shortage of low-income and working-class housing. In measuring the recovery of New Orleans, significant progress is due in large measure not to government intervention but to the army of volunteers and NGOs that want to make a difference. As neighborhoods in New Orleans and the Gulf Coast region get rebuilt, there is no question the best green technology available and sustainable practices must be employed. However, it is imperative that rebuilding, green or otherwise, be fair, just, equitable, inclusive, and carried out in a nondiscriminatory way.

REFERENCES

Abrams, R. 2005. "Helping Small Businesses in the Wake of Katrina." *USA Today.* September 1.

Babington, C. 2007. "FEMA Slow to Test Toxicity of Trailers." *USA Today.* July 19.

Becker, A. 2005. "Storm-resistant Homes a Long Time Coming: Left Homeless Last Year Still Holed Up in Temporary Housing." *Dallas Morning News.* August 28, 6A.

Bolin, R., and P. A. Bolton. 1986. *Race, Religion, and Ethnicity in Disaster Recovery.* Boulder: Institute of Behavioral Science, University of Colorado.

Boyce, J. K. 2000. "Let Them Eat Risk? Wealth, Rights, and Disaster Vulnerability." *Disaster* 24 (3): 254–261.

Braumbach, R., and E. Borah. 1981. *The Second Battle of New Orleans: A History of the Vieux Carré Riverfront-Expressway Controversy.* Tuscaloosa: University of Alabama Press.

Bullard, R. D. 2005. *The Quest for Environmental Justice: Human Rights and the Politics of Pollution.* San Francisco: Sierra Club Books.

———. 2006. "A Twenty-Point Plan to Destroy Black New Orleans." *San Francisco Bayview.* February 1.

———. 2007a. *Growing Smarter: Achieving Livable Communities, Environmental Justice and Regional Equity.* Cambridge, MA: MIT Press.

———. 2007b. *The Black Metropolis in the Twenty-first Century: Race, Power, and the Politics of Place.* New York: Rowman and Littlefield.

Bullard, R. D., J. E. Grigsby, and C. Lee. 1994. *Residential Apartheid: The American Legacy.* Los Angeles: UCLA Center for African American Studies Publication.

Bullard, R. D., G. S. Johnson, and A. O. Torres (eds.). 2000. *Sprawl City: Race, Politics, and Planning in Atlanta.* Washington, DC: Island Press.

Chang, J., T. Soundararajan, and A. Johnson. 2005. "Getting Home Before It's Gone." *Alternet.org.* September 26. Available at http://www.alternet.org/katrina/25930 (accessed June 1, 2008).

Comerio, M. C. 1998. *Disaster Hits Home: New Policy for Urban Housing Recovery.* Berkeley: University of California Press.

Daniels, R. L., D. F. Kettl, and H. Kunreuther. 2006. *On Risk and Disaster: Lesson from Katrina.* Philadelphia: University of Pennsylvania Press.

DeNavas-Walt, C., B. D. Proctor, and R. J. Mills. 2004. *Income, Poverty, and Health Insurance Coverage in the United States: 2003.* Washington, DC: U.S. Census Bureau.

Duchon, L., C. Schoen, M. M. Doty, K. Davis, E. Strumpf, and S. Bruegman. 2000. "Security Matters: How Instability in Health Insurance Puts U.S. Workers At Risk." Findings from the *Commonwealth Fund 2001 Health Insurance Survey.* New York: Commonwealth Fund. Available at http://www.cmwf.org (accessed June 1, 2008).

Dymski, G. A. 1995. "The Theory of Bank Redlining and Discrimination: An Exploration." *Review of Black Political Economy* 23 (winter): 37–74.

Edsall, T. B. 2005. "Bush Suspends Pay Act in Areas Hit by Storm." *Washington Post.* September 9.

Frank, T. 2005. "Blanco Pushes FEMA for Hotel Rooms." *USA Today.* September 21.

Gabe, T., G. Falk, M. McCarthy, and V. W. Mason. 2005. *Hurricane Katrina: Social-Demographic Characteristics of Impacted Areas.* Washington, DC: Congressional Research Service Report RL33141, November.

Hughes, A. 2005. "Blown Away by Katrina." *Black Enterprise Magazine* 36, no. 4. November.

Jackson, S. 2005. "Unnatural Disasters, Here and There," *Understanding Katrina: Perspectives from the Social Sciences.* New York: Social Science Research Council.

Lee, A. 2005. "Wind or Water: The Debate Rages, but Who Will Pay?" *Sun Herald (South Mississippi)*. December 21.

Maggi, L. 2005. "Shelter Shutting: Next Steps." *Times-Picayune*. October 14.

National Fair Housing Alliance. 2005. *No Home for the Holidays: Report on Housing Discrimination Against Hurricane Katrina Survivors—Executive Summary*. Washington, DC: NFHA, December 20.

Mulligan, T. S., and R. Fausset. 2005. "Baton Rouge a Booming Haven for the Displaced." *Los Angeles Times*. September 7.

Naughton, K., and M. Hosenball. 2005. "Cash and 'Cat 5' Chaos." *Newsweek*. September 26.

Pastor, M., R. D. Bullard, J. K. Boyce, A. Fothergill, R. Morella-Frosch, and B. Wright. 2006. *In the Wake of the Storm: Environment, Disaster and Race After Katrina*. New York: Russell Sage Foundation.

Paul, P. C. 2005. "You've Got to Make Them Feel Good About Something." *Atlanta Journal-Constitution*. September 18.

Peacock, W. P., B. H. Morrow, and H. Gladwin. 1992. *Hurricane Andrew: Ethnicity, Gender, and the Sociology of Disasters*. Miami: Florida International University, Laboratory for Social and Behavioral Research.

Pickel, M. L. 2005. "Immigrant Workers Rile New Orleans." *Atlanta Journal-Constitution*. October 19.

Quigley, Bill. 2007. How to Destroy an African-American City in Thirty-Three Steps— Lessons from Katrina." Common Dreams News Center, June 28. Available at http://www.commondreams.org/print/23196 (accessed October 18, 2008).

Randolph, N. 2005. "State Will Suffer Sans N.O." *Advocate*. September 11.

Regional Planning Commission of Orleans. 1969. Jefferson and St. Bernard Parishes. "History of Regional Growth of Jefferson, Orleans, and St. Bernard Parishes." November.

Rosenberg, J. M. 2005. "Small Business Loans Help with Rebuilding." *Houston Chronicle*. September 4.

Squires, G. 1996a. Policies of Prejudice: Risky Encounters with the Property Insurance Business. *Challenge* 39 (July).

_____.1996b. Race and Risk: The Reality of Redlining. *National Underwriter (Property & Casualty/Risk & Benefits Management)* 100 (September 16): 63, 70.

Sullivan Commission on Diversity in the Healthcare Workforce. 2004. *U.S. Health Care Professions Separate and Unequal: Sullivan Commission—Lack of Diversity May Be Greatest Cause of Health Disparities*. Durham, NC: Sullivan Commission, Duke University School of Medicine. September.

Tibbetts, J. 2006. "Louisiana's Wetlands: A Lesson in Nature Appreciation." *Environmental Health Perspective* 114 (January): A40–A43.

U.S. Census Bureau. 2002. *Survey of Minority-Owned Business Enterprises*. Washington, DC.

Willis, G. 2005. "Disaster Relief: 5 Tips: How to Call on the Disaster Relief Resources You Need." *CNN/Money*. September 16. Available at http://money.cnn.com/2005/09/16/pf/saving/willis_tips (accessed June 30, 2008).

Witte, G. 2005. "Prevailing Wages to Be Paid Again on Gulf Coast." *Washington Post*. October 27.

Yen, H. 2005. "Minority Firms Getting Few Katrina Pacts." *BusinessWeek*. October 4.

PART I

CHALLENGES OF RACIALIZED PLACE

CHAPTER 1

RACE, PLACE, AND THE ENVIRONMENT IN POST-KATRINA NEW ORLEANS

Robert D. Bullard and Beverly Wright

The year 2005 saw the worst Atlantic hurricane season since record keeping began in 1851 (Cuevas 2005). An average season produces ten named storms, of which about six become hurricanes and two or three become major hurricanes. But 2005 saw the most named storms ever, 27, topping the previous record of 21 in 1933—and 13 hurricanes—breaking the old record of 12 in 1969 (Tanneeru 2005). And on August 29, 2005, of course, Hurricane Katrina laid waste to New Orleans. Katrina's death toll of 1,836 and counting made it the third most deadly hurricane in U.S. history, after the 1928 Okeechobee hurricane in Florida, which killed 2,500, and the 1900 Galveston hurricane, which killed 8,000 (Ho 2005, A1). The disaster in New Orleans after Katrina was unnatural and man-made. Flooding in the New Orleans metropolitan area largely resulted from breached levees and flood walls (Gabe, Falk, McCarthy, and Mason 2005). A May 2006 report from the Russell Sage Foundation, *In the Wake of the Storm: Environment, Disaster, and Race After Katrina,* found these same groups often experience a "second disaster" after the initial storm (Pastor et al. 2006).

Hurricane Katrina demonstrated that negative effects of climate change fall heaviest on the poor and people of color (Brinkley 2006; Dyson 2006; Horn 2006; Pastor et al. 2006). Eighty percent of New Orleans was flooded. Low-income and people-of-color neighborhoods were hardest hit. Pre-storm vulnerabilities limit participation of thousands of Gulf Coast low-income communities of color in the after-storm reconstruction, rebuilding, and recovery. In these communities, days of hurt and loss are likely to become years of grief, dislocation, and displacement.

Hurricane Katrina left debris across a 90,000-square-mile disaster area in Louisi-ana, Mississippi, and Alabama, compared to a 16-acre tract in New York on Septem-ber 11, 2001 (Luther 2006). According to the Congressional Research Service, debris from Katrina could well top 100 million cubic yards, compared to the 8.8 million cubic yards of disaster debris generated after the 9/11 terrorist attacks on New York City.

New Orleans, like most major urban centers, was in peril before Katrina flood-waters devastated the city (Pastor, Bullard, Boyce, Fothergill, Morello-Frosch, and Wright 2006). Katrina was complete in its devastation of homes, neighborhoods, in-stitutions, and communities. The city's coastal wetlands, which normally serve as a natural buffer against storm surge, had been destroyed by offshore drilling, Missis-sippi River levees, canals for navigation, pipelines, highway projects, agricultural and urban development.

Over the past century, more than 2,000 of the original 7,000 square miles of coastal marsh and swamp forests that formed the coastal delta of the Mississippi River have vanished. An average of 34 square miles of south Louisiana land, mostly marsh, has disappeared each year for the past five decades. More than 80 percent of the nation's coastal wetland loss in this time occurred in Louisiana. From 1932 to 2000, the state lost 1,900 square miles of land to the Gulf of Mexico (Tibbetts 2006). Hurricane Katrina pushed New Orleans closer to the coast because of exten-sive erosion at the coastal edge. This is a national problem. A range of groups, in-cluding researchers, policy makers, and environmentalists, for decades have called for restoration of wetlands and barrier islands to help protect New Orleans the next time a hurricane strikes.

BLACK NEW ORLEANS BEFORE
HURRICANE KATRINA

The history of New Orleans is intrinsically tied to the Vieux Carré, the French Quar-ter. In 1718, Jean-Baptiste Le Moyne de Bienville, a French Canadian and governor of the state of Louisiana, and a small group of men, left Mobile, Alabama, to establish a city on the banks of the Mississippi (Regional Planning Commission of Orleans, Jefferson, and St. Bernard Parishes 1969, 13; Baumbach and Borah 1981, 5). Located 90 miles from the Gulf of Mexico, it was named in honor of the Duke of Orleans. La Nouvelle Orléans was initially established as a military outpost, a trading post, and an administrative center for French holdings in Louisiana.

As a result of the official launching of the American slave trade in 1619, blacks began to appear in large numbers in New Orleans. The 1726 census recorded only 300 slaves living in the city, but by 1732, there were nearly a thousand (Wright 1991). New Orleans was unique not only because of its European inhabitants, un-common in most southern cities, but also because of its significant number of "free colored people." The first free blacks were recorded living in New Orleans in the 1720s; and by 1803, there were 1,335.

After the Civil War, New Orleans' black population swelled, with many ex-slaves unable to find work or housing. Consequently, the poorest blacks lived where they could. They lived along the battures, or backswamps. Because New Orleans was built facing the Mississippi River, its shape followed the great crescent bend of the river, hence its nickname, the Crescent City. The batture was "the area on the river-side of the artificial levee without flood protection and without private ownership." The poorest blacks built shacks in the batture away from the dock area. These houses were, however, temporary because the river would periodically overflow and wash away the shacks.

Because New Orleans is a seaport city at the mouth of the Mississippi that largely is below sea level, with flooding its main problem, it is not surprising that whites occupied the highest and best land, protected by natural levees. Poor blacks lived in the backswamps on the inland margin of the natural levee, where drainage was bad, foundation material precarious, streets atrociously unmaintained, mosquitoes endemic, and flooding a recurrent hazard. It is along this margin that a continuous belt of black population developed. Free blacks in New Orleans, many of whom were economically well off, originally lived and owned property in the French Quarter. After the Civil War and the onset of Jim Crow laws, however, they were pushed out of that section.

Many of the blacks moved their families to the Treme, or Sixth Ward, an area adjacent to the French Quarter. As the Sixth Ward became crowded, many moved to the old Seventh Ward, next to the Sixth Ward, making for a natural extension of the black community. These early black residential patterns developed over the years into long-standing, traditionally black neighborhoods, although early New Orleans' residential patterns were peculiarly integrated.

Several inventions influenced the racial geography of New Orleans in the twentieth century. These included the invention of a screw pump and the expansion of the city's public transportation system through use of the streetcar. The Wood Screw Pump is a drainage pump designed by A. Baldwin Wood in 1913. In 1915 the first four of these pumps were installed in New Orleans to help alleviate drainage problems in the city. Thanks to the pumps, the city was able to eliminate some of its flooding problems, allowing residents to settle in areas previously flooded. World War I brought with it a virtual halt in the construction of housing. Until the war, black residents of New Orleans had lived in housing comparable to their white working-class counterparts, but they were now relegated to the less desirable homes in the backswamp area. There was also a large in-migration of rural blacks and whites, attracted by defense jobs in the city.

It became clear in the early 1920s that additional housing units were needed in the city, but there were many early barriers to their construction. There was an apparent drive to improve housing conditions when the 1920 census showed that New Orleans had dropped from twelfth to sixteenth place in population. The loss of population was blamed on the local authorities' inability to solve the housing problems of the city, resulting in many of the townspeople moving out beyond the city's boundaries.

The expansion of the city's streetcar system also affected its racial geography. As public transportation expanded, old black neighborhoods established in the nineteenth-century backswamp areas expanded into the newly drained margins of that area. The expanded transportation system made it possible for blacks to live in areas away from their jobs. The Wood Screw Pump made it possible for whites to move to the suburbs and for blacks, with the aid of the expanded streetcar system, to move closer into the city. The black and white populations, it seems, were moving in opposite directions.

For three decades, beginning in 1978, with the election of Ernest "Dutch" Morial, New Orleans has had an uninterrupted succession of black mayors. In 2002, Orleans Parish (a parish is comparable to a county) had the highest percentage of black residents of any older county in the United States. Roughly 68 percent of New Orleans–area residents were black. "White flight" from New Orleans to the suburbs and continuing racial segregation, poverty, unemployment, crime, and low levels of educational achievements stand in marked contrast to the city's growing black middle class, which has elected to settle in all-black affluent areas to the east of New Orleans, an area known as New Orleans East (Wright 1997).

New Orleans, like most major urban centers, was a city in peril long before Hurricane Katrina's floodwaters devastated the city (Pastor et al. 2006; Dyson 2006). New Orleans (Orleans Parish) had a population of 484,674 in 2000. Of this total, 325,947 (68 percent) were African Americans, 135,956 (28 percent) were non-Hispanic whites, and 22,871 (4 percent) were of other ethnic groups. Like many great cities, New Orleans also had its share of problems. The economic structure of the city made it difficult to provide jobs with wages high enough to support a family. New Orleans' economy was built around low-wage service jobs in the tourism sector.

In the 1970s, New Orleans East was the fastest-growing section of the city. Spurred by the prosperity of the oil industry, construction in the east was at an all-time high. Newly constructed moderate-to-expensive homes and comparable luxury apartments dotted the landscape of New Orleans' newest residential area. Between 1979 and 1980, the oil boom turned to bust, and the city fell into decline. Banks that held the mortgages on large luxury apartment complexes built by contractors who overestimated the housing needs of the city and the ability of the population to pay were losing money. At the same time, the city was facing a housing shortage. The inner-city housing stock was increasingly dilapidated. Public housing was in ruin and in short supply. The city was in deep trouble, and the City Council was desperate for answers.

Population patterns in the 1980s changed the race and class composition of New Orleans East. White residents very quickly began to migrate to St. Tammany Parish, a bedroom community across Lake Pontchartrain. Middle-class African Americans began buying more homes in the eastern suburb, and more and more luxury apartments were becoming filled with poorer African-American New Orleanians on rent subsidies. Interstate 10, designated in 1955 as part of the Interstate Highway System, made it possible for middle-class black New Orleanians to move to the eastern suburbs and for white New Orleanians to move to St. Tammany Parish and drive into the central business district every day for work, taking the city's tax dollars with them. The result of this new migration pattern devastated the city's economy. Suburban New Orleans East, just like its inner city, became increasingly black and with pockets of poverty.

AGRICULTURE STREET LANDFILL COMMUNITY—A BLACK LOVE CANAL

Dozens of toxic "time bombs" along Louisiana's Mississippi River Industrial Corridor, dubbed Cancer Alley, the 85-mile stretch from Baton Rouge to New Orleans, made the region a major environmental justice battleground in the 1990s and early 2000s. For decades, black communities there have been fighting against environmental racism and demanding relocation from polluting facilities (Bullard 2005).

Two mostly black New Orleans subdivisions, Gordon Plaza and Press Park, have special significance to environmental justice and emergency response. Both subdivisions were built on a portion of land that had been a municipal landfill for decades. The Agriculture Street Landfill, covering approximately 190 acres in the Ninth Ward, was used as a city dump as early as 1910. After 1950, the landfill was mostly used to discard large solid objects, including trees and lumber. The landfill was a major source for dumping debris from the very destructive Hurricane Betsy that struck New Orleans in 1965. It is important to note that the landfill was classified as a solid waste site and not a hazardous waste site.

In 1969, the federal government created a home ownership program to encourage lower-income families to purchase their first home. Press Park was the first subsidized housing project on this program in New Orleans. The federal program allowed tenants to apply 30 percent of their monthly rental payments toward the purchase of a family home. In 1987, some 17 years later, the first sale was completed. In 1977, construction began on a second subdivision, Gordon Plaza. This development was planned, controlled, and constructed by the U.S. Department of Housing and Urban Development (HUD) and the Housing Authority of New Orleans (HANO). Gordon Plaza consists of 67 single-family homes.

In 1983, the Orleans Parish School Board purchased part of the Agriculture Street Landfill site for a school. That this site had previously been used as a municipal dump prompted concerns about its suitability for a school. The board contracted engineering firms to survey the site and assess it for contamination of hazardous materials. Heavy metals and organics were detected.

In May 1986, the U.S. Environmental Protection Agency (EPA) performed a site inspection (SI) in the Agriculture Street Landfill community. Although lead, zinc, mercury, cadmium, and arsenic were found, based on the Hazard Ranking System (HRS) model used at that time, the score of 3 was not high enough to place the site on the EPA's National Priorities List (NPL) of hazardous substances, pollutants, and contaminants. Despite warnings, Moton Elementary School, an $8 million state-of-the-art public school, opened with 421 students in 1989 (Lyttle 2000).

On December 14, 1990, the EPA published a revised HRS model in response to the Superfund Amendment and Reauthorization Act (SARA) of 1986. Upon the request of community leaders, in September 1993, an Expanded Site Inspection (ESI) was conducted. On December 16, 1994, the Agriculture Street Landfill community was placed on the NPL with a new score of 50.

The Agriculture Street Landfill community is home to approximately 900 African-American residents. The average family income is $25,000, and the educational level is high school graduate and above. The community pushed for a buy-out of their property and to be relocated. However, this was not the resolution of choice by EPA. A clean-up was ordered at a cost of $20 million, even though the community buyout would have cost only $14 million. The actual clean-up began in 1998 and was completed in 2001 (Lyttle 2000).

Disagreeing with the EPA's clean-up plans, the Concerned Citizens of Agriculture Street Landfill filed a class-action lawsuit against the city of New Orleans for damages and cost of relocation. The case was still pending when Hurricane Katrina struck. It is ironic that the environmental damage wrought by Katrina may force both the clean-up and the relocation of the Agriculture Street Landfill community from the dumpsite, but then again it may not, given the slow pace black New Orleans neighborhoods are being cleaned up and rebuilt and the fact that New Orleans, the defendant in the suit, is bankrupt.

In 2002, the federal EPA sued the city and several companies that owned or operated portions of the landfill where hazardous material was found and to recoup the $20 million it spent on clean-up. The case was settled in federal court in a May 2008 consent decree that called for the city to place a synthetic liner and a soil cap over the site. The city was not required to pay for any clean-up costs or civil penalties since the government determined New Orleans could not afford to pay any part of the settlement due to "extraordinary financial difficulties" after Hurricane Katrina (U.S. Department of Justice 2008, 4).

In 2005, CFI, Inc., and its parent company, IPC, Inc., had already agreed to pay $1.75 million, plus interest, and BFI Waste Systems of North America, Inc., agreed to pay $335,000 plus interest. The U.S. Department of Justice reached tentative settlement agreements with Delta By-Products, Inc., and Edward Levy Metal, Inc., but those negotiations are still in progress (Associated Press 2008).

The EPA and city settlement has no impact on the Agriculture Street Landfill class-action lawsuit judgment issued in 2006 by Civil District Court Nadine Ramsey, who ruled in favor of the residents, declaring the neighborhood "unreasonably dangerous" and "uninhabitable." The judge ordered HANO, the city, and the insurers to pay fair-market value, plus $4,000 to $50,000 for emotional distress, depending on how long a resident had lived in the neighborhood before contamination was found in 1993. The ruling was appealed, and in January 2008, Louisiana's Fourth Circuit Court of Appeals largely upheld Ramsey's ruling but cut the emotional distress awards in half (Hammer 2008a).

Nearly a year after Katrina, the EPA gave the city a clean bill of health. There was one glaring exception—the Agriculture Street Landfill neighborhood. EPA scientists discovered cancer-causing benzo(a)pyrene in residents' yards at levels 50 times the normal level. No new clean-up was in the works, but FEMA trailers were supplied to area residents, who later learned that the trailers themselves posed a health hazard from deadly formaldehyde fumes (Associated Press 2008b).

When Ag Street homeowners applied under Louisiana's $10.3-billion The Road Home program (designed to provide compensation to Louisiana homeowners affected by Katrina or Rita for the damage to their homes) to rebuild, they were refused funds. They were told their applications were put on hold indefinitely because they lived on a Superfund clean-up site. HUD, which financed and guaranteed loans in the neighborhood, also took the position that none of its money could be used to purchase contaminated land (Hammer 2008a). The Road Home officials later placed former residents of the landfill neighborhood back in The Road Home pipeline for consideration pending the drafting of policies toward Superfund neighborhoods—neighborhoods with federally designated hazardous waste sites. Homeowners would have the option of having their Road Home grants calculated based on a regular rebuilding grant, but they would also be allowed to use the money to relocate.

In July 2008, after nearly 15 years of struggle, the Louisiana Supreme Court handed a victory to some 8,000 Ag Street residents who sued the city of New Orleans, its public housing authority, and its school board for putting their homes and school on a toxic waste dump without warning them. In a 5–2 vote, the Louisiana Supreme Court upheld the 2006 ruling of Judge Ramsey (Hammer 2008a).

CLEANING UP AFTER KATRINA

Before Katrina, over 50 percent (some studies place this figure at around 70 percent) of children living in the inner-city neighborhoods of New Orleans had blood lead levels above the current guideline of 10 micrograms per deciliter (mcg/dl) (Mielke 1999). Childhood lead poisoning in some New Orleans black neighborhoods was as high as 67 percent (Rabito, White, and Shorter 2004).

Even 10 mcg/dl is not safe. Some medical and health professionals advocate lowering the threshold to 2.5 mcg/dl (Lamphear 2001). The World Health Organization estimates the effect of lead poisoning to be about 1 to 3 points of IQ lost for each 10 mcg/dl lead level. At higher levels, the effect may be larger. Lead affects almost every organ and system in the body, including the kidneys and the reproductive system.

Katrina has been called one of the worst environmental disasters in U.S. history. A September 2005 *BusinessWeek* commentary described the handling of the untold tons of "lethal goop" as the "mother of all toxic cleanups" (2005). However, the billion-dollar question facing New Orleans is which neighborhoods will get cleaned up, which ones will be left contaminated, and which ones will be targeted as new sites to dump storm debris and waste from flooded homes.

Hurricane Katrina left debris across a vast disaster area in Louisiana, Mississippi, and Alabama. According to the Congressional Research Service, debris from Katrina could well top 100 million cubic yards. Ten months after the storm, FEMA had spent $3.6 billion to remove 98.6 million cubic yards of debris from Katrina (Jordan 2006). This is enough trash to pile two miles high across five football fields. Still, an estimated 20 million cubic yards littered New Orleans and Mississippi waterways— with about 96 percent, or 17.8 million cubic yards, of remaining wreckage in Orleans, St. Bernard, St. Tammany, Washington, and Plaquemines parishes.

The Army Corps of Engineers estimated it would complete its debris mission, including demolitions, by the end of September 2006 (Army Corps of Engineers 2006). Debris clean-up continued three years after the storm. Soon after Katrina, officials from the EPA and the Louisiana Department of Environmental Quality (LDEQ) estimated that 140,000 to 160,000 homes in Louisiana might need to be demolished and disposed (U.S. Environmental Protection Agency 2005). More than 110,000 of New Orleans' 180,000 homes were flooded, and half sat for days or weeks in more than six feet of water (Nossiter 2005).

Government officials estimate that as many as 30,000 to 50,000 homes citywide may have to be demolished, while many others could be saved with extensive repairs. Getting permission to demolish private homes has been drawn out because people are coming back slowly to some heavily damaged areas. Demolishing damaged homes in the hard-hit Lower Ninth Ward proved to be a controversial political issue (Filosa 2006).

After Katrina, 350,000 automobiles had to be drained of oil and gasoline and then recycled; 60,000 boats were destroyed; and 300,000 underground fuel tanks and 42,000 tons of hazardous waste had to be cleaned up and properly disposed of at licensed facilities (Varney and Moller 2005). Government officials peg the numbers of cars lost in New Orleans alone at 145,000 (Dart 2006).

What has been cleaned up, what gets left behind, and where the waste is disposed of appear to be linked more to political science and sociology than to toxicology, epidemiology, and hydrology. Weeks after Katrina struck, the LDEQ allowed New Orleans to open the 200-acre Old Gentilly Landfill to dump construction and demolition waste from the storm (Burdeau 2005). In the 1980s, federal regulators had ordered the unlined landfill closed. The 200-acre dump was being readied for reopening just before Katrina hit in August 2005. By December, after it reopened, more than 2,000 truckloads of hurricane debris were entering the landfill in New Orleans East every day (O'Driscoll 2005).

Just four months after the storm, the Old Gentilly Landfill grew to about 100 feet high (Martin 2006). LDEQ officials insist that the old landfill, which is still operating, meets all proper standards, but residents and environmentalists have disagreed. Even some high-ranking elected officials have expressed fear that reopening the Old Gentilly Landfill could create an ecological nightmare (Russell 2005). In November 2005, four days after environmentalists filed a lawsuit to block the dumping, the landfill caught fire.

In April 2006, the U.S. Army Corps of Engineers and the Louisiana Department of Environmental Quality issued permits that would allow Waste Management Inc. to open and operate a construction- and demolition-related material (C&D) landfill in New Orleans East. The new landfill is located on Chef Menteur Highway, which runs through much of New Orleans East, where the majority of the population is African American. Waste Management pledged to give the city 22 percent of all revenue derived from the site. Every week, Waste Management picks up an average of 45 pounds of trash from each home, 20 more pounds per home than pre-Katrina. The new landfill could accept as much as 6.5 million cubic yards of vegetation and other debris generated by Katrina—including roofing materials, Sheetrock, and demolition debris, which are considered less harmful than other types of waste.

After Katrina, the LDEQ expanded its definition of what is considered "construction debris" to include potentially contaminated material (Luther 2007), but regulators acknowledge the potential toxic contamination threat from storm-related wastes. Much of the disaster debris from flooded neighborhoods in New Orleans has been mixed to the point that separation is difficult or impossible (Luther 2007). David Romero of the EPA says it would be "lucky" if even 30 percent of the hazardous waste was removed from the waste stream. In an October interview on CNN, LDEQ assistant secretary Chuck Carr Brown said hazardous materials were hidden "like toxic needles in a haystack" in the hurricane debris (Pardo 2006).

Nevertheless, government officials assert that the risk of hazardous materials being dumped at the Chef Menteur site is insignificant and that current sorting practices are adequate to keep hazardous waste out of the landfill. They also insist that protective liners are not needed for C&D landfills because demolition debris is cleaner than other rubbish (Eaton 2006). C&D landfills are not required under federal law to have protective liners, but municipal landfills, which are expected to receive a certain amount of hazardous household waste, must. LDEQ's Brown told the *New York Times* in May 2006 that "there's nothing toxic, nothing hazardous" going to the landfill (Eaton 2006).

Landfill opponents think otherwise. Many fear the government's willingness to waive regulations will mean motor oil, batteries, electronics, ink toner, chlorine bleach, drain cleaners, and other noxious material will almost certainly wind up at the unlined landfills (Russell 2006). Government at all levels has done a poor job of policing what goes into landfills—especially after hurricanes where contents from gutted homes get mixed together. Community leaders in New Orleans East beat back two other efforts, in 1990 and 1997, to locate landfills along U.S. 90 near their homes. The Chef Highway Landfill is about four miles west of the Old Gentilly Landfill in a mostly African-American and Vietnamese community (Dunn 2006). More than a thousand Vietnamese-American families live less than two miles from the edge of the new landfill. African-American and Vietnamese-American homeowners see the landfill as a direct assault on their health, their property values, and their efforts to rebuild their lives shattered by the storm.

DESTRUCTION OF LOW-INCOME
AND WORKING-CLASS HOUSING

All eyes are watching New Orleans' rebuilding efforts, especially how it addresses the repopulation of its historically African-American neighborhoods and its strategically sited public housing. The Housing Authority of New Orleans was dismantling traditional public housing for nearly a decade before Katrina through Hope VI, a Clinton-era program that favors vouchers and mixed-income developments. Dramatic population shifts occurred in New Orleans as a result of the Hope VI project, which displaced thousands of public housing residents. Gentrification of historically black areas was becoming a problem for many citizens.

The St. Thomas redevelopment in New Orleans in the late 1990s became the prototype for elite visions of the city's future. Strategically sited public housing projects like the St. Thomas homes were demolished to make way for neo-traditionalist townhouses and stores (in the St. Thomas case, a Wal-Mart) in the New Urbanist spirit. These "mixed-use, mixed-income" developments were typically advertised as little utopias of diversity, but—as in St. Thomas in New Orleans, Olympic Village (formerly Techwood Homes) in Atlanta, and similar places around the country—the real dynamic is exclusionary rather than inclusionary, with only a few project residents being rehoused on the development site.

After Katrina, HUD announced it would invest $154 million in rebuilding public housing in New Orleans and assist the city to bring displaced residents home, but critics fear that government officials and business leaders are quietly planning to demolish the old projects and privatize public housing. Ten months after Katrina, 80 percent of public housing in New Orleans remained closed. Six of ten of the largest public housing developments in the city were boarded up, with the other four in various states of repair.

Over 49,000 people lived in public housing before Katrina, 20,000 in older, large-scale developments such as St. Bernard and 29,000 in Section 8 rental housing (a federal housing program that provides housing assistance to low-income renters and homeowners in the form of rental subsidies), and these were also devastated by the storm. The number of public housing units in New Orleans has been on a steady decline since the mid-1990s. In 1996, the city had 13,694 units of conventional public housing. In 2005, shortly before Katrina, the number had fallen to 7,379.

New Orleans' homeless population has skyrocketed since Katrina—reaching an unprecedented 4 percent of the total population in 2008—12,000 homeless people, nearly double the pre-Katrina count. New Orleans' homeless rate is more than four times that of most U.S. cities. The cities with homeless rates closest to that of New Orleans are Atlanta (1.4 percent) and Washington (0.95 percent), both majority-black cities (Jervis 2008a).

New Orleans faces a severe housing crunch and a growing homeless problem. Plans to rebuild the city's 77,000 rental units lost to Katrina have largely failed (Dewan 2007). There is little money for families who are ineligible for FEMA rental payments. Of the $121.5 billion Louisiana received in the federal community development block grants, $25 million has been spent on homelessness prevention and $72 million for the housing voucher program. The state received a $220 million block grant for social services, of which $100 million went to the Louisiana Department of Health and Hospitals for medical and mental health care. For those families who are eligible for FEMA-financed housing but have been unable to find it, FEMA has agreed to pay for a new case-management program but not direct assistance like furniture, utilities, or deposits (Dewan 2008).

In June 2006, federal housing officials announced that more than 5,000 public housing apartments for the poor would be razed and replaced by developments for residents from a wider range of incomes. The demolition plan would eliminate 4,500 public housing units in the city while building only about 800 units of traditional public housing (Kromm and Sturgis 2008). This move has heightened the anxiety of many low-income black Katrina survivors who fear they will be pushed out in favor of higher-income families (Walsh 2007).

Powerful forces have been trying to demolish public housing in New Orleans for decades. When Katrina emptied New Orleans of public housing residents, the *Wall Street Journal* reported U.S. Congressman Richard Baker, a ten-term Republican from Baton Rouge, telling lobbyists: "We finally cleaned up public housing in New Orleans. We couldn't do it, but God did" (Babington 2005, A04). The demolition of four sprawling public housing projects—the St. Bernard, C. J. Peete, B. W. Cooper, and Lafitte housing developments—represents more than half of all of the conventional public housing in the city, where only 1,097 units were occupied ten months after the storm.

HUD raised by about 35 percent the value of disaster vouchers for displaced residents because the city's housing shortage caused rents to skyrocket. However, Katrina has driven housing prices up as individuals compete for a limited supply that survived the storm and for newly constructed units. The average two-bedroom apartment that would have cost $676 a month before Katrina in 2005 now rents for $990. Housing discrimination becomes rampant when the supply is scarce—hitting African-American renters and home buyers especially hard (National Fair Housing Alliance 2005). A Greater New Orleans Fair Housing Action Center study of the New Orleans metro area after Katrina found discrimination in nearly six out of ten transactions, with African Americans encountering less favorable treatment based on race (Berry 2007). Housing providers often simply didn't return phone calls from African Americans, didn't provide applications to them, or didn't show available rental units to them. With results like these, it is no wonder that African-American Katrina survivors have had difficulty recovering from the storm. Many African-American households began their road to recovery by not returning to work and home but looking for jobs and housing.

Although Katrina did not discriminate, a May 2008 progress report from the Louisiana Family Recovery Corps found a wide disparity in adaptation and recovery between black and white storm victims: "There is great disparity in the progress towards recovery, disruption from the storms and levels of progress between black and white households, even for those with similar incomes. On nearly every indicator, the storm impact and recovery experience for black households is significantly different than for whites, even after examining these issues by income levels" (Alfred 2008, 12).

A June 6, 2008, CNN *Money Magazine* report indicates that the price of the average single-family home in the New Orleans metropolitan area rose to $215,179, up from $195,377 immediately before Katrina. Rents in Mid-City and Lakefronts sections of New Orleans, both of which were flooded, rose to a post-storm average of $1,584 a month from $986 before the storm. As of July 2008, nearly 4,000 displaced New Orleans residents lived in trailers. Some one-fourth of the trailer residents are renters, and 16 percent have special needs. Most of the people still living in trailers three years after the storm are families who have the most challenges in a tight housing market (Jervis 2008b, 4A). In May 2008, black storm victims were more than twice as likely as white storm victims to be still living in trailers (Alfred 2008).

A "SAFE" ROAD HOME

Katrina and the failures of the federal levee system displaced more than 378,000 people from New Orleans, creating "one of the largest disaster diasporas in U.S. history" (Jervis 2008c, 1A). Three years after Katrina, population estimates vary on how many people have actually made it back. Some demographers place the total population of the city between 315,000 and 320,000 residents, estimated by utility and water hookups, mail delivery, and other public service accounts. In August 2008, the Brookings Institution estimated that New Orleans had reached 72 percent of its 453,726 pre-Katrina level (Liu and Plyer 2008). The storm cut deeper for African-American households than for white households as 47 percent of African-American households live someplace different, compared to only 19 percent of white households (Alfred 2008, 16).

Since Katrina, the New Orleans African-American population has plummeted by 57 percent, while the white population has fallen less, by only 36 percent. African Americans now make up 58 percent of New Orleans compared to 67 percent before the storm. New Orleans has been a predominately black city for three decades, but now some well-known African-American communities are a fraction of what they were, and others see their very existence threatened. For example, the Lower Ninth Ward has seen only 9.9 percent of its population return. A traditionally mixed-race neighborhood within the Lower Ninth, Holy Cross, has fared better with a 37 percent return, benefiting from the work of preservationists who seek to restore the federally declared historic district.

The sprawling New Orleans East area, which includes the black upper-middle-class enclave of Eastover and several other communities on man-made lakes, has seen nearly 60 percent of its residents back home—compared with 65–70 percent of the city's total population return. Affluent and mostly white areas are not only back, but they are growing. The population of the Garden District is at 107 percent of its pre-Katrina level, the French Quarter at 103 percent, and an adjacent neighborhood called Faubourg Marigny at 100.3 percent (Gonzales 2008).

Whereas local advocates have focused largely on the demolition of New Orleans public housing, the loss of working-class rental units to Katrina is just as significant. Katrina and Rita, which hit four weeks after Katrina, destroyed more than 41,000 apartments affordable to people earning less than the area's median income, and only 43 percent will be rebuilt under federal programs. Prospects are bleakest for households earning less than $26,150—with only 16 percent of housing affordable to them scheduled for federally funded redevelopment. Working-class families' rents have increased 46 percent and utility rates have risen 33 percent while wages have lagged.

Katrina hit New Orleans' mostly African-American blue-collar workers, individuals who never lived in public housing and who often made ends meet by working two jobs, especially hard. With limited plans to replace rental units lost in the storm, the city is at risk of losing an entire tier of workers. It is no surprise that such a large share of the African-American working-class population is still stranded three years after the storm. This trend can be observed in job vacancy rates in the cleaning and maintenance sector that are up from 4.1 percent before Katrina to 13.1 percent now, in the restaurant sector from 3.6 percent to 13.4 percent, and in other service jobs from 6.3 percent to 16.7 percent (Gonzales 2008b).

The government has been slow to invest in bricks-and-mortar housing for working-class families. By March 2008, FEMA had paid to Louisiana 93 percent of the $6.6 billion infrastructure allocation, but only 47 percent had actually reached localities. Overall, Katrina relief and rebuilding funds have only trickled down to local governments and residents. Given the enormity and urgency of the need, one would think much more would have been done after three years.

FEMA even withheld disaster relief supplies from Katrina victims. In June 2008, nearly three years after the storm, the first truckload of $85 million in federal relief supplies, lost in a bureaucratic hole, arrived in Louisiana and were distributed to those still displaced by Katrina and Rita. The supplies had been stored in Fort Worth for two years, and FEMA finally deemed them surplus goods early in 2008 after the building's owner decided to demolish the structure.

The road home for many Katrina survivors has been bumpy, largely due to slow government actions to distribute the $116 billion in federal aid to residents to rebuild. Only about $35 billion has been appropriated for long-term rebuilding. Most of the Katrina money coming from Washington hasn't gotten to those most in need—and the funding squeeze is stopping much of the Gulf Coast from coming back (Kromm and Sturgis 2007).

Eighteen months after the storm, only 630 homeowners had received checks from Louisiana's The Road Home program, which provides eligible homeowners up to $150,000 in compensation for their losses to get back into their homes. In July 2008, The Road Home program had issued checks to 74 percent of eligible homeowners. It made 114,679 awards totaling $6.7 billion, making it the largest home-rebuilding program in U.S. history. The Road Home is closing an average 3,972 applications per month, down from a monthly average of 9,450 in the latter half of 2007 (Liu and Plyer 2008; Jervis 2008c). The average Road Home award in Louisiana was $58,688 compared to $73,090 in Mississippi.

Although government officials insist that the dirt in residents' yards is safe, Churchill Downs, Inc., the owners of New Orleans' Fair Grounds, felt it was not safe for its million-dollar thoroughbred horses to race on. The Fair Grounds is the nation's third-oldest track. Only Saratoga and Pimlico have been racing longer. The owners hauled off soil tainted by Katrina's floodwaters and rebuilt a grandstand roof ripped off by the storm's wind (Martell 2006). The Fair Grounds opened on Thanksgiving Day 2006. If tainted soil is not safe for horses, surely it is not safe for people—especially children who play and dig in the dirt.

Families who chose to return to rebuild their communities shouldn't have to worry about their children playing in yards, parks, and schoolyards contaminated with cancer-causing chemicals left by Katrina floodwaters. In March 2006, seven months after the storm slammed ashore, organizers of A Safe Way Back Home initiative, the Deep South Center for Environmental Justice at Dillard University (DSCEJ), and the United Steelworkers (USW) undertook a proactive pilot neighborhood clean-up project—the first of its kind in New Orleans (Deep South Center for Environmental Justice 2006). The clean-up project, located in the 8100 block of Aberdeen Road in New Orleans East, removed several inches of tainted soil from the front and back yards, replacing the soil with new sod, and safely disposed of the contaminated dirt.

But residents who choose to remove the topsoil from their yards—which contains sediments left by flooding—find themselves in a Catch-22 situation with the LDEQ and EPA insisting that the soil in their yards is not contaminated and the local landfill operators refusing to dispose of the soil because they suspect it is contaminated. This bottleneck of what to do with the topsoil remains unresolved more than three years after the flood.

The Safe Way Back Home demonstration project serves as a catalyst for a series of activities that will attempt to reclaim New Orleans East after Katrina. It is the government's responsibility to provide the resources required to address areas of environmental concern and to ensure that the workforce is protected. However, residents are not waiting for the government to ride in on a white horse to rescue them and clean up their neighborhoods.

The DSCEJ/USW coalition received dozens of requests and inquiries from New Orleans East homeowners associations to help clean up their neighborhoods block by block. State and federal officials called these voluntary clean-up efforts "scaremongering" (Simmons 2006). EPA and LDEQ officials said that they tested soil samples from the neighborhood in December 2006 and that there was no immediate cause for concern.

According to Tom Harris, administrator of LDEQ's environmental technology division and the state toxicologist, the government originally sampled 800 locations in New Orleans and found cause for concern in only 46 samples. Generally, the soil in New Orleans is consistent with "what we saw before Katrina," says Harris. He called the Safe Way Back Home program "completely unnecessary" (Williams 2006). A week after the voluntary clean-up project began, an LDEQ staffer ate a spoonful of dirt scraped from the Aberdeen Road pilot project. The dirt-eating publicity stunt was clearly an attempt to disparage the proactive neighborhood clean-up initiative. LDEQ officials later apologized.

Despite barriers and red tape, Katrina evacuees are moving back into their damaged homes or travel trailers in their yards. Homeowners are gutting their houses, treating the mold, fixing roofs and siding, and slowly getting their lives back in order. One of the main questions returning residents have is: Is this place safe? They're getting mixed signals from government agencies. In December 2005, the Louisiana Department of Environmental Quality (LDEQ) announced that "there is no unacceptable long-term health risk directly attributable to environmental contamination resulting from the storm." Yet contamination was found all across the city's flooded neighborhoods.

Two months later, in February, the results of tests by the Natural Resources Defense Council (NRDC) came out with different conclusions (Solomon and Rotkin-Ellman 2006). NRDC's analyses of soil and air quality after Hurricane Katrina revealed dangerously high levels of diesel fuel, lead, and other contaminants in Gentilly, Bywater, Orleans Parish, and other New Orleans neighborhoods.

Although many government scientists insisted the soil is safe, an April 2006 multi-agency task force press release distributed by the EPA raised some questions (U.S. EPA 2006). Though it claimed that the levels of lead and other contaminants in New Orleans soil were "similar" to soil-contaminant levels in other cities, it also cautioned residents to "keep children from playing in bare dirt. Cover bare dirt with grass, bushes, or 4–6 inches of lead-free wood chips, mulch, soil, or sand."

Surely, if the federal government can pay for debris removal, blue tarp roofs, and temporary trailer housing (which have already cost an estimated $4.5 billion), it can make funds available to address the "silent killer" of childhood lead poisoning. Making government grants of $2,000 to $3,000 available to homeowners to test and clean up contamination in their yards would be a bargain given the millions of hurricane relief dollars wasted on profiteering, no-bid contracts, and material markups (Varney 2006). The band-aid approach of, for example, covering bare dirt with grass and wood chips stops short of addressing the root problem—environmental hazards found inside and outside of homes.

Now, instead of cleaning up the mess that existed before the storm, government officials are allowing dirty neighborhoods to stay dirty forever. Just because lead and other heavy metals existed in some New Orleans neighborhoods before Katrina doesn't mean that there isn't a moral or legal obligation to remediate any contamination uncovered. Government scientists have assured New Orleanians, including gardeners, that they do not need to worry about soil salinity and heavy metal content. They also say residents need not worry about digging or planting in the soil. But given the uncertainties built into quantitative risk assessments, how certain are these government officials that all of New Orleans' neighborhoods are safe?

In August 2006, nearly a year after Katrina struck, the EPA gave New Orleans and surrounding communities a clean bill of health, while pledging to monitor a handful of toxic hot spots (Brown 2006). EPA and LDEQ officials concluded that Katrina did not cause any appreciable contamination that was not already there. Although EPA tests confirmed widespread lead in the soil—a pre-storm problem in 40 percent of New Orleans—EPA dismissed residents' calls to address this problem as outside the agency's mission.

And in June 2007, the U.S. Government Accountability Office (GAO) issued a report, *Hurricane Katrina: EPA's Current and Future Environmental Protection Efforts Could Be Enhanced by Addressing Issues and Challenges Faced on the Gulf Coast,* criticizing EPA's handling of contamination in post-Katrina New Orleans and the Gulf Coast (U.S. Government Accountability Office 2007). The GAO found inadequate monitoring for asbestos around demolition and renovation sites. Additionally, the GAO investigation revealed that "key information released to the public about environmental contamination was neither timely nor adequate, and in some cases, easily misinterpreted to the public's detriment."

The GAO also found that EPA did not make clear until eight months later, in August 2006, that a major finding in its 2005 report—that the great majority of the data showed that adverse health effects would not be expected from exposure to sediments from previously flooded areas—applied only to short-term visits, such as to view damage to homes (U.S. Government Accountability Office 2007).

In March 2007, a coalition of community and environmental groups collected over 130 soil samples in Orleans Parish. Testing was conducted by the Natural Resources Defense Council (Fields, Huang, Solomon, Rotkin-Ellman, and Simms 2007). Sampling was done at 65 sites in residential neighborhoods where post-Katrina EPA testing had previously shown elevated concentrations of arsenic in soils. Sampling was also done at 15 playgrounds and 19 schools. Six school sites had arsenic levels in excess of the LDEQ's soil screening value for arsenic. The LDEQ soil screening value of 12 milligrams per kilogram normally requires additional sampling, further investigation, and a site-specific risk assessment. It is clear that the levels of arsenic in the sediment are unacceptably high for residential neighborhoods.

DYING FOR A HOME—TOXIC FEMA TRAILERS

Right after Katrina, FEMA purchased about 102,000 travel trailers for $2.6 billion, or roughly $15,000 each (Spake 2007). Soon there were reports of residents becoming ill in these trailers due to the release of potentially dangerous levels of formaldehyde, a known carcinogen (Hampton 2006). In fact, formaldehyde was omnipresent in the glues, plastics, building materials, composite wood, plywood panels, and particle board used to manufacture the trailers.

In Mississippi, FEMA received 46 complaints by individuals who had symptoms of formaldehyde exposure, including eye, nose, and throat irritation, nausea, skin rashes, sinus infections, depression, inflamed mucus membranes, asthma attacks, headaches, insomnia, intestinal problems, memory impairment, and breathing difficulties (Schwartz 2007; Spake 2007; Hampton 2006; Johnson 2007). The Sierra Club conducted tests of 31 trailers and found that 29 had unsafe levels of formaldehyde (Hampton 2006; Damon 2007; Brunker 2006). According to the Sierra Club, 83 percent of the trailers tested in Alabama, Louisiana, and Mississippi had formaldehyde levels above the EPA limit of 0.10 parts per million (Schwartz 2007; Brunker 2006).

Even though FEMA received numerous complaints about toxic trailers, the agency only tested one occupied trailer to determine the levels of formaldehyde in it (Committee on Oversight and Government Reform 2007). The test confirmed that the levels of formaldehyde were extraordinarily high and presented an immediate health risk to the occupants (Committee on Oversight and Government Reform 2007). Unfortunately, FEMA did not test any more occupied trailers and released a public statement discounting any risk associated with formaldehyde exposure.

According to findings from a congressional committee hearing, FEMA deliberately neglected to investigate any reports of high levels of formaldehyde in trailers so as to bolster FEMA's litigation position in case individuals affected by their negligence decided to sue them (Damon 2007; Babington 2007). In fact, more than 500 hurricane survivors and evacuees in Louisiana are pursuing legal action against the trailer manufacturers for formaldehyde exposure. Two years after Katrina, more than 65,000 Gulf Coast families, an estimated 195,000 people, were living in FEMA trailers. The vast majority of the trailers, about 45,000, were in Louisiana (Alberts 2007; Damon 2007; Babington 2007).

In July 2007, FEMA stop buying and selling disaster relief trailers because of the formaldehyde contamination (Johnson 2007). FEMA administrator R. David Paulison admitted that the trailers used by displaced Katrina residents were toxic and concluded that the agency should have moved faster in addressing the health concerns of residents (Cruz 2007). In August 2007, FEMA began moving families out of the toxic trailers and finding them new rental housing. Testing of FEMA travel trailers for formaldehyde and other hazards began in September 2007 (Treadway 2007). The Centers for Disease Control and Prevention was tasked with developing parameters for testing the travel trailers.

In February 2008, more than two and a half years after residents of FEMA trailers began complaining of breathing difficulties, nosebleeds, and persistent headaches, CDC officials announced that long-awaited government tests had found potentially hazardous levels of toxic formaldehyde gas in travel trailers and mobile homes provided by FEMA. CDC tests found that levels of formaldehyde gas in 519 trailers and mobile homes tested in Louisiana and Mississippi were—on average—about five times what people are exposed to in most modern homes (Maugh and Jervis 2008). More than 38,000 families, or roughly 114,000 individuals, were living in FEMA-provided travel trailers or mobile homes along the Gulf Coast at the time of the CDC tests—down from a high of about 144,000 families.

In some trailers, the levels were nearly 40 times customary exposure levels, raising fears that residents could suffer respiratory problems and potentially other long-term health effects. CDC tests showed an average formaldehyde level of 77 parts per billion (ppb), with a low of 3 ppb and a high of 590 ppb. The average level in new homes is 10 to 20 ppb. Long-term exposure to levels of 77 ppb could have serious effects. Exposure to the higher levels can cause eye irritation and coughing and other respiratory problems. These findings come 23 months after FEMA first received reports of health problems and test results showing formaldehyde levels at 75 times the U.S.-recommended workplace safety threshold.

The federal government has approved $400 million to build Katrina Cottages, alternative affordable housing designed to survive a storm (Alberts 2007), but nothing has happened because of internal political fights between the state government and private contractors over what kind of homes should be built.

LET THEM FIND FOOD

Before Katrina, predominantly African-American communities in New Orleans were struggling with the mass closings of shopping centers and grocery stores. Many watched in horror at the explosion of chain-store fast-food restaurants, liquor stores, dollar stores, pawn shops, and check-cashing shops in their neighborhoods. Having to travel great distances for the ordinary amenities of life made life more and more difficult. After Katrina, middle- and upper-middle-class black neighborhoods have fallen victim to the same fate. All must drive long distances to white neighborhoods for supermarkets, shopping centers, and quality restaurants.

In a 2007 survey of low-income Orleans Parish residents, nearly 60 percent were more than three miles from a supermarket while only 50 percent owned cars. Additionally, of those surveyed, 70 percent reported that they "would buy" or "might buy" fresh produce items if they were available in their neighborhoods. Moreover, the study showed that low-income people "like" to eat fruit and vegetables as much as or more than unhealthy foods (The New Orleans Food Policy Advisory Committee 2007).

Access to fresh, nutritious food was inadequate in New Orleans even before Katrina. At that time, there were about 12,000 residents per supermarket while the nation's average was 8,800 residents (New Orleans Food Policy Advisory Committee 2007). Now, nearly three years after Katrina, the availability of these types of foods has only gotten worse. Today, there are nearly 18,000 residents per supermarket (Figure 1.1). There are presently only 18 supermarkets open in New Orleans. Adding to this woeful lack of stores is the fact that the smaller stores that have reopened are not meeting the demand for fresh produce.

In predominantly black New Orleans East, with a current population of 60,000, there is only one supermarket, a Winn-Dixie. In September 2007, news of its reopening created such excitement in the neighborhood that opening day felt like the local jazz festival. People gathered and greeted friends they had not seen since before the storm.

FIGURE 1.1—Supermarkets in New Orleans Before and After Hurricane Katrina

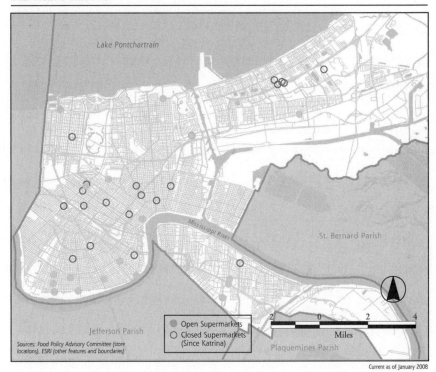

Source: Map created by the Louisiana Public Health Institute for the New Orleans Food Policy Advisory Committee (January 2008). Originally published in *Building Healthy Communities: Expanding Access to Fresh Food Retail. A Report by the New Orleans Food Policy Advisory Committee.* New Orleans: The Prevention Research Center at Tulane University and The Food Trust, March 2008.

The supermarket opening also excited elected officials and business leaders. On opening day, Thursday September 27, 2007, the NASDAQ market's opening bell was rung from that Winn-Dixie. Winn-Dixie CEO Peter Lynch and New Orleans Mayor Ray Nagin rang the bell from the supermarket at 9701 Chef Menteur Highway. The opening bell ceremony was broadcast live on the seven-story NASDAQ MarketSite Tower in Times Square and via satellite to national and international media. This was the first NASDAQ remote opening ceremony from a grocery store and the first ever in Louisiana, which has 18 NASDAQ-listed companies.

Who would have thought that one supermarket could bring such joy? Everyone was chatting with someone they had not seen in a long time. It was time to catch up on stories of loved ones and harrowing tales of survival. This excitement is not uncommon to African-American urban neighborhoods that have become food deserts, without full-service supermarkets, grocery stores, and farmers markets. New Orleans East residents are forced to accept extremely long checkout lines in exchange for access to a full-service supermarket.

Access to fresh healthy foods, like fruits and vegetables, high in nutrients and low in salt, fat, and calories, is vital to the good health of the people in our communities. Research in New Orleans' Central City neighborhood revealed that greater access to fresh vegetables has led to increased consumption of these foods by residents of the neighborhood (New Orleans Food Policy Advisory Committee 2008). Improving access to healthy foods would lead to better dietary practices and the resultant better health of individuals and families in underserved communities. In the rebuilding of New Orleans, we must reverse this trend of poor access to healthy foods leading to poor dietary health.

UNEQUAL LEVEE PROTECTION

The Army Corps of Engineers is working to fix or replace 220 miles of levees and floodwalls, build new flood gates and pump stations at the mouths of three outfall canals, and strengthen existing walls and levees at important points. By May 2008, the Corps had spent $4 billion of the $14 billion set aside by Congress to repair and upgrade the metropolitan area's hundreds of miles of levees by 2011. Some outside experts say that there are leaks in the new levees, that some of the work already completed may need to be redone, and that billions more will be needed (Burdeau 2008).

The latest report including flood maps produced by the Army Corps of Engineers shows no increase in levee protection to New Orleans East residents since Katrina (Army Corps of Engineers Interagency Performance Evaluation Task Force 2007). (See Table 1.1)

A disproportionately large swath of black New Orleans once again is left vulnerable to future flooding. After nearly two years and billions spent on levee repairs, the Army Corps of Engineers has estimated that there is a 1-in-100 annual chance that about a third of the city will be flooded with as much as six feet of water (Schwartz 2007).

Mostly African-American parts of New Orleans are still likely to be flooded in a major storm. Increased levee protection maps closely correspond with race of neighborhoods, black neighborhoods such as the Ninth Ward, Gentilly, and New Orleans East receiving little, if any, increased flood protection. These disparities could lead insurers and investors to redline and think twice about supporting the rebuilding efforts in vulnerable black areas.

The Lakeview-area resident can expect 5.5 feet of increased levee protection. This translates into 5.5 feet less water than what they received from Katrina. Lakeview is mostly white and affluent, New Orleans East is mostly black and middle class. This same scenario holds true for the mostly black Lower Ninth Ward, Upper Ninth Ward, and Gentilly neighborhoods. There is a racial component to the post-Katrina

TABLE 1.1—Interagency Performance Evaluation Task Force Risk and Reliability Report, Army Corps of Engineers, June 20, 2007

Neighborhoods	Average Depth of Flood Water Decrease	Fatalities Decreased	Property Loss Decreased
Lake View	5.5 ft	70%	32%
Upper Ninth	0.5 ft	31%	11%
Lower Ninth	2.0 ft	29%	4%
Gentilly	0.5 ft	19%	5%
N.O. East (West Lake Forest)	NC	NC	NC
Michoud	NC	NC	NC
New Orleans East	1.0 ft	83%	24%

Source: Army Corps of Engineers Interagency Performance Evaluation Task Force (IPET), "Risk and Reliability Report" (June 20, 2007). Available at http://nolarisk.usace.army.mil.

levee protection. Whether you are rich, poor, or middle class, if you are a black resident of New Orleans, you are less protected and you have received less increased flood protection from the federal government than the more white and affluent community of Lakeview.

Racism has taken an unmeasured toll on the lives of minorities and the poor. We say unmeasured because institutionalized racism has influenced policy that discriminates in ways that better serve the white and more affluent populations and communities. Katrina and its impacts, in a very powerful and revealing way, showed the world how race and class are intrinsically tied to policy. Moreover, it pointedly displayed how government policy can actually be harmful to the health and well-being of vulnerable populations (racial minorities, the poor, the sick and elderly, and children).

The scenes of stranded New Orleanians trapped on the roof of the crumbling Superdome and people dying on the street outside the Superdome and the New Orleans Convention Center are visions tragically etched in our collective memory. What was obvious to all was that policies for responding to disasters were woefully inadequate and needed to change.

What the New Orleans recovery process is also showing is that policies intended to be race-neutral can accelerate rather than alleviate the destructiveness of a disaster for the most vulnerable populations if the policies are not also race-sensitive.

More recently, African-American citizens of New Orleans have discovered that another government initiative completely excludes them. FEMA has a Hazardous Mitigation Fund that provides millions of dollars to ease flooding in communities. Site selections are based on participation in the National Flood Insurance Program.

Most homeowners in the city of New Orleans have flood insurance through that program. In fact, the city of New Orleans has a participation rate higher than the national average.

The second part of the equation is where the discrimination kicks in: The number of claims submitted by neighborhoods for flooding is included in FEMA's analysis. Before Katrina, largely white uptown neighborhoods tended to flood every time there was a very hard rain. Before Katrina, largely black New Orleans East and the Lower Ninth Ward, which are much more vulnerable to hurricanes, seldom flooded when it rained.

Consequently, FEMA Hazardous Mitigation Funds that were intended to help the populations most vulnerable to hurricanes will not receive any of the hazardous mitigation monies. Once again, this benefits the more affluent and white populations. What is being experienced in New Orleans is a "policy surge" more powerful than the storm surge that could facilitate a permanent and systematic depopulation and displacement of New Orleans' African-American communities.

CONCLUSIONS

As the waters began to recede, and the light of day was cast on the enormous, unbelievable extent of the damage to New Orleans and the Gulf Coast, speculation on the city's recovery or its demise began to echo across the media. How extensive was the environmental contamination? Had New Orleans become a Superfund site? Was it safe to return? The inability of both federal and state agencies (FEMA, EPA, LDEQ, CDC, ATSDR) to effectively and accurately answer these questions created a quandary that both slowed the recovery and paralyzed the ability of citizens to make a decision on returning.

To date, the information on the environmental safety of residents in New Orleans is nothing short of double talk. The EPA tells citizens that the city is safe, but qualified environmental scientists disagree, as does the agency's own test sampling. The EPA gives the city a clean bill of health, then provides instructions for parents to follow in order to keep their children safe when they play outside. LDEQ attempted to discredit citizen actions to organize to work with labor unions, nonprofit organizations, and volunteers to clean up their own neighborhoods. This schizophrenic response by government bears some of the responsibility for the slow recovery of New Orleans.

We can only speculate on what progress could have been made toward rebuilding New Orleans and returning most of its citizens if the environmental clean-up that we deserved had been done. What if the same priority for clean-up and safety given to the French Quarter, the Central Business District, and the racetrack had been given to the Lower Ninth Ward, New Orleans East, and other hard-hit sections of the city?

Just after the storm, an article in the *Dallas Morning News* quoted the Army Corps of Engineers as saying that it would take the Corps three months to scrape the city clean of all contaminated soil and sediment (Loftis 2005). This, of course, did not happen. What did occur was politics as usual, and the losers were the citizens of New Orleans, with African Americans taking the biggest hit.

Residents of devastated New Orleans neighborhoods do not need government agencies debating the "chicken or egg" contamination argument ("Which came first, the contamination or Katrina?"). They need the government to clean up the mess. All levels of government have a golden opportunity to get it right this time. Clean-up and reconstruction efforts in New Orleans have been shamefully sluggish and patchy, and environmental injustice may be compounded by rebuilding on poisoned ground.

The opportunities are only fading as Katrina slowly slips off the political radar. It is no accident that not one word about Katrina and the Gulf Coast reconstruction was mentioned in President Bush's State of the Union address in January 2007—seventeen months after the devastating storm. Displaced residents need a "road home" program that is not only fair but also safe. It is immoral—and should be illegal—to unnecessarily subject Katrina survivors to contamination—whether the pollution was there before or after the storm.

Clearly, prevention and precaution should be the driving force behind the environmental clean-up in post-Katrina New Orleans. Either we all pay now or we all pay later. It will cost more in terms of dollars and ill health if we wait. The nation cannot allow another immoral, unethical, and illegal "human experiment" to occur in New Orleans and the Gulf Coast. The solution is prevention. In July 2008, FEMA sought immunity from lawsuits over potentially dangerous fumes in government-issued trailers that have housed tens of thousands of Gulf Coast hurricane victims (Kunzelman 2008). Lawyers for the trailer home plaintiffs want the cases certified as a class action on behalf of tens of thousands of current and former trailer occupants in Alabama, Louisiana, Mississippi, and Texas. Such cases and legal wrangling often take years to resolve.

POLICY RECOMMENDATIONS

- Implement environmental justice. Ensure equal funding, equal clean-up standards, and equal protection of public health and environmental response in minority and low-income communities. The EPA, FEMA, and the Army Corps of Engineers need to enforce Executive Order 12898, Federal Actions to Address Environmental Justice in Minority Populations and Low-Income Populations, regarding environmental justice in the clean-up and rebuilding in the hurricane-affected Gulf Coast region.
- Enforce existing environmental and health standards. Clean-up standards should not be weakened or compromised in low-income and minority neighborhoods. Allowing waivers of environmental standards could compound the harms already caused by Katrina and undermine health protection of the most vulnerable members of our society.

- Provide environmental guidance on comprehensive waste management. Provide more detailed guidance to state and local entities in developing a comprehensive waste management plan before and after disasters to better ensure protection of public health and the environment and prevent the creation of future Superfund sites. This guidance should address the selection of landfill sites for disaster debris, including advance selection of potential landfill sites, and practices to consider when making special accommodations for debris disposal in emergency situations. Guidance should be put in place so that public health risks are minimized during the demolition and renovation of buildings containing asbestos, activities that can release asbestos fibers into the air. Further, many thousands of homes being demolished and renovated by or for individual homeowners are generally not subject to EPA's asbestos emissions standards aimed at limiting releases of fibers into the air.

- Provide environmental assessment. Federal and state government agencies should include additional sampling, assessment, and clean-up of toxic sites, establishing an effective process for debris and waste management, and fully informing the public of health risks, including access to protective equipment and treatment, if necessary. The city should ensure that state and federal agencies continue to fully assess health risks for residents returning to contaminated areas before making any official declarations that it is safe for them to do so.

- Conduct independent environmental testing and monitoring. Because of the loss of trust in government, independent testing and monitoring of the water, soil, sediment, and air in the affected areas are needed using the best testing technology and methods available. This testing must provide an assessment of current contamination levels, as well as continuous monitoring.

- Remove contaminated sediments. The city should immediately request that FEMA and the EPA remove contaminated sediment from New Orleans' communities and conduct further investigation and remediation of toxic hot spots.

- Monitor the air and water. There is a need for ongoing monitoring of the air and water quality in New Orleans. In many cases, no data have been available since 2006, yet we know that there were documented problems with mold, endotoxin, heavy metals, particulate matter, and drinking water contamination. These findings need to be followed up to ensure that they have been resolved. EPA should develop a plan for additional air monitoring and evaluate the number and location of the air monitors to ensure sufficient coverage of areas with substantial demolition and renovation activities, both regulated and unregulated. If air monitors are not appropriately located in neighborhoods undergoing demolition and renovation, the monitoring network will not be adequate to ensure that public health is being protected. While the EPA took steps to monitor asbestos after the hurricane—for example, more than doubling the number of ambient (outdoor) air monitors and monitoring emissions at debris-reduction sites—monitors were not placed in areas undergoing substantial demolition and renovation, such as the Ninth Ward.

- Give residents access to treatment for exposure to toxins. The city should demand that the federal Public Health Service and Agency for Toxic Substances Disease Registry provide ongoing medical care and testing to residents exposed to toxins, as required by the Comprehensive Environmental Response, Compensation and Liability Act (section 104[i][1]).
- Ensure safe and healthy schools for returning children. Flood-damaged schools should be rebuilt in a manner that fully protects children's health. It is imperative that schools and the land on which they sit are safe, clean, and free from health-threatening contamination. Rebuilt schools should be LEED (Leadership in Energy and Environmental Design) certified and incorporate guidelines developed by the Collaborative for High Performance Schools for the design of energy-efficient, healthy, comfortable, well-lit schools. Care should be taken to make design, engineering, and materials choices that prevent mold from growing indoors. The city also should guarantee that soil on school grounds is clean and safe by making sure it is tested and cleaned to at least the level of the most protective clean-up guidelines in the country.
- Balance green building and social justice. Rebuilding efforts in the Gulf Coast region should adopt smart growth and green building principles to ensure that past environmental inequities are repaired along with the physical infrastructure. However, greenness and justice need to go together. Green building in New Orleans and the Gulf Coast could involve exorbitant fees for architects, materials, and construction—and greening that fails to address issues of affordability, access, and equity may open the floodgates for permanent displacement of low-income and minority homeowners and business owners.
- Implement an Environmental Training and Green Jobs Initiative. Implement a comprehensive environmental clean-up, restoration, and green jobs training program for local residents who live in environmental hot-spot areas.

REFERENCES

Alberts, S. 2007. "Katrina Survivors Suffer in 'FEMA Dirty Little Secret' Trailers." August 28. Available at http://www.canada.com/nationalpost/news/story.html?id =d3c0b8fa-31d3-4695-a806-5cfd2fef53e5&k=35727 (accessed July 17, 2008).

Alfred, D. 2008. *Progress for Some, Hope and Hardship for Many.* New Orleans: Louisiana Family Recovery Corps. May.

American Society of Mechanical Engineers and the Sewerage and Water Board of New Orleans. 1974. "A National Historic Mechanical Engineering Landmark . . . No. 1 Pumping Station, New Orleans, La." Available at http://files.asme.org/ASMEORG/ Communities/History/Landmarks/5485.pdf (accessed October 10, 2008).

Army Corps of Engineers. 2006. "Questions and Answers: Hurricane Recovery and Levee Issues." January 18. Available at http://www.mvn.usace.army.mil/tgf/Q&A01.htm (accessed July 1, 2006).

Army Corps of Engineers Interagency Performance Evaluation Task Force. 2007. "Risk and Reliability Report." June 20. Available at http://nolarisk.usace.army.mil (accessed July 1, 2008).

Associated Press. 2008a. "Feds Settle with City Over Agriculture Street Landfill Site." *Times-Picayune*. May 29.

_____. 2008b. "Scientists Scrutinize Toxic FEMA Trailers." *USA Today*. February 16.

Babington, C. 2005. "Some GOP Legislators Hit Jarring Notes in Addressing Katrina." *Washington Post*. September 5.

_____. 2007. "FEMA Slow to Test Toxicity of Trailers." *USA Today*. Available at http://www.usatoday.com/news/topstories/2007-07-19-2231201740_x.htm (accessed July 1, 2008).

Baumbach, R., and W. E. Borah. 1981. *The Second Battle of New Orleans: A History of the Vieux Carré Riverfront Expressway Controversy*. Tuscaloosa: University of Alabama Press.

Berry, D. B. 2007. "Testers Play Crucial Role in Exposing Discrimination." *USA Today*. September 28.

Brown, M. 2006. "Final EPA Report Deems N.O. Safe." *Times-Picayune*. August 19.

Brunker, M. 2006. "FEMA Trailers 'Toxic Tin Cans'?" July 23. Available at http://risingfromruin.msnbc.com/2006/07/are_fema_traile.html (accessed August 1, 2006).

Bullard, R. D. 2005. "Katrina and the Second Disaster: A Twenty-Point Plan to Destroy Black New Orleans." December 23. Available at http://www.ejrc.cau.edu/Bullard20PointPlan.html (accessed July 17, 2008).

Burdeau, C. 2005. "New Orleans Area Becoming a Dumping Ground." *Associated Press*. October 31.

_____. 2008. "Leaky New Orleans Levee Alarms Experts." *Times-Picayune*. May 21.

BusinessWeek. 2005. "The Mother of All Toxic Cleanups." September 26. Available at http://www.businessweek.com/magazine/content/05_39/b3952055.htm (accessed December 21, 2005).

Committee on Oversight and Government Reform. 2007. "Committee Probes FEMA's Response to Reports of Toxic Trailers." July 19. Available at http://oversight.house.gov/story.asp?ID=1413 (accessed July 17, 2008).

Cruz, G. 2007. "Grilling FEMA Over Its Toxic Trailers." *Time*. Available at http://www.time.com/time/nation/article/0,8599,1645312,00.html (accessed July 17, 2008).

Cuevas, F. 2005. "Fla. Eyes on Strengthening Wilma." *Atlanta Journal-Constitution*. October 18. A6.

Damon, A. 2007. "FEMA Covered Up Toxic Danger in Trailers Given to Katrina Victims." July 21. Available at http://www.wsws.org/articles/2007/jul2007/fema-j21.shtml (accessed July 17, 2008).

Dart, D. 2006. "Junk Cars, Boats Slow Recovery in Big Easy." *Atlanta Journal-Constitution*. July 5.

Deep South Center for Environmental Justice at Dillard University. 2006. "Project: A Safe Way Back Home." Available at http://www.dscej.org/asafewayhome.htm (accessed July 2, 2006).

Dewan, Shaila. 2007. "Road to New Life After Katrina Closed to Many." *New York Times*. July 12.

_____. 2008. "Out of FEMA Park, Clinging to a Fraying Lifeline." *New York Times*. August 4.

Dunn, M. 2006. "Debris Removal Need Trumps Protest." *Advocate*. May 8.

Dyson, M. E. 2006. *Come Hell or High Water: Hurricane Katrina and the Color of Disaster*. New York: Basic Books.

Eaton, L. 2006. "A New Landfill in New Orleans Sets Off a Battle." *New York Times.* May 8. Available at http://www.nytimes.com/2006/05/08/us/08landfill.html ?ex=1151035200&en=99305c0b4651e848&ei=5055&partner=RRCOLUMBUS (accessed July 15, 2006).

Environmental Science News. 2007. "FEMA's Toxic Trailers Exposed." July 25. Available at http://www.ens-newswire.com/ens/jul2007/2007-07-25-02.asp (accessed July 17, 2008).

Fields, L., A. Huang, G. Solomon, M. Rotkin-Ellman, and P. Simms. 2007. *Katrina's Wake: Arsenic-Laced Schools and Playgrounds Put New Orleans Children at Risk.* New York: NRDC. August.

Filosa, G. 2006. "House Razing Costs to Rise for N.O." *Times-Picayune.* May 22.

Gabe, T., G. Falk, M. McCarthy, and V. W. Mason. 2005. *Hurricane Katrina: Social-demographic Characteristics of Impacted Areas.* Washington, DC: Congressional Research Service Report RL33141. November.

Gonzales, J. M. 2008a. "U.N. Weighs in Against Demolishing Public Housing." Associated Press. February 28.

_____. 2008b. "New Orleans Working Class Hit by Cost Squeeze." *Boston Globe.* January 27.

Hammer, D. 2008a. "Court Upholds Dump Housing Payout." *Times-Picayune.* July 1.

_____. 2008b. "Contaminated Homes Denied Funds." *Times-Picayune.* March 27.

Hampton, M. 2006. "Formaldehyde in FEMA Travel Trailers Making People Sick." August 8. Available at http://www.homelandstupidity.us/2006/08/08/formaldehyde -in-fema-travel-trailers-making-people-sick (accessed July 17, 2008).

Ho, D. 2005. "The Worst Hurricane Season Ever." *Atlanta Journal-Constitution.* November 30.

Jervis, R. 2008a. "New Orleans' Homeless Rate Swells to 1 in 25." *USA Today.* March 17.

_____. 2008b. "New Orleans to Begin Citing Trailer Residents." *USA Today.* July 14.

_____. 2008c. "New Orleans May Have Hit Plateau." *USA Today.* August 4.

Johnson, A. 2007. "FEMA Suspends Use of 'Toxic' Trailers." Available at http://www .msnbc.msn.com/id/20165754 (accessed July 17, 2008).

Jordan, L. J. 2006. "Washington Extends Full Pickup Costs of Hurricane Debris Removal." Associated Press. WWLTV.com. June 29. Available at http://www.wwltv .com/cgi-bin/bi/gold_print.cgi (accessed July 1, 2006).

Kromm, C., and S. Sturgis. 2007. *Blueprint for Gulf Renewal: The Katrina Crisis and a Community Agenda for Action.* Durham, NC: Institute for Southern Studies.

_____. 2008. *Hurricane Katrina and the Guiding Principles of Internal Displacement: A Global Human Rights Perspective on a National Disaster.* Durham, NC: Institute for Southern Studies.

Kunzelman, M. 2008. "FEMA Seeks Immunity from Suits over Trailer Fumes." Associated Press. July 23.

Liu, A., and A. Plyer. 2008. *The New Orleans Index, Tracking Recovery of the New Orleans Metro Area: Anniversary Edition Three Years After Katrina.* The Brookings Institution and Greater New Orleans Community Data Center.

Loftis, R. L. 2005. "Extreme Cleanup on Tap in New Orleans." *The Dallas Morning News.* November 6.

Luther, L. 2007. *Disaster Debris Removal After Hurricane Katrina: Status and Associated Issues.* Washington, DC: Congressional Research Service Report to Congress. June 16, p. 1.

Martell, B. 2006. "Horse Racing Returns to New Orleans." Associated Press. November 23.

Martin, A. 2006. "Katrina's Garbage Rates a Category 5." *Chicago Tribune.* January 4.

Maugh, T. H., and J. Jervis. 2008. "FEMA Trailers Toxic, Tests Show." *Los Angeles Times.* February 15.

Mielke, H. 1999. "Lead in the Inner Cities: Policies to Reduce Children's Exposure to Lead May Be Overlooking a Major Source of Lead in the Environment." *American Scientist* 87, no. 1 (January/February).

National Fair Housing Alliance. 2005. *No Home for the Holidays: Report on Housing Discrimination Against Hurricane Katrina Survivors—Executive Summary.* Washington, DC: NFHA. December 20.

New Orleans Food Policy Advisory Committee. 2008. *Building Healthy Communities: Expanding Access to Fresh Food Retail.* New Orleans: A Report by the New Orleans Food Policy Advisory Committee.

Nossiter, A. 2005. "Thousands of Demolitions Are Likely in New Orleans." *New York Times.* October 2.

O'Driscoll, P. 2005. "Cleanup Crews Tackle Katrina's Nasty Leftovers." *USA Today.* December 11.

Pardo, A. 2006. "The Battle of Chef Menteur: The Movement to Close a New Orleans Landfill Presses On." *Reconstruction Watch.* July 6. Available at http://www.reconstructionwatch.org/index.php?s=20&n=56 (accessed July 15, 2006).

Pastor, M., R. D. Bullard, J. K. Boyce, A. Fothergill, R. Morello-Frosch, and B. Wright. 2006. *In the Wake of the Storm: Environment, Disaster and Race After Katrina.* New York: Russell Sage Foundation.

Rabito, F. A., L. E. White, and C. Shorter. 2004. "From Research to Policy: Targeting the Primary Prevention of Childhood Lead Poisoning." *Public Health Reports* 119 (May/June).

Regional Planning Commission of Orleans. 1969. Jefferson and St. Bernard Parishes. "History of Regional Growth of Jefferson, Orleans, and St. Bernard Parishes." November, p. 13.

Russell, G. 2005. "Landfill Reopening Is Raising New Stink." *Times-Picayune.* November 21. Available at http://www.nola.com/news/t-p/frontpage/index.ssf?/base/news-4/1132559045240640.xml (accessed July 2, 2006).

———. 2006. "Chef Menteur Landfill Testing Called a Farce: Critics Say Debris Proposal 'Would Be a Useless Waste of Time.'" *Times-Picayune.* May 29.

Schwartz, J. 2007. "Army Corps Details Flood Risks Facing New Orleans." *New York Times.* June 20.

Schwartz, S. M. 2007. "Deja Vu, Indeed: The Evolving Story of FEMA's Toxic Trailers." July 16. Available at http://www.toxictrailerscase.com (accessed July 17, 2008).

Shields, G. 2006. "Five Parishes to Receive Help with Debris Cleanup." *Baton Rouge Advocate.* June 30.

Simmons, A. S. 2006. Quoted in Ann S. Simmons. "New Orleans Activists Starting from the Ground Up." *Los Angeles Times.* March 24.

Solomon, G. M., and M. Rotkin-Ellman. 2006. *Contaminants in New Orleans Sediments: An Analysis of EPA Data.* New York: NRDC. February. Available at http://www.nrdc.org/health/effects/katrinadata/sedimentepa.pdf (accessed July 1, 2006).

Spake, A. 2007. "Dying for a Home: Toxic Trailers Are Making Katrina Refugees Ill." *The Nation.* February 15. Available at http://www.alternet.org/katrina/48004 (accessed July 17, 2008).

Tanneeru, M. 2005. "It's Official: 2005 Hurricanes Blew Records Away." CNN.com. December 30. Available at http://www.cnn.com/2005/WEATHER/12/19/hurricane .season.ender (accessed June 22, 2008).

Tibbetts, J. 2006. "Louisiana's Wetlands: A Lesson in Nature Appreciation." *Environmental Health Perspective* 114 (January): A40–A43.

Treadway, T. 2007. "Formaldehyde Testing on Travel Trailers to Start in September, FEMA Tells Hastings, Mahoney." August 23. Available at http://www.tcpalm.com/ news/2007/aug/23/congressmen-question-fema-availability-travel-trai (accessed July 17, 2008).

U.S. Department of Justice. 2008. Proposed Consent Decree: United States of America v. City of New Orleans et al. June 16. Available at http://www.usdoj.gov/enrd/ Consent_Decrees/City_New_Orleans/r_City_Of_New_Orleans_Consent_Decree Final.pdf (accessed June 19, 2008).

U.S. Environmental Protection Agency. 2006. "Release of Multi-Agency Report Shows Elevated Lead Levels in New Orleans Soil, Consistent with Historic Levels of Urban Lead." *EPA Newsroom*. March 4. Available at http://yosemite.epa.gov/opa/admpress .nsf/0/BA5F2460D6C777F58525714600693B5B (accessed July 17, 2008).

U.S. Environmental Protection Agency and Louisiana Department of Environmental Quality. 2005. "News Release: Top State and Federal Environmental Officials Discuss Progress and Tasks Ahead After Katrina." September 30. Available at http:// www.deq.state.la.us/news/pdf/administratorjohnson.pdf#search='katrina%20 debris%20350%2C000%20automobiles (accessed July 2, 2006).

U.S. Government Accountability Office. 2007. *Hurricane Katrina: EPA's Current and Future Environmental Protection Efforts Could Be Enhanced by Addressing Issues and Challenges Faced on the Gulf Coast*. Washington, DC: GAO Report to Congressional Committees. June.

Varney, J. 2006. "Senators Grill Corps, FEMA: Hearing Details Waste in Relief Spending." *Times-Picayune*. April 11, 2006.

Varney, J., and J. Moller. 2005. "Huge Task of Cleaning Up Louisiana Will Take At Least a Year." *Newhouse News Service*. October 2. Available at http://www.newhousenews .com/archive/varney100305.html (accessed July 2, 2006).

Walsh, B. 2007. "Feds Oppose Full Replacement of N.O. Public Housing Units." *Times-Picayune*. September 26.

Williams, L. 2006. "Groups Warn About Arsenic in Soil." *Times-Picayune*. March 24.

Wright, B. 1991. "Black in New Orleans: The City That Care Forgot." In R. D. Bullard. *In Search of the New South: The Black Urban Experience in the 1970s and 1980s*. Tuscaloosa: University of Alabama Press.

———. 1997. "New Orleans Neighborhoods Under Siege." In R. D. Bullard and G. S. Johnson (eds.). *Just Transportation: Dismantling Race and Class Barriers to Mobility*. Gabriola Island, BC: New Society Publishers.

CHAPTER 2

THE OVERLOOKED SIGNIFICANCE OF PLACE IN LAW AND POLICY

Lessons from Hurricane Katrina

Debra Lyn Bassett

Just over a year ago, we saw the televised images of Hurricane Katrina's aftermath—the frightened, mostly African-American, survivors huddling on rooftops awaiting rescue without food or water for five desperate days, then herded into the Superdome with an astonishing lack of planning that left the survivors surrounded by dead bodies, sewage, stench, and inadequate police protection. These horrifying images, televised again and again, helped to bring issues of race and poverty to the forefront of the collective public consciousness.

Hurricane Katrina's aftermath highlighted these same issues, and, perhaps unwittingly, the issue of place. But although Hurricane Katrina provoked subsequent discussions of race and class in America, our mostly unacknowledged, conflicted, ambiguous, and misunderstood question of place remained largely unexamined.

As a general matter, the degree to which we underplay and undermine the significance of place in law and policy is quite remarkable. Although the law does not always ignore place, we tend to approach law from the perspective of general applicability, and therefore the significance of place, with its need to emphasize particulars, fits uncomfortably into discussions of law and policy. Instead, its significance is muted, ignored, or minimized—in the service of generalization. Despite the perils of generalization, the attempts to minimize differences and to find commonality tend to predominate.

Place often is seen as narrowing the reach and applicability of the discussion. Place inserts specificity and boundaries into conversations that are seeking generalities.

Moreover, the insertion of place-based language often is viewed as narrow-minded and parochial. A prominent example is found in discussions of globalization, which celebrates themes of universality and commonality. Discussions of globalization require a diminished sense of place, one that has become diluted, and therefore is no longer of any particular importance. A perhaps unintended consequence of heralding globalization is the homogenization of place, in which place is viewed as interchangeable, a mere neutral backdrop without independent significance.

In empirical studies, researchers control for variables that might have an impact on the outcome. Place might, or might not, be one such variable. If place is not a controlled variable, the researcher has thereby indicated that she considers place irrelevant to the potential outcomes. The same is true in law and policy: When place is not specifically mentioned, that omission reflects a belief that place is irrelevant.

To some degree, law and policy's tendency to seek universality and commonality is understandable and practical. We want laws and policies to have broad, societal applicability rather than narrow, individualized applicability. After all, if too many variables are introduced, a formula, program, or approach becomes too case-specific to have any real utility. The combination of this universalist approach, taken together with our system of majority rule, contributes to the omission of discussions of place. As in some empirical studies, place indeed may be irrelevant in some instances—but there is also a danger that we may sometimes carry unexamined generalizations too far, resulting in unjustified assumptions of similarities that do not, in fact, exist.

Place did receive some attention in the context of Hurricane Katrina, because place mattered during Katrina and its aftermath. Place is more than an interchangeable location. Only particular places felt any impact from the hurricane—so the Gulf Coast region was the focus. In addition, only certain places within the Gulf Coast region suffered serious devastation. There was a geography of vulnerability—place was not irrelevant, because some places were safer, and some were more dangerous, than others.

Who ends up in the places that carry more risk—that are less safe—and why? We know the answer: The people who are more economically and socially vulnerable are the ones shunted into the places that are more geographically vulnerable—including those who are less educated, who are low income, who are elderly, or who are minorities. In New Orleans, the more geographically vulnerable places specifically included the properties most at risk for flooding (Seidenberg 2006). Race, place, and class all overlapped in the city of New Orleans in Katrina's aftermath when the city's poor, largely black, residents could not escape from the water that flooded the lower-lying residential areas.

But another sense of place did not receive the same media attention, and to get to that "place," I want to discuss some additional factors contributing to geographic vulnerability. What is it that makes a particular place geographically vulnerable? In the context of Hurricane Katrina, we saw that geographic vulnerability can include a number of considerations. An initial consideration, of course, is living in a location that is warm, humid, and near a warm sea, such as the Gulf of Mexico, and therefore in a location that is susceptible to hurricanes (or, in other contexts, in areas susceptible to earthquakes, tornadoes, or other natural disasters). Another consideration is living in a location with a low elevation or drainage issues, such that if flooding occurs, the location is at additional risk. Other considerations include season and climate. Katrina hit in August in the Deep South, which meant that the residents were vulnerable to an oppressive combination of heat and humidity from which there was no respite due to the lack of electricity to run the air-conditioning systems.

These considerations are the most obvious sources of geographic vulnerability with respect to hurricanes. But still other factors also contribute to geographic vulnerability. When a location lacks access to technology, communication, and transportation, and when the residents of that location lack the financial means to overcome these issues, this also renders the location geographically vulnerable. A successful evacuation of New Orleans, for example, required access to information and access to transportation. There were residents of New Orleans who never heard the order to evacuate (Hanson and Hanson 2006), and even among the majority who did, we saw the consequences of a lack of available and affordable transportation for thousands of residents who had no means to get out of the city.

In addition to these factors contributing to geographic vulnerability, there is another aspect of place—one which was not the focus of media attention after Katrina. The nation's focus was and continues to be on urban areas, especially New Orleans. Rural areas, in contrast, attracted far less notice—a phenomenon that is true more generally as well as in the specific context of Hurricane Katrina. A recent study has empirically demonstrated the pervasive lack of media attention to rural areas (W. K. Kellogg Foundation 2003). In particular, the plight of the hurricane victims who lived in the urban area of New Orleans received massive, ongoing media attention, whereas the plight of the hurricane victims who lived in the remote rural areas of Mississippi, Louisiana, and Alabama did not. Rural areas are often more vulnerable in disasters, and race often compounds vulnerability—and, of course, the rural South has a large African-American population (Saenz and Peacock 2006). With respect to Hurricane Katrina, as well as more generally, important issues of race and poverty were, and are, exacerbated by the additional issue of place—and rural areas create an additional dimension to issues of place.

One explanation for the common tendency to highlight urban areas and urban events is the reality that urban areas and events typically involve larger numbers of people—and therefore are more newsworthy, or more relevant, or more credible, or carry more significance. But there is an undercurrent, or perhaps more accurately, an underbelly to this rationalization: An urban focus and urban bias accord greater value to urban areas and urban dwellers, and a lesser value to rural areas and rural dwellers. Accordingly, when laws and policies omit any references to place, this omission permits the urban assumption to prevail.

A few news stories recognized the lack of attention to rural areas after Hurricane Katrina. According to one article, "While the nation's recovery effort and media attention has been focused on the Gulf Coast and New Orleans, hundreds of country towns in Mississippi and Louisiana [were] whacked by [Hurricane] Katrina as she beat her way inland. . . . They watch as a parade of relief workers and heavy equipment rumbles through their Main Streets on the way to Biloxi and Gulfport, knowing they'll be the last to see much help" (Jubera 2005). Another writer noted: "The horror [of Hurricane Katrina and its aftermath] is being felt not only in the hell of New Orleans, but also here in rural Mississippi, where most of the victims feel forgotten—by their countrymen, by rescuers and by the media. Nobody brings food. There are no shelters" (Associated Press 2005). And according to another article: "Rural communities in southern Mississippi have been especially hard hit, and unlike their larger counterparts, such as Biloxi, Gulfport and Pascagoula, there seems to be little progress in restoring electricity to these areas" (Zarazua 2005).

Some of the more detailed stories are heartbreaking:

> Bond, Mississippi, isn't a town or a city, just a name on a green signpost along the highway that means little to people who don't live here. But people do live here, back among the pines, in small houses and single-wide trailers. Most are black, and most are poor, and they have been devastated by Hurricane Katrina. But they have been forgotten. They have no food, no water, no gasoline, no electricity, and little hope of getting any anytime soon. "I ain't got nothing to eat and I'm hungry," moaned one 81-year-old resident with diabetes. Clutching at the collar of her thin cotton housedress, the old woman moves between despair and anger. "They got to send us something. We got nothing. People back here are going to starve," she said, her voice picking up an octave. The Red Cross trucks and the National Guard and the local power trucks roar right by this small enclave scattered off Highway 49, about 25 miles inland from the Gulf of Mexico and smack in the path of Katrina's wrath (Hastings 2005).

Everyday assumptions are often rendered erroneous due to the differing practical realities of place. In particular, everyday assumptions routinely held by urban dwellers often do not hold true for rural dwellers. Urban dwellers assume the ready availability of telephone service and further assume that if an individual cannot afford traditional telephone service, accessibility is nevertheless available through a neighbor's phone, cell phone, or local pay phone. However, in remote rural areas a neighbor's phone or pay phone may be several miles away, and cell phone service may not be available at all. Urban dwellers assume the ready availability of Internet access, when in some rural areas high-speed Internet access is unavailable (Drabenstott and Sheaff 2001), and dial-up Internet access not only requires telephone service, but often is available only through a long-distance call (TVA 2001). Urban dwellers assume access to television, but cable television is not available or affordable for all rural dwellers, and without cable, many rural homes are located too far from television stations to receive any signal.

Urban dwellers assume the availability of transportation. Although most people in both urban and rural areas own a car (Pucher and Renne 2004), in urban areas additional, back-up forms of transportation also exist, whether taxicabs, subways, buses, light rail, or some other form of mass transit. Many rural dwellers own older, unreliable vehicles (University of Wisconsin 1998), and in many rural areas no alternative methods of transportation exist (Glasgow 2000). Moreover, although most urban areas have ready access to an airport, nearly 83 percent of rural counties are beyond commuting distance to a major airport (Gale and Brown 2000). We saw, in New Orleans, that forms of mass transit can become disabled and leave people stranded. But in most remote rural areas, alternative methods of transportation are unavailable even before a disaster strikes.

These restrictions on the availability of technology, communications, and transportation increase vulnerability—as do lower levels of education and income. And, it turns out, poverty is also tied to place.

As a political columnist observed, until Hurricane Katrina, the issue of poverty had largely fallen off the public's radar screen (Alter 2005). Typically, poverty is literally out of sight as well as out of mind. For urban dwellers, aside from occasional panhandlers on city streets, most of us do not see poverty. For most of us, poverty is not apparent on our street, at our workplace, or at our health club. We do not encounter poverty because poverty is segregated from most of the more affluent population. Indeed, the poor are so segregated as to render them invisible: "That the poor are invisible is one of the most important things about them. They are not simply neglected and forgotten as in the old rhetoric of reform; what is much worse, they are not seen" (Harrington 1981).

The poor are "politically invisible" as well. Politicians do not court the poor; the poor do not retain lobbyists to promote their interests; the poor do not staff voter registration tables or organize drives to "get out the vote." The poor are both unseen and unheard.

Although various factors, including race, gender, and place, increase the risk of living in poverty, it turns out that place is the most important—in fact, often the determining—variable. America's urban focus extends to a focus on urban poverty as well, despite the fact that *rates* of poverty are consistently higher in rural areas—*and have been every year since 1959* (Economic Research Service 2004).

Place is the most important factor in determining the likelihood that someone will live in poverty. Rural dwellers are significantly more likely to be poor than urban dwellers (Cotter 2003; Weber and Jensen 2004). Of all the counties nationwide with poverty rates above the national level, approximately 84 percent are rural. Moreover, more than 80 rural counties have poverty rates of more than 30 percent; 12 of these counties have poverty rates of more than 40 percent. In fact, counties with high rates of poverty are disproportionately concentrated in rural areas. Not only is the level of poverty striking in rural areas—of the 250 poorest counties in America, 244 are rural (Beeson and Strange 2000)—but poverty becomes more acute in more remote rural areas. Poverty and place have a direct and proportional relationship: the more rural the place, the higher the likelihood of poverty.

The insidious impact of place also contributes disproportionately to minority poverty. Contrary to conventional wisdom, the poverty *rates* for African Americans, Hispanics, and Native Americans are all higher in rural areas than in urban areas (Rural Social Security Task Force 1993). Minorities bear an incommensurate burden from rural poverty, with more than one out of every four rural African Americans, Hispanics, and Native Americans living in poverty (Housing Assistance Council 2002). The connection between race and rural poverty becomes even stronger in counties designated by the federal government as "persistent poverty" counties—those with poverty rates of 20 percent or higher over a 40-year period. The United States currently has 382 "persistent poverty" counties—counties with consistent poverty rates of 20 percent or more in 1960, 1970, 1980, 1990, and 2000. Nearly half of all rural poor blacks and Native Americans live in these persistently high-poverty areas, as do nearly a third of all poor rural Hispanics. By contrast, only an eighth of poor white households live in persistent poverty areas (Beale 2004). Moreover, rural poverty is geographically concentrated in areas that correspond to racial and ethnic dimensions. Three of the highest concentrations of American poverty exist in the rural pocket of the old southern cotton belt (where most of the poor are black), the rural pocket of the Rio Grande Valley/Texas Gulf Coast (where most poor people are Hispanic), and the Native American reservations of the rural Southwest (where poverty is nearly all Native American) (Rural Policy Research Institute 2003).

Race, place, and poverty—even when taken individually, our society has little desire to acknowledge, much less fully address, any of these three issues. Each of the populations embodying these issues—minorities, the rural, and the poor—is itself the subject of neglect and disrespect. The addition of each successive disrespected population correspondingly reduces society's interest even further, rendering the population encompassed by all three of these issues—minorities living in rural poverty—not just powerless, but genuinely forgotten to the point of invisibility.

This phenomenon was painfully evident in the aftermath of Katrina. The media's attention was focused on urban areas, and particularly on New Orleans. And perhaps that focus was eminently reasonable in light of the sheer number of people affected by the flooding. My point is the "invisibility" point: that minorities living in rural poverty are unseen, and that this invisibility is not only a function of race and class. "Rural" adds another factor—another devalued factor. We saw poor black faces on our television screens after Katrina. But we did not tend to see poor black *rural* faces. Many people seemed surprised that those stranded by Katrina were largely poor and black, because we do not see those who are poor and black as a general matter. But the addition of the rural factor heightens invisibility even further—even though, as explained in one recent study, rural residents represented the majority of the population affected by Hurricane Katrina in the state of Mississippi (Saenz and Peacock 2006).

About 38 percent of Katrina's rural disaster area population was African American. Forty percent of those African Americans lived in poverty, nearly three times the rate of white urban residents. African Americans were also less likely to be home-owners, more likely to own mobile homes, less likely to have a telephone, and nearly four times more likely to lack a car (Saenz and Peacock 2006).

Indeed, instead of the five-day wait experienced by survivors in New Orleans—and criticized throughout the nation as being unreasonable and outrageous—the wait experienced by rural survivors stretched into *weeks*. The same lack of attention to rural areas recurred during Hurricane Rita, where the anticipatory focus was a worry about the urban areas of Houston and New Orleans. Hurricane Rita's impact was greatest in rural, rather than urban, communities—and perhaps for that reason, its impact was, and largely continues to be, overlooked.

Despite the preference in our laws and policies to avoid place-specific references, place in fact puts some citizens at higher risks during natural disasters and makes them less able to recover from such disasters. In what ways are rural areas hampered by their place in the context of natural disasters? In addition to higher rates of poverty, in addi-tion to their general invisibility, in addition to the often reduced availability of tech-nology, communication, and transportation, remote rural areas are also hampered by other disadvantages stemming from their place. For example, many remote rural areas have unpaved dirt roads rather than superhighways, which can hinder evacuation ef-forts. Another disadvantage is that due to the dispersion and lower population densi-ties of remote rural areas, attempts to centralize efforts—whether at the warning stage, the evacuation stage, or the remedy stage—do not tend to work effectively in rural areas due to the dispersion of fewer people over greater distances and the related trans-portation issues. The physical and social isolation, and lack of transportation, in many rural communities serves as a major barrier to the delivery of aid to these localities.

Still another disadvantage concerns housing. The American dream is home own-ership. However, low-income and minority families are often funneled into homes that are older, built in more vulnerable areas, constructed with lower-quality materi-als or poorly built generally, constructed to conform to older, less stringent building codes, and are less well-maintained, and this is particularly true in rural areas. One study has reported that people in rural areas affected by Katrina were 14 percent more likely than urban residents to be homeowners, but they were more than twice as likely to be living in mobile homes than were city dwellers affected by the hurri-cane (Saenz and Peacock 2006). Mobile homes provide the opportunity for home ownership at a dramatically lower cost than traditional housing. Most cities have restrictions regarding mobile homes, but rural areas tend to be more lenient in this regard. The problem is that mobile homes create an additional vulnerability—they are less sturdy than traditional housing and more susceptible to extensive damage in natural disasters. As a result of these housing characteristics, rural low-income and minority households are far more likely to suffer disproportionately from the dam-age associated with Katrina.

Because rural areas often are not considered separately—because the unique needs and characteristics of rural areas are not always considered—urban models are often employed in designing policies and programs, even when the intended beneficiaries of those policies and programs include rural dwellers (Fitchen 1993). In designing policies that include the delivery of services, an urban focus or urban model might lead a policy maker to make the assumption that service recipients will effectively and efficiently receive their benefits, and administrative and distribution costs will be lower, by using a centralized location. This assumption, although widely true for cities, is largely untrue for rural areas, where smaller, more geographically dispersed populations, typically lacking any form of mass transit, require lengthy travel to get to so-called centralized locations.

We commonly hear about economies of scale with respect to distribution. However, the concept of economies of scale itself reflects an urban bias. Economies of scale, by definition, require more demand or larger numbers in order to achieve such economies. Such an approach tends to work just fine in urban areas, but often is lacking in rural areas, especially when the rural area is both remote from other population centers and its population is widely dispersed.

More broadly, America generally and lawmakers in particular have embraced economic models and rationales that assume an urban place, and thereby tend to reward urban areas and penalize rural areas. Such economic concepts as economies of scale, profitability, cost effectiveness, cost-benefit analysis, and market efficiencies create justifications for deregulation, privatization, and the promotion of business interests in both law and policy. But rural markets are unlikely to satisfy any of these economic-based concepts. Rural markets tend to be remote, dispersed, and sparsely populated. A dispersed population tends to be more expensive to serve than a concentrated one. Remote and sparsely populated communities often translate into higher transportation costs with concomitant decreases in profitability, cost effectiveness, and market efficiencies.

Although place includes location, place also carries meanings beyond mere location. The general availability, and the specific types and quality, of health care, social services, schools, housing, employment, and basic amenities vary from place to place. Siting, by definition, centers on place, and determines the location of solid and toxic waste dumps, prisons, industrial waste facilities, and other undesirable land uses.

How does all of this factor into our laws and policies? The reality that most laws and policies do not address place was seen in the context of Hurricanes Katrina and Rita. The state of Louisiana's Hurricane Evacuation and Sheltering Plan, for example, notes some of the problems in evacuating New Orleans but does not take note of the problems unique to evacuating rural areas, leaving both the acknowledgment of such issues and the planning to address them to the local parishes. Emergency shelters, not surprisingly, tend to be centrally located, which in rural areas necessarily means that shelters are geographically spread out and require a reliable means of transportation to get there.

In terms of subsequent recovery efforts, low-income households generally, and rural households in particular, have suffered disadvantages. Our laws and policies are counterintuitive—one would think that the neediest households would receive the most government support, but instead, our laws and policies are structured in such a manner that those who had more resources before the hurricanes continue to have more resources after—and those who had fewer economic resources before the hurricanes are likely to continue to have fewer available resources after.

As a matter of policy, our country has chosen to approach disaster relief in an individualized, market-driven manner, so that private property insurance and individual savings are the primary financial resources for repairing or rebuilding. But full insurance coverage and financial reserves are the province of the financially secure, not those who are barely getting by. Indeed, our country's market-based approach to recovery tends to exacerbate the consequences of poverty and discrimination and renders poor and minority households less able to recover from natural disasters (Peacock and Ragsdale 1997).

Relying on an approach to recovery that is market- and insurance-driven disadvantages low-income and rural households—both homeowners and renters—because they are more likely to lack insurance, to have inadequate insurance, and to lack important insurance options—such as flood, hurricane, or earthquake coverage, full replacement value coverage, and coverage for temporary housing expenses. Moreover, studies conducted after 1992's Hurricane Andrew in Florida indicated that minorities were receiving inadequate insurance settlements at a rate more than twice that of whites. This differential was blamed largely on the companies with which individuals were insured—households insured by major carriers fared better than households insured by smaller, less well-known insurance carriers, and, perhaps not surprisingly, low-income households were less likely to be insured by major carriers (Peacock and Girard 1997).

This means that the uninsured, underinsured, and renters are inherently disadvantaged under existing laws and policies—so that although uninsured homeowners' needs are greater than the needs of insured homeowners, uninsured homeowners actually receive less financial assistance to rebuild. Louisiana's The Road Home program, for example, helps only homeowners (not renters) and gives uninsured homeowners only 70 percent of what those with homeowner's insurance would receive from their insurer. In addition, The Road Home program requires, as a prerequisite for assistance, that households must have previously registered with FEMA—thus presenting another hurdle for low-education, low-income households. But despite its flaws, The Road Home program, which is Louisiana's rebuilding plan, is nevertheless superior to Mississippi's rebuilding plan—which simply excludes uninsured homeowners altogether.

Even programs that purport to assist both the insured and the uninsured often fall short in aiding the uninsured. For homeowners without insurance or with insufficient insurance, the low-interest loan program of the Small Business Administration (SBA) can help to cover repairing or rebuilding. Rural households, however, are less likely to have heard of the program, less likely to persevere through the application process, and less likely ultimately to qualify for SBA assistance. The application process can seem daunting to populations with lower levels of education and income, and the SBA prerequisite of a demonstrated ability to repay the loan tends to preclude low-income households. The recipients of these financial resources thus tend to be white and middle-income rather than black and low-income.

Disadvantages to rural households persist all the way to the end of the legal-financial spectrum. Amendments in 2005 to the federal bankruptcy laws restrict access to bankruptcy as a method of discharging debt and starting fresh. A recent study concluded that rural households filing for bankruptcy earn significantly lower incomes and have higher debt-to-income ratios than urban households filing for bankruptcy (Porter 2005). In addition to these financial disadvantages, the new bankruptcy provisions require debtors to undergo credit counseling and complete a personal financial management course, and the new provisions make it more difficult for debtors to keep their cars. These new amendments are particularly burdensome for rural households—credit counseling agencies do not tend to exist in remote rural areas, and completing a personal financial management course is most likely to require travel to a more urban area. Although the law permits the completion of both the credit counseling and the financial management course over the Internet, the Internet is not widely available in remote rural areas. And the potential for rural households to lose their cars in the bankruptcy process is especially troublesome due to the lack of public transportation options (Porter 2005).

During congressional hearings regarding the new bankruptcy amendments, one of our most persistent rural myths surfaced—Senator Charles Grassley stated that the special needs of rural households would be protected due to the availability of a specialized form of reorganization bankruptcy for farmers. Protections for farmers, however, do not equate to protections for rural households generally. Studies have repeatedly shown that only approximately 6 percent of rural dwellers are farmers or earn their incomes through farming operations (Johnson 2005). Accordingly, the needs of 94 percent of the rural population were overlooked in the congressional hearings concerning these new bankruptcy provisions. The myth that "rural equals farming" is a misconception that we see repeatedly in the formation of law and policy, and one that harms the vast majority of rural households by relying on outdated stereotypes rather than the actual needs of today's rural population.

Ignoring place has benefits. In particular, ignoring place reduces the number of factors that must be taken into account, with a concomitant sense (even if that sense is false) of greater consistency and cohesion. Thus, ignoring place tends to promote contentions that seek unity, consistency, and sameness.

However, ignoring place carries perils as well. Ignoring place doesn't make it go away. When no distinctions are drawn, and all are treated as if place were consistent or irrelevant, the lack of distinction carries its own assumptions—assumptions drawn from majority or dominant perspectives. Just as is true of assumptions of maleness and whiteness absent other factors or indicators, similar assumptions adhere with respect to place—and the assumption is that of an urban location. Since approximately

80 percent of the population of the United States lives in urban areas, an urban assumption will often be correct. But an urban assumption presumes, in the more than 20 percent of instances involving a rural setting and rural residents, that a rural location makes no difference. Unquestionably, in some circumstances the urban versus rural distinction does not matter. For example, the premeditated killing of another without justification or excuse is a homicide, regardless of whether the killing occurred in an urban or a rural area. But in other instances, assuming uniformity of place can lead to unjustified or erroneous conclusions—and one such example involves the vulnerability to natural disasters.

Higher rates of poverty, as well as geographical isolation and lack of public transportation, all contribute to render rural populations more vulnerable to natural disasters. The greater vulnerabilities for low-income households generally, and rural households in particular, translate into an increased likelihood of greater damage in a disaster, followed by an increased likelihood of insufficient insurance, inadequate insurance settlements, and less government assistance to repair and rebuild.

Place is a powerful construct that plays an important role in how we identify ourselves, how we relate to others, what opportunities are available to us, and how we live. Hurricanes Katrina and Rita have provided an opportunity for lawmakers, policy makers, and the public at large to take a closer look at the significance of place—and to recognize the broader structural considerations that often tend to favor urban areas, and to impact rural areas more harshly.

REFERENCES

Alter, J. 2005. "The Other America." *Newsweek*. September 19.

American Public Transportation Association. 2006. "Public Transportation: Wherever Life Takes You."

Associated Press. 2005. "In Rural Mississippi, Hurricane Relief Is Scarce." September 11.

Bassett, D. 2003a. "Ruralism." *Iowa Law Review* 88:273–342.

———. 2003b. "The Politics of the Rural Vote." *Arizona State Law Journal* 35:743–791.

Beale, C. L. 2004. "Anatomy of Nonmetro High-Poverty Areas: Common in Plight, Distinctive in Nature." *Amber Waves*. Available at http://www.ers.usda.gov/amberwaves/February04/Features/Anatomy.htm (accessed August 6, 2008).

Beeson, E., and M. Strange. 2000. "Why Rural Matters: The Need for Every State to Take Action on Rural Education." *Journal of Research in Rural Education* 16:63–140, 64. Available at http://jrre.psu.edu/articles/v16,n2,p63-140,Beeson.pdf (accessed October 3, 2008).

Berkes, H. 2005. "Mississippi Rural Areas Still Without Power." September 15. Available at www.npr.org/templates/story/story.php?storyId=4848396 (accessed August 6, 2008).

Bradshaw, T. K. 1993. "In the Shadow of Urban Growth: Bifurcation in Rural California Communities." In T. A. Lyson and W. W. Falk (eds.). *Forgotten Places: Uneven Development in Rural America*. Lawrence: University Press of Kansas.

Bullard, R. D. 1990. *Dumping in Dixie: Race, Class, and Environmental Quality*. Boulder: Westview Press.

Cotter, D. A. 2003. "Addressing Person and Place to Alleviate Rural Poverty." In *Perspectives on Poverty, Policy & Place*. RUPRI Rural Poverty Research Center. August.

Davidson, O. G. 1996. *Broken Heartland: The Rise of America's Rural Ghetto*. Iowa City: University of Iowa Press.

Drabenstott, M., and K. H. Sheaff. 2001. "Exploring Policy Options for a New Rural America: A Conference Summary." Available at http://www.kc.frb.org/PUBLICAT/ Exploring/RC01DRAB.pdf (accessed August 6, 2008).

Economic Research Service. 2004. "Rural Income, Poverty, and Welfare: Rural Poverty."
_____. 2004. "Rural Poverty at a Glance." Rural Development Research Report No. 100. July, p. 6.

Ellison, R. 1952. *Invisible Man*. New York: Random House.

Fitchen, J. M. 1991. *Endangered Spaces, Enduring Places: Change, Identity, and Survival in Rural America*. Boulder: Westview Press.

Gale, F., and D. Brown. 2000. "How Important Is Airport Access for Rural Businesses?" *Rural America* 15 (September): 16–17. Available at http://www.ers.usda.gov/ publications/ruralamerica/sep2000/sep2000e.pdf (accessed August 6, 2008).

Gannon, M. 2005. "Rural Poor Last to Get Help." September 10.

Glasgow, N. 2000. "Older Americans' Patterns of Driving and Using Other Transportation." *Rural America* 15 (September): 26. Available at http://www.ers.usda.gov/ publications/ruralamerica/sep2000/sep2000f.pdf (accessed August 6, 2008).

Grassley, Senator C. 2005. Press Release. "Grassley Renews Effort to Reform Bankruptcy Code: Bill Includes Permanent Chapter 12 Protection for Farmers, New Consumer Protections, Child Support Provisions." February 2.

Hanson, J., and K. Hanson. 2006. "The Blame Frame: Justifying (Racial) Injustice in America." *Harvard Civil Rights Civil Liberties Review* 41:413, 452.

Harrington, M. 1981. *The Other America*. New York: Touchstone.

Hastings, D. 2005. "Forgotten People Grow Desperate in Rural Mississippi." *Decatur Daily News*. September 3.

Housing Assistance Council. 2002. "Executive Summary, Taking Stock: Rural People, Poverty, and Housing at the Turn of the 21st Century." December. Available at http://ruralhome.org/pubs/hsganalysis/ts2000/executivesummary.htm (accessed August 6, 2008).

Johnson, K. 2005. "Reports on Rural America: Demographic Trends in Rural and Small Town America," p. 9. Available at http://www.carseyinstitute.unh.edu/publications/ Report_Demographics.pdf (accessed October 3, 2008).

Jubera, D. 2005. "Rural Towns Recover Outside Spotlight." *Oxford (MS) Press*. September 2.

Miller, K. K., and B. A. Weber. 2004. "How Do Persistent Poverty Dynamics and Demographics Vary Across the Rural-Urban Continuum?" In *Measuring Rural Diversity*. January. Available at http://srdc.msstate.edu/measuring/series/miller_weber.pdf (accessed August 6, 2008).

Murdock, S. H., R. S. Krannich, and F. L. Leistritz. 1999. *Hazardous Wastes in Rural America*. Lanham, MD: Rowman & Littlefield.

Oxfam America. 2005. "Oxfam Partners Assess Katrina's Impact on Rural Communities." September 4. Available at http://www.oxfamamerica.org/newsandpublications/ news_updates/archive2005/news_update.2005-09-04.8683832325 (accessed October 20, 2008).
_____. 2006. "Forgotten Communities, Unmet Promises: An Unfolding Tragedy on the Gulf Coast." Available at http://www.oxfamamerica.org/newsandpublications/

publications/briefing_papers/briefing_paper.2006-08-21.1978258942 (accessed October 20, 2008).

Peacock, W. G., and C. Girard. 1997. "Ethnic and Racial Inequalities in Hurricane Damage and Insurance Settlements." In W. G. Peacock, B. H. Morrow, and H. Gladwin (eds.). *Hurricane Andrew: Ethnicity, Gender and the Sociology of Disasters.* New York: Routledge.

Peacock, W. G., and A. K. Ragsdale. 1997. "Social Systems, Ecological Networks and Disasters." In W. G. Peacock, B. H. Morrow, and H. Gladwin (eds.). *Hurricane Andrew: Ethnicity, Gender and the Sociology of Disasters.* New York: Routledge.

Porter, K. 2005. "Going Broke the Hard Way: The Economics of Rural Failure." *Wisconsin Law Review* no. 4 (2005): 969–1032.

Pucher, J., and J. L. Renne. 2004. *Urban-Rural Differences in Mobility and Mode Choice: Evidence from the 2001 NHTS.* New Brunswick, NJ: Rutgers University.

Rural Policy Research Institute. 2002. "Rural by the Numbers: Poverty in Rural America."

Rural Sociologist Society Task Force on Persistent Rural Poverty. 1993. *Persistent Poverty in Rural America.* Boulder: Westview Press.

Saenz, R., and W. G. Peacock. 2006. "Rural People, Rural Places: The Hidden Costs of Hurricane Katrina." In *Rural Realities.* Available at http://www.ruralsociology.org/pubs/ruralrealities/Issue2.html (accessed August 6, 2008).

Seidenberg, J. 2005. "Cultural Competency in Disaster Recovery: Lessons Learned from the Hurricane Katrina Experience for Better Serving Marginalized Communities." Available at http://www.law.berkeley.edu/library/disasters/Seidenberg.pdf (accessed August 6, 2008).

South Carolina Rural Health Research Center. 2002. *Minorities in Rural America.* Available at http://rhr.sph.sc.edu/report/MinoritiesInRuralAmerica.pdf (accessed August 1, 2008).

State of Louisiana. 2000. "Emergency Operations Plan, Supplement 1A: Southeast Louisiana Hurricane Evacuation and Sheltering Plan." January.

State Profiles: The Population and Economy of Each U.S. State. 1999. C. M. Slater and M. G. Davis (eds.). Lanham, MD: Bernan Press.

Steinhauser, J. 2005. "Smaller Towns Bore the Brunt of Rita's Force." *New York Times.* October 1, p. A1.

Stommes, E. S., and D. M. Brown. 2002. "Transportation in Rural America: Issues for the 21st Century." *Rural America* 16 (March): 2–4. Available at http://www.ers.usda.gov/publications/ruralamerica/ra164/ra164b.pdf (accessed August 6, 2008).

The Road Home Program. 2005. Available at http://www.road2la.org/default.htm (accessed August 6, 2008).

TVA Rural Studies. 2001. "OTA Follow-Up Conference Report: Rural America at the Crossroads." Available at http://www.rural.org/workshops/rural_telecom/OTA_followup_report.pdf (accessed August 6, 2008).

University of Wisconsin. 1998. Center for Community Economic Development, Community Econ. Newsletter. "Transportation Barriers to Employment of Low-Income People." April. Available at http://www.aae.wisc.edu/pubs/cenews/docs/ce258.txt (accessed August 6, 2008).

W. K. Kellogg Foundation. 2003. "Perceptions of Rural America: Media Coverage." Available at http://www.wkkf.org/Pubs/FoodRur/MediaCoverage_00253_03795.pdf (accessed August 6, 2008).

Weber, B., and L. Jensen. 2004. "Poverty and Place: A Critical Review of Rural Poverty Literature." RUPRI Poverty Research Center, Working Paper Series, June.

Weisheit, R. A., D. N. Falcone, and L. E. Wells. 1999. *Crime and Policing in Rural and Small-Town America*. 2nd ed. Prospect Heights, IL: Waveland Press.

Zarazua, J. 2005. "Rural Communities Hit by Katrina Wait in Shadows." September 3. Available at http://www.mysanantonio.com/news/MYSA090305_20A_katrina _miss_1d1107d8_html1349.html (accessed October 3, 2008).

CHAPTER 3

TRANSPORTATION MATTERS

Stranded on the Side of the Road
Before and After Disasters Strike

Robert D. Bullard, Glenn S. Johnson, and Angel O. Torres

Transportation provides access to opportunity and serves as a key component in addressing poverty, unemployment, and equal-opportunity goals while ensuring access to education, health care, and other public services (Garrett and Taylor 1999). Transportation is also a necessary and essential element in emergency preparedness, response, and evacuation from natural and human-induced disasters.

This chapter examines the role of transportation in moving Americans to opportunity and reducing vulnerability to job flight from central cities, economic decentralization, or office sprawl. Our analysis focuses on who is most likely to get left behind economically—during economic recessions and booming times, and natural and human-induced disasters—and why? It also examines the role of personal automobiles and mass transit in emergency preparedness, response, and evacuation planning. American society is largely divided between those with cars and those without cars. Many of the nation's transportation policies and public investments leave some Americans "stranded on the side of the road" (Bullard and Johnson 1997; Bullard 2005, 24).

LEFT BEHIND BY TRANSPORTATION INEQUITY

The modern civil rights movement has its roots in transportation. In 1953, nearly half a century after *Plessy vs. Ferguson* relegated blacks to the back of the bus, African Americans in Baton Rouge, Louisiana, staged the nation's first successful bus boycott. Two years later, on December 1, 1955, Rosa Parks refused to give up her seat at the front of a Montgomery city bus to a white man. In so doing, Parks ignited the modern civil rights movement.

Many of the nation's regional transportation systems are regional in name only—with a good number comprised largely of "separate and unequal" urban and suburban transit operations built along race and class lines. Without a doubt, "transportation apartheid" is firmly and nationally entrenched in American society. For more than a century, African Americans struggled to end apartheid on buses, trains, and highways (Bullard and Johnson 1997).

Clearly, an effective regional transit system is important in connecting workers with jobs, serving a rapidly aging population, and reducing traffic congestion, which has a positive effect on the environment. Americans spend more on transportation than any other household item except housing. Americans spend more on transportation than they do on food, education, or health care. On average, Americans spend 18 cents out of every dollar earned on transportation expenses. Spending on transportation is lowest in metro regions with strong public transit systems (Center for Neighborhood Technology and the Surface Transportation Policy Project 2005). American households earning less than $50,000 spend on average three times more per year on transportation than they do on retirement, pensions, and Social Security.

Low-income households spend an even greater percentage of their income on transportation than their higher-income counterparts. For example, two-person households earning less than $30,000 annually spend 24 percent while households earning $100,000 spent only 10 percent (Center for Neighborhood Technology and the Surface Transportation Policy Project 2005). These transportation spending differentials also hold true for poor and affluent commuters.

The working poor spend a much higher portion of their income on commuting (Roberto 2008). For working-poor homeowners, nearly 25 percent of their household income is consumed by housing and commuting expenses compared with just 15.3 percent for other households. The disparities between the working-poor renters (32.4 percent) and other households (19.7 percent) are even greater.

Rising gas prices increase household transportation costs and take money out of consumers' pockets and food off the table. Again, the pain is not felt uniformly. High gas prices hit low-income and working-class family budgets hardest. In June 2008, gas prices reached a national average of $4 a gallon for the first time. Nationally, American families are now spending about 4 percent of their take-home income on gasoline, but in some rural counties in the mostly black and poor Mississippi Delta, that figure has surpassed 13 percent (Krauss 2008a). Gasoline expenses are rivaling what many families spend on food and housing.

Soaring gas prices are pushing more Americans to take public transit. Some urban public transit systems, like New York and Boston, have seen increases in ridership of 5 percent. Even higher surges of 10 to 15 percent or more are occurring in many metropolitan areas in the South and West, where the driving culture is strongest and bus and rail lines are more limited (Krauss 2008b).

Follow the transportation dollars and one can tell who is important and who is not. Congress passed the Intermodal Surface Transportation Efficiency Act of 1991 (ISTEA) to improve public transportation necessary "to achieve national goals for improved air quality, energy conservation, international competitiveness, and mobility for elderly persons, persons with disabilities, and economically disadvantaged persons in urban and rural areas of the country." In 1998, Congress reauthorized the act under the Transportation Equity Act for the Twenty-First Century, or TEA-21. From 1998 to 2003, TEA-21 spending amounted to $217 billion (Gardner 1998).

TEA-21 expired in September 2003. Congress passed six temporary extensions. TEA-21 created thousands of job opportunities. On August 10, 2005, President Bush signed into law the $244.1 billion Safe, Accountable, Flexible, Efficient Transportation Equity Act: A Legacy for Users (SAFETEA-LU), representing the largest surface transportation investment in U.S. history (U.S. Department of Transportation 2005). The U.S. Department of Transportation (DOT) estimates that every $1 billion invested in public transportation infrastructure supports approximately 47,500 jobs.

Most of the transportation funds are distributed through the state DOT and the local metropolitan planning organization (MPO) for each city. Generally, MPOs are not known for their diversity. The "one area, one vote" voting structure significantly underrepresents racial minorities and urban areas of large MPOs and overrepresents white constituents. Local bodies (and officials) are not representative due to persisting racism and social and institutional barriers encountered by racial minorities (Sanchez, Stolz, and Ma 2003).

The current federal funding scheme is biased against metropolitan areas. The federal government allocates the bulk of transportation dollars directly to state DOTs. Many of these state road-building fiefdoms are no friend to urban transit. Nationally, 80 percent of all surface transportation funds is earmarked for highways and 20 percent for public transportation. Generally, states spend less than 20 percent of federal transportation funding on transit (Sanchez et al. 2003). Although local governments within metropolitan areas own and maintain the vast majority of the transportation infrastructure, they receive only about 10 percent of every dollar they generate (Ashe 2003). Only about 6 percent of all federal highway dollars are suballocated directly to the metropolitan regions (Puentes and Bailey 2003).

The nation's skewed gas tax distribution system creates donor regions. Taxpayers in 54 metropolitan areas lost an estimated $100 million during the six-year period. The top gas tax losers were Los Angeles, Dallas-Fort Worth, Phoenix, Atlanta, Detroit, and New Orleans. New Orleans, with an astounding 27.9 percent poverty rate, received only 53 cents on each dollar paid (Environmental Working Group 2004).

Where people live and where jobs are located do not always coincide. No other group in the United States is more physically isolated from jobs than African Americans (Stoll 2005). UCLA scholar Michael Stoll's research reveals that more than 50 percent of blacks would have to relocate to achieve an even distribution of blacks relative to jobs. The comparable figures for whites are 20 to 24 percentage points lower. Job sprawl exacerbates racial inequality. By better linking job growth with existing residential patterns, policies to promote smart growth could help narrow the spatial mismatch between blacks and jobs and improve their employment over time.

Clearly, transportation is an essential ingredient in moving low-income families from poverty and dependency to self-sufficiency. Transportation investments, enhancements and financial resources, if used properly, can bring new life and revitalization to much-needed urban areas and can aid in lifting families out of poverty. Race and class dynamics operate to isolate millions of African Americans in central cities and away from expanding suburban job centers.

LEFT BEHIND BY NATURAL AND HUMAN-MADE DISASTERS

Transportation is a major component in emergency preparedness and evacuation planning. There is a clear connection between social inequities and the policies, or the lack of concrete plans, to evacuate individuals who do not have the transportation to leave the city. Disaster evacuation plans all across the nation assume that people own a car. Nearly 11 million households in the United States lack vehicles (Wellner 2005). This translates into more than 28 million Americans who would have difficulty evacuating their area in the event of an emergency.

In 1997, to encourage better disaster planning, the Federal Emergency Management Agency (FEMA), under the Clinton administration, launched Project Impact, a pilot program that provided funding for communities to, among other things, assess their vulnerable populations and make arrangements to get people without transportation to safety. The program reached 250 communities and proved quite effective, but the Bush administration ended the program in 2001, and funds once earmarked for disaster preparation were shifted elsewhere (Elliston 2004).

Being left behind has not been headline news for millions of central city residents who have struggled to get dollars allocated for public transit. Cars are not only an essential part of evacuation plans but often make the difference between being employed and unemployed. Unequal access to automobile ownership contributes to the racial economic divide and vulnerability to natural and man-made disasters.

The private automobile is still the most dominant travel mode of every segment of the American population, including the poor and people of color. Car ownership is almost universal in the United States with 91.7 percent of American households owning at least one motor vehicle (Pucher and Renne 2003). Clearly, private automobiles provide enormous employment-access advantages to their owners. Private automobiles are also the principal mode of urban evacuation, and having a car can mean the difference between being trapped by or escaping from natural disasters.

Nationally, 87.6 percent of whites, 83.1 percent of Asians and Hispanics, and 78.9 percent of blacks rely on the private car to get around. Nationwide, roughly 8 percent of Americans reside in a household with no access to an automobile. Lack of car ownership and inadequate public transit service in many central cities and metropolitan regions with a high proportion of "captive" transit dependents exacerbate social, economic, and racial isolation—especially for low-income people-of-color residents who already have limited transportation options.

A great deal of media attention was given to the fact that a large share of New Orleans' population (27 percent, or 130,000 residents) did not own a car and were not able to drive out of Katrina's reach (Renne 2005). The phenomenon of large urban carless populations is not unique to New Orleans since a number of American cities have a higher percentage of carless households, including New York City (56 percent), Washington, D.C. (37 percent), Baltimore (36 percent), Boston (35 percent), Chicago (29 percent), and San Francisco (29 percent). The carless rates in majority-black cities are significantly higher for African Americans than for whites (Table 3.1).

Nationally, roughly 7 percent of white households own no car, compared with 24 percent of African-American households, 17 percent of Latino households, and 13 percent of Asian-American households (Sanchez et al. 2003). African Americans are nearly 3.5 times more likely to lack access to a car than whites; for Latinos it is about 2.5 times. There is a clear racial and economic disparity in who can escape natural disasters by car. It should not be a surprise to anyone that people of color are considerably more likely to be left behind in a natural disaster, since they have lower incomes and fewer of them own cars compared to whites.

The low car ownership of African Americans follows directly from sharp racial differences in household income and poverty (Berube, Deakin, and Raphael 2006, 6). In 2006, almost a quarter (24.3 percent) of African-American households lived below the federal poverty line, compared with 8.2 percent of non-Hispanic whites (DeNavas-Walt, Proctor, and Smith 2007). Median income in 2006 for African-American households stood at $32,000 a year, only 62 percent of the median household income of whites ($52,400).

In addition to lower rates of car ownership, people of color tend to make up a greater proportion of the nation's cities that are at risk of hurricanes: Miami, 79 percent; New Orleans, 73 percent; New York City, 65 percent; Houston, 58 percent (Lui, Dixon, and Leondar-Wright 2006). In *Stalling the Dream: Cars, Race and Hurricane Evacuation* (Lui et al. 2006, 1) the authors arrived at some insightful conclusions on how unequal access to automobiles contributes to the racial divide for African Americans and other people of color. Some fifty years after Rosa Parks ignited the Montgomery bus boycott that set off the modern civil rights movement, "African Americans are still left standing on the side of the road" (Lui et al. 2006, 2). The report concludes:

- In all 11 major cities that have had five or more hurricanes in the last 100 years (Houston, Miami, Fort Lauderdale, Orlando, Jacksonville, St. Petersburg, Tampa, New York City, Providence, Boston, and New Orleans), people without cars are disproportionately people of color.
- In the case of a mandatory evacuation order during a disaster, 33 percent of Latinos, 27 percent of African Americans, and 23 percent of whites say that lack of transportation would be an obstacle preventing them from evacuating, according to the National Center for Disaster Preparedness.
- Evacuation planning tends to focus on traffic management for those with cars and on institutionalized people, not on non-institutionalized people without

TABLE 3.1—Car Ownership Rates in Selected U.S. Cities by Race

	Washington city, District of Columbia	Atlanta city Georgia	Cleveland city, Ohio	Memphis city Tennessee	Baltimore city Maryland	Detroit city, Michigan	St. Louis city Missouri	New Orleans city Louisiana
All Households								
No vehicle available	36.9%	23.6%	24.6%	14.3%	35.9%	21.9%	25.2%	27.3%
1+ vehicle available	63.1%	76.4%	75.4%	85.7%	64.1%	78.1%	74.8%	72.7%
White Households								
No vehicle available	27.0%	9.2%	17.3%	6.7%	22.7%	19.0%	15.7%	15.3%
1+ vehicles available	73.0%	90.8%	82.7%	93.3%	77.3%	81.0%	84.3%	84.7%
Black Households								
No vehicle available	42.1%	34.6%	31.7%	20.3%	44.4%	22.7%	36.2%	34.8%
1+ vehicles available	57.9%	65.4%	68.3%	79.7%	55.6%	77.3%	63.8%	65.2%

Source: U.S. Census Bureau (2000).

vehicles. New Orleans had only one-quarter the number of buses that would have been needed to evacuate all carless residents.

- In the counties affected by Hurricanes Katrina, Rita and Wilma in 2005, only 7 percent of white households have no car, compared with 24 percent of black, 12 percent of Native American and 14 percent of Latino households.
- Eleven percent of African-American families and 21 percent of Latino families have missed out on medical care because of transportation issues, compared to only 2 percent of white families, according to the National Center for Disaster Preparedness.

Generally, public transit in the United States is considered to be transportation of last resort or a novelty for tourists—resulting in dramatic differences in convenience, comfort, and safety between motorists and non-motorists, and therefore between wealthy and poor, white and black, and able and disabled (Litman 2006). Nevertheless, without a car, millions of jobs are unreachable—thereby locking many families into permanent poverty, unemployment, and underemployment.

In June 2006, the Department of Homeland Security (DHS) released the *National Plan Review,* a comprehensive, nationwide assessment of the adequacy of emergency plans for each state and the 75 largest urban areas (Department of Homeland Security 2006). DHS found these plans particularly insufficient with regard to evacuation planning for the carless and special-needs populations—individuals who cannot simply jump into their cars and drive away. Evacuation of low-mobility and special-needs groups, while included in most state emergency operation plans, has been largely unaddressed by state DOTs.

The DHS notes that large swaths of the population have special needs that must be addressed in evacuation plans, including the carless (8 percent of U.S. households), those with a physical or mental disability (13 percent of residents) or language barrier (8 percent), the elderly (40 percent have a disability), and those living in group quarters such as nursing homes and assisted-living facilities (2 percent of residents).

In urban areas, African Americans and Latinos comprise over 54 percent of transit users (62 percent of bus riders, 35 percent of subway riders, and 29 percent of commuter rail riders). Nationally, only about 5.3 percent of all Americans use public transit to get to work. African Americans are almost six times as likely as whites to use transit to get around. Urban transit is especially important to African Americans where over 88 percent live in metropolitan areas and 53.1 percent live inside central cities. Nearly 60 percent of transit riders are served by the ten largest urban transit systems and the remaining 40 percent by the other 5,000 transit systems (Sanchez, Stolz, and Ma 2003).

Evacuation plans that are centered on the premise that the population will use private transportation are faulty policies and will universally fail. These policies privilege middle- to upper-class, able-bodied, and non-elderly households, which are more likely to own cars, and exclude the poor, mostly people of color, disabled, and elderly because many of them lack the physical mobility or transportation to evacuate.

Unequal access to transportation alternatives in disasters heightens the vulnerability of the poor, elderly, disabled, and people of color. Individuals with private automobiles have a greater chance of "voting with their feet" and escaping threats from hurricanes than individuals who are dependent on the government to provide emergency transportation. Too often buses (public transit and school buses), vans (paratransit), and trains do not come to the rescue of low-income, elderly, disabled, sick people, and people of color.

MANDATORY EVACUATION OF
NEW ORLEANS—"YOU'RE ON YOUR OWN"

On August 28, 2005, Mayor Ray Nagin ordered New Orleans' first-ever mandatory evacuation since the city was founded in 1718. Buses evacuated thousands of residents to the Superdome and other shelters within the city (Dyson 2006). It has been the policy of the Red Cross for years not to open shelters in New Orleans during hurricanes greater than Category 2. Red Cross storm shelters were moved to higher ground north of Interstate 10 several years ago (American Red Cross 2005). Before Hurricane Katrina emptied the city of its more than 400,000 population in August 2005, New Orleans was the largest city in the country without a meaningful master plan.

New Orleans' emergency plan called for thousands of the city's most vulnerable population to be left behind in their homes, shelters, and hospitals (Schleifstein 2005). A *Times-Picayune* reporter summed up the emergency transportation plan: "City, state and federal emergency officials are preparing to give the poorest of New Orleans' poor a historically blunt message: In the event of a major hurricane, you're on your own" (Nolan 2005, 1).

The city set up ten pickup stations where city buses were to take people to emergency shelters. The New Orleans Rapid Transit Authority (NORTA) emergency plan designated 64 buses and ten lift vans to transport residents to shelters. Several organizations, including the Red Cross, the U.S. Department of Homeland Security, the New Orleans Public Health Department, the city's Office of Emergency Preparedness, and the nonprofit Unity for the Homeless group, were in the process of creating a strategy to use Amtrak and city buses to evacuate 25,000 to 30,000 people in the event of a hurricane. The plan was incomplete since the city did not have regional agreements in place with the receiving sites when the storm hit. The flood drowned 197 of the NORTA buses and 24 of its 36 lift vans (Renne 2006).

Katrina is likely the most destructive hurricane in U.S. history (Brinkley 2006). According to the *Times-Picayune* (2005, C9), the bill for replacing and repairing the roads and bridges destroyed by the storm could exceed $2.3 billion. Repairing damage to interstate highways and major state roads such as I-10 alone could cost $1.5 billion, to be paid with federal funds. An estimated $77 million of repairs are needed on another 9,000 miles of off-system roads in the disaster area. These roads are not controlled by local government and are not repaired or maintained with federal dollars. The $2.3 billion price tag does not include damage to state ports, airports, levees, or mass transit systems and does not provide funds to relieve traffic gridlock in Baton Rouge streets filled with vehicles from New Orleans evacuees.

NORTA's preliminary analysis indicated that the system will lose more than $94 million in anticipated revenues in 2006, and its capital replacement costs could exceed $750 million. In October 2005, FEMA released $48.4 million to reestablish bus service in New Orleans and along the Mississippi coast and to expand service in Baton Rouge, which experienced significant population growth after Katrina. East Baton Rouge Parish population surged from 425,000 to 1.2 million, making it one of the fastest-growing regions in the country (Mulligan and Fausset 2005). The influx of these new residents to the region created traffic gridlock.

To assist NORTA to redevelop effective public transportation in the region, FEMA funds helped purchase 39 biodiesel buses at a cost of $15 million. The buses were delivered in July 2008, nearly three years after Hurricane Katrina destroyed more than half of the city's 370 buses (Dungca 2008). The biodiesel vehicles were built by the Orion bus company based in Ontario, Canada. The release of the brand-new buses comes at a time of increased reliance on the NORTA. From April 2007 to May 2008, ridership increased 53 percent. Many of the new riders have been using public transportation in light of rising gas prices—currently topping $4 per gallon.

Katrina exposed a major weakness in urban mass evacuation plans. It also shone a spotlight on the heightened vulnerability of people without cars—a population that faces transportation challenges in everyday life (Pastor et al. 2006). The 2000 Southeast Louisiana Hurricane Evacuation and Sheltering Plan called for use of school buses and municipal buses to evacuate people who did not have access to private transportation. The plan states: "The primary means of hurricane evacuation will be personal vehicles. School and municipal buses, government-owned vehicles and vehicles provided by volunteer agencies may be used to provide transportation for individuals who lack transportation and require assistance in evacuating" (State of Louisiana 2000, 13).

Public officials provided little assistance to households that lacked cars (Renne 2005). FEMA also failed to deploy buses in a timely manner for evacuation as planned despite early warnings. In the initial preparations for Katrina, Amtrak offered help but was turned down. In the meantime, a train with 900 seats (seven locomotives and 20 cars) rolled away empty a day and a half before the storm made landfall. After the storm, Amtrak provided a special 12-car train that operated over freight tracks to evacuate 96 people from New Orleans to Lafayette, Louisiana, where passengers were transferred to motor coaches to complete the journey to Dallas and other destinations. The Amtrak trains also brought in essential supplies of food and water. "We have clear tracks and an empty train ready to help get residents safely out of the city," said DOT Secretary Norman Mineta (U.S. Department of Transportation 2005).

One of the reasons for the six-day delay in evacuating some people from the squalid and inhumane conditions inside the New Orleans Superdome after Katrina was serious mismanagement on the part of a Jacksonville, Florida, company (Sturgis 2006). In 2002, Landstar—a company with close ties to the Bush family and the national Republican Party—won a five-year, $289 million contract from the U.S. DOT to shuttle people and relief supplies during national emergencies (Sturgis 2006, 41; Kromm and Sturgis 2008, 20).

Government auditors say Landstar waited until 18 hours after Katrina struck to order 300 buses for the evacuation and placed the order with a subcontractor, Cary Limousine, which in turn relied on yet another subcontractor—costing U.S. taxpayers $137 million, not including a $32 million overcharge by Landstar that government auditors later discovered and forced the company to repay. Despite the problems with its performance, however, DOT in April 2006 presented a plaque to Landstar's president and CEO honoring his company's service to Gulf Coast residents (Sturgis 2006).

In general, urban mass evacuation plans are weak. The problem is not unique to New Orleans and the Gulf Coast. The 2005 evacuation of 2.7 million people from Houston after Hurricane Rita shows that "there is no way to evacuate a large U.S. city quickly and smoothly" (Hsu and Balz 2005, A9). Many motorists ran out of gas after spending more than fifteen hours stuck in traffic. In a 2006 report, transportation expert Todd Litman concludes: "Katrina's evacuation plan functioned relatively well for motorists but failed to serve people who depend on public transit. Rita's evacuation plan failed because of excessive reliance on automobiles, resulting in traffic congestion and fuel shortages. Equitable and compassionate emergency response requires special efforts to address the needs of vulnerable residents. Improved emergency response planning can result in more efficient use of available resources" (Litman 2006, 1).

A September 24th *New York Times* editorial, "Educated by Rita," summed up the flawed transportation response to Katrina and Rita: "If Katrina exposed what happens when many people have no cars to escape danger, Rita seemed to show the other side of the coin. The authorities are going to have to become much more sophisticated about developing evacuation plans that do not put every family on the highway in its own vehicle. But the car-obsessed American public is going to require a lot of education before many will accept the idea that they should flee disaster via mass transit" (*New York Times* 2005, A4).

Tragically, one bus carrying 45 Hurricane Rita evacuees, 38 of them elderly nursing home residents, caught fire near Dallas, killing at least 24. In the case of Katrina, emergency transportation planners failed the most vulnerable of our society, individuals without cars, nondrivers, disabled, homeless, sick persons, elderly, and children. As a result, many vulnerable people were left behind and may have died because they lacked transportation. More than a third of New Orleans' African-American residents did not own a car. Over 15 percent of city's residents relied on public transportation as their primary mode of travel.

Local, state, and federal emergency planners have known for years the risks facing transit-dependent residents (State of Louisiana 2000; Fischetti 2001; Bourne 2004;

City of New Orleans 2005). At least 100,000 New Orleans residents did not have cars to evacuate in case of a major storm (City of New Orleans 2005). A 2002 article titled "Planning for the Evacuation of New Orleans" detailed the risks faced by hundreds of thousands of carless and non-drivers in the New Orleans. Of the 1.4 million inhabitants in the high-threat areas, government officials assumed that only approximately 60 percent of the population of about 850,000 people would be able to leave the city (Wolshon 2002).

Although the various agencies had knowledge of this large vulnerable population, there simply was no effective plan to evacuate these New Orleanians away from rising water. This problem received national attention in 1998 during Hurricane Georges when emergency evacuation plans left behind mostly residents who did not own cars (Perlstein and Thevenot 2004). The city's emergency plan was modified to include the use of public buses to evacuate those without transportation. When Hurricane Ivan struck New Orleans in 2004, many carless New Orleanians were left to fend for themselves, while others were evacuated to the Superdome and other "shelters of last resort" (Laska 2008).

Transporting some 100,000 to 134,000 people out of harm's way was no small undertaking (Litman 2005). Most of the city's 500 transit and school buses were without drivers. About 190 New Orleans Rapid Transit Authority (NORTA) buses were lost to flooding. Most of the NORTA employees were dispersed across the country, and many were made homeless (Eggler 2005). Before Katrina, NORTA employed more than 1,300 people. A year after the storm, NORTA's board of directors laid off 150 of its remaining 730 employees, including 125 of NORTA's 400 operators and 21 of its 162 maintenance employees.

Three years after the storm, 48 percent of all New Orleans public transit routes were open and only 19 percent of the number of pre-Katrina buses were operating. NORTA's average daily ridership dropped from 71,543 in July 2005 to 28,590 in June 2008 (Liu and Plyer 2008, 70). Its core black ridership continues to be scattered.

In November 2006, New Orleans and Jefferson Parish councils met to try to bring the fractured city and suburban bus system in sync (Moran 2006). The two adjoining jurisdictions have always run separate bus systems. Transit riders on NORTA and Jefferson Transit are forced to switch buses at the parish line. Katrina did not wash away the stubborn cultural divide that separates New Orleans from its suburbs. The two jurisdictions had a chance to combine forces a year after Katrina, when Jefferson awarded a three-year contract for management of its public transit system. NORTA made a bid for the job, but Jefferson chose a private Illinois company that offered a better price.

Before Katrina, more than a quarter of New Orleans households did not have a car and relied on public transit as their primary mode of travel. On the other hand, in Jefferson Parish, public transit has been a low priority because most residents own cars. Before Katrina, only 5,300 Jefferson Parish residents used public transit to get to work, while more than 209,000 drove their cars to work.

The flooding of New Orleans after Hurricane Katrina revealed that our society is ill-prepared to respond to people with mobility restrictions. Disaster planners failed the most vulnerable in New Orleans—individuals without cars, nondrivers, the disabled, homeless, sick, elderly, and children. These data confirm what many believe, that Katrina killed the weakest residents (Riccardi 2005). More than 1,800 people perished in Katrina and its aftermath. A disproportionately large number of the fatalities were elderly, with 71 percent of the victims older than 60 and 47 percent over the age of 75 (Cahalan and Renne 2007, 7).

On August 29, 2005, FEMA director Michael Brown instructed emergency service personnel not to send trucks or emergency workers to disaster areas without a specific request from state or local authorities (*Washington Post* 2006). These instructions were given as Katrina made landfall and the levees had already begun to be breached. FEMA officials took over the evacuation coordination three days after the storm struck.

On September 2, five days after the storm, fifteen airlines began flying evacuees out of New Orleans Louis Armstrong Airport to San Antonio. Between September 3 and September 11, more than 24,400 people were evacuated via airlift. Some New Orleans residents waited two weeks to be evacuated from floodwaters. The Coast Guard rescued nearly half of 75,000 people stranded in New Orleans.

FEMA and DOT officials never requested any military assistance in evacuating the city. For example, the USS *Bataan* was sitting off the coast with operating rooms and rooms for 600 patients and could bring on hospital beds for special-needs evacuees such as the elderly, handicapped, and hospital patients. DOT and FEMA failed to live up to their emergency response mandate by failing to foresee the need to muster buses, boats, and aircraft (Hsu 2006, A01).

Hundreds of available trucks, boats, planes, and federal officials were unused in search-and-rescue efforts because FEMA failed to give them missions (Jordon 2006). The first federal order to evacuate New Orleans was not issued until 1:30 a.m., August 31, and came only after FEMA's ground commander in New Orleans, Phil Parr, issued a call for buses after finding water lapping at the approaches to the Superdome, where 12,000 victims were sheltered. Failure of local, state, and federal authorities to coordinate transportation assets required under city and state emergency plans for search and rescue and evacuation resulted in unnecessary loss of life (Johnson 2006, 13).

Emergency evacuation plans need to optimize any and all available transportation assets to provide transit to those who have no means to evacuate themselves. This group includes hospital patients, prisoners, disabled, and other members of society with special needs or requirements. In Katrina, the transportation plan to support evacuation failed miserably. In the end, "lives were lost and undue pain and suffering occurred because people were not evacuated out of harm's way" (Johnson 2006, 4).

The National Council on Disability (2005) estimated that there are more than 155,000 people with disabilities over the age of five, or about 25 percent of the cities' population, living in the three cities hardest hit by Hurricane Katrina: Biloxi, Mississippi; Mobile, Alabama; and New Orleans. Evacuation accessibility is required under the federal Americans with Disabilities Act. Although there are special-needs evacuation plans on the books and posted on official Web sites, they are underdeveloped, and most are not effective.

Lessons learned from Hurricane Katrina identified severe flaws in the way that local, state, and federal authorities coordinated and managed emergency transportation assets. The lethargic response by all levels of government raised questions about environmental justice and emergency management and preparedness (Johnston and Nee 2006). Slow government response disproportionately and adversely affected low-income and ethnic minority populations (Pastor et al. 2006; Wright and Bullard 2007). Thousands of New Orleanians, many without access to personal automobiles, were housed in hospitals and prisons, and many suffered in squalid conditions waiting for relief in shelters of last resort, including the Louisiana Superdome and the Morial Convention Center. Without a doubt, FEMA, DOT, the state of Louisiana, and the city leaders failed these New Orleanians.

THE ROLE OF MASS TRANSIT IN EMERGENCY EVACUATION

The need to safely and efficiently transport people, particularly individuals for whom public transportation is the primary means of mobility, before, during, and after emergencies, is crucial to disaster preparedness. U.S. Department of Transportation Order 1900.9 defines a disaster as "a fundamental disruption of socioeconomic activity resulting from natural or human causes that is characterized by actual or potential significant loss of life . . . interruption of transportation operations or damage to portions of the transportation infrastructure that are beyond the response capabilities of state and local authorities" (U.S. Department of Transportation 2000, 4). FEMA reports that from 1953 to 2007 there have been between 45 and 75 presidentially declared disasters annually—both natural and human caused, that exceed local capacity, require state and federal assistance, and may involve an evacuation (Transportation Research Board 2008, 24). In FY 2003 alone, there were 52 presidentially declared disaster designations. Severe storms account for two-thirds (66 percent) of the total, followed by floods (10 percent), hurricanes (8 percent), and tornados (5 percent). Major disasters are concentrated geographically. Nearly a third of all presidentially declared disasters since 1953 have occurred in only ten states.

On February 11, 1994, President Bill Clinton signed Executive Order 12898, Federal Actions to Address Environmental Justice in Minority Populations and Low-Income Populations (Clinton 1994), which covers a dozen or so federal agencies, including FEMA and DOT, and other government agencies that receive federal funds. It mandates that each federal agency must make achieving environmental justice part of its mission by identifying and addressing, as appropriate, disproportionately high and adverse human health, environmental, economic, and social effects of its programs, policies, and activities on minority and low-income populations.

FEMA and DOT fall under Executive Order 12898. Given the way emergency response to Katrina was handled, both federal agencies failed to live up to the 1994 executive order. On April 15, 1997, the U.S. Department of Transportation issued its Order on Environmental Justice. The DOT order requires the agency to comply with Executive Order 12898 but goes a step further in tailoring actions directed at existing transportation laws, regulations, and guidance (U.S. Department of Transportation 1997). In December 1998, the Federal Highway Administration (FHWA) issued an order requiring the agency to incorporate environmental justice in all its programs, policies, and activities.

In 2005, transit could have played an important role in the evacuation of New Orleans in advance of Katrina. The evacuation plan broke down when few drivers reported to work, transit equipment proved inadequate and was left unattended, and communications and incident command were nonexistent. A 2006 DOT and DHS study examined emergency operations plans in states, territories, and 75 major metropolitan areas and concluded that most plans could be improved to better address the requirements for mass evacuations and that the Gulf Coast region plans for evacuating persons with various special needs generally are not well developed. The study outlines some lessons learned in Gulf Coast evacuations: "An important lesson learned in evacuations associated with Hurricanes Katrina and Rita was the necessity of having food, water, restrooms, fuel, and shelter opportunities along evacuation routes. State and local plans generally recognize the need to have these services prepositioned and available along evacuation routes. However, plans for providing real-time information on the availability and location of these services are not as well developed" (U.S. Department of Transportation and U.S. Department of Homeland Security 2006).

Hurricane Katrina accentuated the need to include all modes of transportation in New Orleans—a city that was unprepared to evacuate so many persons using other modes. Since Hurricane Katrina, however, New Orleans has developed a plan for the use of multiple modes of transportation to evacuate those who cannot evacuate by private vehicle. The plan identifies target populations to be evacuated by bus, railroad, and airplane and how persons will be transported to those modes.

In addition, the city has enhanced its sheltering plan and will provide more information to citizens early in the season. The city has also established a 311 information hotline to register residents with special needs for evacuations. One goal of the plan is to "create and maintain an environment where the decision to evacuate becomes more desirable than remaining behind" (U.S. Department of Transportation and U.S. Department of Homeland Security 2006).

A 2006 U.S. Government Accountability Office report determined that state and local governments are generally not well prepared to evacuate transportation-disadvantaged populations, but some have begun to address challenges and barriers. The report also concluded that the federal government could do more to assist state and local governments to address the needs of transportation-disadvantaged populations (U.S. GAO 2006). A 2006 AARP report concluded that government emergency planning documents or processes at any level—federal, state, or local—rarely mention the needs of vulnerable older persons (Gibson and Hayunga 2006).

The National Council on Disability (2006) reports that local evacuation plans during Katrina failed to adequately provide for the transportation needs of people with disabilities for two reasons. First, many local planners reported they were unaware that people with disabilities have special evacuation needs. Second, when local planners were aware of the need to plan for people with disabilities, the plans failed because people with disabilities had not been involved in their development.

A 2007 study commissioned by the Federal Transit Administration (FTA) Office of Civil Rights found that most of the transit agencies as well as the metropolitan planning organization and state departments of transportation surveyed had taken limited steps to address the needs of vulnerable populations in an emergency; these same agencies have not thoroughly identified the transportation-disadvantaged populations within their areas, and they do not routinely or systematically address their needs (Milligan and Company 2007, 42).

Similarly, a 2008 Transportation Research Board (TRB) study examined strategies to improve the role mass transit systems can play in disaster preparedness and response, especially for people without cars or those with special needs. According to the study, "Emergency plans that inadequately represent transit or are poorly executed risk significant loss of life, particularly among those who are dependent on transit for evacuation out of harms way" (Transportation Research Board 2008, 1).

The study was requested by Congress and funded by the FTA and the Transit Cooperative Research Program, and conducted by a committee of experts under the auspices of the TRB. The committee broadly defined transit as bus and rail systems, paratransit and demand-responsive transit, commuter rail, and ferries. After reviewing 38 urban areas' emergency response and evacuation plans, the TRB (2008, 4–12) found the following:

- The majority of the emergency operations plans for large urbanized areas are only partially sufficient in describing in specific and measurable terms how a major evacuation could be conducted successfully, and few focus on the role of transit.
- Even among localities with evacuation plans, few have provided for a major disaster that could involve multiple jurisdictions or multiple states in a region and necessitate the evacuation of a large fraction of the population.
- In those areas where transit is a full partner in local emergency evacuation plans, transit agencies have been involved in the development of such plans and are part of the designated emergency command structure.
- Transit can play multiple roles in an emergency evacuation, but these roles depend on the nature of the incident and its location in a region; the availability of transit operators and equipment at the time of the incident; and the extent of damage, if any, to transit equipment and facilities.
- Emergency managers, elected officials, and the general public should be realistic in their expectations regarding the role that transit can play in an emergency

evacuation, particularly for a no-notice incident that occurs during a peak service period.

- Transit has a unique role to play in evacuating the carless and people with special needs (e.g., the disabled, the elderly, special-needs populations with pets)
  during an emergency. However, these groups are inadequately addressed in
  most local emergency evacuation plans.
- The capacity and resilience of transit and highway systems as they affect evacuation capability in an emergency incident are poorly addressed in current
  funding programs.

Overall, the committee found that transit has a role to play in each of the four
major elements that make up an emergency response plan—mitigation, preparedness, response, and recovery. More planning at local levels and greater guidance from
the federal government is needed to ensure that public transit systems will be effective in helping to evacuate residents of large urban areas during disasters. Local governments have the primary responsibility for responding to emergency incidents,
and if necessary ordering an evacuation. However, there is a role that the federal government can play.

The committee recommended that the Department of Homeland Security and
Department of Transportation provide more guidance to state and local governments on regional evacuation planning. Emphasis was given to meeting the needs of
people without cars and those with special needs, such as the disabled and poor, as
top priorities and the Achilles heel in local emergency evacuation and response plans.
Federal funding should be provided to help cities develop regional evacuation plans,
and grant recipients should be required to report on their progress.

CONCLUSIONS

Transportation is essential to nearly every aspect of daily life and continues to be a
major civil rights and human rights issue. Transportation plays a key role in workers'
ability to find and retain employment. Population and jobs have become increasingly decentralized. Improvements in transportation investments are of special concern to low-income families and people of color who are spatially concentrated in
neighborhoods away from major job centers. Instead of being a bridge to opportunity, some transportation investments have cut wide paths through poor neighborhoods, physically isolated residents from their institutions, displaced thriving
businesses, and subsidized suburban sprawl.

Too often race and class dynamics operate to isolate many central city residents
from expanding suburban job centers. Transportation investments, enhancements, and
financial resources, if used properly, can bring much-needed revitalization to urban
areas, and aid in lifting families out of poverty. Transportation is a key ingredient in
smart growth—building economically viable and sustainable communities. Changing
our development patterns with better planning toward more compact communities

can save energy, generate less air pollution, including greenhouse gases, and create healthier and livable communities with more alternatives to driving.

The nation is largely divided between people with cars and those who are carless. This fact alone makes the need for public transit essential in preventing families from being stuck in low-opportunity neighborhoods away from jobs, or stranded on roof-tops after natural and man-made disasters strike. Katrina highlighted the mobility problem many of our nation's non-drivers and transit-dependent residents face every day. Emergency transportation planners failed the most vulnerable of our society.

Rising fuel prices are stranding millions of Americans on the economic sidelines, forcing them to alter their budgets, rethink their driving patterns, and change their mode of travel. Soaring gas prices are pushing more Americans to take public transit and ditch their cars. This transit ridership increase is noteworthy because it occurred when the economy was declining and fares were increasing. Families in rural com-munities where transit is nonexistent are forced to dig deeper into their wallets—with gasoline rivaling what many spend on food and housing.

Clearly, all levels of government, local, state, and federal, failed New Orleanians, who were left on their own after Katrina and the levee breech flooded 80 percent of their city. Katrina demonstrated that disaster planners are ill-prepared to respond to people with mobility restrictions. It also clarified the need to include all modes of transportation in evacuation plans, including transit, school buses, community center vehicles, Amtrak, etc. This tragedy was most acute for special-needs and vulnerable populations, including people without cars, non-drivers, disabled, homeless, sick per-sons, elderly, and children.

Transportation is a crucial aspect of disaster preparedness. The everyday challenges of people who do not own cars and who are dependent on public transit become ur-gent in an emergency situation. It is one thing for individuals to miss their bus on the way to work. They can always catch the next one. However, it is entirely a different matter for buses not to show up in a disaster to evacuate transit-dependent riders—as in the case of New Orleans after the flood. Not showing up for work could mean loss of a job. Buses not showing up during a disaster could mean loss of life.

During Katrina, local hurricane emergency evacuation plans failed to optimize all available transportation assets to provide transit to those that have no means to evac-uate themselves. Serious mismanagement of emergency transportation by a federal contractor also created delays in evacuating thousands of flood victims from inhu-mane conditions in the New Orleans Superdome. Special-needs evacuation plans were underdeveloped and ineffective. The end result was chaos and unnecessary loss of life.

This is a national problem—rather than one unique to New Orleans or the Gulf Coast. Even three years after Katrina, state and local governments are generally not well equipped to evacuate transportation-disadvantaged populations. The primary means of emergency evacuation in most disaster plans is the personal automobile. However, mass transit has a role to play in an emergency response plan—mitigation, preparedness, response, and recovery. Many transit agencies as well as metropolitan planning organizations and state departments of transportation have not identified the transportation-disadvantaged populations. With federal assistance, some government entities, including the New Orleans city government, have begun to address challenges and barriers, but the federal government could do more.

Disaster planners should take steps to incorporate transit in local emergency evacuation plans; make transit a full partner; encourage transit's multiple roles in an emergency evacuation but remain realistic; integrate the requirement of carless and special-needs populations into evacuation planning; fund evacuation-related capacity enhancements to transportation; and conduct research (Transportation Research Board 2008). States should take the lead to see that plans are implemented, coordinating with appropriate regional entities—metropolitan planning organizations (MPOs). And special-needs populations, such as persons with disabilities, should be involved in the development of emergency response plans in order to enhance their success.

REFERENCES

Abt Associates, Inc. 1999. *Adverse Health Effects Associated with Ozone in the Eastern United States.* Washington, DC: Clean Air Task Force.

American Lung Association. 2007. *State of the Air—2007.* Washington, DC: American Lung Association. Available at http://lungaction.org/reports/stateoftheair2007.html (accessed June 1, 2008).

American Red Cross. 2005. "Hurricane Katrina: Why Is the Red Cross Not in New Orleans?" September 2. Available at http://www.redcross.org/faq/0,1096,0_682 _4524,00.html (accessed June 1, 2008).

Ashe, V. H. 2003. "Testimony to the U.S. House of Representatives Transportation and Infrastructure Committee." May 7.

Atlanta Regional Commission. 2006a. *Population and Housing in the Atlanta Region.* Atlanta: ARC.

_____. 2006b. *Envision 6: Envision Our Future.* Atlanta: ARC.

_____. 2007. "Metro Stats—Black History Month 2007." Atlanta: ARC.

Bourne, J. K., Jr. 2004. "Gone with the Water." *National Geographic.* October. Available at http://magma.nationalgeographic.com/ngm/0410/feature5/ (accessed June 27, 2008).

Brinkley, D. 2006. *The Great Deluge: Hurricane Katrina, New Orleans, and the Mississippi Gulf Coast.* New York: William Morrow.

Bullard, R. D. 2005. "Transportation Policies Leave Blacks on the Side of the Road." *The Crisis* 112 (1): 24–25, 27.

_____. 2007a. Growing Smarter: Achieving Livable Communities, Environmental Justice and Regional Equity. Cambridge, MA: MIT Press.

_____. 2007b. *The Black Metropolis in the Twenty-First Century: Race, Power, and the Politics of Place.* New York: Rowman & Littlefield.

Bullard, R. D., and G. S. Johnson (eds.). 1997. *Just Transportation: Dismantling Race and Class Barriers to Mobility.* Gabriola Island, BC: New Society Publishers.

Bullard, R. D., G. S. Johnson, and A. O. Torres (eds.). 2000. *Sprawl City: Race, Politics, and Planning in Atlanta.* Washington, DC: Island Press.

_____. 2004. *Highway Robbery: Transportation Racism and New Routes to Equity.* Cambridge, MA: South End Press.

Cahalan, C., and J. L. Renne. 2007. "Emergency Evacuation of the Elderly and Disabled: Safeguarding Independent Living." *Intransition* (spring). Available at http://www.connectingcommunities.net/documents/useful/evacelderly.pdf (accessed July 30, 2008).

Center for Neighborhood Technology and the Surface Transportation Policy Project. 2005. *Driven to Spend: Pumping Dollars Out of Households and Communities.* Chicago: CNT.

City of New Orleans. 2005. *City of New Orleans Comprehensive Emergency Management Plan.* Available at www.cityofno.com (accessed June 27, 2008).

Clinton, W. J. 1994. "Federal Actions to Address Environmental Justice in Minority Populations and Low-Income Populations." *Federal Register* 59 (32). February 16. Available at http://www.archives.gov/federal-register/executive-orders/pdf/12898.pdf (accessed July 30, 2008).

DeNavas-Walt, B., D. Proctor, and J. Smith. *Income, Poverty, and Health Insurance Coverage in the United States: 2006.* Washington, DC: U.S. Bureau of the Census, Current Population Reports. August.

Department of Homeland Security. 2006. *National Plan Review Phase 2 Report.* Washington, DC: DHS (June 16). Available at http://www.emforum.org/news/06061601.htm (accessed June 3, 2008).

Dreier, P., J. Mollenkoph, and T. Swanstrom. 2001. *Place Matters: Metropolitics for the Twenty-First Century.* Lawrence: University Press of Kansas.

Dungca, N. 2008. "New Biodiesel Buses Report for Duty Today." *Times-Picayune.* July 10.

Dyson, M. E. 2006. *Come Hell or High Water: Hurricane Katrina and the Color of Disaster.* New York: Basic Books.

Earth Policy Institute. 2002. "Air Pollution Fatalities Now Exceed Traffic Deaths by 3 to 1." September 17. Available at http://www.earth-policy.org/Updates/Update17.htm (accessed June 3, 2008).

Eggler, B. 2005. "RTA Back on Track Slowly, Surely." *Times-Picayune.* October 14, p. B1.

Elliston, J. 2004. "Disaster in the Making." *Orlando Weekly.* October 21.

Environmental Working Group. 2004. "Metropolitan Areas Get Short End of Federal Gas Tax Funds." Available at http://www.ewg.org/reports/gastaxlosers/analysis.php (accessed June 2, 2008).

Ewing, R., K. Bartholomew, S. Winkelman, J. Walters, and D. Chen. 2008. *Growing Cooler: The Evidence on Urban Development and Climate Change.* Washington, DC: Urban Land Institute.

Fischett, M. 2001. "Drowning New Orleans." *Scientific American* (October). Available at www.sciam.com (accessed June 3, 2008).

Frumkin, H., L. Frank, and R. J. Jackson. 2004. *Urban Sprawl and Public Health.* Washington, DC: Island Press.

Gardner, D. C. 1998. "Transportation Reauthorization: A Summary of the Transportation Equity Act (TEA-21) for the Twenty-first Century." *Urban Law Journal* 30 (1097): 1099–1101.

Garrett, M., and B. Taylor. 1999. "Reconsidering Social Equity in Public Transit." *Berkeley Planning Journal* 13 (1): 6–27.

Gibson, M., and M. Hayunga. 2006. *We Can Do Better: Lessons Learned for Protecting Older Persons in Disasters.* Washington, DC: AARP Public Policy Institute. May.

Gillham, O. 2002. *The Limitless City: A Primer on the Urban Sprawl Debate.* Washington, DC: Island Press.

Glaeser, E. L., M. Kahn, and C. Chu. 2001. *Job Sprawl: Employment Location in U.S. Metropolitan Areas.* Washington, DC: Brookings Institution, Center on Urban and Metropolitan Policy.

Health Effects Institute. 1995. *Diesel Exhaust: A Critical Analysis of Emissions, Exposure, and Health Effects.* Cambridge, MA.

Hill, E. W., B. Geyer, K. O'Brien, C. Robey, J. Brennan, and R. Puentes. 2003. *Slanted Pavement: How Ohio's Highway Spending Shortchanges Cities and Suburbs.* Washington, DC: Brookings Institution. March.

Hsu, S. S. 2006. "Katrina Report Spreads Blame." *Washington Post.* February 12.

Hsu, S. S., and D. Balz. "Ins and Outs of Emergency Evacuation." *Washington Post.* September 24.

Jargowsky, P. A. 2002. "Sprawl, Concentration of Poverty, and Urban Inequality." In G. D. Squires (ed.). *Urban Sprawl: Causes, Consequences, and Policy Responses.* Washington, DC: Urban Institute Press, p. 39–71.

Johnson, R. P., Jr. 2006. "Should the National Response Plan Be Changed to Divide the Transportation Responsibilities Under Emergency Support Function #1? Lessons Learned from Hurricane Katrina Show That Transportation Support for Emergency Response Needs Revision." Carlisle, PA: U.S. Army War College Strategy Research Project. March 15.

Johnston, E., and B. Nee. 2006. "A Methodology for Modeling Evacuation in New Orleans." Department of City and Regional Planning, University of California. May. Available at http://www.bnee.com/wp-content/uploads/2006/10/New_Orleans _Evacuation.pdf (accessed July 29, 2008).

Jordon, L. J. 2006. "FEMA Failed to Use Many Katrina Resources, New Documents State." *Patriot News.* January 26.

Krauss, C. 2008a. "Rural U.S. Takes Worst Hit As Gas Tops $4 Average." *New York Times.* June 9.

_____. 2008b. "Gas Prices Send Surge of Riders to Mass Transit." *New York Times.* May 10.

Kromm, C., and S. Sturgis. 2008. *Hurricane Katrina and the Guiding Principles of Internal Displacement: A Global Human Rights Perspective on a National Disaster.* Durham, NC: Institute for Southern Studies.

Lang, R. E. 2000. *Office Sprawl: The Evolving Geography of Business.* Washington, DC: Brookings Institution.

Laska, S. 2008. "What If Hurricane Ivan Had Not Missed New Orleans?" *Sociological Inquiry* 78 (2): 174–178.

Lewis, J. 2004. "Foreword." In R. D. Bullard, G. S. Johnson, and A. O. Torres (eds.). *Highway Robbery: Transportation Racism and New Routes to Equity.* Cambridge, MA: South End Press.

Litman, T. 2005. *Lessons from Katrina and Rita: What Major Disasters Can Teach Transportation Planners.* Victoria, BC: Victoria Transport Policy Institute, September 30.

_____. 2006. *Evaluating Transportation Equity: Guidance for Incorporating Distributional Impacts in Transportation Planning.* Victoria, BC: Victoria Transport Policy Institute, March 8.

Liu, A., and A. Plyer. 2008. *The New Orleans Index, Tracking Recovery of the New Orleans Metro Area: Anniversary Edition Three Years After Katrina.* The Brookings Institution and Greater New Orleans Community Data Center. August.

Lui, M., E. Dixon, and B. Leondar-Wright. 2006. *Stalling the Dream: Cars, Race and Hurricane Evacuation.* Boston: United for a Fair Economy. January 10.

McCosh, J. 2001. "MARTA Calls on Marketers for Image Air: Can Soft Drinks Fill Empty Seats?" *Atlanta Journal-Constitution.* February 11, p. A1.

Milligan and Company. 2007. *Transportation Equity in Emergencies: A Review of the Practices of State Departments of Transportation, Metropolitan Planning Organizations, and Transit Agencies in 20 Metropolitan Areas.* Washington, DC: Federal Transit Administration. May.

Moran, K. 2006. "Public Transit on Agenda at Joint N.O., Jeff Session." *Times-Picayune.* November 6.

Mulligan, T. S., and R. Fausset. "Baton Rouge a Booming Haven for the Displaced." *Los Angeles Times.* September 7.

National Council on Disability. 2005. "National Council on Disability on Hurricane Katrina Affected Areas." September 2. Available at http://www.ncd.gov/news room/publications/2005/katrina.htm (accessed July 30, 2008).

———. 2006. *The Impact of Hurricanes Katrina and Rita on People with Disabilities: A Look Back and Remaining Challenges.* Washington, DC: NCD. August.

New York Times. 2005. "Educated by Rita." September 24, p. A14.

Nolan, B. 2005. "In Storm, N.O. Wants No One Left Behind." *Times-Picayune.* July 24.

Orfield, M. 2002. *Metropolitics: The New Suburban Reality.* Washington, DC: Brookings Institution Press.

Pastor, M., R. D. Bullard, J. K. Boyce, A. Fothergill, R. Morello-Frosch, and B. Wright. 2006. *In the Wake of the Storm: Environment, Disaster and Race After Katrina.* New York: Russell Sage Foundation. May.

Perlstein, M., and B. Thevenot. 2004. "Evacuation Isn't an Option for Many N.O. Area Residents." *Times-Picayune.* September 15, p. A1.

Prakash, S. R. 2007. "Beyond Dirty Diesels: Clean and Just Transportation in Northern Manhattan." In R. D. Bullard (ed.). *Growing Smarter: Achieving Livable Communities, Environmental Justice and Regional Equity.* Cambridge: MIT Press, pp. 273–298.

Pucher, J., and J. L. Renne. 2003. "Socioeconomics of Urban Travel: Evidence from the 2001 NHTS." *Transportation Quarterly* 57 (3): 49–77.

Puentes, R., and L. Bailey. 2003. *Improving Metropolitan Decision Making in Transportation: Greater Funding and Devolution for Greater Accountability.* Washington, DC: Brookings Institution.

Puentes, R., and R. Prince. 2003. *Fueling Transportation Finance: A Primer on the Gas Tax.* Washington, DC: Brookings Institution.

Renne, J. 2005. "Car-less in the Eye of Katrina." *Planetizen.* September 6. Available at www.planetizen.com/node/17255 (Accessed July 3, 2008).

———. 2006. "Evacuation and Equity: A Post-Katrina New Orleans Diary." *Planning Magazine.* May. Available at http://myapa.planning.org/katrina/reader/plannning may2006.htm (accessed July 20, 2008).

Riccardi, N. 2006. "Many of Louisiana Dead over 60." *Atlanta Journal-Constitution.* November 6, p. A6.

Richards, L. 2001. "Alternatives to Subsidizing Edge Development: Strategies for Preserving Rural Landscape." *Terrain.org: A Journal of the Built & Natural Environment* 10 (fall/winter).

Roberto, E. 2008. *Commuting to Opportunity: The Working Poor and Commuting in the United States.* Washington, DC: Brookings Metropolitan Policy Program. February.

Rusk, D. 2001. *The Segregation Tax: The Cost of Racial Segregation on Black Homeowners.* Washington, DC: Brookings Institution Center on Urban and Metropolitan Policy.

Sanchez, T. A., R. Stolz, and J. Ma. 2003. *Moving to Equity: Addressing the Inequitable Effect of Transportation Policies on Minorities.* Cambridge, MA: The Civil Rights Project, Harvard University.

Saporta, M. 2003. "Transportation Funds Must Be Shared Fairly." *Atlanta Journal-Constitution.* February 24, p. E3.

_____. 2004a. "Transit Funding in Mass. Opens Eyes of Atlantans." *Atlanta Journal-Constitution.* May 17, p. E6.

_____. 2004b. "Transit 'Catch-22' Is Bad for Atlanta." *Atlanta Journal-Constitution.* August 16, p. E3.

Schleifstein, M. 2005. "Preparing for the Worst." *Times-Picayune.* May 31.

Stanford, D. 2003. "Metro Roads Shortchanged: Funding Formula Steers Cash to Rural Highways at the Expense of Gridlocked Atlanta Motorists." *Atlanta Journal-Constitution.* September 28.

State and Territorial Air Pollution Program Administrators and Association of Local Air Pollution Control Officials. 2000. "Cancer Risk from Diesel Particulate: National and Metropolitan Area Estimates for the United States." March.

State of Louisiana. 2000. Southeast Louisiana Hurricane Evacuation and Sheltering Plan. Baton Rouge: State of Louisiana. Available at www.ohsep.louisiana.gov/plans/EOPSupplementala.pdf (accessed June 2, 2008).

Stoll, M. A. 2005. *Job Sprawl and the Spatial Mismatch Between Blacks and Jobs.* Washington, DC: Brookings Institution.

Stolz, R. 2000. "Race, Poverty & Transportation." *Poverty & Race.* March/April.

_____. 2006. "A National Transportation Equity Movement for Real Human Needs." *Race, Poverty & the Environment.* Winter 2006.

Sturgis, S. 2006. "Katrina Bus Fiasco Reveals Contracting Weakness." In *One Year After Katrina: The State of New Orleans and the Gulf Coast.* Durham, NC: Institute for Southern Studies/Southern Exposure.

Surface Transportation Policy Project. 2004. *Mean Streets: How Far Have We Come.* Washington, DC: STPP. Available at http://www.transact.org/library/reports_html/ms2004/pdf/Final_Mean_Streets_2004_4.pdf (accessed July 28, 2008).

Thayer, K. 2002. "Detroit Draws Closer to Regional Transit System: Speedlink Rapid Bus System Advances." *Great Lakes Bull. News Serv.* January 4. Available at http://www.mlui.org/transportation/fullarticle.asp?fileid=11932 (accessed June 22, 2008).

Times-Picayune. "Road Damage May Exceed $2.3 Billion." September 18.

Transportation Research Board. 2008. *Special Report 294: The Role of Transit in Emergency Evacuation.* Washington, DC: National Research Council.

Trowbridge, R. 2002. "Racial Divide Widest in U.S.: Fewer Metro Detroit Neighborhoods Are Integrated Than 20 Years Ago." *Detroit News.* January 14.

U.S. Census Bureau. 2006. "Estimated Daytime Population." Washington, DC: Population Division, Journey to Work and Migration Statistics Branch. December 6.

U.S. Department of Transportation. 1997. "Department of Transportation (DOT) Order to Address Environmental Justice in Minority and Low-Income Populations." 62 Federal Register 18,377 (No. 5610.2).

_____. 2000. "Order 1900.9, U.S. Department of Transportation Research and Special Programs Administration." Washington, DC: U.S. DOT. April.

_____.2005. "Department of Transportation Arranges for Amtrak to Begin Evacuating Residents from New Orleans Starting Tonight." DOT 119–05. September 5. Available at http://www.dot.gov/affairs/dot11905.htm (accessed July 30, 2008).

_____. 2005. "A Summary of Highway Provisions in SAFETEA-LU." FHWA. August 25. Available at http://www.fhwa.dot.gov/safetealu/summary.htm (accessed June 2, 2008).

U.S. Department of Transportation and U.S. Department of Homeland Security. 2006. *Catastrophic Hurricane Evacuation Plan Evaluation: A Report to Congress.* Washington, DC: U.S. DOT and U.S. DHS. June 1.

U.S. Government Accountability Office. 2006. *Transportation-Disadvantaged Populations: Actions Needed to Clarify Responsibilities and Increase Preparedness for Evacuations.* Washington, DC: U.S. GAO. December.

Wald, M. L., and K. Chang. 2007. "Minneapolis Bridge Had Passed Inspection." *New York Times.* August 3.

Washington Post. 2006. "Hurricane Katrina: What Went Wrong." September 11. Available at http://www.washingtonpost.com/wp-dyn/content/custom/2005/09/11/CU2005091100067.html (accessed July 30, 2008).

Wellner, A. S. 2005. "No Exit." *Mother Jones.* September 13.

Wolch, J., M. Pastor, and P. Dreier. 2004. *Up Against the Sprawl: Public Policy and the Making of Southern California.* St. Paul: University of Minnesota Press.

Wolshon, B. 2002. "Planning for the Evacuation of New Orleans." *Institute of Transportation Engineers Journal* 72 (2): 44–49.

Wright, B., and R. D. Bullard. 2007. "Black New Orleans: Before and After Hurricane Katrina." In R. D. Bullard (ed.). *The Black Metropolis in the Twenty-First Century: Race, Power, and the Politics of Place.* New York: Rowman & Littlefield, pp. 173–198.

CHAPTER 4

KATRINA AND THE CONDITION OF BLACK NEW ORLEANS

The Struggle for Justice, Equity, and Democracy

Mtangulizi Sanyika

Hurricane Katrina and its disastrous aftermath exposed and revealed the profound socioeconomic contradictions already existing in the fabric of New Orleanian society. The hurricane and flood merely exacerbated the socioeconomic conditions of the majority-black population, and it worsened the municipal infrastructure system, which was also in serious disrepair. What we witnessed on television as the 40,000 suffering poor mostly black people trapped and neglected in the Superdome and the 20,000 to 30,000 at the Convention Center was the manifestation of deep, lingering historical race-class-gender inequities and disparities (Quigley 2006).

Two-thirds of the black population of roughly 353,000 persons were either in poverty, or constituted the working class/working poor and the underclass or were marginalized, with the remaining one-third constituting the middle class. Most black Orleanians were a marginal, at-risk population, living separate and unequal before the storm (U.S. Bureau of Census 2000). It is recognized that other ethnic groups (such as the Houmas, Latinos, Isleños, Vietnamese, Filipinos, Cajun, and Anglo communities) and other Gulf South locations also experienced devastation and suffering due to Katrina's fury (Dyson 2006). However, this chapter focuses primarily on the story and conditions of African Americans because of the particular suffering and treatment of black Orleanians before, during, and after Katrina. It is recognized that there were times when impacted Orleanians of all races and ethnicities collaborated together as allies, and times when each group found it necessary to articulate its own particular issues and concerns.

PRE-KATRINA LEADERSHIP DYNAMICS

The New Orleans population was quite aware of the bifurcated class system of haves and have-nots based largely on race, but this social reality had been masked from the national consciousness by images of Mardi Gras, the jazz festival, the Bayou Classic, the Essence Music Festival, and other cultural and entertainment events. Katrina forever changed the external perception of New Orleans from the city that care forgot, to the city that was simply forgotten by lack of care, from the Big Easy to the "Un Easy."

Local governments in New Orleans have historically attempted to address and resolve the race-class contradictions of its black citizens and simultaneously play levee roulette with the hurricane protection system based on the availability of federal funding. That system was precarious and vulnerable to levee breaks and catastrophic flooding for some time, resulting from the lack of proper maintenance by the Army Corps of Engineers.

In 2005, $71 million had been cut from the budget of the New Orleans District of the Army Corps of Engineers, thus denying needed improvements to the levees (Dyson 2006). Funding to improve the levees and to regularly maintain them had only increased slightly, and in a gradual fashion by Congress (presumably because the administration had other funding priorities, such as Iraq). It was just a matter of time before the game of roulette would end, as it dramatically did between August 29 and September 3, 2005.

According to the Mardi Gras Index, the failure of the levee system resulted in the flooding of over 80 percent of the city, the loss of over 1,500 lives, severe damage to 183,000 housing units, the loss of 150,000 jobs, and an estimated $200 billion in economic damage.[1] It is the convergence of the socially disastrous conditions of black New Orleans with the failure of the levees and the breakdown of local, state, and federal emergency response systems that resulted in the human suffering and loss of life and property associated with Katrina. New Orleans survived the storm but could not survive the flood.

The human agony exposed by Katrina and the subsequent struggle that emerged was preceded before the storm by the efforts of black Orleanians to prevent a perceived threat by the white elites to recapture politics and power from the black majority—a perceived white takeover. The story of how black evacuees and returnees fought after the storm to ensure that the 250,000-plus dispersed citizens were able to return emerged as the dominant historical struggle of modern-day New Orleans. It evolved as a continuation of the pre-Katrina struggle that had began to crystallize into a maturing social movement.

The pre-Katrina and post-Katrina struggles merged into a battle for New Orleans waged courageously by heroic black citizens of all classes, faiths, genders, neighborhoods, and social strata, as well as dispersed residents across the country from the newly formed involuntary diaspora. Not since the Civil Rights era had so many Orleanians of all socioeconomic strata been involved in the social justice movement.

The struggle to ensure the right of return, justice, equity, and democracy for all Orleanians is the untold story that will potentially shape the future of social relations in the post-Katrina environment. While the total human suffering, pain, and brokenness from Katrina can never be fully determined, the city must focus on both its human and its physical capital if it is ever to reclaim its place as a world-class cultural city. Not only must it rebuild its physical infrastructure, it must sensitively repair the brokenness of its people, the disruption of its rhythm, and the social infrastructure of its communities as well. Only then can it legitimately reclaim its place as a global destination that has made unparalleled contributions to human civilization (Pastor et al. 2006).

Despite the progress that has been made for some black Orleanians, large numbers of them are relegated to the status of the underclass and the working poor, are in poverty, or are marginalized. New Orleans has long been a city deeply troubled by the persistent patterns of low-wage work, racial disparities, systemic inequalities, and socioeconomic injustices. Simply stated, New Orleans was a city deeply divided along racial and class lines, and constantly living on the edge of social disaster. It was a city separate and unequal, despite the positive gains from the civil rights movement.

Given these social realities, the black community initiated a serious movement to challenge the incumbent administration of Mayor C. Ray Nagin to do more for the marginalized black population. In 2002, Nagin won election with 85 percent of the white vote and 35–40 percent of the black vote, thus leading to the conclusion that his policy orientation would favor business and the white population. Activists and organizers were critically examining the conditions of black residents, institutions, and neighborhoods and searching for strategic solutions to the black condition, prompting a comparative examination of the Nagin era with his black predecessors in the city's modern political history. The results of that examination are beyond the scope of this chapter, but the following summary is suggested as a context for understanding the leadership problem.

In May 1978, the city inaugurated Ernest N. "Dutch" Morial (Morial I), as its first mayor of African descent (1978–1986) and thus ushered in a new era of political leadership in the city. New Orleans next elected its second African-American mayor, Sidney Barthelemy (1986–1994), its third, Marc Morial (Morial II: 1994–2002), and its fourth, C. Ray Nagin in 2002 and 2006. Thus, over the last thirty years, African Americans have served as the highest municipally elected official to govern New Orleans. This fundamental change in political leadership from a white-controlled to an African-American–controlled city government has also been accompanied by a change in the complexion of the seven-member City Council from predominantly white to predominantly black. (After the 2007 election, however, the council has four whites and three blacks.) After three decades of black political leadership, the fundamental question confronting black Orleanians has been what difference has it made to black reality. The central concern, question, and topic of everyday conversation for black Orleanians has been how has black control of politics translated or not translated into improvements in the life chances, life opportunities, and quality of life of everyday black citizens. This question was of especial interest during Nagin's first term, and it resurfaced with a fierce intensity after the storm.

As the numbers would suggest, the depths of problems experienced by large segments of the black community were not resolved by black control of the highest municipal political offices. To be sure, black political power in New Orleans as elsewhere has resulted in notable differences, including more black government employees, increased contracts to black professionals, more black department heads, black police chiefs and more black police, and modest increases in black ownership and wealth (Colburn 2005).

All four black mayoral regimes could make these claims to varying degrees. However, because Nagin in his first term was elected primarily by the white population and business interests, significant questions arose regarding his policy positions as evidenced by new problems such as the affordability of the city, developer subsidies, job availability and access, and minority and small business inclusion. Regardless of who is in power, however, it is clear that black municipal power—in New Orleans or elsewhere—does not automatically resolve the intractable problems of poverty and systemic inequality.

These problems may be beyond the reach of a municipality and may require local, state, and federal interventions as well as citizen and market interventions. Despite this reality, black constituents expect a mayor to be the advocate for blacks in general and to address many of the problems of residents at the bottom. At the time of Katrina, there were widely divergent views as to whether the Nagin administration had fulfilled the minimum mandate of black politics. Social movements began to emerge to challenge specific policy proposals of his administration and to argue the need for a different direction.

The schools were deteriorating, police accountability appeared to be highly problematic, gentrification and displacement were rampant, public housing seemed vulnerable to elimination, affordable housing was rapidly vanishing, violence and drugs appeared out of control, the number of dropouts and the rate of unemployment were skyrocketing, and the jails continued to fill up. The state of black New Orleans appeared dismal without the prospect of an immediate resolution.

These and similar conditions led to the public statements of discontent with the Nagin administration and calls for alternative policies and alternative black candidates. Bishop Paul Morton and the (black) Greater New Orleans Coalition of Ministers even called Nagin a "white man in black skin." The strategic assessment and reflective process that began in 2002 led many community planners, activists, and organizers to ask profound questions about the past, present, and future of black New Orleans. As a result of that assessment, new voices began to emerge to argue the need for justice, equity, and democracy in the New Orleans political economy. African Americans had control of the political apparatus, but without control or significant influence over the economic apparatus, where effective power appeared to reside.[2] The Nagin administration now faced the responsibility of responding to this contradiction in black political leadership.

STRATEGIC ORGANIZING RESPONSES:
THE AALP AND OTHER INITIATIVES

It is within this leadership context that the African-American Leadership Project (AALP) emerged as an "action-oriented, community-based think tank" in 2002–2003 to further the black community's capacity to strategically harness its resources and direct them to its own self-interests. A new paradigm was evolving that challenged government, rather than relying on government as the agency of black liberation. Initially, this was a radical departure from the norm of black political dynamics.

The AALP is now a growing five-year-old nonpartisan network of African-American community, business, and religious leaders and representatives that focuses on agenda building, organizing, policy analysis and advocacy, strategic dialogue, consensus building, and neighborhood planning and development. Prior to the Katrina disaster, it had spent two years developing and building consensus on an African American Agenda (AAA) of common interests to potentially guide future policy choices and community actions to foster justice, self-determination, and liberation for black and poor people in the city. That agenda was approved one month before Katrina. Because of the disaster, the AALP shifted its emphasis to constructing a new post-Katrina agenda.[3]

During the spring and summer of 2005, broad-based African-American movements were actively organizing and engaging in advocacy related to several hot-button issues, including schools and quality education, the residency rule, police accountability, street violence, crime and drug reduction, gentrification and displacement, affordable housing, public housing revitalization, neighborhood revitalization, economic ownership and wealth creation, local benefits from tourism, respect for black cultural traditions, and quality health care.

In addition to the AALP, other on-the-ground formations included the Millions More Movement (self-help, crime, and police accountability), the Greater New Orleans Coalition of Ministers (government accountability), the Residency Rule Coalition (the municipal residency rule policy), the NAACP (racial discrimination and inequality), the Urban League (jobs/workforce and small business), the Southern Christian Leadership Conference (SCLC; racial justice), Rainbow-PUSH (minority business and wealth creation), the People's Institute (anti-racist campaigns and organizing), Families Against Police Brutality, Central City Youth Against Violence (street violence and crime), and the Mardi Gras Indian Coalition (cultural traditions). All of these groups and others were in motion organizing and challenging the incumbent administration to broaden its emphasis to include more benefits for African Americans and working people in its policies and programs.

In July 2005, a month before Katrina, the AALP and the New Orleans Local Organizing Committee for the Millions More Movement held demonstrations during the Essence Music Festival to expose the levels of black suffering in the city. Families Against Police Brutality and the NAACP were also conducting demonstrations against police violence and racism in the French Quarter. Educational advocates were challenging the school board and often disrupting its meetings to compel debate on the delivery of quality education to black children and to resist a power-elite takeover.

The Residency Rule Coalition was demanding the retention of the rule that municipal employees live in New Orleans. New Orleans was in the midst of an emerging multiclass social change movement, the likes of which had not been witnessed since the days of the civil rights movement.[4] Katrina occurred in August 2005 in the midst of this "siege against racism" and momentarily disrupted the progress of this emerging movement. Everyone was now confronted with immediate survival issues and compelled to regroup and reposition resources to meet the new survival challenges.

Immediately after the storm, new formations and voices emerged to challenge local government and the white power elites to rebuild an equitable and just New Orleans. These new formations included the People's Hurricane Relief Fund (PHRF) and the Common Ground Collective, both of which were engaged in highly important grassroots organizing and service delivery to Katrina survivors/evacuees. In 2008, the PHRF terminated its existence.

LEVEE ROULETTE AND SOCIAL NEGLECT

For years, scientists, meteorologists, journalists, policy analysts, and government officials had wondered aloud, "What if the Big One hits New Orleans?" It was no secret that a major Category 5 hurricane might one day strike the city and leave it devastated by tidal surges of as high as 25 feet. No less than ten major media sources had conducted analysis of the impacts of a major hurricane on New Orleans or had written articles predicting massive devastation and destruction of the city in the event of a Category 4 to 5 hurricane (Dyson 2006). Numerous media sources had published articles and analysis on the possibility of a devastating hurricane.

Furthermore, the city and state had even conducted a simulation of such a hurricane, PAM, in which it was predicted that 127,000 Orleanians were vulnerable because of their lack of transportation out of the city (Heerden 2006). Yet, despite all the predictions and simulations, when Katrina struck, neither the local, state, or federal governments appeared ready to respond to its challenges. The rate and fury of Atlantic hurricanes had been increasing for some time due to climate change and melting polar caps and the destruction of the coastal wetlands. There was little doubt that the Big One would come. The question often asked by the public was whether officials had properly prepared for it (Heerden 2006).

Some analysts and citizens contend that if Nagin had declared an emergency evacuation earlier, lives and property could have been saved. There probably is some truth to this assertion, but the levee breaches would have occurred regardless of when the evacuation took place. The city had no functional plan to move the 127,000 transit-dependent persons out of the city, and it failed to execute the plan that was supposedly in place based on the PAM simulation model (Heerden 2006). Another critical debate has persisted regarding whether the Industrial Canal levee breach resulted from Katrina's wrath, or whether it was deliberately blown up. Although there is neither definitive nor absolute proof of a deliberate breach, anecdotal and histori-cal evidence are cited as the basis of a plausible hypothesis of an intentional breach.

Some claim that they heard loud sounds similar to explosions and wonder why there was a barge in that location at that time. After all, during the great flood of 1927, it was the deliberate and formal public policy of the government to blow up the levee to save uptown and the central business district (Barry 1997). Similar argu-ments have been made about the levee breaks during Hurricane Betsy in 1965, which also "drowned" the Lower Ninth Ward. Regardless of the explanations of why the Ninth Ward levee break occurred, it is clear that disaster managers and public of-ficials did not anticipate the breaches that occurred at the 17th Street Canal, the Or-leans Avenue Canal, and the London Avenue Canal. Nor did they anticipate or prepare for the flooding problems caused by the Mississippi River Gulf Outlet (MRGO) that destroyed New Orleans East (Heerden 2006).

In addition to the serious problems related to the pace of the evacuation and the levee breaks, the most significant failure was the slowness of the federal government's response to the disaster once it occurred (Heerden 2006; Dyson 2006). The record makes it quite clear that the feds were on vacation and did not properly respond un-til Mayor Nagin blasted President Bush and demanded action. Whether the response was due to bureaucratic wrangling between President Bush and then Governor Kathleen Blanco, or whether it was due to Michael Brown's misread (FEMA) or Michael Chertoff's aloofness (Homeland Security) will be debated forever.

The bottom line is that over 30,000 or more mostly black New Orleanians were trapped between the Superdome and the Convention Center without food, water, sanitation, ice, medical care, and the basics of life for four days. They were left and abandoned to survive on their own, without the help or assistance of their national government. This was the breach that will be most remembered long after the levees are fixed. The federal government abandoned and neglected its own citizens during the worst (human-made) natural disaster in U.S. history. Historians will debate whether the government's failure was a result of incompetence, mismanagement, bu-reaucratic wrangling, and or race/class indifference and insensitivity. Some combina-tion of each of these variables is probably an appropriate and plausible explanation of the events.[5]

As a result of this calamity of bureaucratic blundering, systems failure, and hu-man error, over 1,500 people died, and 300,000 people were dispersed to 47 states, many of whom remain dispersed. It is estimated that initially more than 240,000 evacuees landed in Houston and another 60,000 landed in Atlanta (Quigley 2006). Most Orleanians left with the expectation that they would return to their homes within three to five days of the storm. During a typical hurricane, residents move to higher ground or leave the city and return home within three to five days. However, this episode was different in that residents were literally locked out of the city due to the flooding, with no date certain when they could return.

What was thought to be a temporary evacuation became a form of permanent re-settlement without consent. The most resource-limited populations and those who were trapped in the Superdome and Convention Center now faced the challenge of forced exile to foreign environments, allegedly for their own safety. There is a new diaspora of approximately 200,000 to 250,000 Orleanians, mostly black, who remain scattered and dispersed across the United States.

RESPONSE OF THE LOCAL ELITES: KATRINA CLEANSING

New Orleans survived the storm, but it could not survive the levee breaks that literally drowned 80 percent of the city. Uptown New Orleans, the French Quarter, and the central business district survived the drowning and are intact and functioning, whereas the lower parts of the city in downtown New Orleans (Lower Ninth, the East, and Gentilly) remain significantly unpopulated and dysfunctional. This distinction between downtown or wet neighborhoods and uptown or dry neighborhoods serves as a metaphor for racial and class dynamics in the city: Downtown is primarily black, and uptown is significantly white.

The levees have been restored to their pre-Katrina levels but remain vulnerable to another hurricane of Katrina's magnitude. At the same time, if a hurricane attacks the city from the west rather than from the east, then uptown and Metairie are likely to drown. The levees must be built up to withstand a Category 5 hurricane, and the flood protection system must be substantially upgraded. The technology exists to develop and implement a comprehensive flood management system that will protect the city against catastrophic flooding: Whether the political will exists to do so remains to be seen. The Dutch have intelligently proven that such a system can be designed and successfully operated, and they are 15 to 22 feet below sea level (Heerden 2006). New Orleans is about two feet below sea level.

After overcoming their shock, surprise, and dismay at the level of devastation resulting from the flooding, the white power elites soon summoned their energies to respond to the disaster.[6] A meeting of business leaders was planned and convened in Dallas shortly after the storm and its aftermath to discuss and plan the future of the city—a plan that would completely reshape it demographically, geographically, and politically. Subsequent discussions focused on whether it was wise to rebuild New Orleans at all, or whether it made more sense to "reduce its footprint" by converting the Lower Ninth Ward and New Orleans East to flood protection zones or green spaces. By doing so, it was said, these converted areas would protect the rest of the city from future catastrophic flooding.

Upon hearing of such a proposal, black citizens who were now dispersed all over the country were totally outraged that the elites would publicly or privately engage in such a conversation and that Mayor Nagin did not categorically and unequivocally repudiate such thinking on the spot. After all, there was no debate about rebuilding Lower Manhattan after 9/11 or of rebuilding San Francisco after the Loma Prieta Earthquake. Additionally, speculation regarding the future of New Orleans was publicly voiced by the congressional leadership of the Republican Party. Republican Congressman Richard Baker from Baton Rouge was quoted as saying that pub-lic housing in New Orleans had finally been cleaned up. "We couldn't do it, but God did." Many black citizens concluded that, flood-protection issues notwithstanding, the brazen speculation to "reduce the city's footprint" was occurring because New Orleans was a black and poor city that also traditionally voted for the Democrats. Subsequently, the mayor appointed a new entity to develop plans to rebuild and reconstruct New Orleans, the Bring New Orleans Back (BNOB) Commission. In the opinion of the on-the-ground citizen forces, BNOB was nonrepresentative of the citizens and appeared to be dominated by business and corporate interests.[7]

In its deliberations, the BNOB never effectively included the voices of the black poor, or those who were displaced by Katrina. Its far-reaching areas of concern cov-ered sweeping proposals to remake the city and local government based on the elite's wish list for "good government" reforms rather than on the best interests of the city's majority African-American population. BNOB's span covered education, infrastruc-ture, health care, the environment, culture and the arts, criminal justice, housing, and governance. In its final report, its Land Use Committee, which was chaired by a Bush ally and major banker/real estate developer, also recommended footprint re-duction. It argued that the city might not have the capacity or resources to provide services to all of the neighborhoods; therefore, tough decisions needed to be made regarding which neighborhoods were "viable" and which were not (Bring New Or-leans Back Commission 2006). The black response was swift and vocal: "No foot-print reduction of any kind."

Officially and unofficially, there were now proposals to convert the most devas-tated areas into swamps, green spaces, condos, theme parks, and numerous other schemes that would reduce the geography and population of the city. Obviously all such proposals were suspect in the black community because the neighborhoods and areas so affected were predominantly black: the Lower Ninth, the East, Gentilly, Pontchartrain Park, and, for good measure, parts of the upper-income predominantly white devastated area of Lakeview (Bring New Orleans Back Commission 2006).

The assertion that the footprint-reduction proposal was inherently racist derives from this disproportional impact of the proposal on black residents and homeown-ers. The commission went on to recommend a four-month process of neighborhood planning to determine which neighborhoods were coming back. With little guidance or structure, residents then took the initiative on their own to start the planning pro-cess to determine how "viable" their neighborhoods would be. This was a vote of no confidence in the commission and the elites.

The elites touted their proposals as the salvation of the city and even suggested that God was on their side. While this debate was raging in the city, the AALP and other groups initiated broad discussion with displaced residents and citizens groups to develop a citizens' perspective and vision. The emerging statement was to serve as a statement of fundamental rights and be an appropriate response to "Katrina cleansing"—the elite effort to permanently displace much of the New Orleans black population.

A CITIZEN RESPONSE:
THE CITIZENS' BILL OF RIGHTS

The response of the elites to the disaster served to crystallize the opinions of displaced Orleanians and activists-organizers on the ground that the right of return was a fundamental issue of transcendent importance. The Katrina disaster was one of the most tragic events to occur in the history of the United States in that most of the city was physically destroyed, and its people and culture were significantly compromised. Yet, the failure of local, state, and federal government and their emergency response systems and the response of the white power elites did not diminish the will of the people to survive and triumph.

Those who suffered through and survived Katrina and its aftermath have been referred to by many names—survivors, evacuees, refugees, the dislocated, the dispersed, exiles, new immigrants, and the diaspora. Under international covenants and law, the most appropriate term might be "internally displaced persons," which encompasses the range of legal and political rights of persons forcibly dispersed from their homeland within a country by a natural disaster. In the diaspora cities outside of New Orleans, the most frequently used term is "evacuee," although New Orleanians simply say, "I'm from New Orleans."

Displaced persons argued that this was a new time, a historic moment requiring us to dig deeply into our God-given human capacity and rise from the depths of the water to build a new and different city . . . a new Jerusalem if you will. The emerging vision was that perhaps a "new" city could be built based on justice, equity, sustainability, democracy, and a radical improvement in the quality of life for all those who choose to return/remain as citizens. The exiled diaspora constantly expressed its desire to return and build a city free of racism, poverty, marginality, injustice, and any obstacles that impeded the full realization of human potential. The Citizens' Bill of Rights (CBOR) is thus the result of a broad-based dialogue and consensus on the values and principles that should guide the efforts on the ground.[8]

As the AALP listened to these aspirations and concerns from all over the country, it became evident that a new agenda was emerging from the bottom up and that our task was to give voice and form to these aspirations. The first element of the new agenda was the development of a consensus on what the exiled diaspora preferred in the redevelopment of the city. Diaspora citizens concluded that the rebuilding and reconstruction of the city was an important historical, practical, and cultural imperative for the United States today. New Orleans is arguably the U.S. city that most displays African cultural retentions and traditions, effortlessly blended into everyday life.

The Crescent City is one of the world's great cultural cities, with a grand musical, culinary, architectural, religious, life rhythmic, folk, artistic, linguistic, and literary tradition comparable to any in the world. Indeed, New Orleans represents an indigenous people's way of life and an extraordinarily unique human civilization. The agenda-building process also reiterated what the locals always knew, that despite its great cultural assets, it is also a city with deep racial and class divisions, rooted in the history of slavery, racial segregation, and socioeconomic disparities and inequalities. The faces of Katrina gave living expression to the numbing statistics on the quality of life for a significant number of African Americans.

There was broad agreement that perhaps rebuilding the city offered a unique historical and practical opportunity to promote racial justice, equity, and healing after centuries of racial oppression and exploitation, that is, to humanize the city. The displaced African-American community and low-income households of all races can be integrated into the new New Orleans economy in ways never imagined in the past. If the city is rebuilt, it must address such inequities so that the displaced population perceives New Orleans as a city of quality, opportunity, and justice with a dramatically improved quality of life.

The conclusion was that the hundreds of billions of dollars in state, federal, and private resources should be targeted to improving human development and capacity in areas like literacy, social entrepreneurship, job skills, cultural history and traditions, and multiculturalism; rebuilding the physical infrastructure such as roads, power, levees, flood barriers, bridges; and rebuilding quality, affordable institutional services and systems such as health care, education, housing enterprises, and the cultural economy. New Orleans could become a model of a just, equitable, democratic, and sustainable city in the global era. Based on this reasoning, the following principles and the Citizens' Bill of Rights were then developed by the AALP as the framework and value orientation that should guide the recovery, rebuilding, and reconstruction process.[9]

All displaced persons should retain the right of return to New Orleans as an international human right. A person's socioeconomic status, class, employment, occupation, educational level, neighborhood residence, or how they were evacuated should have no bearing on this fundamental right. This right should include the provision of adequate transportation to return to the city by a similar means that a person was dispersed. The city should not be depopulated of its majority African-American and lower-income citizens, and must be rebuilt to economically include all those who were displaced. The following are central points in the Citizens' Bill of Rights:

1. All displaced persons must retain their *right of citizenship* in the city, especially including the right to vote in the next municipal elections. Citizen rights to the franchise must be protected and widely explained to all dispersed persons. The provisions of the Civil Rights Act of 1965 should be examined and enforced in this regard.
2. All displaced persons should have the *right to shape and envision the future* of the city. Shaping the future should not be left to elected officials, appointed commissions, developers and/or business interests alone. We the citizens are the primary stakeholders of a re-imagined New Orleans. Thus we MUST be directly involved in imagining the future. Provisions must be included to insure this right.
3. All displaced persons should have the *right to participate in the rebuilding* of the city as owners, producers, providers, planners, developers, workers, and

direct beneficiaries. Participation must especially include African-Americans and the poor, and those previously excluded from the development process.

4. In rebuilding the city, all displaced persons should have the *right to quality goods and services based* on equity and equality. Disparities and inequality must be eliminated in all aspects of social, economic and political life. It should be illegal to discriminate against an individual due to their income, occupation or educational status, in addition to the traditional categories of race, gender, religion, language, disability, culture or other social status.

5. In rebuilding the city, all displaced persons should have the *right to affordable neighborhoods,* quality affordable housing, adequate health care, good schools, repaired infrastructure, a livable environment and improved transportation and hurricane safety.

6. In rebuilding the city, workers, especially hospitality workers should have the *right to be paid a livable wage* with good benefits.

7. In rebuilding the city, African-Americans should have the *right to increased economic benefits and ownership.* The percentage of Black owned enterprises MUST dramatically increase from the present 14 percent, and the access to wealth and ownership must also be dramatically improved.

8. In rebuilding the city, African-Americans and any displaced low income populations should have the *right to preferential treatment* in cleanup jobs, and construction and operational work associated with rebuilding the city.

9. In rebuilding the city, the *right to contracting preference* should also be given to Community Development collaboratives, community and faith-based corporations/organizations, and New Orleans businesses that partner with nonprofit service providers and people of color. No contracts should be given to companies that disregard Davis-Bacon, affirmative action and local participation. Proposed legislation to create a "recovery opportunity zone" should specifically include Community Development organizations and minority firms as alternatives to the no bid multi-national companies. Over the last 30 years, community-based nonprofits have demonstrated their capacity to successfully build hundreds of thousands of quality affordable housing, and neighborhood commercial, business and service enterprises.

10. In rebuilding the city, priority must be given *to the right to an environmentally clean and hurricane safe city,* rather than the destruction of Black neighborhoods or communities such as the lower 9th ward. Priority must also be given to environmental justice, disaster planning and evacuation plans that work for the most transit dependent populations and the most vulnerable residents of the city. A comprehensive flood management system should be developed and implemented including category 5 level levee protection.

11. In rebuilding the city, priority must be given to the *right to preserve and continue the rich and diverse cultural traditions of the city,* and the social experiences of Black people that produced the culture. The Second Line, Mardi Gras Indians, brass bands, creative music, dance foods, language and other expressions

are the "soul of the city." Therefore, the rebuilding process should preserve these traditions. *THE CITY MUST NOT BE CULTURALLY, ECONOMI-CALLY, OR SOCIALLY GENTRIFIED INTO A "SOULLESS" COLLEC-TION OF CONDOS AND TRACT HOME NEIGHBORHOODS FOR THE RICH.*

This Citizens' Bill of Rights found its way into the national dialogue along with the National Urban League's Katrina Bill of Rights as developed by Marc Morial, former mayor of the city. The Citizens' Bill of Rights has remained at the center of major organizing efforts and serves as a measuring stick for the progress we have or have not made in rebuilding a humanized city. In addition to citizen responses, it was also necessary to codify the newly emerging values as public policy, which gave rise to City Council actions on equitable rebuilding.[10] Three years after the storm, the Bill of Rights continues to guide and inform our approach to the recovery.

A PUBLIC POLICY RESPONSE: REBUILD ALL DEVASTATED NEIGHBORHOODS—THE NEIGHBORHOOD REBUILDING EQUITY ORDINANCE (NREO)

Even as the AALP was developing the Citizens' Bill of Rights, the City Council began the debate regarding the viability of neighborhoods and subsequently passed a resolution on equitable rebuilding of neighborhoods. It was that resolution developed by Councilperson Cynthia Willard Lewis that became the basis for an ordinance developed jointly by the AALP and the councilperson to legally ensure the equitable treatment of neighborhoods by the city without penalizing the devastated neighborhoods because of the damage they had sustained. Thus, the AALP designed such an ordinance to ensure that the devastated black neighborhoods would not be eliminated by reducing or withholding resources required to rebuild such neighborhoods. Withholding resources emerged as a more sophisticated version of the crude "footprint reduction" proposals of the Bring New Orleans Back Commission; thus it was vehemently opposed. The NREO would also give priority to local residents seeking jobs, to local nonprofits, to African-American disadvantaged business enterprises (DBEs), and to women-owned firms seeking contracts within the city's jurisdiction.

Since Katrina, further and intense public discussion has occurred regarding how to rebuild the city. There are discussions and proposals to eliminate entire black neighborhoods such as the Lower Ninth Ward and New Orleans East, and there have been specific proposals to phase in or exclude some neighborhoods from simultaneous rebuilding. Most of these proposals argue that the low-lying areas of the city such as the Lower Ninth and New Orleans East are below sea level and should thus not be rebuilt because of their vulnerability to flooding. Proposals include conversion to marshlands, public parks, open areas, buffer zones, and other supposed flood protecting. Regardless of the planning logic of these proposals, the effect of any such shrinkage is the depopulation of the city's African-American and working-class majority, which for many displaced residents is an undesirable outcome. Furthermore, if the city is made hurricane safe and flood efficient, there would be no need to discuss modifying the city's configuration for any reason whatsoever.

Therefore, the ordinance was needed to codify as law the council's intent for the equitable treatment of *all* neighborhoods in the rebuilding of New Orleans and to ensure that no neighborhood is discriminated against in the allocation of public resources (local, state, or federal) because of the extent of Katrina-related damage it suffered. The ordinance would also codify as law the equitable allocation of contracts and jobs to locals, racial minorities, nonprofits, DBEs, women, and small firms.

The NREO would make it the policy and intent of the city of New Orleans to approve the timely and simultaneous inclusion of *all* neighborhoods in the rebuilding of the city. Those neighborhoods hit hardest by Katrina and the subsequent flooding (the Lower Ninth Ward, New Orleans East, Gentilly, Pontchartrain Park, and parts of Hollygrove Mid-city and Lakeview) would receive equal treatment in the allocation of public resources and would not be discriminated against because of their level of damage. The rebuilding of the above neighborhoods would take place simultaneously with the postdisaster rebuilding or redevelopment of the rest of the city and would not be subject to any time limits, phasing, or planning contingencies that restrict or limit the neighborhood's redevelopment based on its level of damage or pace of recovery. The NREO makes it the policy of the city to consistently and uniformly distribute public resources based on defined needs and not any plan to shrink the city's footprint or reduce its population. Furthermore, it is the city's policy to award rebuilding contracts, professional contracts, employment opportunities, and jobs on an equitable and fair basis to residents of the city, locally based firms, DBEs, minority, small, and women-owned firms, nonprofits, and community development organizations. If prime contractors in these targeted categories lack the capacity to complete the scope of work alone, partnerships must be formed to deliver the required services.

This ordinance became effective immediately and remains in effect for as long as the City Council determines that the city is involved in the postdisaster rebuilding process, or for as long as any emergency ordinances, resolutions, or declarations created after September, 1, 2005, apply to any part of the city of New Orleans. The implementation rules and guidelines for this ordinance were developed pursuant to City Council directives to specific departments and agencies of the city. Councilperson Lewis's resolution was unanimously adopted on December 17, 2005, and the ordinance was unanimously adopted by the council on April 20, 2006, and signed into law by Mayor Nagin on April 26, 2006.[11] A comprehensive evaluation of the effect of the NREO has not been undertaken, but it is clear that there will be no footprint reduction and that it is illegal to discriminate against a neighborhood based on its damage level. A review of the city-awarded recovery and rebuilding contracts and jobs appears to be in order.

THE ELECTORAL RESPONSE:
RACE CONTINUES TO MATTER—THE MAYOR'S
RACE AS A CIVIL RIGHTS PROTEST

The April 2006 primary and May 2006 runoff elections in the city were a supreme test of post-Katrina black political will and determination. The major issues that had defined African-American existence since the storm were now subject to open public debate and discussion. Sensing the possibility of retaking political power in the city, the white elites advanced several good-government initiatives that would effectively dilute black political power, regardless of the stated intent. They included (1) consolidation of the seven assessors to one citywide assessor, (2) consolidation of civil and criminal sheriff's offices and divisions, and (3) takeover of the Orleans Parish Public school system by the state. In addition, the elites fielded opponents against two black candidates for City Council who had consistently opposed footprint reduction, and they fielded several "major" white candidates against Nagin whom the elites were increasingly abandoning because of his perceived ineptitude and his refusal to be manipulated by them.

The State Legislature and courts refused to allow satellite voting in the major locations where dispersed Orleanians resided such as Houston, Atlanta, Jackson, and Memphis, settling instead for satellite voting only within Louisiana. Even to accomplish this limited satellite voting, the Louisiana Legislative Black Caucus was forced to walk out of the Legislature in protest. The black community felt under massive racial attack by the white power elites and was threatened by its moves. Black voters felt a specific and serious challenge to the Voting Rights Act of 1965, and a danger to hard-fought-for civil rights victories. As many said, "They can vote for Iraqi politicians who are 10,000 miles away, but we can't vote for Mayor right here in the U.S." The boldness and arrogance of the threat did not go unnoticed by black voters, who responded by supporting black and progressive candidates against the elite-supported black and white challengers.[12] Although many political observers regarded Nagin's runoff opponent Mitch Landrieu as the more liberal of the two, ideological labels meant little when racial threats were perceived.

In the primary, Nagin was challenged by five major candidates (four white and one black) and 16 minor candidates. He edged out all opponents by capturing 38 percent of the vote, while Mitch Landrieu—the current lieutenant governor and son of the last white mayor of the city, Moon Landrieu, and brother of the current U.S. senator from Louisiana, Mary Landrieu—finished second with 29 percent of the vote. Thus the stage was set for a showdown between the black incumbent and a high-profile white liberal challenger. Earlier in January 2006, during a King holiday celebration, Nagin uttered the now famous "Chocolate City" phrase, which reminded the public that New Orleans was a black city before the storm, and by extension it should remain so now by re-electing him to a second term. His comments infuriated and alienated significant numbers of white voters but did more to consolidate his support among black voters than any policy speech or debate ever could. For the first time, Nagin had unequivocally and publicly affirmed the political rights of the black majority, thus repudiating the footprint reduction elites, many of whom he had appointed to the planning bodies that had originated the demographic racial-change logic.

He reiterated his position at a March forum for evacuees sponsored by the NAACP, thus consolidating the view that despite the efforts to force him to "crawfish" (back down), he refused to do so. As stated by many folks on the street, he finally stood up and started sounding like a brother. Thus, despite media efforts to make him appear to be an out-of-control buffoon, once again, Nagin proved the pundits wrong, as he did when he cussed out the president. In both incidents, he shrewdly achieved his objective of dramatically shifting the playing field when more polite efforts had failed. He had now converted a perceived disadvantage (black dispersion and indifference) into an enormous advantage that drew the line—black control of city hall was the issue. A massive march in April 2006 organized primarily by Reverend Jesse Jackson and Reverend Al Sharpton attracted over 10,000 participants from across the country to show support for voting rights. This had emerged as a principal historical challenge because thousands of black voters were dispersed in Houston, Atlanta, Dallas, Jackson, Baton Rouge, and other cities with their voting status in doubt. This mobilization demonstrated the groundswell of support for the "Chocolate City" and all that that term had come to epitomize regarding the fundamental rights of black citizens as articulated by the Citizens' Bill of Rights. That following May, Nagin won the runoff with 52 percent of the vote, securing 80 percent of the black vote and a 20 percent conservative white vote, whereas Landrieu received 80 percent of the white vote and 20 percent of the black vote.

Race continues to be the predictor variable when racial interests are perceived as at risk and threatened. Thus, Nagin's re-election was secured with the overwhelming support of black voters who viewed the election as a civil rights issue that transcended particular candidates and specific policy proposals. In the primary, he finished first with 38 percent of the total vote, securing 66 percent of the black vote and 15 percent of the white vote. In 2002, the situation was reversed, when Nagin won with 85 percent of the white vote and 35 percent of the black vote.

The question that was on many people's mind was which policy orientation would Mayor Nagin govern from, and which constituency would he most consistently represent. Would he be the mayor of the black majority that elected him in 2006, or the mayor of the white minority that elected him in 2002, or would he fashion a synthesis of policies that favored his new black constituency, while simultaneously making concessions to white business interests?

Black voters elected Nagin overwhelmingly to beat back the attempted white takeover, but did so without an explicit agenda that defined their specific policy preferences. The right to return and rebuild the devastated neighborhoods was generally supported by Nagin, but not with the passion and consistency of his major black opponent in the primary, Reverend Tom Watson. Nevertheless, the right of return emerged as the de facto black agenda in the primary and carried over into the runoff.

However, there was not a formal platform of specific proposals that translated the rhetoric into tangibles consistent with what black voters needed and expected. The assumption based on campaign rhetoric was that Nagin would fight to bring dispersed black citizens home and involve them in rebuilding the city for all of its former residents. That was the meaning of his "Chocolate City" remark.

The greatest fear of ground organizers and advocates was that racial symbolism would triumph over policy substance and that skin-color politics would leave black voters with little to show for their support. The white elites had already articulated their position favoring a smaller, leaner, whiter, and richer New Orleans (footprint reduction), and Nagin's response was not as swift and definitive as some would have preferred in rejecting this position. The elites were quite specific in advocating for a New Orleans from the 17th Street Canal to the Industrial Canal, which would thus eliminate the Lower Ninth Ward and New Orleans East. One such advocate, Rob Couhig, a conservative Republican who ran for mayor and subsequently endorsed Nagin, was a key member of Nagin's transition team. However, to his credit, since his re-election, Nagin has never supported the footprint reduction proposal nor given it any credence as a viable option. Instead, he has consistently advocated for the return of displaced Orleanians and the rebuilding of all of the city's neighborhoods.

The politics of racial symbolism is often void of policy substance, frequently depriving the black electorate of substantive policy gains and programs that benefit the neediest in the black community. Because Nagin won without an explicit black-oriented policy agenda and platform, it was imperative that a movement be organized to ensure the accountability of the mayor and the City Council to the interests of black voters. Therefore, the African-American Leadership Project convened three policy summits to develop such an agenda. Over 250 citizens attended the summits, representing a broad range of community leaders and neighborhood groups, to develop the agenda in ten core areas: housing, jobs/employment, economic development, the environment, education, hurricane safety, police-public safety, neighborhood planning, youth, and cultural equity. Initially, over 250 specific resident- and citizen-sensitive policy statements or recommendations have been generated for discussion with the City Council, and subsequently with the mayor. Some of the recommendations are under active consideration, while others are being analyzed for future action.[13]

The hope is that the progressive forces on the ground can assist in developing a policy and program culture that will ensure that displaced poor and working-class residents are the primary beneficiaries of the rebuilding process. The policy recommendations are also intended to attack poverty and eliminate disparities and inequalities as we seek to build a just, equitable, democratic, and sustainable New Orleans. The electorate thwarted the elite takeover bid, but the present challenge is to convert the electorate's intent into specific policies and programs.

The black electorate is in the early stages of shaping its self-interests in the politics of policy formation and has already encountered the resistance of the white power elites to such a new black policy paradigm. The black community won the mayor's office, but translating electoral victory into substantive benefits and changes for the people remains a serious challenge. Justice, equity, and democracy were among the primary concerns of black New Orleans before Katrina, and are of even greater concern today.

CHALLENGES TO THE GOVERNMENT

Since Katrina in August 2005 and the mayoral elections in May 2006, a number of key and highly visible public issues have surfaced that were simmering before and after Katrina. The recovery, rebuilding, and revitalization of the city are the dominant public policy concerns three years after the storm and flood. The levee repair can't be trusted, schools are still troubled, health care remains inadequate, street violence continues, contract decisions and jobs for locals are questionable, the prisons are overcrowded with black youth, and political control of City Hall remains tenuous. It is beyond the scope of this chapter to adequately treat all of the issues, but there are at least seven that are sometimes less obvious and require additional analysis and public debate by all sectors.

First, there is no consensus among the stakeholders about the future of the city. One of the first rules of recovery after a disaster is development of a consensus on a vision for the future. That never happened in New Orleans because the elites attempted to impose their vision of a smaller, whiter, richer city on the body politic. The black citizenry was not consulted, has never agreed to this vision, and thus does not trust the motives of the elites.

The behavior of the elites continues to suggest that they remain interested in footprint reduction rather than in the right of return and the building of a just, equitable, and democratic city open to all its citizens. This lack of consensus initially set the recovery back by at least nine to twelve months. Furthermore, the capacity to manage a recovery may be in direct proportion to the presence or absence of a consensus among the body politic. There is no shortage of recovery plans; what is missing is the citywide plan that reflects the vision of the majority African-American population. While the formal planning process has momentarily helped to define a vision, evidence suggests that the elites continue to challenge perceived black and/or public interests.

Recent elite-backed efforts reveal a fundamental difference in vision between the business and power elites and the many citizens regarding what is the public good and the desired future of the city. The preliminary evidence includes the demolition of public housing in favor of mixed-income units (read gentrification); efforts to change the name of the Convention Center by minimizing Dutch Morial's name on the letterhead and logo; efforts to semi-privatize the airport and use the proceeds for downtown projects; proposals to change the composition of the Sewerage and Water Board and reduce the mayor's influence; efforts to change the charter to reduce the City Council's role in land-use decisions and the mayor's role in appointing the City Planning Commission. New Orleans remains a city without an agreed-upon vision and is divided by race and class divisions that may not be resolved anytime soon. Dialogue is difficult because of the elite's inability to accept power sharing with the black and working-class majority.

A second issue is the crystallization of the public housing crisis, and the uncertain future of its residents. Before Katrina, 14,000 families occupied public housing in the city. Since Katrina, virtually all of the public housing projects have remained closed, although they only sustained first-floor water damage, with no apparent structural damage. HUD has proclaimed its intent to reopen approximately 2,100 of its total of 5,000 units, and to demolish the St. Bernard, C. W. Peete, Magnolia, and Lafitte projects. Former public housing residents and their allies have opposed the proposed closings and argued for a reopening of all the developments.

The debate about reopening and/or demolishing public housing is symptomatic of the intensity of the race-class tension revealed by Katrina. Public housing in New Orleans as elsewhere is a black and poor people's issue. After Katrina, the former St. Thomas project was redeveloped as a gentrified white upper-income housing development with very limited affordability. Nevertheless, the city of New Orleans has unanimously voted to demolish the remaining large public housing developments (except Iberville) and has proceeded to do so. Allegedly, mixed-income developments will replace the former units, but this remains to be seen.

A third issue is the ongoing concern for public safety. Crime and the murder rate in the city are sensitive issues for all populations and stakeholders. However, it is time to end the labeling of any city as the murder capital of the United States. New Orleans is no worse than any other city plagued with the socioeconomic problems of drugs, guns, and violence. Instead of the per-capita homicide rate, which is limited and incomplete, perhaps another indicator might be more useful as a comparative measure of criminality and violence—the marginality index. This index would assess the access to resources of a criminal population and would compare the levels of a city's mis-education, joblessness, housing, social capital, and opportunities of marginal populations.

When such a marginality index is used, New Orleans is as safe as any major American city. Labeling the city as a murder capital when compared to places like Atlanta, Chicago, Detroit, Miami, and Houston is highly misleading and inaccurate. New Orleans, however, may be regarded as the capital of socioeconomic marginality, but it is merely one of the many homicide capitals in America, and not *the* capital. Most of its homicidal and violent crimes are localized to drug spots and "hot spot" areas of high criminal activity. The nearer one is to a criminal hot spot, the more likely will be an incident of criminal behavior. The locals know the spots, but visitors looking for a thrill may be less likely to respect the knowledge of the locals in such matters and venture into dangerous territory on their own.

After a weekend spree that led to five homicides in 2006, the mayor and governor called in the National Guard to assist in improving public safety in the city. The public was told that the Guard would patrol in the abandoned areas to protect property and thus free up the NOPD to attack crime and violence at the hot spots. Evidence to date does not suggest that the homicide rate has dramatically declined as a result of the

Guard's presence. In 2006, four homicides were committed in an area not known as a hot spot, suggesting that homicides may not necessarily be localized—they can occur anywhere in the city. It is not clear how long the Guard will remain in the city, nor is it clear that their presence reduces the sources or causes of crime and drug-related violence.

The Guard itself was recently accused of robbery of citizens during routine traffic stops. Everyone wants a safe living environment, but police and Guard forces must be held strictly accountable for their actions. In the post-Katrina environment, we are no closer to eradicating the causes of violent crime than we were before Katrina. There is little credible evidence that ex-offender recidivism rates are any lower despite the new economic resources that are flowing due to the recovery.

A fourth and highly contentious issue was the development of the recovery plan and strategy for both neighborhood-specific plans/projects and citywide infrastructure repair. Unfortunately, the federal dollars for the recovery were sent not to the city but instead to an appointed state-created entity, the Louisiana Recovery Authority (LRA), which has emerged as the "heavyweight" in the recovery effort with direct control of more than $10 billion of the federal recovery funding, which has been poorly administered. Residents have encountered nightmarish problems in applying for and receiving LRA funds for their home repair.

The City Council initiated a neighborhood planning process—the Lambert Advisory plans—primarily in the "wet" or more devastated (and predominantly black) neighborhoods of the city to support and facilitate the initiatives taken by residents to plan for their neighborhood recovery. FEMA chose not to fund the City Council planning initiative, and the LRA then pursued independent funding of its own planning citywide and neighborhood planning initiative through the Greater New Orleans Foundation (GNOF) and the Rockefeller Foundation. More important, decision making, coordination, and resource allocation were potentially housed in this collaborative, and the projects of the wet neighborhoods might be delayed until the dry neighborhoods have completed their process.

Many felt the plan would dilute the power of the mayor and council. Many on the council in effect constitute a shadow government. In part, this conclusion was based on both public and private statements of the LRA/GNOF operatives that suggested a lack of confidence in the ability of either this mayoral administration or the City Council to effectively manage the recovery effort. This intervention by the LRA/GNOF collaborative has led to the suspicion that the elites were once again attempting to exert control over elected officials and dilute black interests. A broad perception in the black community was that at stake was a determination of which neighborhoods were viable, or the resurfacing of the footprint reduction proposal, or the capture of the federal infrastructure dollars for the private sector's desired development projects. Whatever the original intent, or the intended motives, the LRA/GNOF process morphed into the Unified New Orleans Plan (UNOP), which was in fundamental conflict with the neighborhood dynamics of the City Council's Lambert Advisory plans and projects. This conflict resulted in enormous confusion and further racial and class animosity, some of which remains to this day.

A fifth issue is related to the implementation of the recovery strategy that resulted from the planning initiatives after the completion and acceptance of the Lambert Advisory neighborhood plans by the City Council and LRA. In June 2007, the city also adopted a required parish-wide plan, the Orleans Parish Strategic Recovery and Revitalization Plan (OPSRRP). The parish plan was to be a synthesis of the GNOF/UNOP citywide and neighborhood plans and the Lambert Advisory plans and projects for the wet neighborhoods, and the LRA-backed UNOP citywide, infrastructure, and neighborhood plans. The OPSRRP was to be implemented by the newly created Office of Recovery and Development Administration (ORDA), headed by a nationally recognized planner, Dr. Ed Blakely.

The AALP had invited Dr. Blakely and other prominent African-American planners to visit New Orleans on three occasions and assess its potential for recovery and rebuilding. These scoping visits and assessments provided Dr. Blakely with the opportunity to observe the damage firsthand and conclude that all of New Orleans could be rebuilt and that footprint reduction was unnecessary. Eventually these assessment visits led to Mayor Nagin's decision to retain Dr. Blakely as the executive director of the recovery effort. Originally the office was called the Office of Recovery Management but was merged with the former Department of Economic Development and Planning to create ORDA.

The implementation plan for the OPSRRP divides the city's Katrina-impacted neighborhoods into three categories based on level of damage and treatment required. It then prioritizes 17 target development zones, with the Lower Ninth Ward, the East, and Gentilly at the top of the list. Initial funding from the LRA of $117 million has been committed along with about $294 million from other disaster loan waiver payments for projects in the neighborhoods and the city.

There is tension regarding what percentage of the disaster funds should be allocated citywide and what percentage should be allocated to the neighborhoods. There is also tension about the appropriate roles and capacity of the newly reconstituted New Orleans Redevelopment Agency (NORA) in property transfer and property development versus the appropriate roles of the ORDA. It is beyond the scope of this chapter to conduct a thorough review of the problems and arguments regarding the implementation of the OPSRP, but clearly many issues bear close scrutiny and monitoring.

A sixth major issue is the tension between indigenous workers and the immigrant Hispanic workers who have been brought in by contractors under highly questionable circumstances.

Unfortunately, local contractors have exploited Hispanic workers, many of whom are undocumented workers simply seeking a better life for themselves and their families. That economic interest often clashes with the interests of African-American stakeholders who have been excluded from the rebuilding workforce.

The working and housing conditions that are often accepted by immigrant workers are unacceptable to indigenous African Americans, who know that U.S. labor laws and regulations are being significantly violated by such avaricious contractors. The 2006 report of the Advancement Project suggests avenues for intervention in the interests of both indigenous African Americans and immigrant workers (Advancement Project and National Immigrants Law Center 2006). It is in the interests of blacks, Latinos, and all progressive and human-centered peoples to support enforcement of worker protections and the right of black workers to access jobs in the rebuilding of New Orleans.

A seventh and final issue is the capacity of some return of residents to the city after three years. There are many residents in the diaspora who have now settled in their adopted city and may choose not to return. Rents in the city are out of control and are beyond the reach of most low-income citizens in the diaspora. Since public housing developments are being demolished and gentrification has not abated, there are serious problems of affordability of the city to its former residents. For instance, a two-bedroom apartment that formerly rented for $450 a month now goes for $750; a three-bedroom apartment formerly renting for $700 to $800 a month now goes for $1,200 to $1,300 a month. Home prices have also jumped by as much as 25 to 30 percent in some areas of the city.

These seven issues are not intended to be exhaustive but only indicative of day-to-day problems in the post-disaster rebuilding environment. New issues and problems are certain to arise as we attempt to recover, rebuild, and recalibrate the relationship between the citizens, government, business, and other stakeholders.

CONCLUSIONS

New Orleans has been traditionally regarded as the Big Easy, a place to come to relax, forget your cares, and indulge in the sensuous and celebratory pleasures of life such as food, music, and dance and letting the good times roll, "Laissez les bontemps rouler." To others, it is also the most African city in North America with a human-centered ease of life, a colorful expressiveness, a comfortable blend of the sacred and the secular, and respect for ancestral tradition and values. New Orleanians are accustomed to this dual coexistence but remain acutely aware of the burden of a deep, racially based class schism between the haves and the have-nots. The pre-Katrina socioeconomic statistics were numbing—two-thirds of African-American households in the city led a day-to-day marginal existence on the edge of constant economic disaster. Katrina exposed the level and depth of the disastrous and marginal condition of the most vulnerable segments of the black community.

Immediately after the storm, white elites sensed an opportunity to accelerate their efforts to recapture the city through gentrification and displacement. Katrina offered such an opportunity: first in the political arena, and subsequently through control of space such as real estate and land. Black citizens perceived such efforts as an attack on their civil rights and their space, beat back the political challenge, and slowed down the egregious attempts at land grabbing and permanent displacement.

However, the battle for the real estate and neighborhood lands remains unsettled. Mayor Nagin's re-election victory partially settled the political arguments, although it did not resolve the broader problem of ownership, wealth inequality, and the persistent disparities in the quality of life in the neighborhoods. The battle for the soul of New Orleans in the neighborhoods is just beginning in earnest with the various approaches to neighborhood planning and infrastructure. Issues such as the revitalization of the demolished public housing, expanding affordable rental units, increasing affordable homeownership opportunities, rebuilding the public school system, health care, public transit, and expanding job and contracts opportunities for African Orleanians will dictate the future of the city.

There is beginning evidence that the citizens and local government are in agreement that a new New Orleans is appropriate to pursue if it improves on the old system of racially based inequality. However, ensuring equity and justice is not a given—the cost of living in the city has skyrocketed and has priced many black, working-class, and poor residents out of the city. In that sense, new is not necessarily better for everyone. Never before in modern American history has there been a city that was 80 percent drowned and forced to rebuild.

There are specific plans in place to rebuild the city, but the battle continues to rage over the pace of rebuilding in the low-lying, primarily black neighborhoods. That is the ongoing challenge to the movements on the ground—to continue to rebuild and expand a broad social movement that will compel the rebuilding of a just, equitable, sustainable, and democratic New Orleans that welcomes back its black and working-class citizens.

The national lesson of Katrina is that African-American communities across the country are especially vulnerable to any major disruptions in the political economy because of the persistent patterns of inequality and unequal access to life-sustaining resources. Katrina taught us that under such circumstances, government cannot be relied on exclusively to protect us or rescue us from disastrous conditions. Perhaps the neglect and abandonment by the federal government is a stark reminder that we as citizens must accept the responsibility to organize our resources to do some things for ourselves, in addition to the continuous battle to force government accountability.

Nearly every major city in this country has a Lower Ninth Ward in its midst, as well as the socioeconomic conditions that led people to the Superdome and Convention Center. Cities have been undergoing transformation for decades and displacing their low-income residents to lower-cost suburbs, as suburban populations return to the city. Gentrification and displacement are central elements of urban real estate dynamics in all major American cities today. Disasters such as Katrina and the Loma Prieta Earthquake of 1989 further suggest that New Orleans may be not the exception but increasingly the norm.

The recent floods and levee failure in the Midwest, the bridge collapse in Minnesota, wildfires in California, unpredictable tornadoes—all suggest that we need to rebuild both New Orleans and America. Market dynamics and elite power brokers are driving resource-limited and economically marginal populations out of the city altogether, or farther out to the metropolitan periphery. Disasters such as Katrina simply hasten this process.

The African-American and progressive battle to save New Orleans for its black, working-class, poor, and marginal citizens is of national significance to all Americans and to citizens of the world, especially in the developing countries. We all must join the struggle to make New Orleans more just, equitable, democratic, and sustainable for its Katrina victims of all races and ethnicities and genders. The world is watching how we respond to the deepest internal contradictions of the modern-day city in contemporary American history. Our claim to democracy may rest in the balance.

NOTES

1. Mardi Gras Index: This is one of the most comprehensive yet succinct sources of data on the effects of Hurricane Katrina. It covers demographics, housing, infrastructure, economy, education, environment, health, justice system, and culture.

2. This conversation was occurring in the barber shops, beauty parlors, businesses, selected churches, the projects, among lawyers, and across multiple social strata. It was this growing concern about benefits and change for black Orleanians that galvanized the on-the-ground movement for change.

3. The African American Agenda was not released to the public but is available from the AALP.

4. New Orleans has been perceived by some organizers as a city without a politically conscious social movement. Quite the contrary is the case; however the incubation period for social movement in New Orleans follows an idiosyncratic rhythm different from other locations in the United States. In the months before Katrina, the movement for change was proceeding so rapidly from simultaneous directions that it was dubbed the "siege against racism."

5. The social ecology of the Katrina disaster suggests that black Orleanians were at greater risk than others because of their income and transit-dependent status. Thus when the disaster struck, they were disproportionately victimized. This structural inequality can be legitimately termed disaster-induced structural racism. Whether this impact is intended or not is irrelevant to the description of the outcome.

6. The term "white power elite" refers to those white individuals and institutions that exert disproportionate control and influence over the polity of the city. Although there is no single or official structure, the power elites in New Orleans consist of selected business persons, media (especially the daily newspaper), academics, religious leaders, bankers and developers, Mardi Gras Krewes (clubs), civic groups, philanthropists, good government advocates, and various commissions. An additional commentary on the elites can be found in comments by Mike Davis in "Who Is Killing New Orleans?" *The Nation,* April 10, 2006, p. 14.

7. The BNOB was initially comprised of eight black and eight white members, but dominated by white elite interests. The president of the City Council (Oliver Thomas), who is black, was subsequently added to the BNOB. All eight whites and some of the black members represented the elites or were from the business and corporate sectors. There was virtually no representation from grass-roots voices or working-class organizations. The complete roster and their interests can be found at "Bring New Orleans Back Commission," 2008, http://en.wikipedia.org/wiki/Bring_New_Orleans_Back_Commission.

8. The AALP conducted discussions with its constituency and displaced persons in Houston, Atlanta, Baton Rouge, Shreveport, Dallas, Jackson, Memphis, Austin, San An-

tonio, Charlotte, and Atlanta to determine the content and character of the Bill of Rights.

9. The Citizens' Bill of Rights first appeared as a published document of the AALP in October 2005. Its content was presented at the Millions More Movement march in October 2005, based on the findings from its constituent discussions.

10. The AALP utilized a similar dialogue- and consensus-oriented process to translate the values and principles in the CBOR into a specific recovery policy, the Neighborhood Rebuilding Equity Ordinance.

11. City of New Orleans Ordinance # 022194 and # 022195, April 27, 2006.

12. For a fuller treatment of Nagin's re-election and the 2006 elections, see Mtangulizi Sanyika, "The Anatomy of Nagin's Re-election," *Louisiana Weekly,* 80 (37), June 5–11, 2006, p. 1.

13. The complete findings and recommendations from Policy Summits 1, 2, and 3 can be obtained from the AALP.

REFERENCES

Advancement Project and the National Immigrants Law Center. 2006. *Labor Conditions in New Orleans After Katrina.* Available at http://www.advancementproject.org/ourwork/other-initiatives/hurricane-katrina/ontheground.php (accessed July 28, 2008).

Barry, J. M. 1997. *Rising Tide: The Great Mississippi Flood of 1927 and How It Changed America.* New York: Simon and Schuster.

"Bring New Orleans Back Commission." 2008. Available at http://en.wikipedia.org/wiki/Bring_New_Orleans_Back_Commission.

Bring New Orleans Back Commission Urban Planning Committee. 2006. "Action Plan for New Orleans: The New American City." Report. January 11. Available at http://www.bringneworleansback.org/Portals/BringNewOrleansBack/Resources/Urban%20Planning%20Final%20Report.pdf.

Colburn, D. R. (ed.). 2005. *African American Mayors: Race, Politics and the American City.* Champaign: University of Illinois Press.

Davis, M. 2006. "Who Is Killing New Orleans?" *The Nation.* April 10, p. 14. Available at http://www.thenation.com/doc/20060410/davis (accessed July 28, 2008).

Dyson, M. E. 2006. *Come Hell or High Water: Hurricane Katrina and the Color of Disaster.* New York: Basic Books.

Filosa, G. 2006. "Low Wage Laborers Exploited During Recovery." *Times-Picayune.* July 7.

Heerden, I. 2006. *The Storm.* New York: Penguin Group.

Pastor, M., R. D. Bullard, J. K. Boyce, A. Fothergill, R. Morello-Frosch, and B. Wright. 2006. *In the Wake of the Storm: Environment, Disaster, and Race After Katrina.* New York: Russell Sage Foundation.

Quigley, W. P. 2006. "Six Months After Katrina." *Mardi Gras Index; A Special Report by the Gulf Coast Reconstruction Watch.* Institute of Southern Studies/Southern Exposure. February/March.

Sanyika, M. 2006. "The Anatomy of Nagin's Re-election." *Louisiana Weekly.* June 5–11, p. 1. Available at http://www.louisianaweekly.com/weekly/news/articlegate.pl?20060605k (accessed July 28, 2008).

U.S. Bureau of the Census. 2000. U. S. Census of Population and Housing, Orleans Parish. Available at http://www.census.gov/index.html.

PART II

HEALTH AND ENVIRONMENT POST-KATRINA

CHAPTER 5

CONTAMINANTS IN THE AIR AND SOIL IN NEW ORLEANS AFTER THE FLOOD

Opportunities and Limitations for Community Empowerment

Rachel Godsil, Albert Huang, and Gina Solomon

New Orleans has always been a study in contradictions. Those on the outside have known it for its cultural distinctiveness, creative energy, architectural beauty, and good living but also for its poverty rate, toxic environmental hazards, and crime. Hurricane Katrina, and the disaster that ensued, focused the world's attention on the underside of the Crescent City—and renewed sobering questions concerning our nation's commitment to its most vulnerable citizens.

Hurricanes Katrina and Rita claimed more than 1,000 lives, displaced millions of people, and destroyed homes and livelihoods across broad stretches of Louisiana, Mississippi, and Alabama. In the aftermath of the storms, New Orleans now faces both a humanitarian and an environmental disaster. Nearly the entire city was inundated with sewage, toxin-laced floodwaters, and contaminated sediment, and the moisture caused dangerous levels of mold in hundreds of thousands of homes (NRDC 2005a).

In the wake of the storms, authorities received reports of 575 oil and toxic chemical spills. Of these, ten major oil spills, with the total volume spilled approaching eight million gallons, fouled the Mississippi River from Chalmette to Venice and west to Port Fourchon (Table 5.1). The flood-affected area contains some 2,200 underground fuel tanks, an unknown percentage of which ruptured in the storm (Claren 2005). Additionally, the hurricanes were responsible for generating more than 100 million cubic yards of debris—enough to cover a thousand football fields with a six-story-high

TABLE 5.1—Locations of Major Oil Spills

Facility, Location	Spill (gallons)
Murphy Oil, Meraux, La.	819,000
Chevron Empire Terminal, Buras, La.	983,000
Bass Enterprises, Cox Bay, La.	3,780,000
Shell, Pilottown, La.	1,070,000
Dynegy, Venice, La.	24,822
Sundown Energy West, Potash, La.	13,440
Sundown Energy East, Potash, La.	18,900
Bass Enterprises, Point à la Hache, La.	461,538
Shell Pipeline Oil LP, Nairn, La.	136,290
Chevron, Port Fourchon, La.	53,000
TOTAL	**7,359,990**

Source: L. Fields, A. Huang, G. M. Solomon, M. Rotkin-Ellman, and P. Simms. 2007. *Katrina's Wake: Arsenic-Laced Schools and Playgrounds Put New Orleans Children at Risk*. New York: NRDC, August, p. 17.

mountain of trash. Post-storm testing by local and national environmental groups, as well as by the Environmental Protection Agency (EPA) and state officials, confirmed that formerly flooded areas are seriously contaminated with pathogens and toxic chemicals, often with concentrations many times higher than federal and even lax state safety guidelines.

Our nation is now confronted with an unparalleled challenge to clean up and rebuild these devastated areas. So far, the federal government appears to be largely ceding its leadership over the clean-up and rebuilding to state and local authorities. As this chapter details, the EPA has the legal authority necessary to clean up the significant environmental contamination caused by the hurricanes. Unfortunately, the EPA has waived its vast clean-up powers and has instead chosen to defer to poorly resourced local authorities, which are under significant pressure to say everything is safe.

In an ideal world, decentralizing authority over rebuilding and clean-up would be a positive, forward-looking approach that would stimulate collaboration and community involvement. The environmental justice movement is rooted in a grassroots model of decision making, and many believe that this approach would enable the citizens of New Orleans and those currently displaced from their homes to have more access to state officials than they would to federal officials. However, the federal government's decision to avoid responsibility cannot be evaluated in a vacuum.

Unfortunately, as the Katrina tragedy illustrated, we are living in a far from ideal world. The current fate of New Orleans, and particularly people of color in New Orleans, is the result of more than a century of government failure—at both the federal and state level. In the early twentieth century, federal policies helped create a racially segregated city in which many poor and working-class African Americans were isolated and cut off from the city center. The harm caused by residential segregation was made acute by a web of Jim Crow laws that denied African Americans access to education, jobs, and public facilities. In the second half of the century, the state colluded with numerous industries in efforts to locate polluting facilities in African-American communities along the river corridor between Baton Rouge and New Orleans—now commonly known as Cancer Alley (Wright 2005).

We argue in this chapter that the EPA should recognize the federal government's complicity in the current disaster and the state of Louisiana's abysmal record of not protecting its residents from toxic pollution. Under President Bill Clinton, the EPA took positive steps toward recognizing the tenets of environmental justice. Yet in March 2004 and again in September 2006, the EPA's inspector general issued scathing reports concluding that the agency had failed to implement even the basic requirements of Clinton's executive order on environmental justice (EPA Inspector General 2004; EPA Inspector General 2006).

In the setting of a long history of overt local racism and the current blatant federal disregard for environmental justice, a strong coalition of local and national activists attempted to force needed action. Despite scientific evidence of harm, a unified voice, and a clear set of goals and objectives, there was limited leverage available to help force unwilling agencies to take action. The nation's environmental laws and policies have allowed major victories in the environmental justice sector, preventing damaging activities (such as incinerator sitings), but have weak requirements in place that make it difficult to force agencies to act affirmatively to clean up existing problems. The situation in New Orleans suggests a serious weakness in national environmental laws that must be remedied before justice can prevail.

In a well-publicized proclamation from Jackson Square, President Bush pledged to the people of New Orleans that the federal government would "do what it takes, we will stay as long as it takes, to help citizens rebuild their communities and their lives. And all who question the future of the Crescent City need to know there is no way to imagine America without New Orleans, and this great city will rise again" (Think Progress 2005). In order to rise again, the EPA must ensure that returning residents are protected from toxic contamination.

HISTORY OF ENVIRONMENTAL INJUSTICE

Prior to the 2005 hurricanes, New Orleans was struggling with severe environmental health threats and injustices. In the older and poorer neighborhoods, concentrations of lead in the soil were documented at dangerous levels (Mielke et al. 1997; Mielke et al. 1999). The city and nearby areas contained at least 31 listed hazardous waste sites, including the notorious Agriculture Street Landfill Superfund Site in the By-water neighborhood, which contained the incinerator ash generated by debris from 1965's Hurricane Betsy and which housed an elementary school and low-income housing built directly on top of the landfill.

The State of Louisiana ranks fifth in the nation in oil production, generating about 4 percent of total U.S. crude oil (Energy Information System n.d.). The state has nearly 20,000 producing oil wells, and a large network of crude oil, liquefied petroleum gas pipelines, refineries, and storage facilities. The inevitable byproduct of these industries is hazardous waste, and Louisiana ranks second behind Texas among the 50 states in the quantity of hazardous industrial waste generated. When calcu-lated on a per-capita basis, Louisiana leads the nation (Bureau of Applied Research in Anthropology n.d.). Rather than imposing and enforcing meaningful environ-mental standards, however, the state government has generally catered to industry, even going so far as to promote the state's southern bayous as a potential disposal area for other states' hazardous waste.

Louisiana has been identified as a locus of poor environmental quality for decades (Moshman and Hardenbergh 2006). The vast majority of people in Louisiana are at risk as a result of the contamination of drinking water from underground aquifers and from the Mississippi River. Most telling, the river corridor between New Or-leans and Baton Rouge is known as Cancer Alley because of the high number of in-dustrial facilities.

These toxic hazards and the particularly acute harm to poor black neighborhoods are not random. Rather, they are the result of decades of actions and inaction by gov-ernment and private actors—set in motion by the federal government. A series of decisions by federal agencies led New Orleans to follow the pattern of many urban centers in the United States, which went from reasonably integrated to dramatically racially and economically segregated. New Orleans was once an amalgamation of fairly racially mixed residential neighborhoods.

During World War II, however, the federal government responded to wartime housing shortages by building racially segregated housing projects (Mahoney 1990). Several of these projects, such as St. Bernard, were located in an isolated, low-lying area, which eventually became known as the Ninth Ward. The areas to which poor people and people of color were relocated were then underserved generally by government—lacking especially necessary storm protection. The devastation wrought by Katrina is therefore an act not of nature but of government.

For whites, public housing was a way station toward private housing and eventual home ownership. This path was paved largely by federal government intervention in the form of jobs, mortgage guarantees, and highway programs (Frug 1996; Smerk 1965). These federal programs were enormously helpful to white working- and middle-class families, who could afford to buy homes in larger numbers than ever before in history, but they explicitly excluded black people and led to dramatically increased racial segregation (Massey and Denton 1993; Oliver and Shapiro 1995).

During the postwar period, the federal government loan programs began a practice known as redlining, in which neighborhoods were judged according to their racial homogeneity (Bullard, Grigsby, and Lee 1994). Early programs awarded loans only to the top two categories, which were described as either "new, homogenous, and in demand in good times and bad" or "areas that had reached their peak, but were still desirable and could be expected to remain stable" (Massey and Denton 1993). The programs considered suspect any areas not inhabited by white people; indeed, even areas that were primarily Jewish were suspect, but areas in which blacks lived or might live in the future were redlined (literally coded with red to designate a high-risk area that should not receive loans) on area maps. This practice was then adopted by the private banking industry. Perhaps not surprisingly, the racist treatment that began in the federal government permeated all housing financing.

Federal programs using redlining practices had the effect of subsidizing white flight from cities and aided in the creation of white suburbs. The programs that were most effective in creating white suburbs were the Federal Housing Administration (FHA) and Veterans Administration (VA) home ownership loan programs, and the federal subsidization of highways (Jackson 1987). The highways made suburbs accessible and had the long-term effect of facilitating the out-migration of whites. The highways might have had a race-neutral effect, however, were it not for the racist implementation of FHA and VA loan programs.

Both the FHA and VA programs guaranteed loans made by private banks to prospective homebuyers. Both programs guaranteed 90 percent of the value of a home as collateral for loans from private banks, which allowed new purchasers to buy homes with only a 10 percent down payment (as opposed to the norm of at least 33 percent and often 50 percent). Because the FHA and VA guarantees reduced risks to banks, the banks were able to lower interest rates and extend repayment periods. The combination of lower down payments, lower interest rates, and longer repayment periods allowed home ownership to become available to many more people than ever before (Massey and Denton 1993).

Federal policies were far from race neutral, however. The standards used to determine whether to guarantee loans were biased toward suburban land-use practices. Even more troubling, the federal agencies adopted redlining policies and did not guarantee loans in black or mixed neighborhoods. The vast majority of FHA and VA mortgages thus went to white, middle-class suburbs. Without FHA guarantees, even middle-income people of color faced difficulty in obtaining mortgages, which resulted in a massive capital disinvestment in inner cities. The lack of mortgage capital in minority communities also made it impossible for people to sell their homes, or to repair them. This caused a downward spiral of "disrepair, deterioration, vacancy, and abandonment" (Godsil 2004).

This national pattern was reflected in the experience of New Orleans and its suburbs. As Martha Mahoney has demonstrated, following World War II, suburbs surrounding New Orleans were closed to blacks by individual discrimination and the government refusal to adopt race-neutral policies. Mahoney quotes a New Orleans municipal assessor who recalled that "10,000 GI's returned to New Orleans ready to settle down. And they could not get a mortgage in central city, the Irish Channel, the Lower Garden District [the older sections of the city with historically racially mixed population patterns]." Many of these men went to the new subdivisions in Gentilly or Jefferson Parish, he continued, and "now we are missing a generation in the older areas" (Mahoney 1990).

The effect of these programs was not only to create racially segregated suburbs but also to cause a dramatic deterioration of housing conditions in black neighborhoods, as black families were forced to share housing and limited geographical areas. Indeed, in the years after World War II, the Housing Authority had upwards of 46,000 pending applications for public, low-rent housing (Mahoney 1990).

The last public housing project in New Orleans built by the federal government was the ironically named Desire Project. Desire was built in 1964 with the last of the funds from the postwar Housing Act. It was located on a geographically isolated tract, cut off from the rest of New Orleans by two canals and two sets of railroad tracks but near a preexisting small neighborhood of very modest houses occupied by African-American renters and homeowners. This site was built adjacent to and partially on top of the Agriculture Street landfill created with the incinerated ash from Hurricane Betsy, and in 1994 the area was declared a Superfund site. Desire was a huge project, consisting of 262 buildings and 1,860 apartments, one of the largest projects in the country built with federal funds (Mahoney 1990). Located in the Upper Ninth Ward, Desire quickly became a haven of violence and despair and was especially hard hit by Katrina. According to news reporter George Talbot (2005):

In contrast to other areas of New Orleans, where flooding swelled like water in a tub, there were signs that something far more violent swept through the Desire. Around 8 a.m. on the morning after Katrina made landfall, the canal levee was breached, and water rushed out of a turning basin used to service a nearby port terminal. Inside the neighborhood, which includes roughly 100 acres on the city's east side, the torrent blasted houses from their foundations and tossed cars like casino dice. Residents either unwilling or unable to evacuate scrambled to their attics and rooftops, where the lucky were plucked away by helicopter rescue teams (Talbot 2005).

The Desire neighborhood has since been found to be heavily contaminated with cancer-causing chemicals dislodged from the nearby Superfund site by the flood waters. This area has still not been cleaned up and remains uninhabitable.

Whereas the federal government played a critical role in the creation of segregated, contaminated, and disenfranchised sections of New Orleans in the post–World War II era, the state's culpability spans an even longer period. Louisiana, like other states in the Deep South, amended its constitution to disenfranchise virtually all black people. It also enacted a web of laws that segregated the races with respect to transportation, public accommodations, cemeteries, hospitals, prisons, and, infamously, drinking fountains.

Indeed, Homer Plessy, the plaintiff in the infamous *Plessy v. Ferguson,* challenged Louisiana's state law mandating that black and white people ride in separate rail cars. The city of New Orleans also enacted a residential segregation ordinance that prohibited persons of a different race from moving into a block consisting of a majority of one race unless they obtained consent from the majority of people living in the area (Godsil 2006). In 1917, the Supreme Court struck down a similar residential segregation ordinance from Louisville, Kentucky, in *Buchanan v. Warely*. Yet New Orleans political officials ignored the Supreme Court's ruling and enacted a residential segregation law in the 1920s (Bernstein and Somin 2004).

It is no surprise then that the flooding of New Orleans disproportionately affected low-income communities and communities of color, which tended (with some exceptions) to be in the lower-lying areas of the city and were also the communities that housed most of the toxic sites and historical lead contamination. From an environmental health perspective, the flooding represented a fork in the road, exacerbating the environmental contamination in New Orleans by spreading contaminated material throughout the neighborhoods and introducing new contaminants that were not there before the storm. At the same time, the evacuation of the city and rebuilding process opened a window of opportunity to address the environmental injustices in New Orleans directly and definitively.

A just approach to addressing the disaster of the failed levees would have been wide-ranging. It would have included:

- a full analysis of the health risks from environmental contaminants,
- ongoing monitoring of air, water, and sediment pollution,
- provision of adequate warnings and free protective equipment to returning residents,
- broad-scale removal of contaminated sediments and soil from flooded neighborhoods,
- assistance with gutting and decontamination of flooded homes in low-income neighborhoods,
- a sustainable strategy for debris removal and disposal,
- and a public process for rebuilding that fully engaged local residents in planning the future of their communities.

Unfortunately, the process post-Katrina has instead exacerbated the long history of environmental injustices. Residents who are well-insured or have sufficient resources have been able to remediate their homes and yards, whereas impoverished residents have generally faced the choice of returning to toxic areas or staying away completely. Several model efforts, however, have helped to illustrate how the recovery could be done right and have offered hope to the communities.

COALITION BUILDING

After the levees broke and New Orleans flooded, local environmental justice leaders were scattered to temporary shelters throughout the Southeast and beyond. This extreme situation illustrated some of the opportunities inherent in forging collaboration between local and national groups. In this case, a national environmental organization established contact one-by-one with local leaders via cell phone, and connected them with each other on conference calls in which people could share their stories and exchange necessary information. This series of weekly conference calls in the aftermath of Katrina allowed everyone to learn about the needs on the ground.

Local partner groups identified the issues that were of most concern to local residents, provided a liaison with affected communities, and shared the historical and political context for the current environmental and public health crisis. Partners such as the Deep South Center for Environmental Justice, Advocates for Environmental Human Rights, Louisiana Environmental Action Network, the Holy Cross Neighborhood Association, and the Louisiana Bucket Brigade identified contaminated floodwater and sediment, debris removal, air quality, and safe drinking water as key issues that required priority attention. In turn, a national group, the Natural Resources Defense Council (NRDC), was able to provide staff time, funding, logistical support, scientific support, and assistance with legal and policy questions.

The coalition of local environmental justice groups and the national environmental group developed and published a community-driven ten-point plan of action designed to serve as a template for ongoing work in the region (Advocates for Environmental Human Rights et al. n.d.). The plan identified a number of critical short- and long-term tasks facing the city, including cleaning up contamination, publicizing health risks, ensuring safe schools, strengthening health care services, and reconstructing levees. The plan also emphasized the need for the city to ensure environmental justice for the hardest-hit communities, help displaced residents return, and ensure meaningful public participation in all decision making.

The role of scientific testing quickly became central to the early response, when local leaders expressed mistrust of the government's reassurances about environmental safety. It was clear that there was a need for independent testing, as well as for independent analysis and critiques of the government testing data and of the government's interpretation of the results.

THE ROLE OF SCIENCE

The scientific response to the disaster in New Orleans included evaluation of air quality, sediment and soil contamination, and drinking water quality. Soon after the flooding, the EPA began some testing of floodwaters, sediment, and air in the city. Initially, the agency did not make the results public, necessitating advocacy efforts to obtain the data. After public pressure, the EPA posted the data on its Web site, but the results were presented in a format that was unclear and difficult to interpret. In response, scientific staff working with NRDC summarized the results of the early EPA testing in fact sheets that were distributed to local leaders.

Sediment Contamination

In October and November 2005, a Louisiana chemist working with community and national groups collected samples of sediments left behind by the flooding, discovering widespread contamination. The EPA also conducted tests and posted its results in an almost incomprehensible format on its Web site. The levels of arsenic in 95 percent of the sediment samples collected by the EPA in the greater New Orleans area were high enough to pose a significant cancer risk under EPA guidelines. Thirty percent of samples could trigger clean-up under the weaker Louisiana guidelines.

In a February 2006 report, *Contaminants in New Orleans Sediment: An Analysis of EPA Data,* scientists with the NRDC re-analyzed the new EPA data and issued maps and a more understandable report of the EPA findings and the independent testing (Solomon and Rotkin-Ellman 2006). Health effects from long-term exposure to the various toxins discovered in the sampling of sediment after the flooding include an increased risk of cancer, as well as neurological damage and other chronic health problems. Arsenic is toxic to humans and is known to cause cancer; no amount is considered fully safe.

An August 2007 NRDC report, *Katrina's Wake: Arsenic-Laced Schools and Playgrounds Put New Orleans Children at Risk,* co-released with community partners, described sediment throughout the city contaminated with arsenic, lead, diesel fuel, and polycyclic aromatic hydrocarbons (PAHs). Two years after the storm, arsenic levels were still present in the soil at several locations in New Orleans, including schools, playgrounds, and residential areas. Tests conducted by the NRDC in March 2007 revealed that 25 percent of the 35 New Orleans playgrounds and schoolyards tested may be classified as arsenic hot spots (Fields, Huang, Solomon, Roitkin-Ellman, and Simms 2007, 4).

NRDC's tests also found two playgrounds and four residential areas sitting on arsenic hot spots, where the levels of arsenic exceed EPA and Louisiana Department of Environmental Quality (LDEQ) clean-up guidelines. Thirty percent of the samples taken from schools and 13 percent of samples taken from playgrounds exceed the Louisiana and EPA clean-up levels (Table 5.2). LDEQ clean-up level is 12 mg/kg. U.S. EPA Region 6 arsenic soil clean-up level for residential areas is 0.39 mg/kg to protect against cancer.

The government has been unresponsive to contamination dangers. Despite potentially hazardous levels of arsenic in New Orleans soil, not one clean-up of contaminated sediments has been conducted by the EPA or the LDEQ since the storm struck three years ago. The excuse given by both agencies is that the arsenic was there before the storm, and therefore they do not have any legal authority to clean up schoolyards, playgrounds, and other contaminated areas. However, as illustrated in

TABLE 5.2—Arsenic in Hot Spots in New Orleans Today

District	Sampling Location	Arsenic Concentration (mg/kg)*
Gentilly	Alexander Milne Playground	18
Gentilly	Schabel Playspot	19.3
Lakeview	Residential Neighborhood	14.3
Bywater/St. Claude	Drew Elementary School	20.3
Mid-City	Residential Neighborhood	41
Mid-City	Craig Elementary School	16.1
Mid-City	McDonogh #42 Elementary School	34.4
Mid-City	Dibert Elementary School	22.8
New Orleans East	Residential Neighborhood	23.6
New Orleans East	Residential Neighborhood	30
Uptown/Carrollton	Medard H. Nelson Elementary School	12.4
Uptown/Carrollton	McMain Magnet Secondary School	12.6

*Sites where arsenic concentrations exceeded the clean-up levels.

Note: Based on sampling done in March 2007. LDEQ clean-up level = 12 mg/kg. Region 6 EPA arsenic clean-up level for residential areas is 0.39 mg/kg to protect against cancer.

Source: L. Fields, A. Huang, G. M. Solomon, M. Rotkin-Ellman, and P. Simms. 2007. *Katrina's Wake: Arsenic-Laced Schools and Playgrounds Put New Orleans Children at Risk.* New York: Natural Resources Defense Council, August, p. 4.

Table 5.3, NRDC's analysis of "archived soil samples demonstrates that the arsenic discovered post-Katrina was generally not present before the storm" (Fields et al. 2007, 10).

Not only does the government have a legal responsibility to clean up the toxic contamination left behind by the storm, it has a moral obligation to protect the public's health and the environment. There is no excuse for leaving arsenic on schoolyards and playgrounds when it can be safely cleaned up. By not cleaning up the contamination, the government is allowing children, a sensitive and vulnerable population, to be exposed to elevated health risks that can be avoided (Solomon and Rotkin-Ellman 2006).

The toxins likely came from multiple sources, including storm-related releases and spills of petroleum, pesticides, and other chemicals; toxic sediment from lake and river bottoms stirred up by the storm; flooding of hazardous waste sites; household hazardous wastes, such as cleaning agents, home pesticides, and so on; abandoned automobiles; and more.

TABLE 5.3—Present-Day Arsenic Levels in Some Parts of New Orleans

Sampling Locations	Percentage of sites sampled that were hot spots	Number of hot spots exceeding clean-up levels*	Average Arsenic (mg/kg)	Minimum Arsenic (mg/kg)	Maximum Arsenic (mg/kg)	Number of sites sampled
Elementary/Middle Schools	30%	6	6.9	0.40	34.4	20
Playgrounds	13%	2	6.8	0.45	19.3	15
Residential Neighborhoods	5%	4	3.4	0.41	41.0	81
Total	**10%**	**12**	**4.4**	**0.40**	**41.0**	**116**

*Clean-up level = 12 mg/kg

Source: L. Fields, A. Huang, G. M. Solomon, M. Rotkin-Ellman, and P. Simms. 2007. *Katrina's Wake: Arsenic-Laced Schools and Playgrounds Put New Orleans Children at Risk.* New York: Natural Resources Defense Council, August, p. 9.

In addition, the testing identified a number of hot spots where contamination from specific toxic sites moved into residential neighborhoods and had the potential to create very serious health problems. For example, the testing identified high levels of banned pesticides that had been carried by floodwaters from an abandoned pesticide-blending facility into a residential neighborhood in Mid-City, as well as high levels of cancer-causing PAHs traveling onto the grounds of a senior citizens' center near the Agriculture Street Landfill Superfund site in the Desire neighborhood.

Air Quality

The combination of the late summer 2005 heat and flood waters created the perfect environment for mold, and testing revealed extremely high levels of mold spores in the air. Mold exposure can cause congestion, sneezing, runny or itchy nose, and throat irritation; more serious symptoms include major allergic attacks, cough, asthma attacks, and hypersensitivity pneumonitis (a pneumonia-like illness with symptoms including difficulty breathing and fevers). Some studies have shown that outdoor levels of mold spores are directly associated with childhood asthma attacks requiring a visit to an emergency room. Studies that have reported links between outdoor mold spore levels and childhood asthma attacks have found these respiratory effects even in areas where the daily airborne spore counts were relatively low (Natural Resources Defense Council 2005). Mold also poses a special threat to people with allergies and asthma, as well as to immunosuppressed individuals.

Children in New Orleans may be especially vulnerable to mold because of the city's very high asthma rate. A recent study pre-Katrina revealed that children who live in New Orleans have a one-in-four chance of developing asthma during their early lifetime (Mvula et al. 2005). The combination of mold and a high incidence of asthma could prove deadly. According to one study, the risk of death from asthma is 2.16 times higher if mold spore counts are greater than 1,000 spores per cubic meter (Natural Resources Defense Council 2005). In comparison, NRDC's testing in New Orleans after Katrina revealed mold spore counts that averaged around 70,000 spores per cubic meter outdoors and were as high as 650,000 spores per cubic meter in flooded homes.

Government agencies did not test for mold in the aftermath of the flooding. In fact, the EPA claimed that mold is an indoor air-quality problem and is therefore outside the agency's jurisdiction. Community groups pressed hard for mold testing, since the mold growth was visually obvious and significant, and the smell of mold was overpowering even in outdoor air. Independent testing by NRDC scientists in partnership with community leaders found indoor and outdoor mold spore levels in the air in New Orleans to be extremely high, so much so that they could pose a serious health threat, particularly to individuals who are allergic to molds, or who have asthma or other underlying respiratory disease (Natural Resources Defense Council 2005b).

Using standard classifications established by the National Allergy Bureau, mold spore counts outdoors in most flooded neighborhoods were classified as very high, with estimated average daily spore counts well over 50,000 spores per cubic meter.

Such outdoor mold spore concentrations could easily trigger allergic or asthmatic reactions in sensitive people. In contrast, more distant comparison sites in Metairie and in Mandeville on the north shore of Lake Pontchartrain had significantly lower mold spore concentrations.

Indoor testing in flooded homes yielded extremely high mold readings, so high that they would be considered dangerously uninhabitable by any definition. Tests in homes that had been flooded and subsequently undergone some remediation— including removal of contaminated furniture and carpets, and some removal of drywall—found lower but still dangerously high mold concentrations.

Homes that had been fully remediated—including removal of all furniture, carpets, and drywall down to the studs, airing, and mold treatment—found mold spore counts that very nearly matched outdoor air. These tests showed that simply washing walls with bleach (as many residents were being told to do by insurance companies) did not solve the problem. The results of the testing were publicized by posting them on the Internet, making public presentations, and generating extensive national and local news coverage. The coalition followed up the release by issuing an advisory with specific recommendations for returning residents to safely remove mold from their homes.

Drinking Water

Another challenge confronting the Gulf Coast is the provision of clean water to residents. In the days immediately following Katrina, at least 2.4 million people were without access to safe drinking water. EPA estimated that as many as 185 of the 683 drinking water facilities in Louisiana were either not operational or unable to provide water that met EPA standards (Benfield et al. 2005).

In addition to damage at sewage plants and water treatment facilities, the damage from falling trees and tearing tree roots caused tens of thousands of water main breaks (Krupa 2006). These breaks in the pipes can result in contaminants entering the system and contaminating the water between the treatment plant and the tap. The city of New Orleans was pumping out more drinking water than before the storm only to see the bulk of it vanish underground (Krupa 2006).

Lack of certifiable drinking water has until recently kept residents of the Lower Ninth Ward from returning to reclaim their homes. FEMA has rejected funding requests from the New Orleans Sewerage and Water Board (S&WB) for repairs. FEMA rejected the requests because repairs were not "directly related to the storm" and therefore are not eligible for reimbursement (Krupa 2006).

Independent testing in September and October 2006 found that despite the massive water leaks throughout the city, the residual chlorine was sufficiently high throughout the system. No *Escherichia coli Giardia* or *Cryptosporidium* was detected. The disinfection byproducts were all well below regulatory limits (Memorandum from Gina M. Solomon 2006). However, heterotrophic plate count (HPC) in three of the 30 samples were significantly above the EPA guideline value—in one case by more than ten-fold, and one sample contained coliform bacteria but not pathogenic *E. coli*. Although HPC and one positive coliform sample is of uncertain health significance, it is an indicator of poor system maintenance and therefore should be taken seriously.

RESPONSE TO THE SCIENCE

The advocacy community followed up release of the scientific sampling by issuing a public health advisory, which advised returning residents and clean-up workers on how to protect themselves from the environmental contamination. Activists obtained personal protective equipment such as coveralls, respirators, and gloves and distributed them to people on street corners in the Lower Ninth Ward (Oxfam America 2006).

In March 2006, a coalition of more than a dozen civil rights, religious, and environmental justice groups petitioned the EPA, the Agency for Toxic Substances and Disease Registry, the Centers for Disease Control and Prevention (CDC), and FEMA to take immediate action to clean up the toxic contamination in New Orleans (Letter to Administrator Stephen Johnson 2006).

The Deep South Center for Environmental Justice and the United Steelworkers Union used the results of the sediment analysis and created the Safe Way Back Home project, in which they highlighted the failure of government agencies to clean up the contaminated sediment by taking the clean-up into their own hands in an ambitious and highly successful volunteer-based demonstration effort in the community of New Orleans East (Gyan 2006).

FEDERAL AND STATE RESPONSE TO KATRINA'S ENVIRONMENTAL IMPACTS AND RISKS

After this natural disaster of unprecedented scope and scale, the affected communities looked to their local, state, and federal government for support and assistance. Communities not only sought immediate disaster response assistance but also guidance and assurances from government on whether it was safe to return home, to their communities, and to the places where they worked. There was also an expectation by residents that if the government found toxic contamination, it would exercise its authority to the fullest extent to clean up the contamination and protect residents.

These expectations were not unfounded. EPA is the nation's primary repository of expertise and regulatory and enforcement authority for controlling and responding to environmental toxic threats to the public's health. As such, it was assumed that the agency would take on the bulk of the responsibility for assuring, after the massive spills and releases of oil and hazardous substances in the wake of Katrina, that the health of citizens living in or returning to the affected communities was fully protected. In fact, EPA itself noted on its Katrina home page, "In emergency situations such as this, *EPA serves as the lead Agency* for the clean-up of hazardous materials" (U.S. Environmental Protection Agency 2005).

Surprisingly, EPA repeatedly stated after the hurricanes that it was not the agency's obligation to decide whether environmental conditions in New Orleans and other areas affected by toxins and oil pollution were so dangerous as to warrant continued quarantine or additional clean-up prior to general repopulation of the affected areas. In short, EPA was refusing to make any explicit public statements about whether it was safe for the public to return to New Orleans and other hard-hit areas. EPA's reluctance to make any such statements was especially puzzling in light of the staggering amount of its own sampling data, as well as independent data, demonstrating significant toxic contamination.

Instead of exercising its authority, EPA decided early on to punt. In a November 8, 2005, interview on PBS (Online News Hour 2005), EPA Administrator Stephen Johnson was asked what governmental agency was responsible for declaring New Orleans safe for return. He responded, "It's not the EPA's decision. It's the responsibility of the state and local officials to make the decision. You know they're the ones that made the decision to evacuate. They're the ones appropriately to make the decision to come back in."

This statement, made months after Hurricanes Katrina and Rita hit, seemed to contradict EPA's role as lead agency in addressing environmental hazards during emergencies. Instead, EPA appeared to be passing the buck in two major ways. First, it declared that it had no authority or responsibility to monitor or address indoor air pollution and declared that the mold threat was an indoor air problem despite NRDC monitoring data demonstrating extremely high levels even in outdoor air in flooded areas (Chen 2005; Bowser 2005). Second, with regard to the toxic sediment, EPA deferred to local authorities the responsibility to protect citizens' health in the wake of the massive Katrina-related oil and hazardous chemical releases.

Generally, these local authorities, such as the Louisiana Department of Environmental Quality, did not have a significant staff of environmental health experts or access to the array of expertise and scientific information and resources that EPA has. They were also under enormous political pressure to allow rapid repopulation of the toxin-soaked areas.

It was not until August 17, 2006, one year later, that EPA officially made the explicit public statement that "adverse health effects would not be expected from exposure to contaminated sediments from the previously flooded areas, provided people use common sense and good personal hygiene and safety practice." When the announcement was finally made, an estimated 190,000 residents had already returned to previously flooded areas and were potentially already at risk (Louisiana Public Health Institute 2006).

EPA Legal Authorities and Obligations to Respond to Natural Disasters

EPA's decision to defer to local agencies to make determinations of whether it was safe to return appeared to undermine the agency's legal authority under such laws as the

Clean Water Act (CWA), Resource Conservation and Recovery Act (RCRA), Comprehensive Environmental Response, Compensation, and Liability Act (CERCLA, or Superfund), and Oil Pollution Act (OPA). Moreover, under its own National Contingency Plan (NCP) regulations, EPA carried the lead responsibility for evaluating and acting to remedy environmental health threats.

In particular, the NCP regulations impose numerous obligations on the agency to ensure that its response to releases of hazardous substances or oil protect exposed citizens. For example, the NCP requires that after an oil spill, "defensive actions *shall* begin as soon as possible to prevent, minimize, or mitigate threat(s) to the public health or welfare of the United States or the environment." Moreover, if "the discharge poses or may present a substantial threat to public health or welfare of the United States, the [EPA representative] *shall* direct all federal, state, or private actions to remove the discharge or to mitigate or prevent the threat of such a discharge, as appropriate." Similarly, RCRA states that once the EPA knows of hazardous waste at any site which presents an "imminent and substantial endangerment to human health or the environment," then the EPA "*shall* provide immediate notice to the appropriate local government agencies" and "*shall* require notice of such endangerment to be promptly posted at the site where the waste is located."

Under these laws, the EPA bears the lead responsibility for evaluating and acting to remedy environmental health threats. While it is clear that local and state authorities also share in the legal obligation to ensure that local residents are protected from such environmental health threats, under federal law, when there is such a declared national emergency and a significant threat from hazardous substances and oil, the EPA bears the responsibility of being *"the lead agency"* for assuring public health protection from these environmental health threats.

EPA has also often relied upon its Superfund authorities and funding for hazardous waste removal actions and relocations of entire at-risk populations, but the Superfund is now largely bankrupt because Congress has ended the fee on the chemical and oil industry that funded it. Consequently, all clean-up and relocation costs now must come directly from the EPA's budget and ultimately from the general taxpayer. This has served as political disincentive for the EPA to exercise these authorities to clean up and protect residents from environmental hazards.

In addition to Superfund, each of the EPA's major statutes (the Safe Drinking Water Act [SDWA], RCRA, Clean Air Act, CWA, etc.) includes a plenary "imminent and substantial endangerment" provision that allows the EPA to go to court and/or issue administrative orders to force essentially any action that the EPA believes is necessary to protect public health or the environment from an imminent and substantial endangerment due to a release or threatened release of hazardous chemicals or petroleum. The term "imminent and substantial endangerment" has been read by the courts very broadly to favor EPA intervention whenever there is a reasonable question about the safety to the public posed by toxic pollution. RCRA, for example, lets the EPA sue or issue orders to force action "as may be necessary" to protect the public from waste pollution.

The SDWA provides the EPA broad authority to issue orders or sue to force action to protect public health from possible contamination of water supplies or underground water. Similarly, the CWA gives the EPA authority to respond to such endangerment by suing for actions "as may be necessary" to force anyone causing or contributing to pollution to take any action needed to protect public health or the environment.

In the past, the EPA has relocated people from contaminated homes and has sometimes even relocated entire communities (such as Times Beach in Missouri, Love Canal in New York, public housing residents in Portsmouth, Virginia, and more recently a large number of pesticide-contaminated homes in Mississippi, Louisiana, and other states) due to hazardous substance contamination. EPA has also tested air quality inside private homes in the past. In 1994, the agency took samples in 9,000 houses in Ohio after a highly toxic pesticide was illegally sprayed in the community. The EPA eventually decontaminated 1,000 homes (Bowser 2005). Yet in New Orleans, the EPA claimed it did not have the authority or responsibility to test for contamination inside homes or to decontaminate homes. Taken together with numerous other legal authorities, it is clear that Congress intended for the EPA to have the authority to take sweeping actions as lead agency in the case of such nationally declared emergencies to protect the people of New Orleans and other communities from toxic contamination.

EPA Failure to Exercise Legal Authorities

After the tragic events of the September 11 terrorist attacks on the World Trade Center, a lawsuit was brought against the EPA for its failure to act on its legal authorities to clean up environmental contamination. Throughout the litigation, the EPA denied that the agency had any explicit responsibility to act in response to the disaster. Specifically, the EPA argued that it was not required to act to protect workers or the public from environmental contaminants but could do so voluntarily at its own discretion. The statement, although shocking, was also extremely revealing regarding the EPA's reluctance to exercise the multitude of legal authorities it possessed to clean up and protect people from environmental contaminants in a time of disaster. The court found that in the case of the September 11 attacks and under the six provisions of the NCP the plaintiffs relied upon, the plaintiffs did not identify a mandatory duty to act under the provisions of the NCP. In other words, the court decided that residents do not have a legal right to force the EPA to use its authority. Instead, the EPA is free to decide.

The court did, however, recognize a valid Fifth Amendment substantive due-process claim against EPA administrator Christine Todd Whitman for her public statements that it was safe to return to areas she knew continued to pose a grave danger to public health. Plaintiffs' claim alleged a violation of their "substantive due process rights to bodily integrity and, more specifically, their right to be free of official government policies that increase the risk of bodily harm." The court upheld this claim and noted that the agency's inaction and statements that the area was safe, when there was ample evidence contradicting that statement, might put people at risk of bodily harm and might rise to the level of an affirmative act that shocks the conscience.

The September 11 litigation provides helpful insight into explaining why EPA chose not to exercise its legal authorities after Katrina. After September 11, it was clear that the EPA recognized it had the authority to protect workers and the public from toxic contaminants but was unwilling to take any action while under political pressure to say everything was OK.

In the case of Katrina, a larger environmental disaster in scale and scope, the EPA was even more careful to avoid making statements regarding the safety of returning residents. The EPA, at first, avoided making any formal declarations regarding the safety of returning to previously flooded areas. However, at the same time, it also released advisories recommending that residents take all precautions that one would take if there were significant toxic contamination (EPA News Release 2006). The advisories ranged from recommending that people shower often, wash their hands regularly, change clothes often, and use washable doormats, to encouraging the use of respirators in previously flooded areas and avoiding activities that generate dust.

EPA's careful attempt to walk the line between saying it was safe or unsafe was clear early on. Shortly after the hurricanes, Administrator Johnson responded to exactly this question by saying:

> Well, unfortunately it's not a yes or a no answer because, again, what we're seeing in the sediment area is that we're seeing some of those sediments highly contaminated with petroleum products and for those areas that have high contamination you really shouldn't be coming in contact with it. For those areas with very low contamination there's probably not a health consequence . . . but still prudent advice would be—common sense advice would be to avoid exposure, take precaution.

By sending mixed signals that on the one hand it was safe to return, but on the other hand people should significantly alter their normal daily behavior to guard against toxic exposure, the EPA performed a grave disservice to returning residents by allowing them to be exposed to known environmental hazards. Furthermore, Johnson's admission that high contamination was a problem in some areas in New Orleans is troublesome in light of the agency's decision to not take any clean-up actions regarding the contaminated sediment.

The EPA might have concluded that its flaw in the 9/11 context was its failure to recognize the risk and to protect victims from the harm. Instead, it appears that the EPA concluded that a safer route (for the agency) was to equivocate about safety and to disclaim any responsibility at all.

LESSONS LEARNED

The experience in New Orleans offers vital lessons regarding the importance of history in setting the stage for present-day events, the role of partnerships between local community groups and national environmental groups, and the necessity and limitations of science. Ultimately, the experience in New Orleans starkly displays the fundamental failure of our nation's core environmental laws to serve the needs of the environmental justice community at a critical moment of need.

The Role of History

As a nation, we are far from overcoming our history of government-sanctioned and government-sponsored racism. Until the middle of the twentieth century, federal, state, and local governments used a variety of legal mechanisms to separate people by race. Even as the Supreme Court began to dismantle the express use of race beginning with *Buchanan v. Warely* and culminating in *Brown v. Board of Education,* local and state governments colluded in private racism. By the 1960s, residential segregation in New Orleans, like many other cities in this country, was firmly entrenched.

In Louisiana, the state government then compounded the harms of racial segregation by welcoming toxic industry into vulnerable communities and failing to provide any semblance of environmental protection from the toxic assault. As many have noted, the events that followed Hurricanes Katrina and Rita exposed the world to the conditions residents had been experiencing for decades. Now, the homes and communities that former residents of New Orleans constructed despite the challenges are mired in a literally toxic soup.

Partnerships Between Community and National Groups

Environmental justice (EJ) is in many ways local in nature, but national environmental groups can make valuable contributions to ongoing EJ efforts if they approach this work with the appropriate respect for local organizations' and communities' goals and priorities. In light of the tremendous need for additional resources for EJ struggles, and the shrinking pool of money available for community-based EJ efforts, national green groups must renew their commitment to serving the communities that disproportionately bear the brunt of our nation's toxic pollution. Collaborative relationships with EJ communities will serve to strengthen forward-thinking national green groups and provide opportunities for transformative alliances that connect with and are of service to a broader social movement.

National green-group participation in EJ efforts, however, should move beyond the traditionally limited role of case-specific litigation support to reflect a longer-term commitment to EJ. National groups should offer a broader range of institutional resources to support EJ initiatives, including legal resources, policy advocacy, communications support, and scientific and technical expertise.

Successful EJ partnerships between national environmental groups and EJ groups

- must derive from and be accountable to the local community groups;
- should involve multidisciplinary support, incorporating an array of expertise and resources;

- should include a commitment to build short- and long-term institutional capacities within local and regional organizations, so that EJ initiatives can become self-sustaining; and
- should be considered part of a larger movement, and adhere to the movement's established Principles of Environmental Justice adopted at the First National People of Color Leadership Summit in September 1991.

Ultimately, relationships with local and EJ partners will complement and strengthen local groups and create new opportunities for national green groups to address important environmental and human health issues in communities that bear the brunt of the nation's toxic pollution.

The Role and Limitations of Science

The partnership between NRDC and local groups primarily focused on collecting scientific data to demonstrate the scope of the contamination left behind in New Orleans. Without such data, it would have been almost impossible for the community to advocate for a clean-up, or even to know whether such advocacy was warranted. Unfortunately, the interpretation of the scientific data differed between the environmental community and the government agencies. For example, the community compared the contamination to "acceptable" cancer risk numbers of one-in-a-million, whereas the LDEQ announced that in this case, a cancer risk as high as one-in-ten-thousand was perfectly acceptable and required no clean-up, even though hundreds of thousands of people were returning to the city.

Similarly, there was a major debate over how much of the contamination predated the flooding. The government agencies claimed that virtually all of the contamination was present pre-Katrina, despite evidence to the contrary, and therefore claimed that there was no need for a clean-up even if the levels were unsafe. Thus the scientific findings were necessary but not sufficient to force a necessary clean-up of the toxic contamination in the city. Scientific data are always subject to interpretation, and an overlay of politics is always present when there is any need to determine a "safe" level of toxic contamination. Thus the major scientific effort by the coalition after Katrina was helpful in providing information to community members about personal protective measures but was ultimately not enough to push for the necessary action.

The Failure of Environmental Laws

Five years after the September 11 attack in New York, there is now a substantial body of evidence demonstrating that the destruction of the World Trade Center and the Ground Zero fires that continued burning for months did in fact adversely affect the health of tens of thousands of New Yorkers. The evidence also demonstrates that a majority of the heroic first responders—firefighters and other workers who were present at the WTC site in the weeks and months after 9/11—suffered serious health problems for years after the disaster. The federal government was wrong to insist at the time—and today—that the area was safe for people to return. The EPA was also wrong when it concluded that there was no need to exercise the government's wealth of legal authorities to clean up toxic contamination and protect the health of workers and residents.

Along with the more dramatic government failures to protect New Orleans residents from the flood and its aftermaths, the federal government's inaction around the public's health after 9/11 raised questions about the government's environmental response to hurricanes Katrina and Rita. Local leaders in New Orleans were not assuaged by the government's reassurances about environmental safety right after the hurricanes. These local leaders were careful to call for independent testing, as well as for independent analysis and critiques of the government testing data and government's interpretation of the results. The skepticism was warranted when the analysis of the government's data and independent data demonstrated significant toxic contamination.

It is not too late. The federal government still has an opportunity to renew the public's faith by doing right by displaced residents and those seeking to remake their lives in New Orleans. As this chapter illustrates, a host of federal laws provide the legal authority for federal government agencies, namely, the EPA and CDC, to clean up toxic contamination and take the necessary steps to protect workers and residents after natural disasters. The federal government's failure to exercise these authorities, especially in light of 9/11 and the history of racism and discrimination in New Orleans, only further undermines the confidence of the citizenry that the government is here to protect its citizens from environmental health hazards.

The government's abdication of its legal and, indeed, moral obligations to protect its most vulnerable populations is particularly troubling in light of its complicity in their condition. Many will never forget the images of poor African-American citizens abandoned to the flood. The government's actions immediately after the flood sent a powerful message that some people do not matter. Words alone will never erase that message.

As more and more people return to New Orleans, the opportunity for the federal government to "do the right thing" quickly closes. As news articles have documented, the government's failure to address environmental contamination may have the tragic result of discouraging displaced residents from returning, preventing tourists from visiting the city (one of the city's largest economic revenue generators), and slowing much-needed businesses from investing in the rebuilding of the Crescent City (Warner 2006).

To date, the federal government has not released any comprehensive report to address the widespread toxic contamination its own data revealed, nor has the federal government taken any steps to remove the highly contaminated sediment in previously flooded areas of the city.

Returning residents and activists on the ground intend to rebuild their city. In some cases, groups such as the Deep South Center for Environmental Justice and the

United Steelworkers Union are taking matters into their own hands and recruiting community members to clean up contaminated sediments in their own backyards. These activists did not wait for the federal government; they obtained their own protective equipment, distributed it to local residents, and took it upon themselves to protect their community from environmental contamination. These self-help remedies are impressive, but they are unlikely to be sufficient to ameliorate the full scope of the contamination.

When a citizenry must take matters into their own hands, it points out a colossal failure of the government to exercise its responsibilities to its people. We hope that this failure by the government will not become another chapter in a long history of neglect and malfeasance.

REFERENCES

Advocates for Environmental Human Rights et al. (n.d.). "Rebuilding New Orleans: A 10-Point Plan of Action." Available at http://www.nrdc.org/legislation/katrina/leg_06011001a.pdf.

Benfield, K., et al. 2005. *After Katrina: New Solutions for Safe Communities and a Secure Energy Future*. New York: Natural Resources Defense Council. Available at http://www.nrdc.org/legislation/hk/hk.pdf.

Bernstein, D., and I. Somin. 2004. Book Review. *Judicial Power and Civil Rights Reconsidered: From Jim Crow to Civil Rights: The Supreme Court and the Struggle for Racial Equality* by M. J. Klarman. *Yale Law Journal* 114:591–606.

Bowser, B. A. 2005. "The Environmental Impact of Katrina." PBS Online Newshour, November 8. Available at http://www.pbs.org/newshour/bb/science/july-dec05/neworleans_11-08.html (accessed November 18, 2006).

Bullard, R. D., J. E. Grigsby II, and C. Lee. 1994. *Residential Apartheid: The American Legacy*. Los Angeles: UCLA Center for African Studies Publication.

Bureau of Applied Research in Anthropology. (n.d.). "Environmental Problems." Available at http://www.gulfstorms.org/Environment.html. Per-capita calculation credited to biologist Florence Robinson.

Chen, M. 2005. "Unaddressed Health Hazards Persist As New Orleans Slowly Rebuilds." *New Standard*. December 5. Available at http://newstandardnews.net/content/index.cfm/items/2646 (accessed August 8, 2008).

Claren, R. 2005. "The Entire Community Is Now a Toxic Waste Dump." *Salon Magazine*. September 9. Available at http://www.earthshare.org/KATRINA/Salon_toxicwastedump.pdf (accessed August 8, 2008).

Energy Information System. (n.d.). Official Energy Statistics from the U.S. Government. Available at http://72.14.203.104/search?q=cache:YuQABWQz77QJ:tonto.eia.doe.gov/oog/info/state/la.html+louisiana+oil+production&hl=en&gl=us&ct=clnk&cd=1.

EPA Inspector General. 2004. *EPA Needs to Consistently Implement the Intent of the Executive Order on Environmental Justice*. March 1. Available at www.epa.gov/oig/reports/2004/20040301-2004-P-00007.pdf (accessed November 23, 2006).

_____. 2006. *EPA Needs to Conduct Environmental Reviews of Its Programs, Policies and Activities*. September 18. Washington, DC: EPA Office of Inspector General.

EPA News Release. 2006. "Environmental Responders Distribute 2 Million Flyers to Southern Louisiana Residents January 27." Available at http://yosemite.epa.gov/opa/admpress.nsf/fdd0bac26e8db73e852572a000655939/fb760f46b3f78aef8525 71060068112f!OpenDocument.

———. 2006. "Release of Multi-Agency Report Shows Elevated Lead Levels in New Orleans Soil, Consistent with Historic Levels of Urban Lead." April 4. Available at http://yosemite.epa.gov/opa/admpress.nsf/a7b2ee8e45551c13852573590040444/ ba5f2460d6c777f58525714600693b5b!OpenDocument.

Fields, L., A. Huang, G. M. Solomon, M. Rotkin-Ellman, and Patrice Simms. 2007. *Katrina's Wake: Arsenic-Laced Schools and Playgrounds Put New Orleans Children at Risk*. New York: NRDC. August.

Frug, J. 1996. "The Geography of Community." *Stanford Law Review* 48:1047–1068.

Godsil, R. D. 2006. "Race, Nuisance: The Politics of Law in the Jim Crow Era." *Michigan Law Review* 105 (3): 505–558.

———. 2004. "Viewing the Cathedral from Behind the Color Line: Property Rules, Liability Rules, and Environmental Racism." *Emory Law Review*, p. 1808.

Graham-Felsen, S., and K. Vanden Heuvel. 2006. "Sweet Victory: Uniting to Clean Up NOLA." *The Nation BLOG*. March 2. Available at http://www.commondreams .org/views06/0403-25.htm.

Gyan, J., Jr. 2006. "Project Brings Green to N.O.: Joint Initiative to Help Cleanup, Reach Out to Neighborhood." *The Advocate*. March 24.

Jackson, K. T. 1987. *Crabgrass Frontier: The Suburbanization of the United States*. New York: Oxford University Press.

Krupa, M. 2006. "Volume of Water Leaks Cut in Half." *Times-Picayune*. September 20.

———. 2006. "FEMA Bounces Water Board Jobs." *Times-Picayune*. September 26.

Letter to Administrator Stephen Johnson from ACORN, New Orleans; Advocates for Environmental Human Rights; W. Haywood Burns Environment Education Center, Albany, NY; Deep South Center for Environmental Justice, Dillard University, New Orleans; Earthjustice, Washington, DC; Holy Cross Neighborhood Association, Lower 9th Ward, New Orleans; Lawyers Committee for Civil Rights Under Law, Washington, DC; Louisiana Bucket Brigade, New Orleans; Louisiana Environmental Action Network, Baton Rouge; NAACP, Washington Bureau; National Black Environmental Justice Network; Natural Resources Defense Council; 9/11 Environmental Action, New York; Oxfam America; Physicians for Social Responsibility–Louisiana; and Sojourners, Washington, DC. March 15, 2006. Available at http://72.32.110 .154/media/pressreleases/060315.asp (accessed November 18, 2006).

Louisiana Public Health Institute. *2006 Louisiana Health and Population Survey. New Orleans, LA*. Available at http://popest.org/popestla2006/ (accessed November 23, 2006).

Mahoney, M. 1990. "Law and Racial Geography: Public Housing and the Economy in New Orleans." *Stanford Law Review* 42 (5): 1251–1290.

Massey, D., and N. A. Denton. 1993. *American Apartheid and the Making of the Underclass*. Cambridge, MA: Harvard University Press.

Memorandum from Gina M. Solomon, M.D., M.P.H. October 5, 2006.

Mielke, H. W., D. Dugas, P. W. Mielke Jr., K. S. Smith, and C. R. Gonzales. 1997. "Associations Between Soil Lead and Childhood Blood Lead in Urban New Orleans and Rural Lafourche Parish of Louisiana." *Environmental Health Perspectives* 105 (9): 950–954.

Mielke, H. W., C. R. Gonzales, M. K. Smith, and P. W. Mielke. 1999. "The Urban Environment and Children's Health: Soils as an Integrator of Lead, Zinc, and Cadmium in New Orleans, Louisiana, U.S.A." *Environmental Research* 81 (2): 117–129.

Moshman, R., and J. Hardenbergh. 2006. "The Color of Katrina: A Proposal to Allow Disparate Impact Environmental Claims." *Sustainable Development Law and Policy* 6 (3): 15.

Mvula, M., M. Larzelere, M. Kraus, K. Moisiewicz, C. Morgan, S. Pierce, R. Post, T. Nash, and C. Moore. 2005. "Prevalence of Asthma and Asthma-Like Symptoms in Inner-City Schoolchildren." *Journal of Asthma* 42 (1): 9–16.

Natural Resources Defense Council. 2005a. "New Testing Shows Widespread Toxic Contamination in New Orleans Soil, Neighborhoods." December 1. Available at http://www.nrdc.org/media/pressReleases/051201.asp.

———. 2005b. "New Private Testing Shows Dangerously High Mold Counts in New Orleans Air." Press Release. November 16. Available at http://www.nrdc.org/media/pressReleases/051116.asp.

Oliver, M. L., and T. M. Shapiro. 1995. *Black Wealth/White Wealth: A New Perspective on Racial Inequality*. New York: Routledge.

Online News Hour. 2005. "Environmental Impact of Katrina." Available at http://www.pbs.org/newshour/bb/science/july-dec05/neworleans_11-08.html.

Oxfam America. (2005). "Hurricane Cleanup and Recovery Kit." Available at http://www.oxfamamerica.org/whatwedo/emergencies/hurricane_katrina/news_publications/oacontent.2005-10-15.2251461580 (accessed July 23, 2008).

Smerk, G. M. 1965. *Urban Transportation: The Federal Role*. Bloomington: Indiana University Press.

Solomon, G. M., and M. Rotkin-Ellman. 2006. *Contaminants in New Orleans Sediment: An Analysis of EPA Data*. Natural Resources Defense Council. February. Available at http://www.nrdc.org/health/effects/katrinadata/sedimentepa.pdf.

Talbot, G. 2005. "Is Desire Strong Enough to Draw Evacuees Back?" *Newhouse News Service*. September 26. Available at http://www.newhousenews.com/archive/talbot092705.html (accessed June 1, 2008).

Targonski, P. V., V. W. Persky, and V. Ramekrishnan. 1995. "Effect of Environmental Molds on Risk of Death from Asthma During Pollen Season." *Journal of Allergy and Clinical Immunology* 95 (May): 955–961.

Teaford, J. C. 1990. *The Rough Road to Renaissance: Urban Revitalization in America*. Baltimore: John Hopkins University.

Think Progress. 2005. "Bush Advisor to Reporter: Katrina Has Fallen So Far Off the Radar Screen, You Can't Find It." Available at http://thinkprogress.org/2005/12/11/katrina-off-radar.

U.S. Environmental Protection Agency. 2005. "Response to 2005 Hurricanes." Available at http://www.epa.gov/katrina/index.html.

Warner, C. 2006. "NOLA Safe for Visitors, Residents, DEQ Says." *Times-Picayune*. November 13.

Wright, B. 2007. "Living and Dying in Louisiana's 'Cancer Alley.'" in R. D. Bullard (ed.). *The Quest for Environmental Justice: Human Rights and the Politics of Pollution*. San Francisco: Sierra Club Books, pp. 87–107.

CHAPTER 6

INVESTING IN HUMAN CAPITAL AND HEALTHY REBUILDING IN THE AFTERMATH OF HURRICANE KATRINA

Sheila J. Webb

Health disparities that exist among Americans are an indicator of the inequality in health status found among the races in this country. Health disparities refer to the disproportionate burden of disease, illness, and preventable deaths borne by African Americans and other minorities in the United States. In 1985 U.S. Department of Health and Human Services (HHS) Secretary Margaret Heckler released the landmark report on black and minority health drawing national attention to this problem. Twenty years later on August 29, 2005, Hurricane Katrina struck the southeastern coastal line of the United States leaving a trail of destruction significantly affecting the region. Hardest hit were the coastal areas of Louisiana and Mississippi. While both states experienced widespread damage and destruction, the impact of this disaster was felt throughout the nation and touched the world.

The portrayal of the massive destruction and its toll on human capital was played out before the nation and the world on television, radio broadcasts, and through worldwide electronic and print media. The plight of human suffering could be seen on the faces of the victims who awaited rescue efforts in the days that followed the catastrophe. The city of New Orleans and state of Louisiana were front and center as the mounting devastation of Hurricane Katrina unfolded daily. While hundreds of thousands of people were affected by this storm, the poor and underserved populations were disproportionately impacted and significantly bore the brunt of loss, devastation, and injustice. New Orleans, with its majority African-American population and large percentage of individuals living below the federal poverty line, became the embodiment of disproportional impact.

THE BURDEN OF INEQUALITY

Unfortunately, history reveals the ravages of disasters on disenfranchised peoples. Marginalized by social, economic, and racial injustices, these individuals are often further victimized by disasters. There is general agreement among experts in the international community that the poor are disproportionately affected by the global disasters we have all witnessed in recent years. In the case of the Indian Ocean tsunami (2004), although many countries were affected, the most vulnerable was probably Somalia. This is a very poor country (GNI per capita about $100) with very limited resources located in East Africa, with an ineffective governmental structure (Clay 2004).

The failure of public policy to provide for and protect its most vulnerable citizens in times of a disaster is somehow inconsistent with images of a world superpower. Quigley (2006), in an article titled "Who Was Left Behind Then and Who Is Being Left Behind Now," refers to the Katrina evacuation in New Orleans as a "totally self-help operation." He suggests that those with resources, a car, money, and a place to go left on their own—that was about 80–90 percent of the population. As for the rest, "The people left behind in the evacuation of New Orleans after Katrina are the same people left behind in the rebuilding of New Orleans—the poor, the sick, the elderly, the disabled, and children, mostly African American." Unfortunately, these are the same people who are left behind in the world and in our nation, the people who seem to pay again and again.

The cumulative effects of poverty, inequality, social isolation, and racism on a people have a mounting effect. These social determinants are closely linked to the poor health outcomes experienced by many African Americans and other minority populations in the United States. Health disparities are the ultimate price that often results in decreases in the quality and years of healthy life for many Americans.

The unequal burden of disease and death is illustrated in substantial differences in life expectancy in the United States from 1970 to 2003. Figure 6.1 charts life expectancy for white non-Hispanic females at 80.5 years, African-American non-Hispanic females at 76.1 years, white non-Hispanic males at 75.4 years, and African-American non-Hispanic males at 69.2 years. This finding suggests a range of a low—seven months' longer life expectancy for African-American women compared with white males—and a high—eleven years longer in life expectancy for white females, compared with African-American males (National Center for Health Statistics 2004).

Disparities in mortality rates for Louisiana women diagnosed with breast cancer from 1982 to 2005 per 100,000 population are illustrated in Figure 6.2. Louisiana breast cancer death rates for both white and African-American women were slightly higher when compared with national rates for their respective racial groups. However,

FIGURE 6.1—Life Expectancy at Birth, by Year—United States, 1970–2003

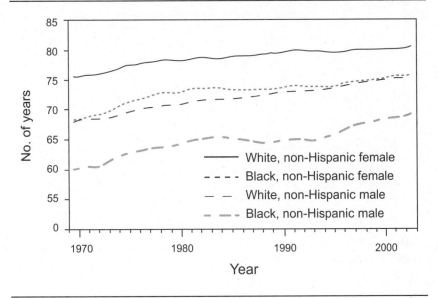

Source: The National Center for Health Statistics.

breast cancer mortality rates overall were significantly higher for African-American women in Louisiana and in the United States, when compared with their white counterparts. Furthermore, as illustrated in Figure 6.2, the gap in breast cancer mortality rates between African-American women and white women has been consistently wider in Louisiana compared to the national gap (National Vital Statistics System).

POVERTY

The U.S. Census Report (2000) identified Louisiana as the poorest state in the nation, with the largest percentage of its residents with incomes below the Federal Poverty Level (FPL). This finding, unfortunately, reflected no change in ranking since the 1990 Census Report. In August 2005, when Katrina hit the Gulf region, 22 percent of Louisiana residents and 23 percent of New Orleans residents were living in poverty ($16,090 for a family of three).

Almost 50 percent of Louisiana residents live at or below 200 percent of the FPL. The child poverty rate for the New Orleans metropolitan statistical area (MSA) was the highest in the nation in 2005 (Annie E Casey Foundation 2005). Consistent with this finding, single-parent households were predominant with 62 percent of children living with single parents compared with 43 percent of all children living in Louisiana and 31 percent of all children living in the United States in 2004.

FIGURE 6.2—Historical Trends in Breast Cancer Mortality Rates for
Females, All Ages, 1982–2005

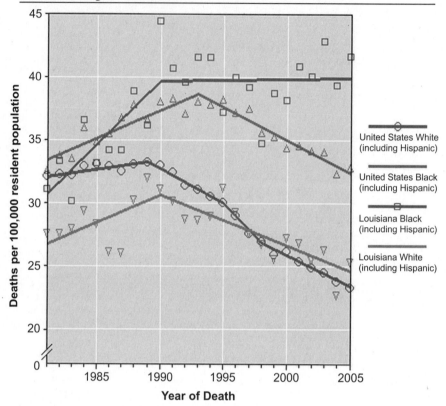

Created by statecancerprofiles.cancer.gov on 10/30/2008, 2:33 p.m. Regression lines calculated using the Joinpoint Regression Program.

Source: Death data provided by the National Vital Statistics System public use data file. Death
rates calculated by the National Cancer Institute using SEER*Stat. Death rates (deaths per
100,000 population per year) are age-adjusted to the 2000 US standard population (19 age
groups: <1, 1–4, 5–9, . . . , 80–84, 85+). Population counts for denominators are based on
Census populations as modified by NCI.

The average family income for New Orleans residents ($36,465) was 33 percent
lower than the U.S. average family income of $53,692. For families with children,
the average family income was 42 percent lower ($30,112 compared to $51,187)
than the national average. New Orleans unemployment rates for the same reporting
period were 7 percent as compared to a 5 percent rate for the state and the United
States (U.S. Census Report 1990, 2000; Zedlewski 2006).

The economic status of children in Louisiana and New Orleans shows limited
prospects for improvement given low salaries, large numbers of single-parent fami-

lies, and fertility rates highest among single women. Seventy percent of all births in New Orleans and 47 percent of all births in the state, compared to 29 percent of all births in the U.S., were to unmarried females. Along with high rates of poverty in New Orleans and Louisiana are high rates of uninsured individuals. Approximately 21 percent of the state's population (900,000) does not have health insurance. The Medicaid rate for the state is 19 percent, the third highest in the nation, providing coverage for children and pregnant women up to 200 percent of the FPL (Louisiana Department of Health and Hospitals 2005).

High rates of poverty and single female heads of households for many women remain consistent throughout the life cycle. Webb (2004) conducted a study on the "Relationship of Selected Cultural Attributes to Knowledge, Beliefs, and Behaviors for Early Breast Cancer Detection Among African-American Women in New Orleans." In a sample population of 189 women ages 40–80 years, Table 6.1 shows 69 percent of the study population reported being single, divorced, or widowed.

TABLE 6.1—Sociodemographic Characteristics of the Sample

(N=189)

Demographic Characteristics	Frequency	Percentage
Marital Status		
Single	49	25.9
Married	58	30.7
Divorced	41	21.7
Widowed	41	21.7
TOTAL	**189**	
Income		
$5,000–9,000	74	39.6
$10,000–19,000	38	20.3
$20,000–29,000	38	20.3
$30,000–39,000	14	7.5
$40,000–49,000	9	4.8
$50,000–59,000	6	3.2
$60,000 and above	8	4.3
TOTAL	**187**	

Source: Sheila J. Webb. 2004. "Development and Exploration of a Culturally-Enhanced Breast Health Measure and the Relationship of Selected Cultural Attributes to Knowledge, Beliefs, and Behaviors for Early Breast Cancer Detection Among African-American Women." Baton Rouge: Southern University Dissertation. May.

Only 31 percent of the women reported being married. Forty percent of the women's annual household incomes were below $10,000. Another 41 percent of the women reported incomes between $10,000 and $30,000 annually. Only about 20 percent of the women reported incomes over $30,000, and two individuals reported household incomes of less than $5,000 annually.

HEALTH STATUS

Louisiana ranks among the lowest of the 50 states in several health indicators: 44th for teen birth rate, 47th for infant mortality rate, and 49th for low birth weight. Louisiana has the fourth highest cardiovascular disease (CVD) death rate in the nation. CVD is the leading cause of death in Louisiana, accounting for about 40 percent of all deaths. Louisiana has a high incidence of diabetes, with approximately 7 percent of adults in the state diagnosed in 2004. Cancer incidence in the state is also higher. Louisiana's overall ranking of 49th in the nation for health status places it next to the bottom with only its neighbor Mississippi ranking worse. Infant mortality rate in 2002 for the state was 10.2 and in Orleans Parish 13.0 per 1,000 live births. Louisiana is ranked sixth in the nation in percent of the population lacking access to primary health care (BRFSS, 2004; Louisiana Office of Public Health, 2005).

HEALTH DISPARITIES

African Americans and other minorities in Louisiana, similar to other states in the United States, are disproportionately affected by illness and disease. Cardiovascular disease, cancer, and diabetes are among the leading causes of death in the state. African Americans are consistently at greater risk with generally higher morbidity and mortality rates. African-American women have a 40 percent higher chance of dying of cardiovascular disease than white women. In the case of breast cancer, African-American women have lower rates of disease incidence but higher mortality rates when compared to white women in the state.

African Americans have the highest prevalence of diabetes, with a 10.9 percent diagnosis rate, compared to 7.9 percent of Hispanics and 7 percent of the white population. Infant mortality rates per 1,000 live births for African-American infants were 14.1 in the state and 10.4 in New Orleans, just over two times the rate for white infants. Of the persons who are living with a diagnosis of HIV/Aids in the state and parish, African Americans comprise 66 and 60 percent respectively compared to a national rate of 42 percent (BRFSS, 2004; Louisiana Office of Public Health, 2005, 2006).

The burden of inequality as previously discussed in relation to poverty, health status, and health disparities begs the question "Do place and race matter?" These health status data suggest that if you lived in Louisiana you were at risk for living in poverty and having poor health outcomes. However, if you lived in Louisiana and were African-American, you were at increased risk for living in poverty and having poor health outcomes. On the other hand, if you lived in New Orleans you were more than likely African-American and you were at an even greater risk of having poorer health and living in poverty.

PLACE MATTERS

On August 29, 2005, Hurricane Katrina hit the costal areas of Louisiana, Alabama, and Mississippi. Louisiana and Mississippi both experienced widespread damage and destruction. However, the historic city of New Orleans felt the greatest impact from this disaster, with major flooding resulting from a failed levee system. The shaded areas of the map in Figure 6.3 indicate flooding to 80 percent of the city, destroying over 180,000 homes, the health care delivery system, schools, businesses, jobs, and a way of life for so many.

African Americans in New Orleans' poorest communities, renters, and the unemployed were disproportionately impacted by Katrina's floodwaters. Quigley (2006) reported that damaged areas were populated by 46 percent African Americans compared to 26 percent African Americans in the rest of the city. Forty-six percent of the population in the most damaged areas were renters compared to 31 percent in the rest of the city, and 21 percent lived below the federal poverty level compared to 15 percent in the rest of the city. If you lived in New Orleans and were African-American, you were at

FIGURE 6.3—The Flood Zone: Orleans Parish September 11 Flood Extent with Neighborhoods and Major Roads

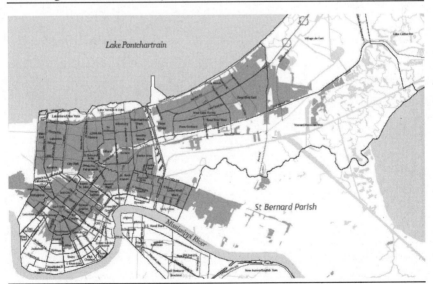

Source: U.S. Army Corps of Engineers.

increased risk for sustaining storm-related damages and losses. Pastor et al. (2006) suggest groups of individuals lacking access to resources, power, and information are usually further disenfranchised before, during, and after a disaster.

New Orleans residents evacuated to 44 different states; the poorer you were the greater the likelihood you ended up in a location not of your own choosing and the farther away you landed. A significant number of evacuees, however, ended up in Baton Rouge, Louisiana, the state's capital. According to a report from the Federal Emergency Management Agency (FEMA) (2005), the total number of evacuees reporting addresses with Baton Rouge zip codes in October 2005 was 202,042. Baton Rouge is 84 miles west of New Orleans and ranks third among cities with the most evacuees. Individuals are at risk for poor health and social outcomes based on where they live. There is substantial research that suggests place matters.

The data in Table 6.2 display a demographic comparison among West and East Baton Rouge parishes and Orleans Parish. Compared to Orleans' 484,674, the combined parishes of West and East Baton Rouge populations were slightly smaller, with 434,453. Baton Rouge had a slightly smaller elderly population, comprising 10 per-

TABLE 6.2—Demographic Comparison

	West Baton Rouge	East Baton Rouge	Orleans
Total Population	21,601	412,852	484,674
Age 65 years & over (%)	9.7	9.9	11.7
White Race (%)	62.8	56.2	28.1
African-American Race (%)	35.5	40.1	67.3
Asian Race (%)	0.2	2.1	2.3
Hispanic (%)	1.4	1.8	3.1
Owner-Occupied Housing Units (%)	78.8	61.6	46.5
High School Graduates (%)	73.4	83.9	74.7
Bachelor's Degree or Higher (%)	11.1	30.8	25.8
Median Household Income (1999)	37,117	37,224	27,133
Families Below Poverty Level (%)	13.2	13.2	23.7

Source: U.S. Census Bureau, *Summary File 1 (SF 1) and Summary File 3 (SF 3)* (2000).

cent for people age 65 or older compared to 12 percent for New Orleans. Stark contrasts are noted in the white and black racial makeup of the populations. Whites accounted for 63 and 56 percent of the population in West and East Baton Rouge compared with 28 percent for Orleans Parish.

African Americans comprised 36 and 40 percent of West and East Baton Rouge Parishes compared to 67 percent for Orleans. Asians and Hispanics were less than 5 percent of the population in all three parishes. Seventy-nine and 61 percent of the housing units were owner occupied in West and East Baton Rouge compared to 47 percent for Orleans Parish. High school graduation rates for all three parishes were above 70 percent. Bachelor's degrees and higher were highest at 31 percent for East Baton Rouge and lowest at 11 percent for West Baton Rouge; Orleans Parish was 26 percent.

Median annual household incomes were $37,000 for Baton Rouge compared to $27,000 for New Orleans. Interestingly, the lower attainment of bachelor's degrees in West Baton Rouge had no effect on median household income. Families living below poverty in Baton Rouge comprised 13 percent of all families compared to 24 percent of families in Orleans Parish (U.S. Census Data 2000). This demographic comparison suggests that if you lived in Baton Rouge instead of New Orleans you would have greater earning potential, which would decrease your risks for living in poverty and possibly increase your potential and opportunity for home ownership. These findings indicate that place does matter. As individuals attempt to rebuild their lives, of major consideration is the concern for an improved and more equitable quality of life for all.

THE AFTERMATH

Before Katrina, New Orleans was the epicenter of medical commerce in the state. In the immediate aftermath of the storm, state and local governments focused all attention on emergency response activities in providing health care services to the hundreds of thousands of evacuees across the state. U.S. Public Health Service officials led the charge in reassembling the collapsed health care delivery system in Orleans, St. Bernard, Jefferson, and Plaquemines Parishes. Health care planning and systems redesign discussions in the aftermath of the disaster have taken on a life of their own.

Health care providers, planners, consultants, and government officials alike are spending inordinate amounts of time and energy in the frenzy of planning. These planning processes are constrained by efforts to include and involve the appropriate stakeholders in the face of blistering deadlines. Earlier planning activities under the Governor's Health Reform Panel, Louisiana Recovery Authority, Public Health and Health Care Taskforce, and Mayor Ray Nagin's Bring New Orleans Back Commission, all provided leadership and a focal point for health care delivery systems revamping activities. These former activities laid the groundwork and helped frame issues for the Louisiana Healthcare Redesign Collaborative.

At the urging of HHS Secretary Mike Leavitt, the collaborative was created by legislative authority to design a new waiver request that addresses the rebuilding of the health care delivery system in the New Orleans region and influences health policy statewide. The mission of the collaborative was "to develop, and oversee the implementation of, a practical blueprint for an evidence-based, quality driven health care system for Louisiana. This blueprint will serve as a guide for health care policy in Louisiana and to the rebuilding of health care in the hurricane-affected areas of the state."

Significant in the charter of the collaborative is the expectation that the waiver will go much farther than the previous Medicaid Health Insurance and Flexibility Act (HIFA) waiver application, be tailored to respond to the loss of infrastructure and population shifts, and include a Medicare demonstration as part of the design. The significance of the latter is that Medicare is 100 percent financed through the federal government. The blueprint was scheduled for presentation to Secretary Leavitt, the governor, the Legislature, and the Louisiana Recovery Authority in late 2006. As of 2008, there have not been any changes to the blueprint.

HEALTH CARE INFRASTRUCTURE

Nearly a year after the storm, in areas sustaining the greatest devastation such as New Orleans and the lower-lying parishes of St. Bernard and Plaquemine, the health care delivery system was greatly fractured. By August 2006, only three of the 12 acute-care hospitals in Orleans Parish had reopened their doors. Acute inpatient care was provided among the nine hospitals operating in Orleans and Jefferson parishes. Service capacity was static with the number of operating hospitals, while demand increases with the returning population. Many services were limited, particularly sub-specialty care. Psychiatric beds were in great demand with mental health needs a number-one priority.

New Orleans Adolescent Hospital opened in June 2006 with ten pediatric psychiatric beds and 20 acute adult psychiatric beds formerly housed at the Medical Center of Louisiana at New Orleans (MCLANO). Access to care for the uninsured remains a great challenge. MCLANO continues to provide emergency services for this population from the New Orleans Centre, formerly the Lord and Taylor Department Store. Veterans Administration Hospital is operating ambulatory care clinics while the inpatient facility remains closed. An agreement between the Veterans Administration and Louisiana State University (LSU) Health Care Services Division is in negotiations for the building of a joint facility. Nearly a year later, private hospitals reported significant losses in earnings as a result of uncompensated-care expenditures, increased lengths of stay resulting from the absence of continuum of care providers such as nursing homes, and low Medicare Diagnostic Reimbursement Group (DRG) payments.

By early spring of 2008, there were nineteen primary-care clinics in Orleans Parish opened or reinvented (Greater New Orleans Community Data Center 2008). There were nine mobile units serving adults and children in Orleans and Jefferson Parishes, with additional mobile units slated for rollout in the near future. Crippled by significant layoffs and damage to its infrastructure, the New Orleans Health Department is operating only four of its nineteen clinics.

Four school-based health centers are operating, one in Orleans Parish and three in Jefferson Parish (Louisiana Public Health Institute 2007). Mental health services are available at community and school sites through primary-care clinics and the Metropolitan Human Service District (Louisiana Department of Health and Hospitals 2007). Federally funded (FEMA) mental health counseling services through Louisiana Spirit are provided in storm-affected areas across the state and metropolitan New Orleans.

This fledgling patchwork delivery effort, although commendable under the circumstances, constitutes only a fraction of pre-storm capacity. The city is largely without a mental health service model designed to address the tremendous need on a publicly available basis. Katrina survivors in all parishes and across all income levels indicate needing help to manage stress and overcome depression (Alfred 2008, 12). In June 2008, nearly three years after the storm, only 13, or 57 percent, of the state-licensed hospitals in New Orleans were open, compared to the 23 that were opened in 2005 before the storm (Liu and Plyer 2008, 71). It is hardly adequate to meet the current service delivery demands. Health workforce shortages also remain significant and are critical to infrastructure repair.

HEALTH WORKFORCE

According to some reports, primary-care physician availability for the insured population is now less of an issue. For the uninsured population, there are shortages of primary-care physicians, psychiatrists, and dentists. Nursing and pharmacy shortages have increased since the storm. Nursing support staff such as licensed practical nurses, certified nurse aids, and other support staff is also short. Academic institutions serving in the role of preparing a qualified workforce scurry to reestablish functionality.

LSU Health Science System is challenged to fulfill its dual missions of medical education and caring for the underserved. Both LSU and Tulane Medical schools are operating with stable student enrollment for incoming students. LSU Dental School remains in Baton Rouge. Dillard University will be back at its Gentilly campus, and Xavier University is open and operating. The three other colleges with schools of nursing in New Orleans—Charity Delgado, Holy Cross, and William Carey—are open.

However, in order to continue operating, most academic institutions have cut programs with faculty and staff layoffs. The open doors of these institutions are encouraging indeed, in a sea of daily disappointments and discouragement. Unfortunately, the pipeline between education and practice does not afford an immediate solution to the severe shortages of today. Some health professionals fed up with the struggles of recovery choose to leave. The health care workforce, as a major artery of the health care delivery system, continues to hemorrhage.

MENTAL HEALTH

Mental health needs are at the top of the chart in the aftermath of the disaster. The immediate stress and trauma experienced by many individuals are now manifesting in the form of depression and anxiety disorders. Individuals with chronic mental illness conditions are exacerbated in the absence of stability in their lives, treatment facilities, and medical providers. In a survey conducted of evacuated families still in Louisiana in February 2006, mental health problems were significant. The survey documented nearly half of the parents reporting behavior or emotional problems observed in their children after the storm (Abramson and Garfield 2006). Based on results from a standardized mental health screening tool, more than half of the mothers scored at a level consistent with a psychiatric diagnosis. The deputy coroner of Orleans Parish recorded almost a threefold increase in suicide rates, from 9 per 100,000 before Katrina to 26 per 100,000 in the four months after Katrina hit. In 2006, the murder rate was about the same as before the storm.

There are also reported increases in domestic violence cases. In a report from the *Journal of the American Medical Association,* only 22 of the 196 psychiatrists are practicing in New Orleans, with drastic reductions in inpatient beds (Weisler, Barbee, and Townsend 2006). The poor, the uninsured, the elderly, the homeless, and people of color are disproportionately impacted in the situations and circumstances they currently face in post-Katrina life.

HEALTHY REBUILDING AND
INVESTING IN HUMAN CAPITAL

In the healthy rebuilding of New Orleans and the entire Gulf Region, extraordinary leadership is needed from all sectors of government, the private sector, business community, nonprofits, academia, the faith-based community, and from citizens in general. The rebuilding of the region will require broad-based participation, commitment, and resources. Governmental funding and resources are essential, but rebuilding efforts will be greatly stymied without additional resources and assistance from the other societal sectors.

The entire region experienced what has been termed the worst disaster in our nation's history, and it is still dazed by the might of the impact. The wounds of destruction are visible and appear as gaping holes seen and felt throughout the region. The people of the region are substantially affected and need time and unprecedented support to assist in their healing and recovery. The most vulnerable received the greatest impact and are suffering disproportionately. These individuals need even more support and assistance as they attempt to piece their lives and communities back together. Investing in human capital in rebuilding lives, families, and communities is what is needed in the days that follow.

Another immense challenge, nearly one year after Katrina, is the redesign of a health care delivery system under very extraordinary circumstances, a feat Louisiana could not accomplish under normal conditions. While the Health Care Redesign Collaborative focuses on health systems redesign, Louisiana also grapples with parallel problems of the collapsed health care system in New Orleans, serious health workforce shortages, and the fiscal crisis experienced by the remaining operating hospitals within metropolitan New Orleans.

There is no one solution to this myriad of very complicated problems. The approaches and solutions needed are both long and short term and will more than likely require many years to be phased in. How will Louisiana establish the future political will to carry a long-range plan to fruition, when elected officials and policy makers serve four-year terms? There is no shortage of studies, reports, and expert recommendations on what needs to be done to fix the broken system. However, long-term commitments from federal, state, and local governments that transcend four-year terms of office are needed. The appropriate levels of accountability through monitoring and evaluation feedback loops with flexibility to change are also needed. Consistency in leadership and accountability at all levels of development, implementation, and evaluation are vital to the challenge of designing and building a system that is accessible, patient centered, efficient, quality driven, and cost effective. A most obvious need is a unified approach in the form of public policy and the available mechanisms and resources to accomplish such an unprecedented task.

The rebuilding of healthy communities in New Orleans will involve reestablishing schools, businesses, housing, transportation systems, infrastructure, and faith-based institutions. The difficult task faced by all who are impacted and involved in the rebuilding effort is to build better communities and systems in the face of such daunting challenges. A number of community-level planning processes have engaged homeowners and neighborhood associations in designing and planning their future neighborhoods. It is yet to be seen how this input will translate into public policy decisions and the allocation of resources.

Renters are less advantaged as the options for rental units are limited by the scarce availability of rental property and escalating costs. Public housing units have been closed to previous occupants, making it nearly impossible for the return of these individuals and families to New Orleans. Policy decisions regarding the repopulation of the city should include affordable housing options for renters and homeowners, mixed-use neighborhoods with ample green spaces for walking, recreation, and biking. All neighborhoods should be cleaned and free of environmental contaminants and hazardous substances.

Finally, sustainable employment opportunities with a living wage should be the central focus of policy decisions regarding the building of healthy communities. Addressing many of the social and economic determinants of health will go a long way in eliminating health disparities. This moment in history should be embraced as an unparalleled opportunity for change. In the resulting paradigm shift, the future New Orleans will be incompatible and incommensurate with what existed before the devastation.

REFERENCES

Alfred, Dana. 2008. *Progress for Some, Hope and Hardship for Many.* New Orleans: Louisiana Family Recovery Corps, May.
Annie E. Casey Foundation. 2006. *Kids Count Data Book: State Profiles of Child Well-Being.* Baltimore: Annie E. Casey Foundation.

Bring New Orleans Back Commission. 2006. "Action Plan for New Orleans: The New American City." Urban Planning Committee Report. New Orleans: Bring New Orleans Back Commission.

Centers for Disease Control. National Center for Health Statistics. 2000. "State Cancer Profiles. Louisiana Facts."

City of New Orleans Emergency Operations Center. 2006. "Rapid Population Estimate Project." January.

Foundation for the Mid South Indicator Web site. 1999. *Louisiana: Poverty Rate, by Age.* Available at www.fmsindicators.org.

Greater New Orleans Community Data Center. 2008. "Map & Directory of Primary Care Community Clinics in Orleans and Surrounding Parishes." February 29. Available at http://www.gnocdc.org/maps/orleans_clinics.pdf (accessed August 1, 2008).

Henry J. Kaiser Family Foundation. 2006. "Medicaid and the Uninsured." January.

Louisiana Department of Health and Hospitals. 2005. *2005 Louisiana Health Report Card.*

_____. 2007. *2006–2007 Annual Report of the Adolescent School Health Initiative.* Available at http://www.dhh.louisiana.gov/offices/reports.asp?ID=255&Detail=525 (accessed August 2, 2008).

Louisiana HIV/AIDS Quarterly Report. 2006. First Quarter.

Louisiana Public Health Institute. 2007. School-Based Health Centers in the New Orleans Metropolitan Area. Available at http://www.lphi.org/home2/section/3-30-32 -90-91/locations-and-map (accessed August 2, 2008).

National Center for Health Statistics. 2004. "Life Expectancy at Birth, by Year—United States, 1970–2003."

National Vital Statistics System. n.d. "Historical Trends in Breast Cancer Mortality Rates for Females, All Ages, 1982–2005."

Pastor, M., R. Bullard, J. Boyce, A. Fothergill, R. Morello-Frosch, and B. Wright (eds.). 2006. *In the Wake of the Storm.* New York: Russell Sage Foundation.

Quigley, B. 2006. "Who Was Left Behind Then and Who Is Being Left Behind Now?" *Dissident Voice.* February.

U.S. Bureau of the Census. 2000. "Supplementary Survey. Ranking Table—Percent of People Below Poverty Level in the Past 12 Months." Available at www.census.gov/ acs/www/Products/Ranking /2000 (accessed August 2, 2008)

_____. 2005. Federal Emergency Management Agency. Reported Locations of Katrina/ Rita Applicants from Louisiana, Mississippi, Alabama and Texas Disasters as of 10-31-05.

U.S. Department of Health and Human Services. 1985. "Report of the Secretary's Task Force on Black and Minority Health. DHHS publication No. (PHS). 1985."

Webb, S. 2004. "Development and Exploration of a Culturally-Enhanced Breast Health Measure and the Relationship of Selected Cultural Attributes to Knowledge, Beliefs, and Behaviors for Early Breast Cancer Detection Among African-American Women." Southern University Dissertation. May.

Weisler, R. H., J. G. Barbee, IV, and M. H. Townsend. 2006. "Mental Health and Recovery in the Gulf Coast After Hurricanes Katrina and Rita. *Journal of the American Medical Association* 296 (5): 585–588.

Zedlewski, S. 2006. *Pre-Katrina New Orleans: The Backdrop.* The Urban Institute. April.

CHAPTER 7

MAKING THE CASE FOR COMMUNITY-BASED LABORATORIES

A New Strategy for Environmental Justice

Earthea Nance

This chapter introduces community-based environmental laboratories as a new paradigm for achieving environmental justice. The existing environmental justice paradigm, rooted in the ideology and methodology of the civil rights movement, has succeeded in carrying the environmental justice movement to this point, but continued progress will require a diversity of approaches. The post-disaster context of New Orleans, which simultaneously presents a long history of environmental injustice and the largest city-rebuilding effort in U.S. history, is an ideal site for observing the possibilities for community-based laboratories.

THE POST-KATRINA ENVIRONMENT

In New Orleans, testing by the U.S. Environmental Protection Agency (EPA) and the Natural Resources Defense Council (NRDC) following Hurricanes Katrina and Rita revealed the presence of a range of contaminants in soils and sediment at levels high enough to pose potential health risks to residents (EPA-LDEQ 2006; Solomon 2006). As unsettling as these results are, even more disturbing is the fact that little is being done to clean up the contamination. Most residents who want to know more about their environmental risk exposure do not have access to the information they need to protect themselves and their families. Many people would benefit from this information.

Given the uncertain environmental health risks in many areas of the city and the thousands of individuals who are rebuilding their homes and coming into frequent contact with potential hazards, people ideally should have direct access to nonprofit environmental testing services. People should also have access to household-level inspection and remediation assistance to help them clean up any contamination that is discovered, restore their property, and monitor the results over time. People should also be given the opportunity for training in how to inspect their house and property, proper respirator use, safe work practices, how to take samples, and local environmental conditions. These three key services—testing, remediation, and education—could be provided by community-based laboratories on a sliding scale. By offering on-demand, direct services to residents, community-based laboratories would fill a niche that private for-profit and university laboratories cannot fill.

Community-based laboratories could be a vital new strategy in the struggle for environmental justice. Bringing science directly into people's neighborhoods gives them another tool in their struggle to deal with environmental injustices of the past—injustices such as the contamination of communities along the Mississippi River between New Orleans and Baton Rouge, an intense chemical corridor known as Cancer Alley (Nixon 2001). Community-based laboratories would also give people the capacity to prevent future environmental injustices before they get started. With community-based laboratories, residents could better understand and respond to the potential environmental health risks in their homes and neighborhoods. Sooner is better than later. If community-based laboratories had been available 25 years ago, the residents of Cancer Alley would have been able to make informed decisions about where to work and live, and they would have been armed with analytical information early on in the fight against polluting industries. Community-based laboratories also make sense from the viewpoint of ecological democracy and sustainable urban development. These principles are based on the democratization of information, technology, and decision making to achieve more equitable outcomes in terms of environmental health impacts (Hester 2006; McGranahan and Satterthwaite 2000; McGranahan et al. 2001).

New Orleans presents a unique combination of historical, social, political, economic, and environmental circumstances that make it the ideal place to introduce the notion of community-based laboratories. The Deep South region, Louisiana in particular, has a well-documented history of environmental injustice, whose primary form has been the inequitable siting of locally unwanted land uses in neighborhoods of color and poverty (Bullard et al. 2007; Bullard 2005). These neighborhoods have been constructed near or on top of landfills and have been disproportionately targeted as sites for landfills, incinerators, and other polluting land uses. A case in point is the Agriculture Street Landfill, on which a housing subdivision and elementary school were constructed. In 1994, the EPA declared the area a Superfund site, one of the 1,275 locations across the country that have been contaminated by hazardous waste and are in need of clean-up because of a risk to human health and the environment (Agency for Toxic Substances and Disease Registry n.d.; Lyttle 2003). Other examples are the New Orleans East neighborhood, which is riddled with landfills and illegal dumps (Malek-Wiley 2008; USA Today 2007), and the disproportionate exposure and overrepresentation of African-American residents in areas of New Orleans with high lead contamination (Campanella and Mielke 2008).

The storms of 2005 turned up and distributed contaminant-laden bottom sediments from local water bodies, and scattered unknown contaminants that had been stored in barrels at industrial sites throughout the region (Esworthy et al. 2005). As a consequence, all areas touched by the contaminated flood waters are potentially contaminated. For the first time in the history of the United States, the public is facing environmental hazards of unprecedented scope and uncertainty. An unknown cocktail of polluted material has blanketed a metropolitan region already unable to enforce environmental regulations effectively and unable to protect its most vulnerable population groups. It is time for a new strategy to cope with this set of interrelated problems.

THE PRE-KATRINA ENVIRONMENT

Any notion of environmental injustice in New Orleans must be grounded in an understanding of the injustices of pre-Katrina conditions. In some cases, drums of hazardous waste were allowed to sit on industrial sites throughout the region instead of being properly disposed under the Resource, Conservation, and Recovery Act. These industries were effectively allowed to transfer their environmental costs onto nearby residents, who were exposed to higher health risks without their knowledge or approval. Careless industrial practices, lax enforcement of environmental regulations, numerous spills, leaking tanks, improper waste disposal, and past common use of dangerous pesticides, solvents, and heavy metals have resulted in widespread soil pollution and high background contaminant levels (especially lead and diesel-range organics) as documented by the EPA, the NRDC, and independent researchers from Tulane University (Laidlaw and Mielke 2004). Many of these sites could be considered unidentified brownfields with no plans for clean-up, representing another tacit transfer of environmental burdens onto the population without their knowledge or approval.

Following slavery, African-descended people in the region were forced (by law) to live in low-lying areas such as the Lower Ninth Ward, which put them at higher risk of flooding and water-related contamination. This represented another tacit transfer of environmental burdens onto specific population groups. Access to flood protection (levees, insurance, evacuation, and so on) was unevenly distributed, leaving many of these same communities at higher environmental risk today even after the construction of the levee system. Recent maps issued by the Army Corps reveal disproportionate levels of risk still faced by different New Orleans neighborhoods (Army Corps of Engineers n.d.; Advocates for Environmental Human Rights 2007). The areas of the city most at risk of flooding—New Orleans East, Lower Ninth Ward, and Gentilly—are primarily inhabited by people of color.

In addition to these historically rooted environmental injustices, Hurricanes Katrina and Rita brought a continuation of injustice. Poor people and people of color were more vulnerable during the disaster (Pastor et al. 2006; Mann 2006; Hartman and Squires 2006). They were impacted and displaced by the storms and floods at disproportionately higher levels, and they received lower levels of government assistance. Women, the elderly, the disabled, the carless, and non-English speakers were also disproportionately affected. Those who returned to New Orleans after the storms were potentially exposed to contaminants that were released into the air and water and spread across the soils and sediments. Some of these contaminants were perceptible (by sight and smell), but many were not immediately perceptible. Access to environmental information is critical because of the possibility of widespread contamination, significant hot spots, and cumulative risk. Without this information, people have little incentive to mobilize around the environmental issues that directly affect their lives. This is, however, a continuation of the status quo—they never have this information until it is too late. The reports of exposure to dangerous levels of formaldehyde by inhabitants of FEMA trailers are a case in point. The injustices only continued to pile up after the disaster, as the inequitable distribution of impacts became clear and as the government initiated a botched response to the disaster. Soil/sediment and air were the primary mediums of contamination. Mold levels in the air reached unprecedented levels for months after the storms and continued to be a concern in the most devastated areas for over a year (Reichel 2006). But there are no clear-cut maximum contaminant levels for mold, so people were not able to understand the risks faced by mold exposure. In the case of mold, there is not enough science to guide clean-up and restoration action.

Based on independent soil sampling throughout New Orleans, the EPA and NRDC agreed that the most widespread contaminants in soils and sediments are arsenic, lead, diesel fuel, and benzo(a)pyrene (EPA-LDEQ 2006; Solomon and Rotkin-Ellman 2006; EPA 2007; Fields 2007). All of these contaminants have known health impacts and health-based screening and guideline levels. But despite agreement about the presence of contamination, the EPA and NRDC disagreed strongly about the need for clean-up and the risks faced by returning residents. While the NRDC and other organizations issued strong warnings to returning residents (Solomon and Rotkin-Ellman 2006; PEC-AEHR-PSR 2005), the EPA declared it had no responsibility or authority to sample, test, or clean up private property no matter how bad the contamination was (many environmental activists have noted the EPA's similar response to the September 11 disaster in New York) (Ware 2006; Elkins 2006).

In the case of soil contamination, people are frustrated by the lack of clean-up action in the face of available scientific information, which only perpetuates their mistrust of government after the failure of the federally funded levees in New Orleans. One year after the disaster, all parts of the New Orleans drinking water system had been certified by officials, but as of late 2008, confidence in the water system has not been restored. The condition of the water distribution system and the quality of the water continue to be monitored by environmental groups and other concerned nongovernmental organizations (Solomon 2007). All of the city's sewer pumps are still in a state of disrepair three years after the storms. These ongoing substandard conditions contribute to an overall lack of confidence in government. In many cases, people have taken it upon themselves to recover from the disaster, relying on family, friends, neighbors, volunteers, community groups, and nonprofit organizations for assistance. As a result, the civil society sector in New Orleans has become one of the most active and well-organized in the United States.

The EPA's sampling program documented widespread contamination and potential health threats in general, but residents still do not have access to enough household-level guidance on what to do if contamination is present or suspected in their home, workplace, school, or park. The cost of education, sampling, testing, and remediation is prohibitively high. Only wealthier people can afford to pay upwards of $500 to have their property tested for a range of contaminants. Most people have no choice but to pay for these risks with their (and their children's) lives and health, which is a continuation of the status quo of injustice.

The EPA and the Louisiana Department of Environmental Quality failed to establish a program of sampling and testing homes that were potentially contaminated after Katrina. Moreover, the sampling protocols used by the EPA are suspected of underreporting the actual level of contaminant exposure. While EPA samples typically draw several inches of soil, the primary concern in terms of human exposure is surface contamination, which only occurs in the top few centimeters of soil (Agwaramgbo 2008; Mielke et al. 2007). Deeper samples have the effect of diluting the overall result. In addition to this deficient sampling effort, there are systemic flaws in the environmental regulatory system. Nothing in the regulations requires clean-up. When contamination is found, all that is required is further testing and monitoring. And when clean-up is done, benchmarks are negotiated because there are no established clean-up standards. This means that citizens and clean-up workers cannot take proper precautions and make informed decisions about working in the area, moving back to their homes, and rebuilding. The Community Right-to-Know Act of 1986 substantiated people's right to know about the contaminants, toxics, and hazards in their immediate environment, their neighborhood, and their workplace. Beyond this, people should have access to technical assistance to decide what to do if contamination is found on their property, in their home, in their workplace, or in their neighborhood. This is especially true in New Orleans, where the potential risk is high and where the EPA's environmental protection efforts have been lacking (GAO 2007).

A comprehensive assessment of the storm's impacts (Pastor et al. 2006) found that the environmental vulnerability of poor and black New Orleans neighborhoods is systematically ignored by policy makers, the media, and the public. The report by Pastor et al. views the Katrina disaster as an acute version of an ongoing crisis and finds that race was the most significant predictor of environmental disparities in many studies. People of color and poverty were more likely to be vulnerable, marginalized, and underserved by governments and relief agencies, but other segments of the population—such as the elderly, women, immigrants, and the disabled—were also vulnerable. The Pastor et al. report concludes that disaster preparedness and environmental policy are both in need of deep reform and that environmental justice principles should guide policy to instill fairness in terms of social justice and economic equity.

Several conclusions can be drawn from this overall state of affairs. First, the status quo of not knowing about environmental hazards is unacceptable because it facilitates the unjust transfer of environmental burdens onto vulnerable population groups. Second, existing institutions for dealing with environmental contamination in New Orleans have systematically failed to protect people of color, the poor, and other vulnerable population groups affected by the storms and flood. These same institutions cannot be expected to change suddenly. Third, governmental agencies make decisions and take action in the public interest in principle, but in practice these agencies do not represent all citizens. This is a crisis of representation, a crisis of democracy.

STRATEGIES AND TACTICS OF THE ENVIRONMENTAL JUSTICE MOVEMENT

Many people recognized the crisis of democracy long ago when the U.S. environmental justice movement emerged in the early 1980s (Bullard 2005; Bullard et al. 2007). The core strategy of the movement's first 25 years has been to extend democracy by increasing representation and compelling existing institutions to be more inclusive. Tactics include creating new forms of representation, primarily environmental nongovernmental organizations and grassroots groups; producing alternative reports to counteract "official stories" and shape public opinion; exerting pressure on Congress, the EPA, and industry via lobbying, the media, and so on; and, most important, litigating.

The core environmental justice strategy has resulted in much successful litigation and many settlements, as well as the assessment of fines, sentences, and required clean-ups. The environmental justice problem has become more visible as a policy issue as a result of the environmental justice movement. And where pressure is exerted, government agencies and industries are made to be more accountable. But a number of critical observations should also be mentioned. First, only the worst-case instances of environmental injustice make it into the media or the courts. And by definition, these cases are only examined after the damage is done. The class-action lawsuit against the Murphy Oil Refinery in New Orleans is a case in point. Also, recognition of the environmental problems in New Orleans appears to be decreasing, not increasing, as the severity of the environmental hazard is publicly denied by authorities even in the face of their own evidence. A good example of this is the EPA's assurance that it is safe for residents to return even though the EPA's sampling results show contamination hot spots at tens, hundreds, and even thousands of times higher than screening and health-based guideline levels. The EPA appears to be relying on widespread ignorance on the part of the public. How else could it make such a claim?

Despite the success of the environmental justice movement in general, accountability in New Orleans also appears to be getting weaker, not stronger, as exemplified by the waiving of FEMA Road Home reconstruction funds from environmental clean-up requirements (Elkins 2006). This allows and condones reconstruction on contaminated sites, showing no accountability for imposing environmental health risks onto the unknowing public. And despite the clearly increased environmental risk that now exists in the region, the public's ability to mobilize around environmental issues in New Orleans is probably lower, not higher. The many barriers to mobilizing include lack of access to and lack of understanding of environmental information, competing priorities and needs in a disaster context, and widespread displacement of residents and disintegration of communities. The existing core strategy of the environmental justice movement—largely based on exposing and litigating the most egregious cases—is more important than ever after Katrina. But it also needs to be supplemented and complemented with new strategies.

Two central concepts from the international development field should be brought to bear on the environmental justice issues and crisis of democracy problems facing people in New Orleans: participatory development and appropriate technology. Under the principle of participatory development, infrastructure and other urban services can be co-produced by civil society and the state in order to increase citizen voice and accountability of government. The principle of appropriate technology is based on diversifying the infrastructure options available for the purpose of meeting locally defined needs and improving environmental health conditions on the ground. Participatory development and appropriate technology should be considered key elements of a new strategy to address the overwhelming environmental problems present in New Orleans. In New Orleans, the most vulnerable population groups shoulder most of the environmental burdens, and the conventional technologies for addressing these environmental problems (such as large-scale sampling and testing at accredited laboratories, extensive borehole drilling and testing, pump and treat systems, soil excavation and disposal methods, bioremediation treatment techniques) are extremely expensive and require cadres of highly trained experts and complicated, expensive equipment. The existing solutions to the problem are out of reach for the average citizen, not to mention poor and low-income citizens. Furthermore, the existing environmental policy context offers solutions for clean-up of commercial properties (such as the EPA Brownfields Program) and clean-up of extremely contaminated sites (such as the EPA Superfund Program) but no systematic solutions for the clean-up of residential properties that pose health risks to children at a range of contamination levels.

Community-based laboratories constitute a new strategy that fills the existing environmental policy gap and that is based on the principles of participatory development and appropriate technology. The strategy addresses contamination at the grassroots level using low-cost technologies that are implemented by community-based organizations. The strategy complements the core environmental justice strategy (which gives people direct access to law/legal protection) by giving people direct access to science. Community-based labs attempt to change the status quo of not knowing about environmental hazards, the status quo of environmental science and technology being out of reach and unaffordable, and the status quo of people having to rely on government agencies and private industries that have systematically failed them in the past. Community-based laboratories would offer environmental testing

directly to residents at sliding-scale prices, as well as appropriate household-level remediation techniques that could be implemented by residents at the household level.
Community-based laboratories would also serve local organizations that are working
with New Orleans communities. These organizations need access to a nonprofit laboratory to assess the extent of household contamination and to monitor the long-
term effectiveness of a range of remediation and restoration practices, including
conventional techniques (for example, material removal, scrubbing) and experimental techniques (for example, phyto- and bioremediation) at sites they have already established. Environmental education and technical advice is the third fundamental
component of the community-based lab strategy. Increasing the general level of environmental literacy is an important element of the strategy.

Community-based labs could address the previously mentioned crisis in democracy
in three ways. First, they would democratize information by offering environmental
information and direct access to technical advisors in people's communities. Second,
community-based labs would democratize technology by offering people intermediate
technologies and appropriate solutions they can control and afford without only relying on government agencies and private firms. And third, community-based labs
would democratize decision making by offering people more decision-making power
so that their status as "victims" is not reproduced in the disaster management and reconstruction process.

In summary, the U.S. environmental justice (EJ) movement has responded to the
race, class, and environmental dimensions of inequality. The core strategy driving action has been primarily reactive, based on litigation after the damage is done, with
the overall objective being to extend democracy to the victims. A new strategy is proposed that views the crisis as rooted in democracy itself along multiple dimensions
including race, class, environment, gender, age, citizenship status, disability, and so
on, and with an expanded objective of empowering the public to take action to defend their health and protect their property. The new strategy moves beyond the civil
rights discourse of the U.S. EJ movement and adopts the broader perspective embraced by the global environmental health movement, which includes participatory
development, appropriate technology, and human rights. The new strategy is proactive rather than reactive, based on community-driven sampling, testing, and remediation. Combined with the core EJ strategy, community-based labs can fulfill the
same fundamental goal of extending democracy to previously marginalized, excluded, and victimized segments of the population by legitimizing the role of people
in science and the role of scientists in communities. Both strategies together will
likely be stronger and more effective than either one alone.

COMMUNITY-BASED LABORATORIES—A NEW
STRATEGY FOR ENVIRONMENTAL JUSTICE

Under the current status quo, whole segments of the population do not know about
the environmental conditions in their homes, workplaces, schools, and parks. People

everywhere have the right to this information as an extension of the Community Right-to-Know Act of 1986. One principle behind community-based labs is that people should demand this information and come to expect it.

The current status quo in the environmental testing industry is a high-tech, high-cost operation attuned to the needs and pocketbooks of the military, the government, universities, and large industries. It is inaccessible to people even though individual residential properties represent the largest number of potential clients. People everywhere should have access to affordable and reliable environmental testing facilities and scientific advisers in order to protect and defend themselves and their property. The community-based lab strategy is based on the principle that the environmental testing industry should be directly accessible to the public.

And finally, the current status quo gives government and its agents a corner on the market for remediation and clean-up, having established a system of high-tech, high-cost approaches that do not serve the entire population. Equal protection under environmental law does not exist because many environmental laws are not enforced in poor neighborhoods and communities of color. People everywhere should have direct access to appropriate remediation technologies that can be implemented at the household level. Implementing the proposed community-based lab strategy will put these technologies into widespread use and will contribute greatly to overall clean-up of the urban environment.

Several early innovators of community-based remediation have appeared in New Orleans, including the Deep South Center for Environmental Justice (DSCEJ), Lead Lab, Common Ground Bioremediation Project, and the People's Environmental Center (PEC). The DSCEJ is a university- and community-based nonprofit organization that has been in operation since 1992. As one of the leading centers for environmental justice in the United States, DSCEJ focuses on curriculum development and community projects in the areas of environmental clean-up and hazard materials training. DSCEJ's model is known as the communiversity, which brings scholarship and grassroots knowledge together to overcome the injustices along the Mississippi River Corridor and throughout the Gulf Coast. Since Katrina, DSCEJ has prioritized the environmental remediation of neighborhoods through its award-winning Safe Way Back Home program. This is a program that residents who are interested in remediating their property can apply for directly. The process involves a statement of the criteria for neighborhood clean-up guidelines, a written application, a signed consent form, and a job order. DSCEJ has successfully remediated household properties using soil removal techniques followed by placement of clean soil and sod.

Lead Lab is a nonprofit organization established by Howard Mielke and colleagues of Tulane University's Center for Bioenvironmental Research. The need for a nonprofit organization grew out of Mielke's applied research on lead contamination in New Orleans' soil and its impacts on children. Lead Lab was established as a resource for conducting neighborhood-scale remediation projects that were sites for Mielke's research program. With Lead Lab, Mielke and his colleagues were able to successfully remediate households by placing clean soil and sod on top of contaminated soil. His approach also included pre-and post-remediation monitoring of lead levels in soil and blood.

The Common Ground Bioremediation Project was established immediately after Katrina by Common Ground Relief. With thousands of volunteers from across the United States, Common Ground has been perhaps the most successful grassroots startup in post-Katrina New Orleans. The group's main project areas are medical clinics, house gutting, and remediation. Common Ground's remediation approach primarily involved the use of plants, fungi, and worms to draw contaminants from soil.

The People's Environmental Center was established as a community-based environmental center after Katrina. Its goals are to offer environmental education, laboratory testing, and remediation services to residents and other nonprofit groups. Professors, environmental professionals, students, and residents are involved in the PEC. The PEC is striving to become one of the first nonprofit, community-based laboratories offering direct access to analytical testing of air, water, soil, and mold samples; household-level remediation, inspection, monitoring, and technical assistance; and workshops and training about how to take samples and understanding local environmental conditions, test results, and health impacts.

These early innovators are part of a network of experts and organizations focused on environmental contamination in New Orleans, including the Louisiana Environmental Action Network, Louisiana Bucket Brigade, the Natural Resources Defense Council, Wilma Subra Environmental, Inc., the Sierra Club, Tulane Bioenvironmental Research Center, Louisiana State University (LSU) Agricultural Center, Dillard University, and others. A common challenge that has emerged is the lack of institutional infrastructure for nonprofit laboratories. There is no model to follow, no systems in place for scientists and engineers to work directly with community groups, no federal support, and few well-developed intermediate remediation technologies. The existing model for nonprofit environmental organizations, based on advocacy, public education, and litigation, is easier to follow and is more widely practiced.

Another unique challenge is the severe shortage of local expertise in post-Katrina New Orleans. Funders often want to see local hiring, but the reality is that New Orleans has a significant shortage of local expertise. There needs to be recognition that this problem pre-existed the disaster. Organizations should not be penalized for using outside workers. The free market funding rationale is another challenge faced by almost all nonprofit organizations. Nonprofit start-ups follow an economic logic in which many small start-ups compete in the philanthropy market for extremely limited funding. This model can create disincentives to coalition building. It can also slow the growth of individual organizations and prevent any one group from getting large enough to achieve financial stability. With very limited ability to hire permanent staff, the success of many nonprofit organizations is tied to the personal circumstances of its founding members. And despite the low funding levels, funders still expect significant, visible results over a short time with very small grants. "Grassroots" effectively means operating in a constantly underfunded condition.

CONSOLIDATING THE NEW STRATEGY

Interest in establishing community-based laboratories is expected to grow fastest in areas where lax environmental enforcement and environmental health issues are well-documented, such as along the U.S.-Mexican border and in the Deep South, including New Orleans. In addition, most older U.S. cities, including New Orleans, have widespread lead-contaminated soils as a result of past use of leaded gasoline and paint (Laidlaw). The experience in New Orleans thus far has yielded some important lessons. The most significant to date is the lack of nonprofit funding to support community-based environmental initiatives in general, and community-based laboratories specifically. The EPA's Environmental Justice Small Grant Program issues on average less than $20,000 per grant annually (based on 1,030 grants totaling $18,780,545 since 1994), and the grants carry high administrative burdens that make them difficult for some community groups to manage. Philanthropic organizations such as the Rockefeller Philanthropy Advisors have shown leadership in supporting community-based laboratories through its Gulf Coast Fund for Community Renewal and Ecological Health, but these grants have also been very small (on the order of $20,000–$40,000 each).

To be viable, community-based laboratories need grants of $100,000–$500,000 in order to establish themselves, attract the scientists and engineers they need, and leverage adequate equipment and instruments. Recognizing this problem, the city of New Orleans is proposing to set aside special recovery funds that will be distributed to local groups for the purpose of remediating neighborhoods. Given the city's well-documented history of childhood lead poisoning and recent research that links lead poisoning to crime (Nevin 2007), the city's Lead Safe Communities Initiative proposes to focus on lead contamination. The initiative intends to fund the development of lead-safe areas. A lead-safe area is defined as a contiguous area in which all sources of lead contamination—soil, dust, paint, water systems, consumer products—have been effectively mitigated and where a lead-safe level has been established, monitored, and maintained. New Orleans' Lead Safe Communities Initiative was inspired by Norway's national action plan for lead remediation, which sets lead-safe levels that are protective of children and requires remediation of all areas inhabited by children, including parks, schools, playgrounds, and homes (Ottesen 2008).

The New Orleans program seeks to enhance the capacity and capability of the community to reduce the risk and level of poisoning from lead-hazard conditions. The objective of the Lead Safe Community Initiative is both to develop this local capacity and to effectively develop model lead-safe areas in New Orleans. New Orleans is interested in developing a cadre of local organizations that are capable and qualified to contribute to environmental remediation of lead contaminants both inside and outside the home. Nonprofit and for-profit groups with expertise and interest in creating lead-safe communities are encouraged to form consortiums to ensure that they have all of the necessary qualifications and resources to meet the objective, which is the creation of model lead-safe areas. Nonprofit environmental groups are especially encouraged to respond in collaboration with universities, private firms, unions, laboratories, foundations, and other entities. By incorporating rather than outsourcing the analytical and remediation components, and by working directly with residents in a defined community, these consortiums would effectively implement the community-based laboratory model. The city of New Orleans is also supporting the creation of phytoremediation research gardens (contaminant extraction from soil by plants) by partnering with local non-profit groups to conduct field tests on the use of sunflowers and other plants. A total of $4 million is being proposed for the Lead Safe remediation and phyoremediation research efforts, enough to make a significant local impact by establishing the viability of a new paradigm for community-based clean-up. These initiatives combined with the ongoing efforts of New Orleans' environmental organizations make New Orleans the most innovative site in the nation for community-based remediation.

CONCLUSION

Community-based laboratories have been presented as an innovation in the environmental justice movement. The essence of the innovation is bringing scientists and engineers into communities to make environmental testing widely available on a not-for-profit basis. This approach is similar to the community-clinic model, but broad support including federal and state funding will have to be made available for the innovation to succeed at scale. This will require a transition away from a liability paradigm, in which clean-up is perpetually delayed out of fear of admitting that contamination exists, and a willingness to accept the need for widespread clean-up, public education about environmental contamination, and access to affordable remediation services at the neighborhood level. The rebuilding of New Orleans offers an ideal opportunity for community-based laboratories to emerge. As a result of Hurricanes Katrina and Rita, New Orleans is now among the most well-organized cities in the United States. Neighborhood-based organizations and national nonprofits proliferate across the city, helping people to rebuild, monitoring and watch-dogging government agencies, and experimenting with new ways to deal with environmental hazards. And like all other major urban centers, New Orleans' soil is contaminated with legacy contaminants that were once in widespread legal use, such as lead. These contaminants, but lead in particular, are directly harmful to children and must be controlled. People have the right to know about the contaminants in their environment, and community-based laboratories offer a new instrument in the struggle for environmental justice. Community-based laboratories increase people's access to knowledge by putting them in direct contact with scientists and engineers and by giving them affordable techniques for clean-up. While past environmental justice struggles have taken place largely on the streets and in courtrooms, the future site of environmental justice may be in community-based laboratories.

REFERENCES

Advocates for Environmental Human Rights. 2007. "Flood Levels During Hurricane Katrina, by Neighborhood." December 11. Available at http://www.ehumanrights .org/media_newsroom_news_releases.html (accessed July 29, 2008).

Agency for Toxic Substances and Disease Registry. n.d. "Public Health Assessment: Agriculture Street Landfill." Available at http://www.atsdr.cdc.gov/hac/PHA/agriculture street/asl_p1.html (accessed July 29, 2008).

Agwaramgbo, L. 2008. "Lead Mobility and Bioavailability in Three Louisiana Soils: Implications of Its Bioaccumulation in Edible Plants and Health Risks." Presented at the 2nd Annual National Symposium on Race, Place, and the Environment After Katrina, New Orleans, May 15–18. Available at http://www.dscej.org (accessed July 29, 2008).

Army Corps of Engineers. n.d. "IPET Risk and Reliability Report: Interactive Maps." Available at http://nolarisk.usace.army.mil (accessed July 29, 2008).

Bullard, R. D. (ed.). 2005. *The Quest for Environmental Justice: Human Rights and the Politics of Pollution.* San Francisco: Sierra Club Books.

Bullard, R. D., P. Mohai, R. Saha, and B. Wright (eds.). 2007. *Toxic Wastes and Race at Twenty, 1987–2007.* Cleveland: United Church of Christ.

Campanella, R., and H. W. Mielke. 2008. "Human Geography of New Orleans' High-Lead Geochemical Setting." *Journal of Environmental Geochemistry and Health* 30 (6): 531–540.

Elkins, S. 2006. "Notice of Finding of No Significant Impact and Notice of Intent to Request Release of Grant Funds." Baton Rouge: Office of Community Development.

Environmental Protection Agency. 2007. "Citizen's Guide to Lead Issues: New Orleans Area Agencies." Dallas: Environmental Protection Agency.

Environmental Protection Agency and Louisiana Department of Environmental Quality. 2006. "Summary Results of Sediment Sampling Conducted by the Environmental Protection Agency in Response to Hurricanes Katrina and Rita." Available at http://www.epa.gov/katrina/testresults (accessed July 29, 2008).

Esworthy, R., L. J. Schierow, C. Copeland, and L. Luther. 2005. *Cleanup After Katrina: Environmental Considerations.* Congressional Research Service. No. RL33115. Washington, DC: Library of Congress.

Fields, L., A. Huang, G. Solomon, M. Rotkin-Ellman, and P. Simms. 2007. *Arsenic-Laced Schools and Playgrounds Put New Orleans Children at Risk.* Natural Resources Defense Council, Inc.

Government Accountability Office. 2007. *Hurricane Katrina: EPA's Current and Future Environmental Protection Efforts Could Be Enhanced by Addressing Issues and Challenges Faced on the Gulf Coast.* Report to Congressional Committees. No. GAO-07-651. Washington, DC: Government Accountability Office.

Hartman, C., and G. D. Squires (eds.). 2006. *There Is No Such Thing As a Natural Disaster: Race, Class, and Hurricane Katrina.* New York: Routledge Press.

Hester, R. T. 2006. *Design for Ecological Democracy.* Cambridge, MA: MIT Press.

Laidlaw, M. A. S. "Association Between Soil Lead and Blood Lead." Available at http://urbanleadpoisoning.com/maps.html (accessed July 29, 2008).

Lyttle, A. 2003. "Agriculture Street Landfill: Environmental Justice Case Study." Available at http://www.umich.edu/~snre492/Jones/agstreet.htm (accessed July 29, 2008).

Malek-Wiley, D. 2008. "Trails of Trash: Landfills." Presented at the 2nd Annual National Symposium on Race, Place, and the Environment After Katrina, New Orleans, May 15–18. Available at http://www.dscej.org (accessed July 29, 2008).

Mann, E. 2006. *Katrina's Legacy: White Racism and Black Reconstruction in New Orleans and the Gulf Coast.* Los Angeles: Frontlines Press.

McGranahan, G., and D. Satterthwaite. 2000. "Environmental Health or Ecological Sustainability? Reconciling the Brown and Green Agendas in Urban Development." In C. Pugh (ed.). *Sustainable Cities in Developing Countries: Theory and Practice at the Millennium.* London: Earthscan Publications.

McGranahan, G., P. Jacobi, J. Songsore, C. Surjadi, and M. Kjellen. 2001. *The Citizens At Risk: From Urban Sanitation to Sustainable Cities.* London: Stockholm Environmental Institute and Earthscan Publications.

Mielke, H. W., G. Wang, C. R. Gonzales, E. T. Powell, B. Le, and V. N. Quach. 2004. "PAHs and Metals in Soils of Inner City and Suburban New Orleans, Louisiana, USA." *Environmental Toxicology and Pharmacology* 18:243–247.

Mielke, H. W., E. T. Powell, C. R. Gonzales, P. W. Mielke, Jr., R. T. Ottesen, and M. Langedal. 2006. "New Orleans Soil Lead (Pb) Cleanup Using Mississippi River Alluvium: Need, Feasibility, and Cost." *Environmental Science and Technology* 40 (8): 2784–2789.

Mielke, H. W., E. T. Powell, C. R. Gonzales, and P. W. Mielke, Jr. 2007. "Potential Lead on Play Surfaces: Evaluation of the 'PLOPS' Sampler as a New Tool for Primary Lead Prevention." *Environmental Research* 103 (2): 154–159.

Nevin, R. 2007. "Understanding International Crime Trends: The Legacy of Preschool Lead Exposure." *Journal of Environmental Research* 104 (3): 315–336.

Nixon, R. 2001. "Toxic Gumbo: In the 'Cancer Belt,' Louisiana Black Communities Fight Industrial Polluters." *SeeingBlack.com.* Available at http://seeingblack.com/x040901/toxic_gumbo.shtml (accessed July 29, 2008).

Ottesen, R. T. n.d. "Soil Pollution in Day-Care Centers and Playgrounds in Oslo, Norway: National Action Plan For Mapping And Remediation." Available at http://www.ngu.no/upload/Arrangement/Internasjonale%20dager%202008%20-%20foredrag/Pollution_Ottesen.pdf (accessed July 29, 2008).

Ottesen, R. T., J. Alexander, M. Langedal, T. Haugland, and E. Høygaard. 2008. "Soil Pollution in Day-Care Centers and Playgrounds in Norway: National Action Plan for Mapping and Remediation." *Environmental Geochemistry and Health* 30 (6): 623–637.

Pastor, M., R. D. Bullard, J. K. Boyce, A. Fothergill, R. Morello-Frosch, and B. Wright (eds.). 2006. *In the Wake of the Storm: Environment, Disaster, and Race After Katrina.* New York: Russell Sage Foundation.

People's Hurricane Relief Fund (PEC), Advocates for Environmental Human Rights (AEHR), and Physicians for Social Responsibility (PSR). 2005. "We Have the Right to Return to Healthy and Safe Neighborhoods." New Orleans (pamphlet produced and distributed in New Orleans after Katrina).

Reichel, C. 2006. *Mold Removal Guidelines for Your Flooded Home.* Disaster Information Resources Pub. 2949-B. New Orleans: Louisiana State University Agricultural Center.

Solomon, G. M. 2007. *Drinking Water Quality in New Orleans, June–October 2006.* New York: Natural Resources Defense Council.

Solomon, G. M., and M. Rotkin-Ellman. 2006. *Contaminants in New Orleans Sediment: An Analysis of EPA Data.* New York: Natural Resources Defense Council.

USA Today. 2007. "Katrina Debris Adds to Illegal Dumps." March 26. Available at http://www.usatoday.com/news/nation/2007-03-25-katrina-dumps_N.htm (accessed July 29, 2008).

Ware, P. 2006. "Hazardous Waste: Sediment from Katrina Poses Little Risk, EPA Says in Final Summary of Sampling." *Bureau of National Affairs.* No. 160.

PART III

EQUITABLE REBUILDING
AND RECOVERY

CHAPTER 8

POST-KATRINA PROFITEERING

The New Big Easy

Rita J. King

In Katrina's devastating immediate aftermath, business as usual was suspended. The Federal Emergency Management Agency (FEMA), crippled by cutbacks and gutted of personnel, faced the job of finding qualified companies to help with basic and pressing needs. There was no time, FEMA said, to solicit and weigh bids, and so a more recent variation of "business as usual" took over: The lucrative contracts to clean up New Orleans and the Gulf Coast went to a bevy of familiar faces, some of the same corporations who have "cleaned up," literally and figuratively, in Afghanistan and Iraq. The lack of a competitive bidding system in the earliest days and continuous chaos on the Gulf Coast hindered the effort to impose any meaningful accountability on those companies staking claim to the billions in federal recovery dollars.

By the first anniversary of Katrina, Congress had appropriated $85 billion for hurricane relief, various foreign governments had contributed around $100 million, and FEMA's Disaster Relief Fund had received $36.5 billion for Katrina and $1.5 billion for Hurricanes Rita and Wilma (Congressional Testimony from Department of Homeland Security 2006). Administered primarily by FEMA and the Army Corps of Engineers, a chunk of that money was divvied up into thousands of contracts for local, national, and multinational corporations.

Within six months of Katrina, FEMA had issued $7 billion in related funds to other federal agencies, such as the Army Corps of Engineers, the Environmental Protection Agency (EPA), the General Services Administration (GSA), and the Department of Housing and Urban Development (HUD). A total of $28.6 billion was

---

This chapter is based on the report "Big, Easy Money: Disaster Profiteering on the American Gulf Coast," published by CorpWatch in August 2006.

assigned by Congress to various federal agencies. As federal and local governments continue to duke it out over a grand plan for rebuilding the region, the lion's share of the funds allocated for the purpose by Congress remain unused.

The work in the first year mainly included debris pickup, temporary housing, levee repair, stop-gap measures such as blue tarps on damaged roofs and security in the form of private contractors for the devastated region. The Gulf Coast staggered along, wounded, with mattresses still in trees, no reliable electricity, boats on the shoulders of highways, crushed houses slumped and moldering where they fell, and public school instruction held in portable classrooms or tents, if at all, while some hospitals remained understaffed and others, too damaged to ever reopen, stayed saturated with the memory of lost life.

The sheer cost of Katrina and the additional catastrophe of the New Orleans flood caused local, state, and federal agencies to throw up their hands to avoid picking up the tab. But regardless of who is footing the bill, where are the billions in recovery funds going? Major corporations use political clout to win lucrative no-bid contracts and then take advantage of the lack of any functional system of accountability to profit handsomely. This is a major drain on taxpayers, and, many argue, a human rights violation that further curbs the possibility of recovery for the victims of Katrina, most of whom were already afflicted by a broken system of poverty and injustice.

The Department of Homeland Security (DHS), the umbrella organization established in 2002 under which FEMA now operates, spends federal money faster and with fewer controls than any other segment of the government, according to a July 2006 report issued by the United States House of Representatives Committee on Government Reform. The report, prepared for Representatives Tom Davis and Henry Waxman, found that half of all DHS contracts are awarded without full and open competition and that the $34.3 billion DHS has spent on private contracts since its inception has been "plagued by waste, abuse or mismanagement." The committee noted that DHS does not require ethics training for its procurement officers. Between 2003 and 2005, DHS spending exploded from $3.5 billion to $10.5 billion (11 times the rate of increase for the entire remainder of the government), and at the same time the agency actually slashed staff. The report concluded by saying "the cumulative costs to the taxpayer are enormous" (Committee on Government Reform).

Pam Dashiell, 58, activist-president of the Holy Cross Neighborhood Association, lost her home in Katrina. New Orleans, in her eyes, has become a "free-for-all for corporations . . . the big money, as usual, is reserved for the big corporations," Dashiell said. "The usual suspects, including Halliburton and the Shaw Group, are getting the big contracts from FEMA and the Army Corps of Engineers" (author interview).

THE IMMEDIATE AFTERMATH

When bloated bodies floating down the streets of New Orleans were broadcast live on national television days after Hurricane Katrina, a frazzled federal government called on Kenyon International Emergency Services, a wholly owned subsidiary of

Service Corporation International (SCI), a funeral-services firm based in Texas, helmed by Robert Waltrip, a close family friend of the Bush clan and a major donor to President George W. Bush's gubernatorial and presidential campaigns. SCI was at the center of FuneralGate, one of the biggest scandals in Bush's gubernatorial career.

In the two months Kenyon worked in New Orleans, it recovered 535 bodies and billed the state well over $6 million (about $12,500 per victim) (author interview with Robert Johannessen). Meanwhile, local black morticians who volunteered their services to help in recovery and processing of bodies were turned away by FEMA (Black Voice News 2005). Dozens of bodies missed by Kenyon were discovered later by local authorities and, in some cases, family members.

This no-bid, cost-plus contract is but one of dozens of examples of how Katrina created a crisis ripe with opportunity for the well-placed corporation. The revolving door between Capitol Hill and Wall Street has created a cozy club for major contractors and politicians. For example, lobbyist Joseph Allbaugh was once George W. Bush's presidential campaign manager and later head of FEMA. Two of Allbaugh's clients were among the first to receive fat Katrina contracts. One, the Shaw Group, Inc., of Baton Rouge, won several no-bid contracts from FEMA, the EPA, and the Army Corps of Engineers immediately following the storm, totaling $700 million (one $100 million contract has since been rescinded) (Associated Press 2006, "Shaw Group").

Allbaugh's other client, Kellogg, Brown & Root (KBR is a subsidiary of Halliburton, where Vice President Dick Cheney was once CEO), won an initial $30 million contract (Project on Government Oversight) to work on devastated military bases in the Gulf Coast as part of a $500 million naval contract cemented pre-Katrina in July 2004. Allbaugh's Web site offers "assistance to companies engaging the U.S. Government process to develop post-war opportunities," but Allbaugh denies pulling strings to secure contracts for his clients.

"I tell them how to best craft their pitch," he asserted to the *Washington Post,* "to craft their technical expertise so everybody knows exactly what they do." Before the Iraq war began, Allbaugh's client KBR secured a $7 billion noncompetitive contract to repair Iraq's oil fields (U.S. Army Corps of Engineers). An audit by the Department of Defense disclosed in August 2004 that KBR had not adequately accounted for $1.8 billion it was given for work in Iraq and Kuwait (King 2004). The Defense Department paid the bill anyway.

ASHBRITT

Three days post-Katrina, AshBritt, a Florida-based firm, with close ties to Florida governor and presidential brother Jeb Bush, hired the former head of the Army Corps of Engineers, Mike Parker, to help maximize contracts for clean-up. Among the company's other lobbyists were a former Louisiana legislator and Barbour, Griffith & Rogers, a lobbying firm co-founded by former chairman of the Republican National Committee and current Mississippi governor, Haley Barbour. By mid-September, AshBritt had $500 million in debris-removal contracts, plus its guaranteed $56 million contingency fee from FEMA under a preexisting retainer for natural disaster recovery (Javers 2005).

Records show that AshBritt's CEO, Randal Perkins, is a major donor to state and federal GOP candidates (Center for Responsive Politics). AshBritt's $500 million debris removal contract (which has since far exceeded that wishful number) attracted attention from Capitol Hill. In May 2006, the House of Representatives' Committee on Government Reform took a special interest in AshBritt's contract and made it a centerpiece in its evaluation of the contracting system. "They grilled AshBritt's president and he wasn't happy," said Bill Woods, a spokesman for the Government Accountability Office (GAO), of Perkins's testimony before the panel (author interview).

AshBritt has enjoyed meteoric growth since winning its first big debris removal subcontract from Halliburton to help clean up after Hurricane Andrew in 1992 (Cray 2005). AshBritt is an "active status" contractor, having won a competitively bid contract in 2002 through the Army Corps of Engineers to essentially remain on call in case of a natural disaster, terrorist attack, or other emergency. Some of the major contractors say active status is less about cronyism and more about expedience—but the process makes it extremely difficult for small and local companies to get in on the action. A total of 1,230 post-Katrina subcontractors under AshBritt removed 20,000,000 cubic yards of debris and 19,000 tons of spoiled food. But within weeks of AshBritt's arrival in Mississippi, the Corps was so disappointed in its performance it had issued a cure notice threatening to terminate the contract (testimony before the Committee on Government Reform 2005).

AshBritt has also tried to take advantage of federal rules that reserve a certain percentage of contracts for minority and female-owned businesses (set-asides). As recently as October 2005, AshBritt described itself in the Small Business Administration database in both categories, with Perkins's wife, Cuban-American Saily Perkins, listed as the company president (Witte and Merle 2005). But on a list of campaign contributors compiled by the Federal Election Commission for a 2004 donation, Saily Perkins's occupation is listed as homemaker (Federal Election Commission). Randal Perkins has since claimed that the SBA listing was a clerical error (Javers 2005).

AMERICOLD

Another former FEMA director, James Lee Witt, is also a lobbyist. His firm, James Lee Witt Associates, is Louisiana's disaster consultant. Americold Logistics of Atlanta paid $40,000 in fees to retain Witt's firm prior to the hurricane (Center for Responsive Politics). Witt arranged a meeting between Americold executives and FEMA, which resulted in an arrangement for the company to provide ice and cold storage facilities in case of a major storm. Its Katrina contracts totaled over $1.7 billion. Taxpayers for Common Sense (TCS) investigated the contract and criticized Witt for "acting like a gatekeeper." TCS's Keith Ashdown called Witt the "king of disaster lobbying." "The message it sends," Ashdown says, "is that if you're not willing to pay his firm a retainer, you're not going to get a FEMA contract" (Shields 2005). Americold was at the center of controversy when a truck full of ice headed for the devastated region was turned away by disorganized FEMA officials and ended up traveling 1,600 miles before the ice melted, unused (Shane and Lipton 2005).

CARNIVAL CRUISE LINE

Florida-based Carnival won a $236 million no-bid contract to house hurricane victims, despite the nation of Greece offering free use of ships. Jeb Bush pushed for the contract, according to emails made public by Congressman Henry Waxman. Bush, who later claimed to be simply "facilitating communication," forwarded an email from the top Carnival executive directly to then-FEMA chief Michael Brown (Associated Press 2006, "Jeb Bush"). The ships floated half-empty for six months, and the cost per person per week for those housed on the ships (many of them public employees including police officers) worked out to more than twice the cost of a Caribbean cruise vacation for the same period. And that's minus most of the crew, entertainment, fancy banquets, and the cost of actually sailing the ships. Carnival said the cost of canceling booked cruises contributed to the price and that food and other services were also provided (Office of Senator Tom Coburn). "Finding out after the fact that we're spending taxpayer money on no-bid contracts and sweetheart deals for cruise lines is no way to run a recovery effort," Senator Coburn complained (Weisman 2005).

NOT PLAYING FAIR OR PAYING FAIR

A look at FEMA's records shows that about 60 percent of the $6 billion in contracts granted within a year of Katrina went to "small businesses," in keeping with federal procurement law that requires at least 23 percent of such contracts benefit small business. That number is deceiving: A large number of contracts went to small businesses, but their net worth was just 13 percent of the total amount granted by FEMA. The rest went to "other than small business." Five percent of contracts are normally set aside for minority-owned business, but post-Katrina, only about 1.5 percent of the initial major federal contracts went to such firms, in part because federal affirmative action regulations were suspended immediately following the storm. The Department of Labor said the relaxed rules were necessary to cut down on paperwork and get the job done quickly. "It was about saving lives [and] protecting property," said DHS spokesman Larry Orluskie (MSNBC 2005).

Local businesses fared even worse. In the initial aftermath of the storm, a surge of no-bid contracts emanated from FEMA, but only 10 percent (in dollar value) of those contracts went to businesses headquartered in the three worst-hit states, and Virginia alone could lay claim to 30 percent (in dollar value) of FEMA's largesse. Within a year, the percentage for the three worst-hit states had grown to 16.6 percent, or $1.17 billion, of the total contracts awarded nationwide.

Even if a contract was awarded to a small local business, it doesn't necessarily mean the company ever got paid. Ron Kennedy of Coastal Environments, Inc. (CEI), said that the small Baton Rouge–based company was awarded a $3.1 million contract to begin restoring the coastline and wetlands for 16 affected parishes throughout Louisiana with an eye toward redeveloping the areas. CEI was to augment FEMA's Emergency Support Function (ESF) team. Dr. Sherwood Gagliano, CEI's president, was the author of an ambitious 2003 plan to re-divert the Mississippi River and restore coastal barrier islands and marshes along the southern Louisiana coast. Some experts contend that the plan, had it not been suddenly defunded by the federal government, might have prevented the worst of the flooding from Katrina. Post-Katrina, CEI was asked to come up with a recovery plan for the resurrection of St. Bernard Parish, where 65,000 properties had been destroyed and the community was crippled further by the loss of firefighters, hospitals, and emergency care.

Almost as soon as CEI arrived, it was apparent that FEMA's team was unfocused. After only 45 days of ground work, the FEMA crew packed up, pulled out, and left many wondering if the protection of the wetlands, which might prevent massive damage from future storms, is a FEMA priority. "We were paid $150,000 on a $3.1 million contract," said Kennedy. "We're still working, but we're not getting paid. FEMA has offered no explanation. FEMA has hired people from all over the United States. They come to Louisiana and they don't even know where St. Bernard Parish is. We've been doing this for years. We've got historical data and information about what the situation is and how to correct it. Why not have small businesses on active status instead of big corporations?"

"FEMA says they are giving a certain amount of money to small businesses but then they pull it. How many times has this happened? What's the real number of payments made? I can assure you we're not the only ones" (author interview with Ron Kennedy). Convoluted federal record keeping further complicates matters. In some cases the invoices just don't add up. On numerous FEMA spreadsheets, the description fields that correspond to many of the cost line items are left blank. Sometimes it is perfectly clear where the money is going, just not why. In the immediate aftermath of Katrina, FEMA awarded a 30-day contract to Emergency Disaster Services (EDS) of Lexington, Kentucky, to provide three meals per day for 200 to 400 emergency personnel, at a cost of $3.6 million (Department of Homeland Security). Depending on how many people actually showed up to be fed, the meals cost between $100 and $279 apiece.

On September 17, 2005, that contract was extended for another 30 days, although the price dropped to $2.6 million for the same number of people and for the same time frame. When the contract was extended for a third time, the price dropped to $1.6 million. The FEMA spreadsheet does not indicate whether lobster was replaced by meatloaf, or if the diminishing urgency forced the company to reduce its prices. EDS also secured a $329,989 contract for renting six shower trailers for a month, and on March 15, 2006, another contract was granted for $86,536, although FEMA left the space reserved for describing the nature of the goods or services provided blank (Department of Homeland Security). A *Washington Post* analysis of existing Katrina contracts found that contractors inflated their actual costs from 40 percent to 1,700 percent when billing the government (Hsu 2005).

Also making it difficult to follow the post-Katrina money is the layering of sub-contractors on nearly every project. Most major contracts provide for the primary contractor to subcontract work to smaller firms. The layers can be so deep that the person on the ground actually sweeping up storm debris is making pennies on the dollar, if he or she gets paid at all. When the Bush administration suspended a number of federal labor and environmental laws in the immediate wake of the storm, ostensibly to speed up relief efforts, those doing the most back-breaking labor and those who live in the worst-hit areas were suffering the most, while out-of-town contractors reaped the rich rewards of a profligate procurement system. Operation Blue Roof is one example. FEMA paid $6.6 million to All American Poly (Project on Government Oversight) to make the blue tarps that covered so many storm-damaged roofs in the worst-hit areas. FEMA then gave the tarps—free-of-charge—and the contracts to install them to the Shaw Group and Simon Roofing and Sheetmetal of Ohio (Project on Government Oversight). Those companies subcontracted much of the actual work, and those subcontractors further subcontracted. The final cost for each tarp installation averaged out to almost $2,500 per tarp—almost enough to pay for a roof in many cases (the tarps were designed to last only three months). The workers who actually tacked the tarps were probably making closer to minimum wage.

AshBritt's $500 million contract for debris removal amounted to about $23 for every cubic yard of debris removed, according to an NBC television investigation. AshBritt in turn hired C&B Enterprises, which was paid $9 per cubic yard. That company hired Amlee Transportation, which was paid $8 per cubic yard. Amlee hired Chris Hessler Inc. for $7 per cubic yard. Hessler, in turn, hired Les Nirdlinger, a debris hauler from New Jersey, who was paid $3 per cubic yard. "It's a pyramid," Nirdlinger told NBC. "And everybody is taking a piece of the pie as you work your way up, and we're at the bottom. We're doing the work." Responsibility for ensuring adherence to labor laws and federal contracting standards is passed down the line as well, and accountability becomes next to impossible to enforce.

The lure of subcontracting was made even more tantalizing on September 7, 2005, when President Bush suspended the Davis-Bacon Act, which protects minimum wages for federal work, in the region. Without it, primary contractors and their subcontractors could pay laborers lower wages and keep more of the profit. Bush defended the action as necessary to enable the private sector to move quickly and get more done in a shorter time frame. Unfortunately, it also meant local laborers—many of whom had lost everything and were working to rebuild their own communities—were getting their wages cut. Bush was forced to reinstate the law two months later after a public outcry, but his reversal had a caveat: It wasn't retroactive. Any contracts signed during the suspension would still be exempt from the law (Project on Government Oversight).

Private contractors are not alone in their enthusiasm for having someone else do the dirty work. FEMA, short-staffed and underfunded, has actually contracted out the job of awarding contracts, both on the Gulf Coast and elsewhere. Acquisition Solutions Inc. handles the job, with dozens of former federal procurement officers on its staff to advise potential and existing contractors on technical and bureaucratic issues.

It even sent employees to FEMA headquarters to fill in for federal personnel who were sent to the Gulf Coast (Witte and O'Harrow, Jr. 2005). Government records show that FEMA paid the company $1.4 million in fiscal 2004. The company secured $2.4 million in post-Katrina contracts (Department of Homeland Security).

While the Gulf Coast was still soaking up Katrina and Rita's toxic aftermath, the Office of Management and Budget (OMB) and the DHS started "tracking key vulnerability areas for the federal Inspectors General (IGs), as a means to stem hemorrhaging of funds, stop uncontrolled spending, and establish a strong anti-fraud message for companies that were awarded contracts in the first several weeks" (President's Council on Integrity and Efficiency 2005). Testifying before the Senate on April 21, 2006, the DHS's Inspector General Richard L. Skinner said: "The federal government, and in particular FEMA, has received widespread criticism for a slow and ineffective response. Unfortunately, much of the criticism is warranted." Testifying about FEMA's failure, former agency director Michael Brown said that so much emphasis had been placed on terrorism that natural disasters just weren't a priority.

Skinner is in charge of the President's Council on Integrity and Efficiency (PCIE) Homeland Security roundtable, a body of 22 agencies responsible for reviewing the performance of FEMA. On April 30, 2006, the panel released a report. "Because the above pre-disaster planning process did not take place prior to Hurricane Katrina," the report reveals, "FEMA found itself in an untenable position and hastily entered into contracts with little to no contract competition for disaster commodities" (President's Council on Integrity and Efficiency 2006).

In the aftermath of any disaster, a mad scramble to restore order might result in sole source contracts, but as soon as the dust settles, FEMA must ensure that the government gets a fair price on contracts, including the use of free and open competition. Widespread post-Katrina destruction greatly lengthened this period of pandemonium, and FEMA failed to keep tabs on the contracts it awarded early on. In November 2005, FEMA tried to deflect some of the criticism over cronyism and profligacy by promising to re-bid four of the largest contracts awarded without competition to politically connected firms Bechtel, Fluor, Shaw, and CH2M Hill. By March 2006, the contracts had been extended rather than re-bid, even after congressional investigators discovered they had resulted in millions of wasted taxpayer dollars (Associated Press 2006, "FEMA Breaks Promise"). By August, they had ballooned to more than twice their initial worth.

The Congressional Committee on Government Reform reiterated the criticisms in a report on its investigation into DHS contracting. It, too, found widespread abuse and fraud, and blamed the DHS for failing to focus on efficient procurement: "Much like the Byzantine organizational structure of DHS itself, the department's diverse acquisition needs are supported by a disjointed acquisition management structure that stretches across various offices and lacks a single official responsible for managing, administering, and overseeing all DHS acquisition activities. The department also suffers from a lack of trained and skilled acquisition professionals" (Committee on Government Reform 2006). According to the Project on Government Oversight's (POGO) communications director, Jennifer Gore, the failure of DHS to track contractors is a "horrible loophole in an already egregious situation." In Iraq, she said, layered contracts prevented auditors from protecting taxpayers from fraud (author interview with Jennifer Gore). Few expected the same on American soil.

Charlie Cray, executive director of the Center for Corporate Policy, said, "We've been hit over the head for decades with this mantra that the private sector knows best. We should have learned this lesson from Enron. Even after Katrina, they continued to press their message by manipulating reality" (author interview with Charlie Cray). During and after Katrina and Rita, five Superfund sites in New Orleans flooded. Elsewhere in southern Louisiana, an estimated seven million gallons of oil seeped out of gas stations, offshore rigs, and coastal refineries. Sewers burst and flooded, sending a stew of fossil fuels and putrid waste across the landscape. In St. Bernard Parish, home to multiple oil refineries and power plants, an estimated million gallons of oil saturated the parish post-Katrina from 44 spills. The worst was Murphy Oil's Meraux refinery, a 100,000-barrel-a-day facility. Katrina lifted and dislodged a 250,000-gallon above-ground tank, sending an oily, muddy slick through the parish.

Soil samples from St. Bernard Parish taken by the Louisiana Bucket Brigade (LABB), the Natural Resources Defense Council (NRDC), several universities, and other organizations indicated the presence of arsenic, heavy metals, pesticides, diesel, benzene, and other toxic compounds. At FEMA's request, EPA took soil samples in the area, particularly in and around temporary housing areas. In some of the EPA samples, a mélange of substances and chemicals, including arsenic, benzene, the pesticide Dieldrin, diesel, organic chemicals, and thallium, was discovered in volumes exceeding state safety standards. The EPA Web site reveals that exposure to each of the substances in such doses increases an individual's lifetime risk of getting cancer—but at rates which "the EPA has found acceptable in other contexts."

Anne Rolfes, executive director of LABB, said, "The first step in solving any problem is admitting that you have one, but the government is pretending there's no problem." The Bucket Brigade has been working since 2000 to help residents in the area collect soil and air samples to make sure local refineries and chemical plants adhere to emissions limits (author interview with Anne Rolfes). What had been an unhealthy place to live became far worse immediately after the hurricane. A Wackenhut security guard lived in St. Bernard Parish for seven months post-Katrina and said that he was sick for four months with flu-like symptoms, fevers, vomiting, and coughing. It wasn't until he left for Colorado at the end of his assignment that he began to recover. He claimed nearly all of the other 1,500 people in the contractor's temporary camp were also sickened (author interview).

"People need information to make decisions about their lives," said Rolfes. The EPA, she said, has failed to consolidate data in a user-friendly format, and she intends the Bucket Brigade to step into the breach. She compared the EPA's conclusion that St. Bernard parish is "safe enough," considering the circumstances, to its post-9/11 declaration that the air quality in downtown Manhattan was safe. Existing environmental regulations that might have prevented spills like those in St. Bernard Parish simply were not enforced, according to Hugh Kaufman, an EPA senior policy analyst.

"The mayor said New Orleans will 'breathe again.' Yeah, they'll breathe bacteria, viruses and volatizing toxic chemicals," Kaufman told *Newsweek*. "There is no environmental assessment. . . . We don't know what to tell the public in terms of what their risk is when they come back. The public thinks it's safe. It's one of the more reckless and irresponsible government decisions made in the last decade, second only to [former EPA chief] Christie Todd Whitman after [the] World Trade towers came down [saying], 'We've tested the air and it's safe. So ya'll come back.' And now [some] of the people that came back are sick as dogs" (Ong 2005).

St. Bernard, a low-lying, flood-prone area, is also home to some of the poorer communities in southern Louisiana. The marshy delta soil was already overburdened with development driven by its proximity to the coastal shipping lanes. That development, according to Kaufman, has stressed the soil and compromised its natural capacity to disperse chemicals. It will cost Murphy $70 million to clean up the six miles of coastline sullied by the Meraux accident, according to Mindy West, Murphy Oil spokesperson. Within a year of Katrina, the company had already paid $80 million in settlements with homeowners not involved in the suit, averaging $30,000 per home. Critics say it is far too little for the scope of the devastation and the havoc that destroyed homes—and health.

Some 3,500 families affected by the spill who have not accepted settlements from Murphy Oil have filed a class-action lawsuit that is expected to drag on for years and cost the company hundreds of millions. Immediately following Katrina, workers were lured to the Gulf Coast with promises of lodging, food, and decent wages. Some 100,000 Latinos heeded the call. But when Bush suspended the Davis-Bacon wage act, many of the promises evaporated, according to Victoria Cintra, executive director of Mississippi Immigrant Rights Alliance (MIRA). The suspension attracted immediate ire from unions, who fought for and won the protection 75 years ago. AFL-CIO President John Sweeney asked Congress to reverse the suspension: "Taking advantage of a national tragedy to get rid of a protection for workers the corporate backers of the White House have long wanted to remove is nothing less than profiteering."

KBR was among the firms that took advantage of the exemption. Union electricians working on the Seabee Navy base in Louisiana were replaced with undocumented workers (Lovato 2005). "While the practice by subcontractors of employing illegal aliens is damaging under normal circumstances, at this time it is devastating," said Louisiana Senator Mary Landrieu, noting that 478,000 Americans lost their jobs following Hurricanes Katrina and Rita (Statement from Governor's Office 2005). Congresswoman Barbara Lee was equally infuriated: "The aftermath of Hurricane Katrina demonstrated the tragic consequences of having an administration where cronyism trumps competence. The fact that the President would cut wages for impacted workers, while handing out millions in no-bid contracts to well-connected firms, is a perfect snapshot to this administration's priorities" (Halliburton Watch 2005).

According to a report, "And Injustice for All," released on July 6, 2006, by the Advancement Project, the National Immigration Law Center, and the New Orleans Workers Justice Coalition, black and Latino workers in post-Katrina New Orleans are being exploited by a system of "structural racism" that has existed since the days when the city was a slave-trade hub. The report articulates a common fear that future reconstruction of the Gulf Coast will create a theme-park-like region with fewer opportunities for the underclass ("And Injustice for All" 2006). Saket Soni of the New Orleans Worker Justice Coalition interviewed hundreds of workers, many of whom reported having their wages stolen by employers who threatened to deport them if they complained. Others claimed to have been forced to work at gunpoint. "What is happening in New Orleans . . . has revealed a story of race and class that cannot be ignored," said Soni. "The city cannot be rebuilt off the backs of low-wage workers of color and then constructed to exclude them because they are too poor to live there" (author interview with Saket Soni).

Rosana Cruz, Gulf Coast field coordinator for the National Immigration Law Center, said, "People across the rest of the country don't really know what's going on. The level of assault against workers feels like war. There's vulnerability in each successive layer of subcontracting. . . . It's shocking that there aren't millions of people across the United States demanding accountability. This is a microcosm of what's happening around the world. If you're poor and you're brown, we can do whatever we want with you" (author interview with Rosana Cruz). Victoria Cintra said that her small volunteer organization has successfully fought for over $300,000 in pay owed to workers, but the battle is ceaseless. The subcontracting layers are a major part of the problem, since each can't pay the next until it gets paid, meaning the laborers on the bottom rung get paid last, if at all. That was the case with a contract granted to KBR in Mississippi to rehab the Seabee Naval Base.

KBR subcontracted with Tipton Friendly Rollins, which subbed the work to Kansas City Tree before duties were passed on eventually to Karen Tovar Construction. Tovar finally hired the workers, many of whom were immigrants, to do the job. She promised food and board in rickety trailers "not fit for rats," according to Cintra. After paying her employees for a week, Tovar claimed that she couldn't pay or feed the laborers until she was paid by Kansas City Tree.

In the dead of night, she allegedly entered the trailers and awakened the laborers and warned them that immigration agents were soon to arrive. Many of the workers fled. MIRA traced the chain of contracts back to KBR and delivered its research to the U.S. Department of Labor (Mississippi does not have a state department of labor). Eventually, MIRA won the $141,000 in back pay for Tovar's laborers, but many fear deportation or have no permanent addresses and cannot be found.

TEMPORARY HOUSING

The DHS notoriously spent almost a billion dollars on mobile homes and travel trailers, including 10,000 which were left sitting empty in an Arkansas field so long that FEMA had to pay $6 million to have gravel spread to keep them from sinking into the soft ground. It seems the DHS ordered the trailers from countless manufacturers without realizing that federal laws prohibits locating them in a known flood plain, which constitutes a huge swath of the Gulf Coast (Committee on Government Reform 2006). According to the DHS, as of June 30, 2006, more than 102,500 people were still housed temporarily in 37,995 FEMA-provided travel trailers and mobile homes, including 3,242 units compliant with the Americans with Disabilities Act. But some people were forced to leave the Gulf entirely when temporary housing wasn't made available in time. That has led to sharp criticism of the corporations tasked with delivering trailers and mobile homes, often under exorbitant contracts. Louisiana lost more than half of its population in the weeks and months following the storm. CH2M Hill, Fluor, Shaw, and Bechtel (all major donors to the Republican Party) were the first companies tapped to provide temporary housing in the region and were awarded no-bid contracts initially worth about $400 million apiece.

FEMA determined the type of housing each victim would receive, and its contractors were to make sure they got it. Delivery was slow and unreliable, and criticism bloomed around the contracts that had been granted for what seemed, to many, to be poor work. FEMA promised to re-bid the four massive contracts, but ended up extending and expanding them without new competition, despite a GAO audit finding that millions had been wasted by the firms. Like many of the corporations with the largest Gulf Coast contracts, CH2M Hill has enjoyed significant federal work in Iraq, including a contract (a joint venture with Parsons, a major construction firm) worth $28.5 million to oversee the construction of Iraq's public water and electrical utilities by four other contractors (between them the corporations were spending an estimated $1.7 billion in taxpayer funds), including Fluor, which has drawn accusations of conflict of interest.

Fluor Corp. won another of the controversial Gulf Coast temporary housing contracts that had been promised for rebidding but was instead ultimately extended and expanded sans competition. This, despite the fact the federal government fined the company $3.2 million in 1994 for "submitting heavily padded repair bills after Hurricane Hugo." In 2005 it was determined that the company will also pay $12.5 million to settle allegations that it knowingly overbilled the Department of Energy and Defense from 1995 to 1998, according to the *Corporate Crime Reporter*. Connections have helped Fluor score a landslide of deals, including $1.6 billion in reconstructive work in Iraq, according to the *Los Angeles Times*. Suzanne H. Woolsey, a "trustee of a little-known arms consulting group that had access to senior Pentagon leaders directing the Iraq war," joined the board of Fluor Corp in 2004. Woolsey's husband, a former CIA director, R. James Woolsey, is a leading advocate for the war and also serves as a government policy adviser.

As recently as May and June 2006, Fluor was still scoring seven-figure Katrina-related contracts, a review of FEMA records shows. Fluor's share of the total federal budget for bringing the Gulf Coast back is an estimated $1.3 billion. While the 2005 hurricane season and its aftermath exposed the cynical tendency toward profiteering by corporations, much of it was made possible by a bungling federal government that was inexcusably unprepared and outrageously incompetent. Amplified in this way, the cost of profiteering is astonishing. The transfer of resources from taxpayers to federal coffers to corporate entities is akin to a chronic low-grade infection sapping the nation's strength.

Like most federal contracting agencies, FEMA was downsized in the 1990s under the guise of reform. In recent years, the agency has been primarily focused on counterterrorism, not natural disasters, and was crippled after Katrina for this reason, according to former FEMA chief Michael Brown. But the contention—heard from Bush and other top federal officials—that FEMA was incapable of anticipating the severity of the storm or the damage it did is a handy but laughable explanation given the sheer volume of material published on the subject over the years. "Hurricane Katrina underscores the urgent need for government transformation," said David M. Walker, comptroller general of the United States, at a conference on Public Service and the Law in March 2006. "It has become obvious," Walker said, "that the government has been issuing far too many contracts and assistance payments for Hurricane Katrina relief that just don't pass the straight face test." He urged the audience to recall that the "ultimate loyalty" of the private sector is to shareholders, while government was designed as a servant of the greater good.

That federal contracting needs fixing is obvious; how to do it depends upon whom you ask and where their loyalties lie. Billions of dollars remain for resurrecting the Gulf Coast, which means billions remain to be made—or spent wisely, with a focus on justice and basic human decency.

REFERENCES

"And Injustice for All: Workers' Lives in the Reconstruction of New Orleans." 2006. The Advancement Project, the National Immigration Law Center, and the New Orleans Workers Justice Coalition. July 6.

Associated Press. 2006. "FEMA Breaks Promise on Katrina Contracts." March 24.

_____. 2006. "Jeb Bush Asked to Explain Cruise Ship Deal." February 28.

_____. 2006. "Shaw Group Swings to Loss on Katrina. 2006." July 10.

Author interview with Charlie Cray, executive director of the Center for Corporate Policy.

Author interview with Rosana Cruz, Gulf Coast field coordinator, National Immigration Law Center.

Author interview with Jennifer Gore, communications director, Project on Government Oversight.

Author interview with Robert Johannessen, Louisiana Department of Health and Hospitals.

Author interview with Ron Kennedy, Coastal Environments, Inc. (CEI).

Author interview with Anne Rolfes, executive director of the Louisiana Bucket Brigade (LABB).

Author interview with Saket Soni, New Orleans Worker Justice Coalition.

Black Voice News. 2005. "Local Volunteers Refused." October 14.

Center for Responsive Politics. Washington, DC. Available at http://www.opensecrets.org.

Committee on Government Reform. 2006. "Report on Katrina Contracting." July.

_____. 2006. "Waste, Abuse and Mismanagement in Department of Homeland Security Contracts." July 27.

_____. 2006. "Report on Department of Homeland Security Contracting." July 17.

Congressional Testimony from Department of Homeland Security Inspector General Matt Jadacki. 2006. May 6.

Cray, C. 2005. "Disaster Profiteering: The Flood of Crony Contracting Following Hurricane Katrina." *Multinational Monitor.* September/October. Available at http://multinationalmonitor.org/mm2005/092005/cray.html (accessed July 23, 2008).

Department of Homeland Security. http://www.dhs.gov/index.shtm.

Federal Election Commission. http://www.fec.gov.

Halliburton Watch. 2005. "Congress Members Demand Halliburton Suspension." September 27. Available at http://www.globalresearch.ca/index.php?context=va&aid=1010 (accessed July 23, 2008).

Hsu. S. 2005. FEMA Overestimated Costs of Contracts After Katrina. *Washington Post.* November 15. Available at http://www.washingtonpost.com/wp-dyn/content/article/2005/11/14/AR2005111401441.html (accessed July 23, 2008).

Javers, E. 2005. "Anatomy of a Katrina Cleanup Contract." *BusinessWeek.* October 27. Available at http://www.businessweek.com/bwdaily/dnflash/oct2005/nf20051027_8761_db038.htm (accessed July 23, 2008).

King, N. Jr. 2004. "Pentagon Questions Halliburton on $1.8 Billion of Work in Iraq." *Wall Street Journal.* August 11.

Lovato, R. 2005. "Gulf Coast Slaves." *Salon.* November 15.

MSNBC.com. 2005. "Minority Firms Getting Few Katrina Contracts: Most Awards Going to Businesses with an Existing Government Relationship." October 4. Available at http://www.msnbc.msn.com/id/9590752 (accessed July 28, 2008).

Office of Senator Tom Coburn. http://coburn.senate.gov/public/index.cfm?FuseAction=ContactSenatorCoburn.home.

Ong, B. 2005. "A Toxic Gumbo." *Newsweek.* September 15.

President's Council on Integrity and Efficiency. 2005. "Oversight of Gulf Coast Hurricane Recovery." December 30.

Project on Government Oversight. http://www.pogo.org/index.shtml.

Shane, S., and E. Lipton. 2005. "Stumbling Storm Aid Put Tons of Ice on Trips to Nowhere." *New York Times.* October 2. Available at http://www.nytimes.com/2005/10/02/national/nationalspecial/02ice.html (accessed July 23, 2008).

Shields, G. 2005. "Contracts Negotiated by Witt Criticized." *The Advocate.* October 14.

Statement from Governor's Office. 2005. October 24.

Testimony before the Committee on Government Reform. May 2005.

U.S. Army Corps of Engineers. 2003. Contract #DACA63–03-D-0005. March 8.

Weisman, J. 2005. "$236 Million Cruise Ship Deal Criticized." *Washington Post.* September 28. Available at http://www.washingtonpost.com/wp-dyn/content/article/2005/09/27/AR2005092701960.html (accessed July 23, 2008).

Witte, G., and R. Merle. 2005. "Defining Small." *Washington Post.* October 20. Available at http://www.washingtonpost.com/wp-dyn/content/article/2005/10/19/AR2005101902270.html (accessed July 23, 2008).

Witte, G., and R. O'Harrow Jr. 2005. "Short-Staffed FEMA Farms Out Procurement." *Washington Post.* September 17.

CHAPTER 9

REBUILDING LIVES POST-KATRINA

Choices and Challenges in New Orleans's Economic Development

Robert K. Whelan and Denise Strong

On Saturday, December 2, 2006, more than 2,500 New Orleanians gathered for Community Congress II, a large-scale community-planning exercise. The majority of the group met in New Orleans, but there were large groups assembled in Atlanta, Baton Rouge, Dallas, and Houston. Webcasts brought the proceedings to sixteen other cities around the country.

The meeting was part of the Unified New Orleans Plan (UNOP) process. The UNOP is an attempt to incorporate previous planning efforts and to present one infrastructure plan for rebuilding New Orleans to funding authorities. The UNOP is funded, in large part, by the Rockefeller Foundation. The meeting was designed by America Speaks, an organization that designs and facilitates large-scale meetings.

Both the UNOP and America Speaks are run by highly qualified, well-trained professionals. UNOP (2006) background materials include an excellent summary of the jobs and the economy in New Orleans metro region since Hurricane Katrina. The UNOP report notes that over 50 percent of businesses were flooded by two feet or more of water. The Louisiana Quarterly Report (which has to be submitted to FEMA every quarter) estimates 81,000 businesses lost in the Hurricanes Katrina and Rita regions. New Orleans alone lost nearly 100,000 jobs in Katrina, and the metropolitan area lost nearly 400,000 jobs. The report sees the shortage of workers, limited affordable housing, reduced daily flights, and violent crime as challenges for the local economy. However, the local economy is influenced as well by regional and state economies. The numbers of jobs lost and businesses impacted by Katrina and Rita reflect the enormity of the challenge of rebuilding the state's economy and the respective regional and local economies. Residents and businesses struggling to rebuild face related dimensions of the same problem: The availability of housing and employment for residents and the availability of employees for businesses. Returning residents need to know whether they will be able to find a job and a place to live. Businesses need to know whether they will be able to hire and retain an adequate number of employees.

The UNOP sees the short-term city economy as driven by jobs from the port, tourism, energy (oil and gas), and health care. These were the major engines of the New Orleans economy before Hurricane Katrina. The UNOP sees the need for a skilled labor force and workforce housing. The shortage of housing and labor will affect the economic recovery of the tourism and health care industries.[1]

As noted above, UNOP planners and America Speaks organizers are very impressive professionals. In structuring Community Congress II, participants were asked to discuss "six key aspects of rebuilding: (1) flood protection; (2) roads, transit and utilities; (3) neighborhood stability; (4) rental and affordable housing; (5) education and health services; and (6) other public services" (America Speaks 2006). In brief, there was no discussion of jobs and economic development at this national meeting of more than 2,500 New Orleanians. This has been typical of recovery and redevelopment efforts since the storm. Mayor C. Ray Nagin's Bring New Orleans Back Commission (BNOB), reporting a few months after Katrina, gave the economy only cursory attention. Indeed, the economic development subcommittee of the BNOB did not present a full report. A PowerPoint presentation was deemed sufficient.

The lack of attention to jobs and economic development has been observed by several students of the rebuilding process. One of the authors of this chapter (Whelan 2006, 230), writing shortly after the storm, observed that "economic development does not seem to be a high priority at this point." In a forum at the New School in New York City, economist David D. Kallick noted "the absence of a coherent government response" in this policy area (Kallick 2006, 36). A group of economic consultants characterized the economic policy response to Katrina as "slow and disjointed" (Zandi et al. 2006, 115).

On Saturday, January 20, 2007, almost 1,300 New Orleanians gathered for Community Congress III. Again, participants were assembled at the Convention Center in New Orleans and sites in Atlanta, Dallas, and Houston. The number of people attending was approximately half that of the earlier meeting. It is unclear whether the big drop in numbers indicated "participation fatigue," or if many were distracted by the New Orleans Saints appearance in the NFC Championship game the following day. It is also possible that participants recognized widespread agreement on the main goals.

There are signs that economic development may be gaining salience as a priority. The UNOP materials include a discussion of economic development as part of its summary of citywide recovery strategies. First, the UNOP calls for the erection of a new economic development commission, as part of city government. It should be noted that in the 1980s former Mayor Sidney Barthelemy left the economic development function to Metrovision (now GNO, Inc.), a private entity that is now part of the Chamber of Commerce. Second, the UNOP calls for support of sectors that have traditionally been strong in the city's economy: energy, health care, the port, and tourism. The UNOP also wants to develop transient worker housing and to relocate small neighborhood-oriented businesses. The UNOP also asks for the establishment of a seed and early-stage equity capital fund (Unified New Orleans Plan 2007, 13–15). Still, at the meeting, discussion of economic development occurred in a session devoted to a wide range of public services. Economic development issues only came up if participants in the small groups raised them.

One hopeful development is Mayor Nagin's appointment of Dr. Edward Blakely as Executive Director for Recovery Management. Blakely is supposed to coordinate and direct Hurricane Katrina recovery efforts in New Orleans. Blakely is the co-author of the leading textbook on local economic development (Blakely and Bradshaw 2002). In his address to Community Congress III, Blakely laid out a five-point plan to guide the recovery. One of the five points was developing a diverse economy based on international trade, digital media, health systems, and advanced business services. Blakely also noted a reorganized City Hall in which he and other key directors, including the director for development, report directly to Mayor Nagin (Blakely 2007).

On the same day (January 20, 2007) as Community Congress III, Donald Powell, the president's representative as head of the hurricane recovery, announced plans to talk to 100 of the country's top firms into bringing 100 jobs apiece to New Orleans. Powell hoped that these jobs would be available during 2007. Diversifying the city's economy is one of the federal government's goals (Associated Press 2007).

Still, over all, almost three years after the storm, not much has been done as far as economic development is concerned. The rest of this chapter will focus on *why* the economic development response has been lacking. The first section will describe the economy pre-Katrina. This will be followed by a discussion of the economy today. The problems facing businesses include reopening/returning versus closing/relocating decisions, the need for affordable housing, and problems with utilities. These will be discussed in the following section. The prospects for jobs include low-skilled work, which has attracted a substantial new immigrant population. The options for economic recovery include governmental programs and ideas advanced by many policy organizations.

THE NEW ORLEANS ECONOMY PRE-KATRINA

In the 2000 U.S. Census, the eight parishes (counties) comprising the New Orleans metropolitan region had 1.3 million residents. The population of the city, of New Orleans was 485,000. Jefferson Parish, directly neighboring the central city had 455,000 residents and was beginning to exhibit the characteristics of older, declining suburbs around the country. St. Tammany Parish, north of Lake Pontchartrain, had close to 200,000 residents, and was the major growth center. In September 2007, the U.S. Bureau of the Census reported a population of 223,388 in New Orleans (Louisiana Department of Health and Hospitals, and Louisiana Recovery Authority 2006). The

Jefferson Parish population was estimated at 431,361. This was almost returned to its pre-Katrina level. St. Tammany Parish gained population, especially from devastated St. Bernard Parish, and its population was estimated at 230,605 people.

The racial composition of New Orleans contrasts sharply with that of its suburban neighborhoods. In the 2000 Census, two-thirds of the city's population was African American, while almost 75 percent of the suburban population in the Metropolitan Statistical Area (MSA) was white. The most recent population estimates show a greatly changed picture for New Orleans, with 58 percent black, 36.8 percent white, and a growing Latino component (4.1 percent). Jefferson Parish population estimates are 65.7 percent white, 24.4 percent black, and 8.3 percent Latino (U.S. Bureau of the Census American Community Survey 2007). At present, it is clear that New Orleans has a population that is now more white than before the storm. Meanwhile, the African-American population declined—both absolutely and relatively.

The racial polarization is compounded by class polarization. In the 2007 Census estimate, 22 percent of the city's residents lived in poverty, with a high percentage of African Americans in this category. At the same time, a mean household income of more than $63,000 in the city indicated that quite a number of people were doing very well. Jefferson Parish and St. Tammany Parish had lower levels of poverty, as you would expect.

This situation is, of course, hardly unique to New Orleans. Except for a few oil boom years in the late 1970s and early 1980s, New Orleans has not experienced the dynamic growth of other cities in its Sun Belt region, such as Atlanta, Dallas, and Houston. In many ways, the loss of population in the New Orleans metro region (not just in the central city) since 1990 and the lack of dynamism in the regional economy made New Orleans resemble declining industrial regions in the Northeast and Midwest, such as Buffalo, Cleveland, and Pittsburgh.

In recent decades, there were three bases for the New Orleans economy: the port, oil and related businesses, and tourism. In brief, New Orleans employment growth was stagnant in the latter part of the twentieth century. There were actually slightly fewer jobs in 1997 than in 1977. Manufacturing, which never employed a large part of the New Orleans workforce, declined by 50 percent. Containerization and other technology-driven processes led to the displacement of 8,900 workers. As the city lost jobs in these areas, it gained jobs in oil and gas, legal services, health care, tourism-related industries, business services, social services, and education (Whelan, Gladstone, and Hirth 2002).

One way to get a snapshot of the local economy before the storm is by looking at the largest private employers as of 2002. Litton Avondale, a shipbuilding firm, was the biggest private employer. An aerospace firm, Lockheed Martin, was the sixth largest employer. The top ten private employers included a university (Tulane), a health care firm (Ochsner), a casino (Harrah's), two utilities (phone and electric), a restaurant chain headquartered in the area (Copeland's Popeye's), and a vacuum cleaner manufacturer (Oreck). There were no oil companies on the 2000 list, although there had been some in the 1990 Census.

Some observers believe that New Orleans lacks economic plans. In 2001, Greater New Orleans, Inc., the regional economic development agency in the regional chamber of commerce, identified ten existing and emerging industry clusters in the region for attraction and retention strategies. These clusters included manufacturing (food processing, shipbuilding, aerospace, petrochemical, and machinery), maritime, construction, repair services, information services and technology, biomedical research and development, media production/entertainment, tourism, health care, and warehousing distribution. Workforce plans and policies for the region, before Katrina, emphasized targeting these clusters. This approach was in agreement with well-accepted ideas in regional economic development, which suggested the development of occupation clusters built upon existing strengths. In 2001, Greater New Orleans, Inc., suggested a focus on six occupational clusters in which the region had a comparative advantage: maritime, medical, oil and gas, petrochemical and refining, shipbuilding, and tourism (Whelan, Gladstone, and Hirth 2002). We suggest that the problem is not a lack of plans but a lack of implementation of economic development plans.

Before Hurricane Katrina, the problems of racially related poverty seemed especially intractable in the New Orleans area. No one has easy answers for the problems of a substantial underclass in an urban economy that was not especially dynamic. Organizations with excellent track records in other U.S. urban areas have not succeeded in New Orleans. The Annie E. Casey Foundation has sponsored workforce development efforts in many urban areas. As part of their Jobs Initiative program, New Orleans was one of six cities funded by Annie E. Casey in 1995. The New Orleans Jobs Initiative (NOJI) is a major collaborative effort to provide job opportunities. In contrast to the other five cities, the Casey Foundation was frustrated by the slow pace of its New Orleans' efforts.

Another example was the efforts of the Local Initiatives Support Corporation (LISC) to build housing in New Orleans. After considerable success in other cities, LISC began a program in New Orleans in 1993. With a nonconfrontational strategy that emphasized working with banks and established political institutions, and an old housing stock in need of repair and renovation, New Orleans seemed a perfect fit for LISC activity. In an analysis of the first several years of the effort, Ross Gittell and Avis Vidal (1998, 66) noted that "city officials were preoccupied with controversies concerning riverboat gambling and expansion of access to the harbor, and the city lacked a low-income housing strategy." Moreover, Gittell and Vidal observed that "the local government was perceived as paternalistic and corrupt, and there was widespread skepticism that this could be changed. Consequently, accountability and expectations of community development in the city were low" (Gittell and Vidal 1998, 67). LISC pulled out of the New Orleans area after a decade of trying to build housing, with little to show for its efforts.[2] Peter Burns (2007) also makes the point that community organizations have found "success" elusive in New Orleans. Although they have a record of achievement in Burns's view, organizations such as ACORN (Association for Community Reform Now), ACT (All Congregations Together), and Jeremiah "illustrate how unaware and unresponsive government can be toward traditionally excluded groups" (Burns 2007, 72). Burns notes the "scarcity of resources in the city, the elite nature of New Orleans, and the fragmentation of leadership" (Burns 2007, 72). All of these impact the larger situation of economic development as well.

PROBLEMS FACED BY BUSINESSES

One fundamental problem faced by all businesses after Hurricane Katrina is the housing of employees. A majority of the housing stock in New Orleans was damaged or destroyed in the storm. The same is true in Plaquemines and St. Bernard Parishes. A substantial minority of homes on the East Bank of Jefferson Parish were flooded. While problems in St. Tammany Parish resulted from storm surge only, the impacts were considerable by normal standards. Overall, the result is a severe shortage of housing in the region.

It is difficult to find precise figures, but it is clear that there is a substantial housing need—both short-term and long-term. Moreover, the New Orleans situation is complicated. Unlike most cities, New Orleans was a majority-renter city (53 percent to 47 percent) before Hurricane Katrina. Since the storm, governmental assistance programs have focused on homeowners. A substantial minority of the renters lived in public housing. Since Katrina, only six of ten public housing developments have reopened. The Housing Authority of New Orleans (HANO) targeted some of the complexes for redevelopment as mixed-income residential, and four of the largest complexes have been demolished. Not surprisingly, market forces come into play. Residential sales prices rose substantially throughout the region for units that were not flooded. Many landlords raised the rent in unflooded units. Affordable housing was difficult to find in the New Orleans region before Katrina. After the storm, it became almost impossible.

Although there has been a slow but steady increase in residential construction since Katrina, there has been a lack of large-scale development that might make a significant impact. In the fall of 2005, KB Homes, a California development firm, proposed building 20,000 new homes on the West Bank of Jefferson Parish. One year later, these plans were dead. The lapse of the contract was attributed to two factors by a KB Homes official. First, the costs and challenges of laying infrastructure to support neighborhoods were daunting. Much of the property is on wetlands and needed elevation. Second, New Orleans real estate expert Wade Reagas noted the severe loss of jobs in the region and the resulting lower demand for new houses in an analysis for the company (Gordon 2007).

Public programs haven't totally ignored the rental market. The state of Louisiana issued low-income housing tax credits. Observers feel that the private market is moving faster than public programs can. Private investors, mainly from out-of-state development companies, are currently renovating 2,600 of the 7,000 flooded apartment units in New Orleans East. Triangle Real Estate, a Gastonia, North Carolina, company, is a major player. Essentially, private firms are in a race to get their New Orleans East apartments ready. They expect to collect substantially higher rents than they received before the storm. One of the main incentives for private firms is the opportunity to write off the costs of these projects from their income taxes, afforded by the Gulf Opportunity Zone Act, passed after the storm. In addition to private efforts, Providence Community Housing (the development arm of the Archdiocese of New Orleans) is developing 270 units in New Orleans East (Thomas 2007).

In January 2007, the state of Louisiana announced a rental equivalent to The Road Home program for homeowners. The rental repair program is aimed at people who own one to four rental units. The program will provide forgivable loans and incentives to rent to lower-income tenants, among other provisions. The pool of money is estimated to be sufficient for only 18,000 of the 82,000 rental units eliminated by Hurricane Katrina and Rita in southern Louisiana. Thus, there will be a competitive application process (Hammer 2007).

Let us suppose that these programs succeed, and that rental units are constructed and renovated in a timely fashion. The New Orleans metropolitan area still faces an immense problem in replacing lost jobs. In its one-year review of recovery indicators in New Orleans, Brookings Institution researchers found that the metropolitan area lost 80,000 jobs between August 2005 and February 2008. The greatest loss of jobs occurred in education and health services. This sector lost approximately 24,700 jobs. The Brookings report found that hotels and travel had returned to 80 percent of pre-Katrina capacity. The current unemployment rate is very low, at 3.1 percent in February 2008 (Liu et al. 2008).

On an individual basis, there are several reasons why businesses have been slow to rebuild. It took several months before FEMA issued elevation guidelines for the rebuilding process. Many businesses still don't know whether they will be allowed to rebuild, and if so, to what height they have to rebuild to qualify for federal flood insurance. Many homeowners remain unsure as to whether they will rebuild; the same is true for businesses. Another classic problem is that New Orleans has long been an undercapitalized community. Major development projects in New Orleans were usually funded by outside capital. In recent years, many of the local banks merged with larger national (and even international) banks. Moreover, the New Orleans banking community was traditionally very conservative in terms of its lending processes. The question remains: What kind of support will banks and mortgage companies provide as businesses try to rebuild? There is also the problem of insurance. Two insurance companies that accounted for 57 percent of the homeowners' business in the state—State Farm and Allstate—are not writing new policies. A state-sponsored option is available but is more costly (Mowbray 2005).

Small businesses face problems different in kind and degree from large multinational conglomerates. Many small businesses had only enough cash to sustain themselves for 60–90 days. The federal and state governments provide bridge funding for short-term sustenance of businesses. In the aftermath of Katrina, many businesses that applied for these bridge loans, and for Small Business Administration (SBA) loans, could not get the assistance in a timely manner. Periodically, there have been reports that widespread business closures and bankruptcies are imminent. Right after

Christmas 2006, a New Orleans *Times-Picayune* story told of the struggle of many small businesses in the tourism industry. As with rental housing, the State of Louisiana announced a program to provide grants and loans to businesses affected by the storm in December 2006. Loans and grants may help businesses keep afloat, but they cannot deal with a long-term loss of leisure tourists (White 2006).

Hurricane Katrina affected everyone in the region. It is somewhat surprising that, in the storm's aftermath, some zoning, environmental, and regulatory processes were not suspended. It is perhaps less surprising that NIMBY (Not in My Back Yard) politics quickly asserted itself. This has been evident in attempts to use trailers as temporary housing, and in numerous efforts to build apartments in the metropolitan region.

Perhaps the best evidence of NIMBYism is the story of the famed New Orleans restaurant Gabrielle. Chef Greg Sonnier and his wife, Mary, ran and operated the restaurant for thirteen years on Esplanade Avenue in the Mid-City neighborhood. The food rates international acclaim. The restaurant's employees are local people. The restaurant was destroyed by flooding, and the Sonniers sought another location. They found one at 438 Henry Clay uptown. After purchasing the property, the Sonniers were told that it was licensed as a reception hall, but not as a restaurant. Influential neighbors, including Eddie Sapir, a former City Council member, are behind the opposition. The neighbors fear a parking problem and "disruption of the neighborhood's tranquility." If memory serves, Gabrielle was open five evenings a week, and once a week for luncheon. The diners were generally quiet, well-dressed, and affluent. And there are other restaurants in the neighborhood. This is the kind of nonsense faced by businesses that wish to operate in the relatively undamaged parts of New Orleans (Anderson 2007).

Larger companies face different kinds of problems. For many, the key decision is whether or not to stay in the region. One company that has decided to move its manufacturing facilities is Oreck Vacuum. The company's headquarters is located in New Orleans. Several years ago, Oreck moved its primary manufacturing plant to Long Beach, Mississippi. Ten days after Hurricane Katrina, the company reopened the Long Beach plant. Now, Oreck will move almost 500 employees to Tennessee. The company cited two main reasons for its decision to leave: problems in getting insurance for the plant and problems in finding skilled workers. Oreck workers did not return after the storm because they had nowhere to live (Eaton 2007).

Other companies have moved but stayed within the region. Many companies, including Bell South and Shell, relocated employees to higher ground north of Lake Pontchartrain. Chevron, the second-largest oil company operating in New Orleans, announced in May 2006 that it would relocate its offices from the New Orleans Central Business District to Covington in St. Tammany Parish. The company experienced concerns about the city's utilities, levees, and infrastructure. In May 2008, Chevron vacated its downtown New Orleans office building and opened its new regional headquarters in an office park near Covington (Morah 2008).

Overall, the state of business confidence is intertwined with the status of the levee system. In the eastern part of New Orleans, storm surge brought about overtopping of the levees and floodwall failure. Hurricane Katrina's impacts were felt widely through the central part of New Orleans because breaches occurred in several drainage canals. In the year after Hurricane Katrina, the U.S. Army Corps of Engineers repaired 220 miles of damaged levees and floodwalls at a cost of more than $350 million. The Corps built temporary storm surge gates at the lakefront mouths of the canals as a short-term solution to the storm-surge problem. It will take many years to construct systems that will reduce the vulnerability of eastern New Orleans and St. Bernard Parish to storm surge. The needed coastal restoration projects might take decades (Unified New Orleans Plan 2007). In getting this work done, a constant concern is the diversion of funds—to the West Bank of the river or to other parts of the country (Grissett 2007).

RELATIONSHIP BETWEEN ECONOMIC AND WORKFORCE DEVELOPMENT

In this section we discuss workforce development in the rebuilding of post-Katrina New Orleans. According to the National Governors Association, workforce development refers to "education, employment, and job training systems designed to provide the skilled workers employers need to succeed and the education and training individuals to succeed in today's labor market" (Jacobs and Hawley 2003). Jacobs and Hawley propose a definition that reflects the broad public- and private-sector involvement in workforce training: "Workforce development is the coordination of public and private sector policies and programs that provides individuals with the opportunity for a sustainable livelihood and helps organizations achieve exemplary goals, consistent with the societal context" (Jacobs and Hawley 2003, 12).

A workforce development system focuses simultaneously on the training needs of workers and employers and economic forces. A discussion of workforce and economic development and New Orleans' rebuilding challenges will necessarily include an examination of development issues in the region as well as in the state. We also discuss the pre-Katrina context, which affects post-Katrina workforce development.

Conceptually, economic and workforce development are interrelated *and* interactive. The nature and quality of the workforce are important factors in economic development. A newly created robotics manufacturer, for example, may bring the prospect of economic growth to a region, but if the workforce lacks the knowledge and skills required, the manufacturer will not start production in that region. There are indicators that Louisiana has faced such circumstances.

Policy makers and business leaders have long lamented the state of Louisiana's workforce and its lack of preparedness for a twenty-first-century global economy. Studies and legislative reports prior to Katrina pointed to the shortage of adequately prepared employees for then-existing businesses in New Orleans and in the state. The GNO, Inc., conducted a study of employers throughout the state in which the majority indicated they could not fill positions (Council for a Better Louisiana 2004). In addition, these businesses said they were not able to expand as a result of the shortage of adequately trained potential employees.

Conversely, if the workforce in a region has acquired the skills necessary for robotics manufacturing and there is no manufacturer in the region, that workforce may migrate elsewhere if there are no other viable employment opportunities. Concern about Louisiana's "brain drain" has been a long-standing one among some policy makers and business and civic leaders. Thus, it would appear that economic and workforce development policies and strategies would be closely related.

An adequate workforce is essential to the rebuilding of the Louisiana and Mississippi Gulf coasts. As New Orleans struggles to recover and begin the rebuilding process, it has to deal with a short-term conundrum—businesses are unable to open or to resume functioning at full capacity without adequate staffing, while the workforce cannot function without adequate housing, which it cannot secure without employment. Furthermore, public-sector employers, such as the City of New Orleans, must also deal with a diminished tax base and population. The long-term challenge posed by post-Katrina rebuilding is whether New Orleans, and Louisiana, will be able to attract, retain, and develop a workforce that will facilitate sustained economic development. Thus, New Orleans and Louisiana must simultaneously address and integrate short-term and long-term workforce development with economic development.

JOB PROSPECTS AND WORKFORCE DEVELOPMENT

The demand in low-skilled employment categories, such as construction, was high during the massive clean-up required after Hurricane Katrina. There was a paradox in the tension between the need for labor and the availability of labor. New Orleans residents had been evacuated throughout the country, and many who desired to return found it difficult to do so for a variety of reasons, including lack of housing and employment. At the same time there has been a substantial influx of Hispanic and other immigrant workers, especially construction workers. Recent employment figures show gains in diversified employment fields: hospitals, manufacturing, financial services, and professional services. The unemployment rate is low (3.1 percent), although, of course, the number of jobs is still well below pre-Katrina levels.

In particular, Katrina precipitated an exodus of large segments of the New Orleans middle class, particularly the African-American middle class. Thousands of professionals from the region were relocated by the employers. Others lost jobs as the result of institutional closures and layoffs by public-sector employers such as the City of New Orleans, Charity Hospital, the University of New Orleans, and Southern University at New Orleans. In the Orleans Parish school system, for example, there were 4,857 teachers in 2003–2004 (GNODC 2005). In addition, there were 2,000–3,000 other school employees. Almost all of these were laid off after the storm.

Many of these professionals found employment in other places. In these situations, it is middle-class professionals with technical and entrepreneurial skills who will most easily find employment elsewhere. As a result, this category may be the most difficult to recruit back to New Orleans, which will make it difficult to re-staff hospitals, schools, and government agencies. Even if they had housing in New Orleans, would these teachers want to return to a school situation without tenure and benefits? Similar scenarios exist for health care professionals and for many in the area's universities.

Workers in nonprofessional occupational categories for months after Katrina were in such demand that large employers were paying bonuses up to one year later. Fast-food restaurants were forced to increase starting wages and offer signing bonuses. McDonald's increased hourly wages from $7 to $10 per hour and offered signing bonuses and medical and dental benefits (Guillet 2006). The restaurant industry still needs many employees because of the lack of affordable housing, day care, and public transportation.

People without education and skills face a different set of problems. Many may find work in the "new" New Orleans. However, they need a place to live, as noted above. Moreover, poor people rely on public transportation. As of February 2008, only 49 percent of all pre-Katrina public transportation routes, and 19 percent of buses, are in operation. Essentially, this situation hasn't changed since January 2006 (Brookings Institution, 2008). People without skills will find it more difficult to get jobs in regional centers of the service-based, higher-technology economy, such as Atlanta and Dallas, so may be more likely than professionals to return to New Orleans.

The above are largely short-term concerns. In the long term, the major workforce development issue concerns whether New Orleans and Louisiana will be able to attract, retain, and develop a workforce that will facilitate sustained economic development. This latter issue faced New Orleans before Katrina. Thus, the city must simultaneously address and integrate short-term and long-term workforce issues with economic development.

PRE-KATRINA WORKFORCE DEVELOPMENT

This section discusses the pre-Katrina workforce development system in New Orleans and in Louisiana. Workforce development programs evolved as a result of a range of public policy purposes such as helping displaced workers find alternative employment, reducing poverty, reducing unemployment, reducing welfare rolls, filling a need for skilled workers, and ensuring a competitive workforce. With such varied purposes, workforce development programs were housed in multiple agencies and were not well coordinated. Louisiana, for example, had over 100 job training programs in as many as a dozen state agencies. Furthermore, these programs were implemented by public and private entities ranging from small local nonprofits to major national organizations.

The pre-Katrina workforce development landscape in New Orleans was shaped in large part by broad federal policies as reflected in federal statutes and programs and the local interpretation of such policies. Although there was some discretion in local implementation, local administrators and policy makers were severely constrained in adapting federal programs to local conditions and needs.

Pre-Katrina workforce development programs were inadequate for providing high-skill/high-wage training to New Orleans residents. Some federal programs generally limited training to short-term training. A common complaint among trainees, as well as among employers, was that the training was often for jobs that did not exist. Employers frequently complained that their training needs were not met by the typical workforce development training program. This complaint was directed as well to technical training institutes and community colleges.

New Orleans' workforce development administrators had to contend with a high illiteracy rate, the loss of low-skill/high-wage jobs, a significant growth in low-skill/low-wage service jobs, large numbers of high school dropouts, an aging workforce in high-skill/high-wage jobs, and a brain drain of well-educated and highly skilled people. These factors made it difficult to formulate workforce development strategies that would enable the city and state to attract and retain high-wage employers.

Several other conditions made it difficult for workforce development and economic development strategies to work in tandem. First, there was a significant gap between the type of workforce needed for economic growth and the workforce that was available given the level of literacy, average educational attainment, and educational quality of public schools. As many as 44 percent of adults in New Orleans were at the lowest literacy level, according to a business journal report (Miller 2004). Second, persistent employment discrimination limited entry into the workforce and limited the upward mobility of a significant portion of the working-age population. Third, although race and racism were important elements of the political, social, and economic dynamic of New Orleans, the civic culture was such that political and business leaders would not address publicly the challenges posed by such an environment.

Consequently, workforce development policies and programs were mostly ineffectual because they were unable to compensate for the years of educational neglect. At the same time, the city's economic development strategy of expanding the tourist industry and the number of employers that relied on low-skill/low-wage employment reduced the demand for the type of extensive training that could lead to higher wages in the long term.

Further, workforce development programs and administrators were further challenged by the "work first" policy of the 1996 Personal Responsibility and Work Opportunity Reconciliation Act, which limited welfare assistance to five years. The state of Louisiana chose to implement a "work first" strategy, which severely limited the opportunity for welfare recipients to participate in training or educational programs and to limit cash assistance to families to 24 months. Federal and state welfare reform policy was to force poorly educated welfare recipients into the workplace with almost no serious skills training. Workforce development thus became primarily a matter of helping welfare recipients find low-skill/low-wage jobs.

The absence of a highly skilled workforce had consequences in terms of economic development. The economic development ventures that depended on high technology were problematic for New Orleans. For example, when the University of New Orleans Technology Park opened, elected officials such as Councilman James Singleton expressed concern that New Orleans residents would not qualify for many of the positions. He also expressed the view that, nevertheless, such developments were needed so that when educational reform efforts began to improve the quality of education, public school graduates could find good employment in the New Orleans area.

POST-KATRINA WORKFORCE DEVELOPMENT

Post-Katrina workforce development in New Orleans cannot be considered tabula rasa for several reasons. First, the federal workforce development statutes have not changed significantly. Second, service deliverers have not changed, although they may have diminished capacity. Third, despite the decreased population, the pre-Katrina workforce is slowly returning. Finally, the local New Orleans economy is influenced by globalization, technological, and demographic trends (Gordon 2005). So, the pre-Katrina workforce development system and issues will shape the post-Katrina system and issues even though some conditions have changed dramatically.

Post-Katrina workforce development policies and programs must confront pre-Katrina challenges in addition to a whole new set of challenges. Among the new challenges are higher-than-usual labor shortages, a severe housing shortage, which prevents people from returning to New Orleans, a more diverse workforce, and an influx of immigrant workers who may need assistance with English instruction. In addition, the demand for construction workers and skilled craft workers has increased dramatically.

The unprecedented nature of the disaster has compelled state and local government to rethink its strategies and strengthen the workforce delivery systems. If these conditions discussed in the previous section persist, they will impede the economic recovery of New Orleans and the Katrina-impacted areas of the state. In this section we discuss new initiatives that will enable the state to better design programs responsive to employers and employees. The Louisiana Recovery Authority (LRA), the designated state agency for coordinating recovery and rebuilding, developed several new workforce development programs in 2006 and 2007.

The LRA established an Economic and Workforce Development Task Force, thereby creating an organizational structure that would facilitate a synergy between state-funded economic and workforce development projects (LRA Quarterly Report 2006, 9).

The Economic and Workforce Development Task Force identified long-term economic development priorities that included providing financial assistance to businesses, especially the major industries, cultivating an environment attractive to business and investors and supporting emergent businesses (LRA Quarterly Report 2006, 9). The workforce development priorities included creating high-quality jobs in urban and rural areas, taking advantage of the rebuilding efforts to create high-quality jobs.

Governor Bobby Jindal, elected in October 2007, announced that workforce development would be one of his administration's top priorities. He proposed a reorganization of Louisiana's workforce development administrative structures and programs. The challenges prompting this proposal had also been a concern of the previous administration, under Governor Kathleen Blanco, who had appointed a task force to study the workforce development and post–Hurricanes Katrina and Rita rebuilding needs.

The Task Force on Workforce Competitiveness had recommended that the state consolidate and streamline its various programs to facilitate use by employers and citizens. It further identified a need for strategic positioning of workforce development in state government and leadership in coordinating with adult education and economic development (Task Force on Workforce Competitiveness Report to the Governor 2006). With the enactment of House Bill 1104, the Department of Labor has been reorganized as the Louisiana Workforce Commission and will assume responsibility for workforce development programs currently located in other state agencies. The new legislation also establishes rapid-response funds for emergent employment training needs.

SHORT-TERM AND LONG-TERM WORKFORCE DEVELOPMENT STRATEGIES

These state agencies adopted short- and long-term strategies to encourage the return of the workforce to Katrina-impacted areas. An important early step in supporting residents to return to work was the establishment of LA Swift, free daily bus service between Baton Rouge and New Orleans. This service, initially funded by FEMA as a pilot project to allow displaced workers to commute to New Orleans, is now a Louisiana Department of Transportation program. In the first months of the service 72 percent of the riders surveyed said that they had been able to return to their jobs in New Orleans or find new employment for an average of $10 per hour. Other short-term strategies included hosting job fairs and direct job placements.

The $38-million Recovery Workforce Training Program funded by community development block grants is an example of a long-term strategy. This program is a collaborative effort of the Louisiana Recovery Authority, the Louisiana Workforce Commission, and the Louisiana Office of Community Development and is designed to address three priorities: (1) return of workers to Louisiana; (2) retention of the workforce in place; and (3) increase in the skills of the workforce that would strengthen the state's capacity for economic growth. Training programs that prepare people for occupations considered critical in the recovery process will get priority in funding. The six sectors that are critical in the rebuilding process are the oil and gas industry, construction, manufacturing, transportation, health care, and the cultural economy.

PUBLIC/PRIVATE PARTNERSHIPS

The public workforce development funds and programs may be implemented through private-sector—both for-profit and nonprofit—workforce development initiatives. These initiatives may involve public/private partnerships using a combination of public and private funds. Several examples are discussed in this section.

The Salvation Army initiated a job readiness training program for over 13,000 people impacted by Katrina (Salvation Army 2008). The program was offered in conjunction with the National Business Services Alliance. Participants were able to get certified for existing job skills and to acquire skills through certified training courses.

The Business Roundtable, a national organization of 160 chief executive officers of major corporations, announced a program that would train 20,000 people for construction jobs in the Gulf Coast region of Louisiana and Mississippi by 2009. The Roundtable pledged $5 million that would be used in conjunction with $10 million in federal dollars from the U.S. Department of Labor's Pathways to Construction program and National Emergency Grants (Bergeron 2007).

As of May 2007, some 8,500 people had completed the training, and of these 7,500 entered the construction industry or advanced training in one of the crafts. Sixty percent of participants had been residents of New Orleans at the time Katrina hit. However, the slow pace of recovery in New Orleans, according to program administrators, has hindered the placement of graduates on construction projects in the city (Bergeron 2007).

Another segment of the nonprofit sector that is an important source of job training programs is organized labor. The Louisiana AFL-CIO administers a number of apprenticeship programs that provide training and career paths for high-skill/high-wage job opportunities and has been represented on the Economic and Workforce Development Task Force of the Louisiana Recovery Authority.

OPTIONS FOR ECONOMIC RECOVERY

In the aftermath of the storm, many governmental, policy, and activist groups have offered possible courses of action for economic recovery. Although they represent different political orientations, a great deal of common ground exists. First, recovery should be undertaken following sustainable development guidelines. The environmental destruction caused by the petrochemical industry in the river parishes north of New Orleans and the coastal erosion caused by the oil and gas industry should not be repeated in the future. Many of the planners working in the city stress the need for mass transit and for smart-growth development. Second, recovery should aim for a more balanced economy. The New Orleans regional economy has always depended on a few industries; future development should be more diverse and equitable.

Our major proposal to stimulate rebuilding was offered by Representative Richard Baker (R-LA) in the fall of 2005. The Baker bill would have paid off lenders and restored public works. It would have done this by buying up large chunks of property, dividing them up, and selling them off to developers. To carry this out, the bill would have created a federal agency, the Louisiana Reconstruction Corporation. Indeed, the bill was approved by the U.S. House of Representatives Financial Services Committee in December 2005.

In January 2006, the White House announced that it would not support the Baker bill. Two main reasons were given: The bill would have created a federal bureaucracy, and the cost, estimated from $30 billion to $80 billion, seemed high. Given Louisiana's historic corruption, there has been great caution in sending large amounts of money to the state post-Katrina. The White House suggested that Louisiana follow Mississippi's lead in providing grants to homeowners (Nossiter 2006a).

Indeed, this is what transpired. In mid-February 2006, the White House requested an additional $4.2 billion in aid for Louisiana homeowners. Shortly thereafter, the State of Louisiana announced its own program. Using the new billions from the federal government, the state proposed loans and grants to homeowners to start rebuilding. In contrast to the Baker bill, buyouts were de-emphasized. Louisiana's program combines cash and low- or no-interest loans with the purpose of encouraging repairs and rebuilding (Nossiter 2006b).

Unfortunately, as we write three years later, the state's The Road Home program has been a failure. The money did not get to homeowners in a timely fashion. In its April 2008 update, the Brookings Institution noted that in the first quarter of 2008 fewer grants were dispersed and the average award fell, in contrast to the corresponding period in 2007.

There is no need for us to detail The Road Home program here. Suffice it to say that inadequacy of the response has contributed to the local economy's slow pace of revival. Whether the federal government response is a result of incompetence, indifference, or both is a matter of opinion. One thing that is not in doubt is the exceptional work of volunteers from all over the United States and Canada, who have donated their time and effort to rebuilding the Gulf Coast. This work has been organized by churches and civic and nonprofit groups. The efforts are truly appreciated by individuals, neighborhoods, and communities throughout the region.

One grassroots group that has been more visible and assertive since Hurricane Katrina is ACORN (Association of Community Organizations for Reform Now). Through a lawsuit, ACORN has cleaned up and gutted almost 2,000 houses in the Lower Ninth Ward. In addition, a group affiliated with ACORN produced a detailed Ninth Ward Plan. ACORN also helped in the formation of a Katrina survivors organization (Dreier and Atlas 2007).

The plan developed by the ACORN Housing-University Partnership includes some excellent suggestions for economic development of the Ninth Ward. These ideas include the redevelopment of the St. Roch Market as a farmers' market, along with a café, a restaurant, and community meeting space; the creation of a flea market; development of local skills in the building trades through obtaining a YouthBuild grant from the U.S. Department of Housing and Urban Development (HUD); starting a modular housing factory in the area; and general stimulation of economic opportunities (for example, through residential development) (ACORN Housing-University Partnership 2007). Overall, ACORN's ideas emphasize equity and sustainability.

If ACORN represents grassroots thinking from a progressive point of view, the prophets of the New Urbanism (Peter Calthorpe; Andrés Duany and Elizabeth Plater-Zyberk) represent a more elitist viewpoint supported by the state's political establishment. Both the Calthorpe and Duany/Plater-Zyberk firms were brought into Louisiana as major planning contractors after the storm.

Peter Calthorpe's firm, Calthorpe Associates, promotes diverse, mixed-use, and pedestrian-friendly urban environments. Two of its subcontractors are the Brookings Institution and Policy Link Associates. Since the storm, Brookings has published a Hurricane Katrina Index, with indicators of the recovery process on a regular basis. Generally, Brookings supports the development of industry clusters in the region and revamping of the workforce system (Brookings Institution 2005, 2006). Policy Link is a national nonprofit organization promoting equitable economic development. In the Gulf Coast rebuilding efforts, Policy Link is the representative of Living City, a collaboration of leading foundations and banks (including Annie E. Casey, Rockefeller, MacArthur, Ford, J. P. Morgan Chase, Bank of America, and Deutsche Bank).

Calthorpe conducted six workshops around the state in the summer of 2006. On economic development, these workshops supported thorough educational reform, improved government transparency, increased regional cooperation, enhanced and integrated use of Louisiana's multi-modal transportation system, and support for small business and entrepreneurship. Following a long line of previous reports, analyses, and plans, the workshops supported building industries from existing strengths. These include coastal science, new building technologies, the energy sector, alternative fuels, biotechnology, and the film industry. A public outreach and polling process is underway, with a final plan expected in March 2007 (Louisiana Speaks 2007).

Duany and Plater-Zyberk conducted charrettes in Lake Charles, Vermilion Parish, St. Bernard Parish, and in the Gentilly neighborhood of New Orleans. Their recommendations include the development of "smart growth" codes for each jurisdiction. These are essentially neighborhood design plans, emphasizing New Urbanism principles—dense, walkable neighborhoods with stores, mass transit, and traditional housing. Reed Kroloff, dean of Tulane University's Architectural School, has become a critic of New Urbanism, observing: "The development community loves New Urbanism . . . creating higher density per acre allows developers to make more money" (Pogrebin 2006).

CONCLUSION

The economic recovery of New Orleans will not occur in the absence of a readily available and skilled workforce. Given the critical need of employers for a workforce and the critical need of displaced residents who are still trying to return to New Orleans, as well as those who have returned, workforce development should be a top priority in the planning for recovery and rebuilding. To date, workforce development planning has not received the same degree of attention and commitment from government that housing planning has received.

Furthermore, economic development programs are not well integrated with workforce development initiatives and there is an absence of highly visible, well-funded workforce programs. Post-Katrina workforce development will require considerable investment in short-term and long-term strategies for rebuilding the organizational capacity of public and private workforce development organizations. Finally, strategic investments in both economic and workforce development in a coordinated manner would help accelerate the recovery process.

Before Katrina, the New Orleans economy suffered from fundamental problems— a large poverty population lacking basic skills, a lack of a diverse economic base, and a general lack of opportunity and dynamism. Since the storms, many ideas for rebuilding the local economy have been presented. Many of these have merit. Certainly, the ideas presented by New Orleans' "recovery czar," Ed Blakely, in early 2007 have a sound grounding in theory and practice. His ideas could provide the basis for a good New Orleans economic development plan. Still, it is very difficult to be optimistic about this vital aspect of the rebuilding.

First, economic development does not seem to be a high priority at this point. The physical development aspects of rebuilding, especially those centering on home-owners and neighborhood efforts, have provided the major focus. This has been true both for the New Orleans city government and for the state's Louisiana Redevelopment Authority. Economic development may become a high priority, but it is not high on governmental agendas at present.

Second, many believe in the idea of a city-region—or at least in the idea of a city acting as a base for its regional hinterland. Regional government efforts are always difficult, but New Orleans does not have this kind of cooperation in regional governance that many other metropolitan regions have. This is as true in economic development as it is in more polarizing policy areas. No one is approaching economic development from a regional perspective. St. Tammany Parish and Baton Rouge may now be the motors of the regional economy. This reality is not being taken into account. The Mississippi Gulf Coast is a major part of the regional economy, but this fact is not taken into account by policy makers at any level. There is no evidence of multi-state efforts (Louisiana, Mississippi, Alabama, and Texas) to rebuild the regional economy.

Third, there is a significant lack of vision in the political and business leadership. New Orleans Mayor C. Ray Nagin was re-elected in 2006 but has generally kept a low profile since the election. Former Louisiana Governor Kathleen Blanco was faulted for her lack of leadership, and current governor Bobby Jindal implemented many reforms in his first year in office, but economic development was not a major force. Certainly, the greatest visionary leaders in history would have been challenged by the magnitude of this disaster. If jobs and people are going to return to the region, some creative thinking is necessary. Ed Blakely's ideas are a beginning.

The New Orleans economy lacked dynamism before Katrina. The port no longer provided the number of jobs it once did. Oil and gas industries employment was cyclical, with office jobs often moving to Houston headquarters. Tourism had never recovered from the post 9/11 downturn. To bring the economy back to pre-Katrina levels would be a large order. To move to newer levels, as in Blakely's proposal, is a more daunting task. Businesses still face many problems in reopening. Individual job prospects are hampered by the lack of housing and other services, and the need for workforce training. There are good ideas for recovery, but, at this writing, they have not been implemented.

NOTES

1. The material in the opening section comes from Unified New Orleans Plan materials, especially "The Road to Recovery" (2006).

2. The material in this section on the New Orleans economy is based on the earlier work of one of the authors, especially Whelan (2006).

REFERENCES

ACORN Housing-University Partnership. 2007. *A People's Plan for Overcoming the Hurricane Katrina Blues*. February 1.

America Speaks. 2006. *2500 New Orleans Residents Prioritize Recovery Efforts*. December 3.

Anderson, B. 2007. *Food Fight*. NOLA.com: Everything New Orleans. *Times-Picayune*. January 17.

Bergeron, A. 2007. "Post-Katrina Worker Recruitment Program Along Gulf Coast Is Off to a 'GREAT' Start." December 12. McGraw-Hill Companies. Available at http://www.imgreat.org/news/ENR-12-07.pdf (accessed August 7, 2008).

Blakely, E. J. 2007. Untitled. PowerPoint presentation to Community Congress III. January 20. Broadcast via Information and Communications Technology (ICT) to participants in the cities of New Orleans, Atlanta, Baton Rouge, Dallas, and Houston, among others.

Blakely, E. J., and T. K. Bradshaw. 2002. *Planning Local Economic Development: Theory and Practice*. 3rd ed. Thousand Oaks, CA: Sage.

Brady, Raymond J. 2006. "Louisiana Workforce Training Efforts to Rebuild Hurricane Disaster Areas: Forecast of Critical Occupations Requiring Two Years of Less Training in Six Industry Sectors for the Recovery Period 2006–2009." Baton Rouge. August.

Brookings Institution. 2007. *The Katrina Index*. January 17.

Burns, P. 2007. "Community Organizations in a Non-Regime City: The New Orleans Experience." In M. Orr (ed). *Transforming the City: Community Organizing and the Challenge of Political Change*. Lawrence: University Press of Kansas, pp. 56–83.

Council for a Better Louisiana. 2004. "2004 Employer Survey Questionnaire." Available at http://cabl.org/pdfs/CABL_Employer_Survey_Results.pdf (accessed December 3, 2008).

Dreier, P., and J. Atlas. 2007. "This Missing Katrina Story." *Tikkun*. January 2007.

Eaton, L. 2006. "Slow Home Grants Stall Progress in New Orleans." *New York Times*. November 11.

———. 2007. "Vacuum Maker Hailed as Savior Quits Gulf Tour." *New York Times*. January 15.

Fessler, P. 2007. "Red Tape Ties Up Katrina Funds." *All Things Considered*. National Public Radio. February 5.

Fox, S. 2006. "Pre-existing Shortages, Post-Hurricane Cleanup Needs Have Led to the Search for More Labor." *Louisiana Business Reports*. October 10.

Gittell, R., and A. Vidal. 1998. *Community Organizing: Building Social Capital as a Development Strategy*. Thousand Oaks, CA: Sage.

Gordon, E. 2005. *The 2010 Meltdown: Solving the Impending Jobs Crisis.* Westport, CT: Praeger Publishers.

Gordon, M. 2007. "Derailed Building Plan Gave Leaders a Wakeup Call." NOLA.com: Everything New Orleans. *Times-Picayune.* January 2.

Greater New Orleans Data Center. 2005. http://www.gnodc.org.

Grissett, S. 2007. "Details of Bush Levee Budget Revealed." NOLA.com: Everything New Orleans. *Times-Picayune.* February 3.

Guillet, J. 2006. "National Food Chains Are Slow to Rebuild in New Orleans." *New Orleans CityBusiness.* November 20. Available at http://findarticles.com/p/articles/mi_qn4200/is_20061120/ai_n16856630 (accessed November 20, 2008).

Hammer, D. 2007. "Indecision Dogging Road Home." NOLA.com: Everything New Orleans. *Times-Picayune.* February 19.

_____. 2007. "Rental Road Home Gets Rolling." NOLA.com: Everything New Orleans. *Times-Picayune.* January 31.

Jacobs, R. L., and J. D. Hawley. 2003. "Workforce Development: Definition and Relationship with Human Resource Development." In S. A. Lynham & T. M. Egan (eds.). *Academy of Human Resource Development Conference Proceedings* 10:1014–1020. Bowling Green, OH: Academy of Human Resource Development.

Kallick, D. 2006. "Rebuilding a High Road Economy: What Works for Workers." In A. White and P. Eisinger (eds.). *Cities at Risk: Catastrophe, Recovery and Renewal in New York and New Orleans.* New York: Milano School for Management and Urban Policy, The New School, pp. 32–36.

Krupa, M. 2007. "Citizens Say Yes to Unified New Orleans Plan." NOLA.com: Everything New Orleans. *Times-Picayune.* January 21.

Liu, A., M. Fellowes, and M. Mabanta. 2006. *Special Edition of the Katrina Index: A One-Year Review of Key Indicators of Recovery in Post-Storm New Orleans.* Washington, DC: Brookings Institution, Metropolitan Policy Program.

Louisiana Department of Health and Hospitals, and Louisiana Recovery Authority. 2006. *2006 Louisiana Health and Population Survey—Survey Report.* November 27.

LRA Quarterly Report, February 2006.

Mowbray, R. 2005. "Insurance Moratorium Making Home Sales Difficult." NOLA.com: Everything New Orleans. *Times-Picayune.* December 22.

Nossiter, A. 2006a. "Rejection of Building Plan Causes Dismay in Louisiana." *New York Times.* January 26.

_____. 2006b. "Louisiana Unveils a Plan with Cash to Rebuild Homes." February 21.

Pogrebin, R. 2006. "An Architect with Plans for a New Gulf Coast." *New York Times.* May 24.

Rioux, Paul. 2007. "Chevron Starts Work on Tammany Complex." NOLA.com: Everything New Orleans. *Times-Picayune.* January 23.

Salvation Army. 2008. "Success of Katrina Aid Project Leads to Lasting Relationship." Press Release. July 15. Available at http://www.uss.salvationarmy.org/uss/www_uss.nsf/vw-dynamic-index/4F79968A24D739BF802571DA004C2FDF?Opendocument (accessed August 7, 2008).

Staff Report. 2007. "New Orleans Area Regains Some Jobs." NOLA.com: Everything New Orleans. *Times-Picayune.* January 26.

State of Louisiana. Office of the Governor. 2008. "Governor Jindal Signs Workforce Redesign Bill." Press Release. July 3. Available at http://www.gov.louisiana.gov/index.cfm?md=newsroom&tmp=detail&catID=2&articleID=292 (accessed August 7, 2008).

State of Louisiana. 2006. "Task Force on Workforce Competitiveness Report to the Governor." March. Louisiana Workforce Investment Council. Available at http://www.laworkforce.net/content.cfm?id=54.

Thomas, G. 2007. "Private Money Fuels Apartment Renovations." NOLA.com: Everything New Orleans. *Times-Picayune*. January 25.

Unified New Orleans Plan. 2006. "The Road to Recovery." Document prepared for Community Congress II. December 2.

_____. 2007. "Summary of Draft Citywide Recovery Strategies." Document prepared for Community Congress II. January 20.

_____. 2007. *Unified New Orleans Plan*.

Waugh, W. L. Jr., and R. B. Smith. 2006. "Economic Development and Reconstruction on the Gulf After Katrina." *Economic Development Quarterly* 20 (3): 1–8.

Whelan, R. K. 2006. "An Old Economy for the 'New' New Orleans? Post Hurricane Katrina Economic Development Efforts." In C. Hartman and G. D. Squires (eds.). *There Is No Such Thing As a Natural Disaster: Race, Class, and Hurricane Katrina*. New York: Routledge, pp. 215–231.

Whelan, R. K., D. L. Gladstone, and T. Hirth. 2002. *Building a Workforce Development System in New Orleans*. New Orleans: University of New Orleans, College of Urban and Public Affairs.

White, J. 2006. "Small Businesses Teeter on Edge." NOLA.com: Everything New Orleans. *Times-Picayune*. December 26.

Zandi, M., S. Cochrane, F. Ksiazkiewicz, and R. Sweet. 2006. "Restarting the Economy." In E. L. Birch and S. M. Wachter (eds.). *Rebuilding Urban Places After Disaster: Lessons from Hurricane Katrina*. Philadelphia: University of Pennsylvania Press, pp. 103–115.

CHAPTER 10

THE COLOR OF OPPORTUNITY AND THE FUTURE OF NEW ORLEANS

Planning, Rebuilding, and Social Inclusion After Hurricane Katrina

Mafruza Khan

When the levees along the Mississippi broke after Hurricane Katrina in August 2005, too many people in New Orleans were poor, trapped, and unable to flee and find shelter in a safe place. The problem in the Gulf Coast, as this nation was forced to acknowledge, was not a hurricane, but decades of flawed and discriminatory public policies that created concentrated racialized poverty and an unprecedented man-made disaster. More than three years after Hurricane Katrina, survivors, who are largely poor African Americans or immigrants, continue to struggle to return to their homes and rebuild their lives.

Race has been an architect of our institutions and systems and plays a critical role in determining who has access to opportunities. Hurricane Katrina brought to the forefront the fundamental problems of structural racism[1] in this country and its resultant economic, social, and racial segregation. Seen from this perspective, it is not hard to understand why the faces of the abandoned were mostly black and why they are having the most difficulty rebuilding their lives even now.[2]

Though all cities must contend with their physical settings, cities like New Orleans have specific challenges because of their unique geographical, geological, and historical circumstances. What should a rebuilt New Orleans look like, and who will live and work there? What is the best way to plan for rebuilding, and who must be involved in the planning process? How can former residents be effectively included,

60 percent of whom are still displaced? Who are New Orleans' and the Gulf Coast's emergent leaders and what kind of infrastructure is needed to support progressive leadership and democratic practices for rebuilding an inclusive New Orleans? What are the roles and responsibilities of government, particularly the federal government, as well as the private sector and organized civil society? What systems of governance would be most effective and promote transparency and accountability, given systemic corruption and structural problems? Are there effective policy, planning, and governance models that we can build on? Or, do we need a paradigm shift in the way we consider development in order to build sustainable communities that provide opportunities for all?

This chapter considers these issues in rebuilding New Orleans, examines innovative solutions that have emerged from the ground up, discusses important planning and policy issues for addressing structural barriers to opportunity for Hurricane Katrina survivors, and raises some questions about prevailing models of economic development and planning in relation to race, gender, class, and opportunity.

This chapter examines the historical and structural context that transformed New Orleans from a relatively poor but otherwise diverse and vibrant city to an impoverished black-majority one, and how race has driven and shaped exclusionary public policies that have created concentrated racialized poverty in New Orleans. This chapter provides an analysis of structural barriers to opportunity and demonstrates why race needs to be explicit and embedded in both the planning and policy frameworks for rebuilding. Race-conscious policies are critical for facilitating inclusion, participation, and accountability in rebuilding New Orleans, precisely because race-neutral policies may actually perpetuate structural barriers and historical inequities.

Rebuilding New Orleans after Hurricane Katrina involves work at two levels, which are linked: (1) ongoing emergency rebuilding work involving housing, education, health care, transit/transportation, and essential public services (for example, utilities), or, broadly, community infrastructure; and (2) future economic development. Rebuilding offers an opportunity to get it right (or at least do it better!) this time. This chapter looks forward and points to hopeful directions in public policies and strategic community-based planning that have the potential to create vibrant communities and a better quality of life for all, and raises additional questions that need to be explored.

THE FOUNDING OF NEW ORLEANS, POPULATION GROWTH, AND RACIAL GEOGRAPHY

The French established New Orleans as the capital of Louisiana in 1718. The city was laid out in classic eighteenth-century gridiron pattern, the Enlightenment ideal of a new city in the New World. It remained sparsely populated from its founding in 1718 to until about 1810. Economic growth was also slow for the first hundred years. The mercantilist economic policies of the European colonial powers dictated until the Louisiana Purchase in 1803, which finally removed the political barriers hindering its physical, economic, and social development.

From 1803 until 1861, New Orleans' population soared from 8,000 to nearly 170,000. The 1810 census counted a population of 10,000, making New Orleans the United States' fifth largest city, after New York, Philadelphia, Boston, and Baltimore. In 1830, it ranked third after New York and Baltimore; and in 1860, it was the nation's fifth largest city. The Industrial Revolution and the post–Civil War boom transformed the North into an urban-industrial area, but New Orleans was still one of the twelve largest U.S. cities until 1910 (McNabb and Madere, Jr. 2003).

Since its founding, New Orleans, like most old cities, has gone through distinct phases of development. The first African slaves were brought in the 1720s, when labor shortage became acute.

Of the 8,000 people in New Orleans in 1803, almost 5,000 were African Americans. During the nineteenth century, street patterns in New Orleans clearly influenced racial geography.

> Whites built along the main boulevards and avenues, forming super blocks, with African-American domestics and craftsmen and immigrant whites living on small streets within the cores of the super blocks. African-American neighborhoods, until the twentieth century, were small and separated from one another. African-Americans also lived near whites, both rich and poor, which later made for social stability and less racial tension, although some African-Americans were isolated in neighborhoods along the backswamps, or battures, the riverside of the levee (McNabb and Madere, Jr. 2003).

New Orleans continued to be relatively integrated well into the twentieth century. While government policies enabled the creation of a white middle class and white space through land-use and credit policies that promoted suburban and highway development following World War II, acute concentrated poverty and residential segregation are relatively recent phenomena that have been exacerbated by the reorganization of work, industry, and trade both beyond and within national boundaries.

New Orleans' natural settings also compounded the economic vulnerability of the black population in this model of development. For over 60 years, poor people of color were housed in enclaves that lay almost exclusively in the lower-lying, more flood-prone sections of the city.

In 1970, although New Orleans was a poor city, its poor were not highly concentrated in hyper-segregated neighborhoods. As recently as 1976, there were no neighborhoods that were predominantly black (The Brookings Institution 2005, 6). But that is not to say that African Americans in New Orleans did not face systemic and structural barriers to opportunity before the 1970s. The prevailing (suburban and sprawling) model of development imploded after the 1970s, setting off a new era of urban (and suburban) decline, municipal fiscal crisis, and jurisdictional fragmentation that continues today. During the economic boom of the nineties, as cities made a comeback, concentrated poverty declined for the nation overall but was reinforced in cities like New Orleans, with subsidized housing (housing built with Low Income Housing Tax Credits [LIHTC], a federal subsidy) sited in predominantly poor and black neighborhoods (The Brookings Institution 2005, 6).

CONCENTRATED RACIALIZED POVERTY AND OTHER DEMOGRAPHIC AND SOCIOECONOMIC TRENDS IN NEW ORLEANS AND THE REGION SINCE 1970

Between 1970 and 2000, New Orleans lost both population and jobs. As in the rest of the country, mostly poor people of color lived in declining urban centers like New Orleans, which were steeped in drugs, crime, a declining tax base, and a failing public education system. Blacks continued to be economically ghettoized and routinely excluded from opportunities, while immigrant labor provided opportunities for exploitation as standard business practice. Because of an absurdly low federal minimum wage that was completely out of sync with the real cost of living and the dominance of a low-wage service sector industry, the majority of New Orleans' residents had little hope or opportunity of escaping poverty and moving toward a middle-class life even before Katrina (see Figure 10.1).

In 1970, some 54 percent of the region's population lived in the city, but by 2000, the figure was only 36 percent. In 1970, the city was 42 percent black, but by 2000 that number had risen to 67 percent. Between 1970 and 2000, the number of concentrated poverty neighborhoods in the city grew by two-thirds, even though the poverty rates increased by only 2 percent (from 26 percent to 28 percent) during that 30-year period (The Brookings Institution 2005, 6). Between 1990 and 2000, New Orleans was also one of the few metropolitan areas where the physical distance between where the black population lived and the location of jobs actually increased, going against national trends (Raphael and Stoll 2002).

Before Katrina, 28 percent of New Orleanians were poor. While the entire city suffered from low wages, poor education, and unemployment, black residents suffered even more.

- In 2000, median household income for blacks was half that for whites.
- More than three times as many blacks were poor than whites (35 percent compared to 11 percent).
- Poor blacks were five times more likely than poor whites to live in extremely poor areas (43 percent compared to 11 percent).
- Nearly half (44 percent) of black men 16 and older were unemployed compared to less than a third (30 percent) of white men.
- Less than half (41 percent) of black households owned their home compared to more than half (56 percent) of whites (U.S. Census 2000).

FIGURE 10.1—Concentration of Poverty in New Orleans

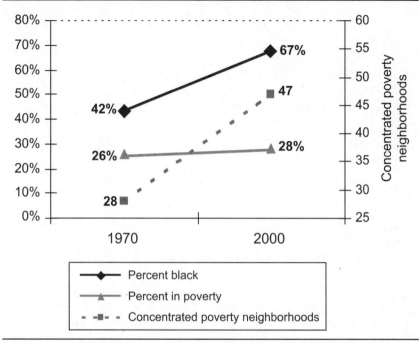

Source: Alan Berube and Bruce Katz, *Katrina's Window: Confronting Concentrated Poverty Across America.* Washington, DC: The Brookings Institution, October 2005, http://www .brook.edu/metro/pubs/20051012_concentratedpoverty.htm. Concentrated poverty neighborhoods (also referred to as extreme or high poverty) are census tracts where 40 percent or more of the population is living at or below the federal poverty line.

THE DISPROPORTIONATE IMPACT OF HURRICANE KATRINA ON POOR PEOPLE OF COLOR

Hurricane Katrina hit a region with significant pre-existing economic disparities and a large vulnerable population that historically has had little or no power in institutional decision making due to racial and/or class bias. When the levees broke and New Orleans flooded, poor people of color, the elderly, and the infirm were trapped and had no means of escaping. Not surprisingly, these populations were the most vulnerable and bore a disproportionate impact of the devastation wrought by Katrina. At the same time, while the overall population in New Orleans has decreased by 34 percent since the hurricane, the percentage of vulnerable individuals living in the Gulf Coast has increased by a dramatic 154 percent (Bill and Melinda Gates Foundation 2006).

Before Katrina and the broken levees:

- Many New Orleanians had disabilities—10.3 percent of 5–20-year-olds, 23.6 percent of 21–64-year-olds, and 50.1 percent of those age 65 and older had disabilities.
- Over 11 percent of New Orleanians were elderly.
- More than 105,000 city dwellers did not have a car during Katrina's evacuation. Nearly one-third (32.7 percent) of black residents did not have a car to help get them out of harm's way compared to less than 10 percent of whites. More than half (52 percent) of poor black residents lacked access to a car compared to only 17 percent of poor whites (U.S. Census 2000).

After Katrina and the broken levees:

- Nearly 30 percent of people hit hard by the flood waters from the broken levees were living at or below the poverty line and another 30 percent were living just above the poverty line (Congressional Research Service 2005). Low-income African-American communities in New Orleans were among the hardest hit by the hurricanes and subsequent flooding.
- Flooded areas were extremely poor—38 of the region's 49 concentrated poverty neighborhoods were flooded after Katrina. Flooded areas of the New Orleans metropolitan region tended to be poorer, have more renters, and were predominantly non-white. In the city of New Orleans, communities of color made up nearly 80 percent of the population in flooded neighborhoods (The Brookings Institution 2005).

REGIONAL ECONOMY AND ECONOMIC BASE

The region's pre-Katrina economy was sluggish and had limited opportunities for low-educated workers. Unemployment among young black men was high—40 percent were not even considered a part of the labor force (those who have been unemployed for six months or more)—and was attributed to inadequate language and math skills, job sprawl (or the relocation of jobs to suburbs that were not accessible to city residents without access to transportation), and disappearing blue-collar jobs. In addition to lacking in education, skills, and experience, black men have borne the brunt of draconian drug laws that penalize nonviolent offenders disproportionately and effectively exclude them from the job market, both because state laws prohibit them from holding certain jobs (or even drivers' licenses) and because most employers are reluctant to hire black men with records (Holzer 2005). (See Figure 10.2.)

Between 1970 and 2000, New Orleans lost jobs, while job growth in the surrounding parishes (suburbs) skyrocketed (157 percent in Jefferson Parish, 431 percent in St. Tammany, and 148 percent in St. Charles). In 1970, the city had two-thirds of

FIGURE 10.2—Jobs and Residents Leave New Orleans

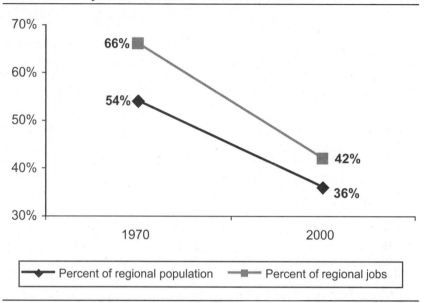

Source: The Brookings Institution, *New Orleans After the Storm: Lessons from the Past, a Plan for the Future.* Washington, DC: The Brookings Institution, October 2005, http://www.brook .edu/metro/pubs/20051012_NewOrleans.pdf.

the region's jobs, but by 2000, the city's share of jobs sank to less than half (42 percent) (The Brookings Institution 2005).

The labor force in the New Orleans region is 30 percent smaller today (Liu, Fellows, and Mabanta 2006) than it was before Katrina, and the unemployment rate remains higher. In order to develop a strong and sustainable regional economic base, rebuilding must be prioritized and coordinated both as a job creation program as well as reconstruction of vital and essential infrastructure that is necessary for jump-starting the economy.

Overall, tourism, higher education, and, to a lesser extent, commercial banking were still important "export" sectors in the city before Katrina. City employment in hotels and motels, for example, represented nearly five times larger a share of local jobs than it did for the nation as a whole in 2000. Similarly, New Orleanians were about 4.5 times as likely to work for colleges and universities and twice as likely to work in commercial banks as their counterparts nationwide. But the broader trend, reflecting national and regional trends, was a shift from high-wage industries such as oil and gas extraction, chemical manufacturing, and ports and related transportation industries to low-wage, service-sector jobs. By 2000, retail and other services comprised 52 percent of all jobs (The Brookings Institution 2005), reflecting the change in the economic base of the region.

SHORT-TERM JOB CREATION

In the shorter term, reconstruction jobs should be prioritized for former residents, and the idea of developing government-funded public works programs (similar to the Civil Works Administration and the Works Project Administration models)[3] with living wages and targeted subsidies (for example, rent) for workers has been proposed by some advocates.

However, the city has, over night, literally changed its hue and ethnicity, as temporary workers are recruited from Latin America and black migrant workers from the Dallas and Atlanta metro areas converge on New Orleans for blue-collar work (Center for Social Inclusion 2007). According to a leading workers' center organizer, this has created a "routine construction of disparity, where Black workers are routinely excluded and immigrants are routinely exploited" (Center for Social Inclusion 2007). Thus, developing an appropriate job/workforce development strategy that is aligned with community economic development requires addressing issues of racial exclusion, and workers' and immigrants' rights explicitly, and is essential for creating a strong regional economy that provides opportunities for all.

FUTURE ECONOMIC DEVELOPMENT PLANNING

In 2003, the Regional Community Audit Project, a partnership including the Louisiana Department of Labor, identified key sectors with growth potentials (see Table 10.1) (MetroVision Economic Development Partnership and DADCO Consulting, Inc., 2003).

Assuming that the analysis in Table 10.1 is correct, in order to transform the region from a low-wage economy to a high-road metropolis in the longer term, an economic development and planning framework for New Orleans needs to consider its strategic sectors and regional industrial clusters and diversify and strengthen its regional economic base in order to have a vibrant local economy that is globally competitive.

The region's competitive advantage lies in industries that have good to high wages and moderate to high growth and are changing to sustainable technologies, such as telecommunications, transportation and logistics, maritime and shipbuilding, and food and consumer industries—offering a real opportunity for rebuilding the region on a more viable and sustainable economic base. Development of the petrochemical and oil and gas industries depends on how the United States charts its energy policy both in the near future and in the longer term. Given New Orleans' cultural significance and its status as a cultural destination point, low-wage service-sector jobs in the entertainment and tourist industry need to be supported with living-wage jobs and adequate benefits and should create pathways for economic and social mobility.

Economic competitiveness is also directly related to a skilled and educated population, which in turn is dependent on a quality education system. Inadequate math and language skills have been identified as one of the major reasons for the extremely

TABLE 10.1—Sectors with Growth Potentials

High Wage, High Growth	Good to High Wages, Moderate Growth	Low Wage, Moderate Growth	Low Wage, Low Growth
• Telecommunications • Warehousing/ Distribution • Petrochemical	• Maritime Shipbuilding • Food and Consumer Products	• Entertainment/ Tourism	• Oil and Gas (high wages for technical and professional workers; good wages for blue-collar workers)

Source: Metro Vision Economic Development Partnership and DADCO Consulting, Inc. 2003. *Making Connections: A Regional Workforce Partnership Community Audit.* U.S. Department of Labor. May 6.

high rates of unemployment among black men in New Orleans. Thus the economic fate of the region is linked to creating a top-notch public education system—both at the K–12 level and beyond.

More broadly, the New Orleans metro region needs to have adequate investment in social, economic, and physical infrastructure along with the right set of policies and governance mechanisms in order to become the great city and region it should be.

PLANNING, REBUILDING, AND SOCIAL INCLUSION IN NEW ORLEANS

Just as public policy choices created concentrated and racialized poverty in New Orleans, rebuilding policies can create opportunities for all, particularly those who have been historically disenfranchised and continue to face structural barriers to opportunity. The twenty-first century holds both new hopes (such as the advent of the Internet and other technology shifts) and old challenges (such as the tension over new immigrants or the persistence of poverty and structural racism) that need to be strategically considered as we rebuild New Orleans.

Our vision of a rebuilt New Orleans builds on its cultural heritage and tangible assets, while protecting it from natural and man-made disasters by investing public and private resources in physical, economic, and social infrastructure. *A rebuilt New Orleans should build on the principles of diversity, sustainability, participation, and accountability to create vibrant neighborhoods/communities that are positioned to thrive in their regional, national, and global context and are informed by strategic community-based planning and led by local leadership.*

This section (a) examines current rebuilding plans and planning processes in New Orleans; (b) grades recovery efforts in housing, utilities, economic development, health services, and education in New Orleans' 13 planning districts; (c) identifies innovative policies and programs that have potentials for success; and (d) underscores the centrality of supporting emergent leaders and organizations that have proved their effectiveness and won the trust of community members and have a vision of a better and fairer New Orleans.

Finally, it comments on the politics of rebuilding and lays out a shared policy platform built on shared principles of diversity, participation, and accountability that needs to be supported in response not only to rebuilding New Orleans and the Gulf Coast but to reimagining and remaking cities and regions.

CURRENT PLANS, PROCESSES, AND OUTCOMES

Neighborhood planning to rebuild New Orleans has been fraught with tension from the beginning. Initial conflict swelled mainly around recommendations by national organizations against rebuilding low-lying areas, like the Lower Ninth Ward, for flood safety reasons. The debate over the size and scope of New Orleans' footprint is not over, though public officials seem to have been sidestepping it for the past several months. A news piece written in late 2006 noted that it "was unclear . . . to what degree the volatile issue of whether to constrict New Orleans' geographic 'footprint' . . . will be explored" (Warner 2006).

A valid question raised by community organizers and residents is the legitimacy of the community planning process when more than half of the pre-Katrina population of New Orleans is still displaced. FEMA parks like Renaissance Village in Baker, Louisiana (with over 600 trailers) have no telephones and more than half of the population are unemployed and cannot afford cellular phones or other means of constant communication (Center for Social Inclusion 2007). How involved is the participation of a city with thousands of new and likely temporary residents? A related point for residents, primarily from low-income and people-of-color communities, has been over the lack of outreach and inclusion in planning discussions and meetings. Well-respected organizations and leaders have also expressed similar feedback on the process: "All the evidence suggests that there is an agenda to keep poor working class folks from returning to the city." "Some plans were more legitimate than others" (Center for Social Inclusion 2007).

There are four main planning processes in relation to rebuilding, though the Unified New Orleans Plan (UNOP) is largely recognized as the most comprehensive of the existing plans (Horne and Nee 2006).

- FEMA's ESF-14, which included local experts and outside consultants, culminated in a nationwide Louisiana Planning Day, which involved displaced residents and returnees.[4] Elements of this plan have not been incorporated in the other major planning processes.
- Mayor Ray Nagin's Bring New Orleans Back (BNOB)[5] plan, the first city-initiated plan, which proposed additional neighborhood-level work by local architects, was politically defeated because it recommended shrinking the footprint of the city and turning the lowest, most flooded, and least populated

neighborhoods to green space. The issue of which areas are the lowest is also disputed, giving rise to further tension among groups.

- The Lambert Plan (or the New Orleans Neighborhoods Rebuilding Plan)[6], initiated by the New Orleans City Council and led by Miami-based housing consultant Paul Lambert, was charged with drawing up plans for 46 significantly flooded neighborhoods in New Orleans. The process got mixed reviews from neighborhood associations. An estimated 7,500 residents participated in the process, which involved 84 public meetings, including three in Houston, Atlanta, and Baton Rouge. The Lambert Plan avoided the concept of neighborhood viability and operated under the assumption that the pre-Katrina neighborhoods should be left intact. The downfall of this process was that it did not offer a unified plan for the entire city and only focused on flooded neighborhoods. Both a unified plan for the entire city and a focus on flooded neighborhoods were requirements of the Louisiana Recovery Authority (LRA).
- The $7.5 million Unified New Orleans Plan or UNOP,[7] completed in January 2007, in theory allows neighborhoods to decide how to implement earlier ideas proposed by other plans, and is supposed to provide a unified plan for the city.[8] (See Figure 10.3.)

FIGURE 10.3—Diagram of the UNOP Process

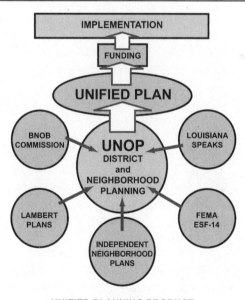

UNIFIED PLANNING PRODUCT

Source: The Unified New Orleans Plan: Citywide Strategic Recovery and Rebuilding Plan. City of New Orleans. 2007, http://www.unifiedneworleansplan.com/uploads/UNOP-FINAL-PLAN -April-2007-15744.pdf.

The main recommendations of UNOP are safer rebuilding; encouraging local and federal housing authorities to rebuild "a sufficient number" of low-income housing, using mixed-income and mixed-use models; providing financial assistance targeted to individuals and businesses in areas with the slowest repopulation and highest risk of future flooding and encouraging "neighborhood clusters"; and restoring city-wide services (including re-visioning the K–12 public education system, redesigning a health care network, and restoring and upgrading the physical and social infrastructure of the entire city).

UNOP has also suffered from issues of representation, participation, and incongruity. There are 15 city planning teams with contracts, but there is no full-time person connecting local activities and planning processes. The general opinion is that leadership in government is lacking. The coordinating organization for the planning process is America Speaks, and it has been said that "The America Speaks budget [$2.4 million], which is more than half the total of all other money allocated for work on the Unified New Orleans Plan, has raised eyebrows in some quarters."[9] Community members, planners, and city leaders have expressed concern that despite its goals, UNOP may omit the priorities of many residents, particularly those who have not yet returned. The demographic disparity between participants at UNOP community meetings versus that of the city before the storm was so great that America Speaks expressed concern about who was not in the room (Krupa 2006).

For example, 75 percent of about 350 participants at an October 2006 UNOP meeting were white, and 40 percent had an annual household income of more than $75,000. Before Hurricane Katrina, 67 percent of the city was African-American, 2 percent of households had incomes over $75,000, and 54 percent earned less than $29,000 per year. Also conspicuously absent were representatives of the city's formerly large youth population (Krupa 2006).

Outreach efforts to maximize community participation for a December 2, 2006, UNOP included using letters to displaced families, information on a Web site, churches, New Orleans neighborhood groups, activist organizations, and city politicians (including Mayor Nagin) to get out the word (Warner 2006).

The final January 25, 2007, meeting fared somewhat better in terms of representation. About 1,300 people participated, including displaced residents in Atlanta, Dallas, Houston, and New Orleans, linked via giant TVs and electronic keypads (Warner 2006). Fifty-five percent were black, 4 percent were Asian-American, 2 percent were Latino, and 34 percent were white. Twenty-four percent had annual household incomes below $24,000, but only 29 percent were renters[10]. Six percent were between 15 and 19 years old and 10 percent were between 20 and 34 years. Of those who attended, 77 percent said they were "satisfied" or "very satisfied" with the process, while 12 percent said that they were "unsatisfied" or "very unsatisfied."

The main actors of UNOP are:

Planning Coordinator: Steven Bingler, Principal, Concordia, LLC. Bingler's New Orleans–based firm, Concordia, is coordinating the planning effort.

Supporters: City of New Orleans; New Orleans City Council; New Orleans Planning Commission; Regional Planning Commission; Louisiana Recovery Authority; and the U.S. Department of Housing and Urban Development (HUD).

Oversight: New Orleans Community Support Foundation (six members) and Community Support Organization (nine members).

Funders: Greater New Orleans Foundation (GNOF), a community foundation that has donated $1 million to UNOP; the Rockefeller Foundation, one of the nation's oldest and largest private foundations, has made the biggest contribution to date at $3.5 million. Other foundations include the W. K. Kellogg Foundation, Rockefeller Brothers Fund, the Carnegie Foundation, the Case Foundation, Surdna Foundation, the Ford Foundation, and the Louisiana Disaster Recovery Foundation.

In June 2007 the *Times-Picayune* reported that "the Louisiana Recovery Authority board accepted New Orleans' citywide recovery plan . . . [which] grew out of the Unified New Orleans Plan, as well as at least seven other planning processes that followed the flood."

COMMON THEMES, GOALS, AND OBJECTIVES IN ESF-14, BNOB, LAMBERT, AND UNOP

Not surprisingly, the most common theme across all the plans is substantial investment in hurricane protection for the city and region. In addition, all four plans propose the following:

- Building/restoring housing for the elderly;
- Creating equitable access to education (UNOP recommends dual use of schools as community centers);
- Providing affordable housing for low-income citizens (BNOB and UNOP recommend mixed-income communities; UNOP recommends mixed-use also);
- Improving health care in the city by distributing the financial burden of caring for the uninsured and creating health care options in more areas throughout the city (UNOP recommends a regional- and neighborhood-serving health care network to meet local health needs by revitalizing the medical district and replacing Charity Hospital).

While the plans have some common goals, they are not always explicit about their objectives or how they will achieve their stated objectives. For example:

Deconcentrating Poverty

The Lambert Plan explicitly mentions deconcentrating poverty as a goal, but does not explain how this would be accomplished. BNOB recommends creating mixed-income communities. UNOP recommends both mixed-income and mixed-use real estate/housing models and inclusionary zoning policies to promote diversity.

Affordable Housing Near Opportunity

ESF-14 mentions building affordable housing but does not discuss location. UNOP offers several suggestions to rebuild housing:

a. Reexamine The Road Home program, which currently presents a prohibitively long and complicated application process, does not address renter needs, and does not provide enough funding to meet construction costs.
b. Provide affordable housing for all displaced former public housing residents, while using mixed-income and mixed-use models.
c. Offer homebuyer assistance and home rehabilitation loans to low- and moderate-income residents.
d. Adopt inclusionary zoning policies to diversify neighborhoods.
e. Develop transient worker housing for those involved in recovery efforts.

Creating a Regional Public Education System

While the plans do recommend creating an equitable public education system, no plan mentions creating a regional, socioeconomically integrated system or grapples with the issues of control and representation in educational structures. UNOP mentions creating an "equitable, competitive and unified elementary and secondary school system" but does not discuss the possibility of a regional public education system.

Creating More Living-Wage Jobs That Provide Opportunities for Career Mobility

ESF-14 and BNOB recommend strategies for workforce development. The BNOB plan goes as far as to suggest building temporary housing units located near job training opportunities and that a living wage be paid to all employees working on all projects receiving government funds. UNOP makes several suggestions for stimulating neighborhood-level economies as well as connecting the city with the region's important industries. Small business incubators and workforce development programs for the "chronically unemployed" are also recommended. The plan proposes relocating small businesses from slowly repopulating areas to more densely populated areas, which might be beneficial for business owners but would likely harm those areas from which this investment is fleeing.

Creating a Regional Transportation System

ESF-14 and BNOB plans outline initiatives to integrate New Orleans with the regional economy through an expanded public transportation systems, labor development, and investment in important industrial sectors. Both plans also explicitly propose investment in small and minority-owned businesses. The Lambert Plan recommends investing in concentrated retail zones near major transportation hubs and neighborhood-level commercial projects such as Main Street programs.

NEW ORLEANS RECOVERY REPORT CARD

Across the city, neighborhoods are still struggling to recover from unprecedented damage and destruction. In addition to the planning processes, physical rebuilding of housing and community infrastructure has been slow and frustrating for most residents, three years after Hurricane Katrina. The Center for Social Inclusion has created a monthly report card for the 13 New Orleans planning districts based on the ability of former New Orleans residents to rebuild their lives (see Table 10.2). The grade is based on performance in five categories: economy, utilities, health, housing, and public education. As of May 2008, the overall grade for New Orleans is D+, with F considered a failing grade.

Many of the planning districts with a failing grade (the Lower Ninth Ward, Village de l'Est, New Orleans East, and Bywater) have over 90 percent persons of color and are facing the most difficulty. These neighborhoods were among the most flooded (Greater New Orleans Data Center 2005) and depended more heavily on systems likely to be disrupted in the event of a disaster, such as public schools and transportation (U.S. Census 2000). Although some wealthier districts with a larger white population also face adversity, these communities were more prepared to rebound from the catastrophe, both because of their financial safety net and lesser reliance on public infrastructure and services.

PROPOSED POLICY PLATFORM
AND RECOMMENDATIONS

What should a rebuilt New Orleans look like? Who needs to be involved in developing, planning, and implementing that vision? What have we learned from the past, and are there promising models that can be tested or adapted in New Orleans? These are some of the obvious questions and challenges faced by residents, planners, policy makers, and organizations working to rebuild New Orleans.

The preceding section provided an overview of current planning and rebuilding work. The following identifies potential policy proposals that would help to achieve desirable outcomes both in terms of immediate rebuilding work and future economic development. It concurs with the common goals of the four plans identified in the previous section. The goal here is not to list a comprehensive set of policy recommendations but to provide a policy framework that will serve as an opportunity builder for people who face systemic and structural barriers by developing race-conscious policies in housing, jobs/economic development, public education, public transportation, and community health in an integrated way.

TABLE 10.2—New Orleans Recovery Report Card

	Report Card												Pre-Katrina Neighborhood Demographics			
	Overall		Utilities		Economy		Health		Rental Housing		Owned Housing		Overall Housing	Public Education		Pop.	% Non-white	Ave. HHI	% Poverty

	Overall		Utilities		Economy		Health		Rental Housing		Owned Housing		Overall Housing		Public Education		Pop.	% Non-white	Ave. HHI	% Poverty
New Orleans Avg.	C-	70%	A+	99%	D+	69%	F	27%	F	41%	A+	100%	C-	72%	F	55%	489,773	74%	43,028	27.34%
Lower Ninth Ward	F	50%	B+	87%	F	56%	F	0%	F	12%	A+	100%	D-	60%	F	48%	19,515	97%	28,867	34.42%
Village de l'Est	F	54%	A+	100%	D-	62%	F	0%	F	20%	A+	100%	F	58%	F	51%	12,912	96%	36,856	29.90%
New Orleans East	F	54%	A+	100%	F	59%	D	0%	F	7%	A+	100%	F	59%	F	54%	79,808	90%	42,951	18.90%
Mid-City	D	64%	A+	100%	D-	61%	F	67%	F	20%	A+	100%	D	46%	F	48%	80,909	88%	27,015	40.51%
Bywater	F	56%	A+	100%	D+	69%	F	0%	F	34%	A+	100%	D	63%	F	49%	42,984	88%	28,873	36.46%
New Aurora/English Turn	D-	61%	A+	100%	D	64%	F	0%	F	60%	A+	100%	B+	89%	F	52%	5,672	83%	62,939	24.80%
Gentilly	D-	60%	A+	100%	D	64%	F	0%	F	18%	A+	100%	C+	78%	F	59%	41,196	74%	47,522	14.58%
Central City/Garden District	B-	81%	A+	100%	B-	82%	A+	100%	D-	63%	A+	100%	C-	73%	F	50%	48,327	73%	36,761	39.51%
Algiers	C	76%	A+	100%	A-	92%	F	50%	D-	62%	A+	100%	B	84%	F	53%	55,857	70%	42,484	24.09%
Uptown/Carrollton	B-	82%	A+	100%	C+	77%	A+	100%	F	51%	A+	100%	C	74%	D-	61%	67,083	53%	57,398	23.99%
Venetian Islands	D-	62%	A+	100%	D-	61%	F	0%	C	75%	A+	100%	A-	91%	F	57%	3,643	47%	40,621	29.93%
French Quarter/CBD	C-	71%	A+	100%	B-	82%	F	40%	C-	71%	A+	100%	C+	78%	F	56%	5,970	21%	60,794	17.26%
Lakeview	D	67%	A+	100%	D+	69%	F	0%	F	46%	A+	100%	B-	83%	B-	82%	25,897	9%	73,716	6.29%

Source: Center for Social Inclusion, *New Orleans Recovery Report Card.* New York: Center for Social Inclusion, 2008. For a complete methodology, see Center for Social Inclusion, *Race to Rebuild: The Color of Opportunity and the Future of New Orleans.* New York: Center for Social Inclusion, 2006, http://centerfor socialinclusion.org/PDF/racetorebuild.pdf.

1. Create Living Wage Jobs for Residents from Rebuilding
   Connect displaced and other residents to rebuilding work (housing, schools, parks, and other civic buildings and spaces) and require living wages for all work.[11]
2. Create Affordable Housing, Mixed-Income Neighborhoods, and Deconcentrate Poverty and Opportunities for Mobility
   a. Rental Housing
   Replace, repair, and relocate public housing.[12]
   Increase voucher support and expand eligible geographic scope.[13]
   Locate future public housing in high-opportunity neighborhoods.[14]
   Create more private affordable housing and locate it in high-opportunity neighborhoods.
   Mandate Regional Inclusionary Zoning.[15]
   b. Home ownership
   Give homeowners who have lost their homes enough support to acquire a home in New Orleans or in their new community if they decide to relocate.[16]
   Expand home-buying opportunities to first-time homebuyers who have low-to-moderate incomes.[17]
   Create a quality regional public education system.
   Develop a quality regional public school system by implementing an economic integration plan with equitable funding for public K–12 schools by allocating more federal resources.
   Provide accessible transportation to regional schools.[18]
3. Transit
   Invest in public transit to provide mobility and access to opportunities to all.
   Invest federal dollars in mass transit (light rail, rapid bus) to connect low-income communities of color to jobs in the suburbs and regional transportation systems that connect neighborhoods within the city and the city to the suburban job centers.
4. Environment
   Adopt an aggressive soil-testing and clean-up program and rethink water management.[19]
   Invest in green infrastructure and green technology.

CONCLUSION: THE POLITICS OF REBUILDING AND SOCIAL INCLUSION

New Orleans epitomizes both our failure as a nation to provide for our most vulnerable and needy as well as the power and resilience of people to come together in times of tremendous crisis. Almost a year and a half after Hurricane Katrina, New Orleans has moved to a phase beyond immediate relief work, notwithstanding the fact that many are still struggling to rebuild their lives.

Government failure and the limitations of the "nonprofit-industrial complex" have been correctly criticized by leaders and community members who continue to struggle with vastly inadequate resources and a complex set of social and economic problems (Flaherty 2006). While the federal government has committed $107.6 billion to the Gulf Coast after Hurricane Katrina, only 43 percent of the authorized dollars have actually been distributed to individuals or recipient governments. More than half of the federal commitment ($57.5 billion) was dedicated to immediate relief. Of the remaining $50 billion for recovery, $41.7 billion is committed to housing and $8.3 billion to other recovery-related activities (Bill and Melinda Gates Foundation 2006).

The nonprofit sector in the Gulf Coast was underresourced relative to other parts of the country before Hurricane Katrina. Despite the tremendous work and leadership of existing nonprofits after the disaster, the capacity of the sector overall is diminished and cannot be restored without additional funding. But only 2 percent (or $2.4 billion) of the total $107.6 billion is available for the nonprofit sector, which again is dominated by large national charities that have received over 80 percent of the total charitable giving and 50 percent of philanthropic giving (Bill and Melinda Gates Foundation 2006).

In addition to funding and capacity, another central rebuilding issue, that of participation and inclusion, remains fiercely contested. Can former residents who want to rebuild their lives in New Orleans have that opportunity, and will they be able to participate in accountable and transparent processes that can facilitate strategic community input and cooperation among diverse stakeholders? More broadly, who will be socially and economically included in a rebuilt New Orleans?

On the one hand, groups that have been working to find innovative solutions to systemic problems (for example, police brutality and community-police relations) well before Hurricane Katrina, as well as other local groups, exude a revitalized social commitment. Equally inspiring are a cadre of new and emergent leaders, who come from diverse social and racial backgrounds and whose commitment to rebuilding a more just and humane New Orleans has been clearly demonstrated.

On the other hand, if the planning process is any indication of what the future bodes, then the people of New Orleans have a tough fight ahead. Most importantly, without the political will and support of elected and other public officials, even the best plan will not yield results. Related and equally flawed is the discussion on the size or footprint of a rebuilt New Orleans. The issue is not about density versus size. A denser New Orleans, if planned thoughtfully, can be viable and better if it allows those who wish to return the opportunity to do so.

But academics, planners, and policy makers who argue that the approximately 175,000 people who have not returned are very poor and can be more easily absorbed in places with vibrant job markets (Nossiter 2007), because the pre-Katrina economy did not have the capacity to employ them, need to consider the reality and politics of projects involving large-scale displacement (relocation!) of the poor. Research shows that this type of displacement has disastrous social and psychological consequences and destroys important social safety networks (Thompson Fullilove 2004).

While some may choose to start their lives anew and build community elsewhere because they have the choice and opportunity to do so, chances are that the majority of the 175,000 very poor displaced New Orleanians whose fates are being determined by others will just continue to be very poor somewhere else and will possibly be worse off than they would be in New Orleans.

New Orleans was the third largest U.S. city in 1830. Where it stands in future as a rebuilt city remains to be seen. Much of its structural problems of racial and economic exclusion that characterize U.S. central cities can be fixed with the right opportunity structures. At the local level, steps toward reforming the police department, led by criminal justice and social justice advocates, constitute a promising move toward governance structures that promote transparency, accountability, and community participation.

What New Orleans (and other equally vulnerable regions across the nation) needs is a renewed federal commitment to provide opportunities for all, particularly those most vulnerable, by promoting the right set of policies and providing the right set of incentives and disincentives for the private sector and organized civil society. If government can live up to its roles and responsibilities, the people and leaders of New Orleans can lead the way to rebuilding a city and region that will be better than before.

NOTES

1. By "structural racism" is meant the blind interaction between institutions, policies, and practices that perpetuate barriers to opportunities and racial disparities.

2. The issue of social/racial and economic exclusion in rural areas is equally important and related but will not be discussed here.

3. In 1933, the U.S. government created the Civil Works Administration (CWA) and put 4.2 million Americans to work in public construction jobs (school repair, sanitation work, road building, and the like). In 1935, the Works Project Administration (WPA) replaced the CWA. Over its seven-year span, the WPA put eight million Americans to work, built or improved 5,900 schools, 2,500 hospitals, and 13,000 playgrounds. Scott Myers-Lipton, Gulf Coast Civic Works Project, November 11, 2006, *Social Solutions to Poverty Weekly,* http://solvingpoverty.blogspot.com/2006/11/gc.html.

4. Louisiana Speaks, http://www.louisianaspeaks-parishplans.org/indparishhome page.cfm?EntID=11.

5. Bring New Orleans Back Fund, http://www.bringneworleansback.org.

6. New Orleans Neighborhood Rebuilding Plan, http://www.nolanrp.com.

7. United New Orleans Plan, http://www.unifiedneworleansplan.com.

8. Ibid.

9. Ibid.

10. About 53 percent of the population were renters before Katrina.

11. Proposed policies include:

- Hiring preferences to community development collaboratives, community and faith-based organizations and New Orleans businesses that partner with nonprofit service providers and people of color. African-American Leadership Project, Letter to the Congressional Black Caucus, 9/22/05, "AALP Perspective on the Rebuilding of the City."

- Prohibiting companies that disregard Davis-Bacon, affirmative action, and local participation from receiving or keeping rebuilding contracts. Ibid.
- For transportation-related jobs, agencies should use provisions in the new federal transportation bill to create local hiring ordinances that allow communities to require that large construction projects rely on a minimum percentage of workers from nearby communities. Smart Growth America, *The Hurricanes' Legacy: Redevelopment in the Gulf Coast and the Nation* (Washington, DC, 2005).

12. While the most detailed policy proposals have been on housing issues, the issue of public housing and rental housing remains contentious. Residents rightly point out that in a city with a majority renter population, the needs of renters are being largely ignored—both in privately owned and in public housing. The fact remains that many, including elected officials, are blatantly prejudiced about public housing and public housing residents because they are largely poor people of color. Noteworthy is U. S. Representative (R-LA) Richard Baker's comment, "We finally cleaned up public housing in New Orleans. We couldn't do it, but God did."

13. Proposed policies include:

- Provide displaced families with Section 8 vouchers eligible for use throughout the Gulf Coast. Center for American Progress, "Rebuilding Homes and Lives: Progressive Options for Housing Policy Post Katrina" (October 14, 2005).
- Use Section 8 along with LIHTC to provide more permanent housing. Ibid.
- Ensure subsidies for displaced residents, who were receiving housing choice voucher assistance before Hurricane Katrina. National Policy and Advocacy Council on Homelessness (NPACH), "Reconstruction After Hurricanes Katrina, Rita and Wilma—Housing Needs and Policy Recommendations."
- Appropriate funds for new vouchers (for use in the interim while awaiting permanent public housing support) for previously unassisted households displaced by the Hurricanes.

14. Proposed policies include:

- Restore the HOPE VI program to funding levels prior to the 2003 reduction and increase HOPE VI beyond this level for the Gulf Region. Center for American Progress, "Rebuilding Homes and Lives: Progressive Options for Housing Policy Post Katrina" (October 14, 2005).

Congress created HOPE VI in 1993 to not only address "bricks and sticks" but also the special needs of the families locked in concentrated poverty through a comprehensive approach to community and supportive services. In 1995, HUD changed HOPE VI by creating the mixed-finance development method, a radical departure from traditional public housing development. The mixed finance approach enables public housing authorities to enter into partnerships with private developers to create new mixed-income communities by combining HUD funding with private financing. These new public/private partnerships allow public housing to be produced in privately owned and managed developments that include additional affordable and market-rate housing.

- Guarantee alternative economically integrated housing opportunities for former residents who are displaced by the new developments.
- Fully fund existing housing assistance programs like HOME and Community Development Block Grant (CDBG). Design these to produce high-quality, mixed-income, and mixed-use communities with enough homes to meet the needs of extremely low-income families.

HOME provides federal formula-based grants to states and localities that communities use—often in partnership with local nonprofit groups—to fund a wide range of activities that build, buy, and/or rehabilitate affordable housing for rent or home ownership or provide direct rental assistance to low-income people.

The Community Development Block Grant (CDBG) program was created to ensure decent affordable housing for all by providing services to the most vulnerable in our communities to create jobs and expand business opportunities. The CDBG program accomplishes this through the provision of annual grants on a formula basis to many different types of grantees (individual, state, and local entities/ communities) through several programs (Entitlement Communities, State Administered CDBG, Section 108 Loan Guarantee Program, Renewal Communities/Empowerment Zones/Enterprise Communities, etc.).

- Provide additional funding for the HOME program; include HOME production as part of a package of federal incentives to stimulate the redevelopment of infrastructure and revive economies in the flooded and storm-wrecked areas.
- Leverage federal CDBGs to increase private investment in mixed-income housing developments.
- Amend Section 152 of the federal Housing and Community Development Act of 1992 to designate New Orleans as a participating site for the Moving to Opportunity (MTO) Program, a pilot program to improve the lives of very low-income families by moving them to low-poverty neighborhoods. Joint Statement by Black Social Scientists, "Principles and Priorities for Rebuilding New Orleans," William E. Spriggs, Senior Fellow, Economic Policy Institute, http://www.planning.org/katrina/reader/pdf/PrinciplesandPriorities.pdf.

The "Black Social Scientists" include the Association of Black Sociologists, National Association of Black Social Workers, and the Planning and Black Community Division of the American Planning Association, the Board of the National Organization of Minority Architects, the Executive Director of the National Forum of Black Public Administrators, and concerned black economists.

Moving to Opportunity for Fair Housing is a HUD ten-year research demonstration that combines tenant-based rental assistance with housing counseling to help very low-income families move from poverty-stricken urban areas to low-poverty neighborhoods (and looks at the impact of the program on the housing, employment, and educational achievements of assisted households). Vouchers must be used in areas with less than 10 percent poverty. Families chosen for the experimental group receive tenant-based Section 8 rental assistance that helps pay their rent, as well as housing counseling to help them find and successfully use housing in low-poverty areas. Five public housing authorities (Baltimore, Boston, Chicago, Los Angeles, and New York City) administer HUD contracts under this ten-year demonstration.

15. Policy proposals include:
- Require inclusionary zoning in new developments throughout the metropolitan area. New developments would include substantial rehabilitation and re-use projects. From The Lake to the River: The New Orleans Coalition for Legal Aid & Disaster Relief, "An Alternative Vision for Rebuilding, Redevelopment, and Reconstruction" (2005), http://www.fromthelaketotheriver.org/files/final_report_11.29.pdf.
- Use tiered income targets that match the affordable housing needs of current and future New Orleans residents.
- Tie federal housing funds to local adoption of inclusionary zoning. The Brookings Institution Metropolitan Policy Program, "New Orleans After the Storm: Lessons from the Past," a Plan for the Future.

16. Louisiana's Road Home program addresses some of this need. It provides up to $150,000 (in addition to FEMA aid and insurance recovery) to insured homeowners to

rebuild anywhere in Louisiana. A team of 40 national and Louisiana-based housing finance experts put together an analysis of how to rebuild housing in New Orleans using
CDBG and other federal funding sources. The analysis was requested by a collaborative
(BNOB Housing Subcommittee, New Orleans Neighborhood Development Collaborative, and the Urban Land Institute). Basically CDBG would be used as gap funding to
make up the deficit left by FEMA and insurance proceeds.

For insured homeowners, the grant could cover up to 100 percent of the gap for a
maximum of $150,000 per household. For uninsured homeowners, the grant would
cover 60 percent of the gap for a maximum of $150,000. Homeowners who had homes
in areas deemed not rebuildable would be offered the option to sell their home for a price
equal to the pre-Katrina market value less FEMA and insurance proceeds, and no more
than $150,000. See The Road Home program at http://www.road2la.org.

17. The Brookings Institution has proposed the following federal policy to produce
affordable housing for homebuyers:

• Adopt the Single Family Homeownership Tax Credit. This tax credit would increase
  the supply of single-family affordable homes by up to an additional 50,000 homes
  annually. Single-family developments must be located in a census tract with a median income equal to 80 percent or less of area median income, with occupancy limited to homebuyers in the same income range.

Builders of affordable homes for middle-income purchasers would receive a tax credit
awarded by state housing finance agencies. State housing finance agencies would be given
credit authority equal to the amount provided for LIHTCs, which in 2004 was the greater
of $2.075 million, or $1.80 per capita. The Brookings Institution Metropolitan Policy Program, "New Orleans After the Storm: Lessons from the Past, a Plan for the Future."

18. Paul T. Hill, the director for the Center of the Center on Reinventing Education at
the University of Washington, has proposed creation of a state-federal partnership to
fund New Orleans' schools. The state would continue to provide its per-capita share of
costs (about two-thirds of the total per-pupil expenditure) and the amount it appropri-
ates for capital expenditures. The federal government would combine all its categorical-
aid programs into one lump sum and replace lost local taxes with aid. To cover students
previously in parochial schools, the federal government would have to come up with additional funds. Federal support would continue until local sales and property tax rev-
enues grew to some share of pre-hurricane levels. Paul T. Hill, "Re-Creating Public
Education in New Orleans," *Education Week*, September 21, 2005.

19. An array of policy proposals tackle how best to rebuild New Orleans, taking into
account the fact that it is sinking and the need for sustainable solutions. Three general
models currently exist: (1) the Netherlands model with its complex construction of levees
and dams; (2) the Venetian model of water flow through the city, depositing sediments to
offset erosion; and (3) allowing nature to help restore the wetland buffers between sea and
city. John Bohannon and Martin Enserink, "Hurricane Katrina: Scientists Weigh Options
for Rebuilding New Orleans," *Science* 309, no. 5742 (September 16, 2005): 1808–1809.
Some of the suggested solutions are hybrids combining aspects of more than one of these
categories. One example is protection of smaller areas against extreme hurricane events
with defenses around population centers and wetlands restoration outside of the city to
moderate storm surges; and, in some areas, elevation of buildings to encourage and manage retreat from the coastline. G. Edward Dickey and Leonard Shabman, "Making Tough
Choices: Hurricane Protection Planning After Katrina and Rita," *Resources for the Future*,
no. 160 (Winter 2006): 31, http://rff.org/Documents/RFF-Resources-160-Katrina.pdf.

REFERENCES

Bill and Melinda Gates Foundation. 2006. Gulf Coast Non-Profits: Landscape Analysis and Needs Assessment. August 31.

Center for Social Inclusion. 2007. "Triumph over Tragedy: Leadership, Capacity and Needs in Arkansas, Alabama, Georgia, Louisiana and Mississippi After Hurricanes Katrina and Rita." November. Available at http://www.centerforsocialinclusion.org/PDF/Triumph%20Over%20Tragedy-%20Leadership%20Capacity%20and%20Needs.pdf (accessed July 29, 2008).

Congressional Research Service. 2005. "CRS Report for Congress, Hurricane Katrina: Social-Demographic Characteristics of Impacted Areas." The Library of Congress. November 4.

Entergy New Orleans. n.d. "Electric and Gas Service in New Orleans." Available at http://www.entergy-neworleans.com/your_home/storm_center/storms_katrina.aspx (accessed July 29, 2008).

Flaherty, J. 2006. "Catastrophic Failure–Foundations, Nonprofits and the Continuing Crisis in New Orleans." December 16. Available at http://www.virtualcitizens.com/articles/Catastrophic_Failure.__Foundations_Nonprofits_and_the_Continuing_Crisis_in_New_Orleans.

Greater New Orleans Data Center. 2005. "Orleans Parish Sept. 11th Flood Extent with Neighborhoods & Major Roads." November. Available at http://www.gnocdc.org/maps/PDFs/flood_extent.pdf (accessed July 29, 2008).

Holzer, H. J. 2005. "Back to Work in New Orleans." October. The Brookings Institution.

Horne, J., and B. Nee. 2006. "An Overview of the Unified New Orleans Planning Process." October 18. Available at http://www.bnee.com/wp-content/uploads/2006/10/An_Overview_of_the_Unified_New_Orleans_Planning_Process.pdf (accessed July 29, 2008).

Krupa, M. 2006. "Survey Backs Plan for Smaller Footprint." *Times-Picayune.* October 29.

Liu, A., M. Fellows, and M. Mabanta. 2006. "Special Edition of the Katrina Index: A One-Year Review of Key Indicators of Recovery in Post-Storm New Orleans." Metropolitan Policy Program, The Brookings Institution. August. Available at http://www.brook.edu/metro/pubs/20060822_Katrina.pdf (accessed July 29, 2008).

McNabb, D., and L. E. Madere, Jr. 2003. "A History of New Orleans." November. Available at http://www.madere.com/history.html (accessed July 29, 2008).

MetroVision Economic Development Partnership and DADCO Consulting, Inc. 2003. "Making Connections: A Regional Workforce Partnership Community Audit." U.S. Department of Labor. May 6. Available at http://www.doleta.gov/usworkForce/communityaudits (accessed July 29, 2008).

Nossiter, A. 2007. "New Orleans of Future May Stay Half Its Old Size." *New York Times.* January 21.

The Brookings Institution. 2005. "New Orleans After the Storm: Lessons from the Past, A Plan for the Future." October. Citing Daphne Spain, "Race Relations and Residential Segregation in New Orleans: Two Centuries of Paradox." *Annals of the American Academy of Political and Social Science* 441:82–96. Available at http://www.brook.edu/metro/pubs/20051012_NewOrleans.pdf (accessed July 29, 2008).

Thompson Fullilove, M. 2004. *Root Shock—How Tearing Up City Neighborhoods Hurt America and What We Can Do About It.* New York: One World/Ballantine.

Raphael, S., and M. A. Stoll. 2002. "Modest Progress: The Narrowing Spatial Mismatch Between Blacks and Jobs in the 1990s." Center on Urban and Metropolitan Policy, The Brookings Institution. December. Available at http://www.brookings.edu/metro/katrina.htm (accessed July 29, 2008).

U.S. Census. 2000. SF3.

Warner, C. 2006. "Rebuild Sessions Casting Wide Net: Thousands Expected in Five Linked Cities." *Times-Picayune*. December 1.

CHAPTER 11

HOUSING RECOVERY IN THE NINTH WARD

Disparities in Policy, Process, and Prospects

Lisa K. Bates and Rebekah A. Green

In the aftermath of Hurricane Katrina's flooding of New Orleans, politicians, pundits, and planners wrote off much of New Orleans' low-income, African-American neighborhoods as unsalvageable. In particular, the Lower Ninth Ward was seen as a totally destroyed neighborhood best abandoned. This impression was further reinforced by Federal Emergency Management Agency (FEMA) damage estimates, along with assumptions about residents' desire and capacity to return. Each seemed to confirm that the neighborhoods were damaged beyond repair. Approximately 20,000 residents were displaced from the Lower Ninth Ward alone.

Even before the disaster, black New Orleanians faced problems with housing affordability, access to financing, and substandard subsidized housing. The loss of housing stock after Katrina and the post-disaster policies implemented by FEMA and the Department of Housing and Urban Development (HUD) compounded pre-storm issues of limited housing opportunities. Nowhere was this more evident than in the city's quintessential low-income, African-American neighborhood, the Lower Ninth Ward.

In this chapter, we present an empirical analysis of the reconstruction of residential housing in the Lower Ninth Ward, considering pre-storm problems, flood damage, and policy impediments to recovery. First, we present pre-Katrina data about racial disparities in housing security and affordability. Second, we examine the physical data forming the basis for depopulation plans, reporting the results of a survey of 3,211 residential units for structural damage, flood damage, and recovery activity. We then evaluate The Road Home program's effectiveness in assisting Ninth Ward homeowners' rebuilding.

Finally, we present data on The Road Home applications and funding receipts in the Ninth Ward compared to other New Orleans neighborhoods. Through this examination we argue that due to pre-storm inequities in housing and program specifics, the post-Katrina Road Home program for housing recovery did not provide sufficient access or resources to meet the housing needs of large numbers of low- and moderate-income African-American families in New Orleans' Lower Ninth Ward after Hurricane Katrina.

RACIAL DISPARITIES IN POST-DISASTER RECOVERY

Research on housing-related policies and outcomes after numerous U.S. natural disasters provides a picture of recovery disparities based on race, class, and gender (Peacock, Morrow, and Gladwin 1997; Wisner, Blaikie, Cannon, and Davis 2003; Comerio 1998; Philips and Morrow 2008). In particular, prior disaster experiences suggest that African Americans are particularly vulnerable to housing damage and have more difficulty rebuilding after impact. Reviewing this literature on recovery disparities shows that several issues that arose in housing and recovery disparities for low-income and African-American New Orleanians could have been anticipated.

Recovery and reconstruction after a disaster are essentially a private function, not a governmental one. Because preparing a housing unit to withstand a disaster and rebuilding after the event is often up to the individual owner, outcomes depend heavily on owners' access to resources. Reconstruction of owner-occupied homes requires tremendous resources, including payouts on building, home content, and flood insurance policies as well as personal savings and credit. Residents' access to recovery capital is a critical factor in the speed at which recovery occurs.

In previous U.S. disasters, black owners have experienced difficulty accessing sufficient resources to strengthen their homes prior to the disaster or rebuild their properties after it has occurred. Blanchard-Boehm (1997) reports that financial constraints reduce the likelihood that blacks will make structural improvements so their houses can withstand disasters, resulting in more serious damage to the homes of African Americans. However, the compensation levels for the damage are typically low, due to lower values of black-owned property pre-disaster (Bolin and Bolton 1986). Lower values may be due to the poor condition of the property, physically undesirable location, status of the neighborhood, including its racial makeup, or discrimination in the appraisal process, all of which affect African Americans disproportionately. Blacks also are less likely to qualify for loans and grants made available for rebuilding property (Fothergill et al. 1999, 167).

Most critically, racial and income differences affect a key economic variable of early recovery—adequate insurance coverage. Bolin and Bolton (1986) and Cooper and Laughy (1994) found that limited savings and lower levels of insurance hinder African-American reconstruction efforts. Peacock and Girard (1997) found that blacks and Hispanics tended to receive insufficient insurance settlements unless they were insured by a major national carrier; blacks were the least likely to have such policies, due to insurance redlining of black neighborhoods.

While rebuilding their permanent homes, residents need temporary housing—a place where normal routines can be reestablished after the emergency. Usually, displaced residents find temporary rental housing on the private market, often using government vouchers, or live in temporary trailers provided by FEMA. Research shows that in the temporary housing stage, blacks are most likely to live in large FEMA trailer parks, which is the least satisfactory of temporary housing options (Quarantelli n.d., 10). The parks tend to be poorly run and far from the original housing site.

There are also consistent problems with temporary housing for renters, especially lower-income households, which are disproportionately represented in the black population. It has been shown that if poverty and homelessness were a problem before a disaster, widespread damage can cause a severe housing crunch, as affordable housing is not quickly rebuilt (Comerio 1997, 173–174). Housing vouchers provide enough units only when pre-disaster vacancy rates for affordable housing are high enough to absorb displaced families (Comerio 1997, 175).

Comerio (1997) concludes that the present system works best for well-insured single-family homeowners, who tend to rebuild on the same site. Quarantelli further finds that, with a policy of nongovernmental intervention in existing economic inequalities, "in the long run the housing configuration of the community will not be significantly altered from the pre-disaster situation" (Quarantelli 1991, 10). As such, the pre-disaster housing market determines the post-disaster housing crisis. Where affordability was a problem, it will be exacerbated by housing loss.

Where household budgets were devoted to high housing costs, they will be less able to prepare for disasters with material goods and savings. Fothergill et al. (1999, 166) and Peacock et al. (1997) find that, in the long-term restoration after a disaster, the standard of living for minorities and low-income households often falls. It has become clear through research that inequality in the general social order leads to "unequal access to opportunities and unequal exposure to risk" (Cannon 1994, 14).

RACIAL DISPARITIES IN PRE- AND POST-KATRINA NEW ORLEANS

Problems with post-disaster reconstruction and temporary housing seen in other disasters were present in New Orleans following Hurricane Katrina. The wide geographic extent of Katrina's damage, along with poor evacuation and sheltering plans, caused many black families to be evacuated to distant locations, rather than finding temporary housing with nearby friends and family. The great distance from former homes made it more difficult to join in recovery planning processes, to assess damage to owned properties, and to resume regular employment. The catastrophic nature of the disaster exacerbated the problems expected for African Americans and created new issues, slowing their rehousing process.

Following the immediate emergency period, many survivors of Katrina attempted to resettle in trailers, either on their own lots or in parks, as a temporary housing solution. This allowed the survivors to easily access their hurricane-damaged homes so that they could begin the arduous process of gutting, repair, and rebuilding. However, more than one year after Katrina, many residents of the Lower Ninth Ward still lacked the municipal services necessary for trailer placement. Without basic utilities service (gas, electricity, and water), homeowners in the Lower Ninth Ward were unable to place FEMA trailers on site or reoccupy their homes. As of October 2006, only 1.6 percent of flooded units in the Lower Ninth Ward had received trailer placements, far below the 6.3 percent city-wide average (AHUP 2006).

An option for those who could not place a trailer on their lot or find space in nearby FEMA trailer camps was to temporarily rent housing. Although many residents received rental vouchers to use for temporary housing, rental units were in very short supply after the storm. In the Lower Ninth, 75 percent of rental units were flooded, and the situation was similarly tight in other low- and moderate-income neighborhoods of New Orleans. This supply crunch led to a sharp increase in rents (FEMA 2006) such that HUD's Fair Market Rents in New Orleans—a measure of affordable rent levels—rose by approximately 45 percent after the autumn of 2005 (HUD 2007). The lack of rental housing, especially at affordable levels, became an impediment to reconstruction in the low-to-moderate-income neighborhoods of the Ninth Ward.

Exacerbating black New Orleanians' struggle were resource deficiencies dating to before the storm. New Orleans did not, prior to the 2005 hurricane season, have a particularly strong housing market. Sale prices and rents were well below the national median, and housing abandonment was widespread, with vacancy rates of over 15 percent suggesting that the market was slow and soft. Despite overall low housing costs, black households of low and moderate income, both renters and owners, faced significant problems with housing affordability even before Katrina struck (Bates 2006). New Orleans was not a high-income city, and its black population was disproportionately poor. Average household incomes in the Upper and Lower Ninth Ward were approximately $30,000 one year before Katrina. In the Lower Ninth Ward, nearly a quarter of homeowners were paying over 50 percent of their monthly incomes on housing costs (Bates 2006). Those whose budgets were already stretched thin by high housing cost-to-income ratios had less saved for post-hurricane repairs, rental deposits, and replacement of furniture and other household goods.

Flood insurance coverage can lead to significant disparities in low- and moderate-income neighborhoods. The typical homeowner's policy against hazards does not cover damages from flooding; to repair flood damage, the owner must purchase an additional flood rider. For those within the FEMA-designated 100-year floodplain, the area with a 1 percent chance of flooding each year, coverage is mandated under the National Flood Insurance Program (NFIP). Under NFIP, federally regulated lenders must require flood insurance for any loan to a property in the 100-year floodplain (NFIP 2002, 30). If properties are designated as being outside the floodplain, if the homeowner has a non-federally insured mortgage, or if the owner has no active mortgage (for example, elderly owners), NFIP coverage is not required. Other low-income households may simply not have had the resources for even the low-cost NFIP premiums and let their policies lapse.

In New Orleans' low-income black neighborhoods, homeowners appear to have been underinsured, especially in regards to flood insurance. Being in a historic district, many of the uninsured Lower Ninth Ward households had property mortgages that preceded the 1974 flood insurance regulation or that were not federally insured; others had paid off their property mortgages and were not required to carry flood insurance. It may also be that other low-income households could not afford even the low-cost NFIP premiums and had let their policies lapse.

Although 71 percent of Orleans Parish households in the floodplain held coverage under this program, only about one-third of Lower Ninth Ward households did so (FEMA 2006). Furthermore, a substantial portion of the Lower Ninth Ward was considered outside of the floodplain due to its levee protection, and therefore over 60 percent of owners did not carry flood insurance (see Table 11.1). Despite being outside of the designated 100-year floodplain, these households flooded in Hurricane Katrina. Owners of flooded units in this area had to rely upon disaster relief, private grants, and personal finances to make repairs.

TABLE 11.1—Insurance Rates, Owner-Occupied Houses in Flood-Damaged Areas

	Lower Ninth Ward (%)	Orleans Parish (%)
Flooded, within floodplain*	**33.1**	**65.7**
Fully insured	47.9	70.9
No flood insurance	18.3	15.0
Uninsured	33.8	14.0
Flooded, outside floodplain*	**47.8**	**15.14**
Fully insured	29.7	40.4
No flood insurance	36.3	36.0
Uninsured	34.0	23.5

*FEMA designated 100-year floodplain; adapted from FEMA, 2006.

Source: Adapted from FEMA, 2006. *Current Housing Unit Damage Estimates: Hurricanes Katrina, Rita and Wilma.* Washington, DC: The Office of the Federal Coordinator for Gulf Coast Rebuilding at the Department of Homeland Security.

In examining the recovery of housing in New Orleans after Hurricane Katrina, we now focus our attention on two key issues for the rebuilding of owner-occupied housing in the historically black neighborhoods of the Lower Ninth Ward. First, we evaluate how damage estimation procedures may have contributed to disparities in recovery potential. Second, we consider The Road Home program grant process and funding in terms of potential disparities in recovery assistance.

DAMAGE ASSESSMENTS AND INEQUITY

Estimates of damage in the Ninth Ward were crucial to rebuilding decisions, as they were in other neighborhoods. According to NFIP compliance regulations, when repair costs are greater than 50 percent of pre-damage value, the house must be repaired with elevated foundations for future flood mitigation or rebuilt. Raising foundations adds $20,000 to $30,000 and significant time and complexity to the home repair process. The costs for raising the foundation can be covered through the FEMA home mitigation program, but some houses cannot be raised at all and an above-50-percent damage designation thus means that demolition is mandatory (FEMA 2007; Green et al. 2007).

According to initial inspections, carried out with haste by FEMA subcontractors, over three-quarters of Lower Ninth Ward houses had substantial damage over the 50 percent standard. As part of a community planning process led by the Association of Community Organizations for Reform Now (ACORN) and ACORN Housing Corporation (AHC), Cornell University, Columbia University, and the University of Illinois, Urbana-Champaign, conducted a follow-up assessment of damage and recovery conditions in the Upper[1] and Lower Ninth Ward of New Orleans as part of a neighborhood recovery planning process. [2]

This damage assessment documented building site conditions over 2,500 (863 within the Lower Ninth Ward) uniformly sampled residential parcels, in a stratified sample by neighborhood density. Just under 800 of these parcels (206 within the Lower Ninth Ward) were surveyed for a detailed building evaluation in line with *ATC-45 Field Manual: Safety Evaluation of Buildings After Wind Storms and Floods* (ATC 2004).[3] The survey divided damage into flood damage and structural damage, due to significant differences in the cost of repair for buildings with and without structural damage, and each of these damage types was divided into low/none, moderate, and extensive damage.

When we compare the results of this ground survey with the NFIP percent damage for each unit, we find that variation is considerable. Units measured at or near 50 percent damage by NFIP assessment had very different types of flood and structural damage. Units in the building evaluation sample that were just below the line—those with 45 to 49.9 percent damage that would not be required to elevate their foundations—had mostly minor or moderate flooding, defined as under two feet and two to four feet of flooding, respectively. However, few (39 of 43) units had any visible structural damage, meaning that damage could likely be repaired via gutting and replacement of wallboards, insulation, electrical wires, and flooring materials.

Units just above the substantial damage line—with 50 to 55 percent damage and the requirement to elevate their foundations to the new floodplain requirements—had much greater variation in levels of flood and structural damage. About half (of 176 units) had minor or moderate flooding but no structural damage, just as did the below-50-percent-damage units. With no greater damage than units below the 50 percent line, the rebuilding costs for these units was much higher due to the requirement of elevating the foundation.

Variation in post-disaster damage assessment is common and unavoidable. The speed, extreme conditions, and uncertainty under which these assessments are conducted ensure that results are not entirely consistent or accurate. Even so, the results of such post-disaster damage assessments often dictate what types of repairs will be allowed and the costs the homeowner will accrue. While the variation found in the post-Katrina New Orleans residential housing damage assessment is not surprising, or entirely avoidable, the variation appears to particularly be a problem for the Ninth Ward, where the city's percent damage estimates were not distinguishable for units with very different combinations of flood and structural damage.

To examine whether NFIP damage assessment data in the Ninth Ward neighborhoods were well matched with indicators of flood damage, we compared flood depth and damage assessment values across several representative neighborhoods in New Orleans. We developed five transects crossing moderately and heavily flooded neighborhoods in New Orleans (Uptown, Lakewood, East Orleans, the Upper and Lower Ninth Ward), where flood depth varied from zero to twelve feet without high-velocity water flow that would cause structural damage (see Figure 11.1 for location). A graph of NFIP percent damage estimate by flood depth for these transects, shown in Figure 11.2, suggests that flood depth and damage are not tightly coupled anywhere in the city. Units with similar levels of flooding were assessed as having a wide range of damage. That wind damage from Hurricane Katrina was minimal and the damage was dominated by flood damage (Guillermo et al. 2008) indicates that assessors had significant difficulties obtaining a uniform and consistent assessment.

Figure 11.2 also indicates inconsistencies in damage assessment across neighborhoods. Outside the Lower Ninth, damage tended to increase with flood depth in neighborhoods, as seen by the positive slope on the linear regression. The linear regression for damage estimate on flood depth within the Lower Ninth Ward, however, is almost flat. The majority of structures in the Lower Ninth Ward were estimated at just over 50 percent damage, regardless of flood depth. Thus, units in the Lower Ninth Ward were estimated as having more damage than units in other neighborhoods for similar flood levels. That the analysis excluded units in areas near the levee break and included units that had only experienced similar flooding processes as elsewhere in the city, all suggests that damage in the Lower Ninth was generally overestimated relative to other neighborhoods. Thus, recovery guidelines were stricter in this neighborhood than in others, most often requiring foundation elevation or demolition, options that added costs, time, and difficulty to the recovery process (Green et al. 2007).

FIGURE 11.1—Transects Examined for Disparities in Flood-Damage Estimation

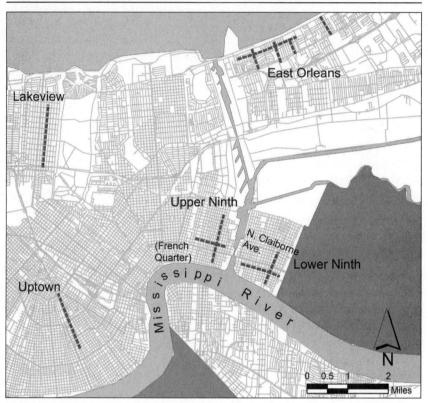

Source: Developed by the authors.

DISPARITIES IN THE ROAD HOME GRANT APPLICATION FOR HOMEOWNER RECOVERY

While NFIP damage assessments strongly framed decisions about repair and demolition, funding sources for individual residential housing recovery were more heterogeneous. Homeowners with flood insurance could often rely upon relatively speedy settlements to begin funding housing recovery. Those with personal savings also had quick access to funding. Low-income homeowners without flood insurance—a majority of Lower Ninth residents—had to wait for federal home repair grants before beginning to rehabilitate their homes.

The Louisiana Recovery Authority's The Road Home program, funded by federal Community Development Block Grant dollars, is the primary grant for rebuilding permanent housing for uninsured or underinsured homeowners. The Road Home grants were intended to close the gap between insurance payouts and the cost of re-

FIGURE 11.2—Flood Height and Damage Estimates for Neighborhoods in New Orleans

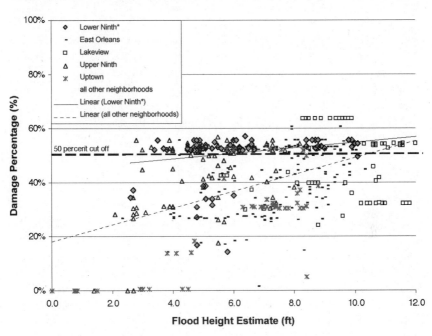

*Units north of N. Clairborne St. excluded due to structural damage from levee failure

Source: Developed by the authors.

pairing or rebuilding a home. The grant funds up to $150,000 for repairs and rebuilding at FEMA standards for base flood elevations for owners who reoccupy their original properties. Other options—to rebuild elsewhere in Louisiana or to leave the state—reduce the maximum grant amount (LRA 2007, 8). The amount of the grant is based on the lesser of the loss of the home's value and its estimated repair cost, itself based on the percent damage estimates from NFIP inspections. Grants are reduced by the amount of any prior insurance payout or other grant received. Low-income homeowners can receive an additional $50,000 forgivable loan, and all homeowners can request a $30,000 elevation grant for raising foundations, as long as the total grant does not exceed $150,000.

While The Road Home program was designed to assist homeowners in need post-Katrina, its implementation has been slow, marred by unforeseen difficulties, and ultimately has not succeeded in ameliorating the serious racial disparities in recovery resources. The first setback for program implementation was in securing funding. Until July 2006, nearly one year after Katrina, the state was awaiting $4.2 billion in federal funds to begin implementation of The Road Home program (LRA

2007, 4). When The Road Home began accepting applications, there was only one application center in Orleans Parish, and no centers providing assistance for home-owners in the diaspora. Many residents who had been displaced to Houston, Atlanta, and beyond—most of whom were African Americans—had to wait until the end of 2006 and early 2007 for centers to open in Houston and Dallas.

Once applications were submitted, the granting process was also slow. In October 2006, only a handful of residents in New Orleans had actually received grants. In Orleans Parish alone, over 24,400 applications had been submitted, but with limited staff capacity there was a caseload backlog of over 10,000 unprocessed applications.

Due to slow application rates from predominantly black neighborhoods in the Ninth Ward, ACORN Housing Corporation was contracted by the state to provide outreach and application counseling starting in the spring of 2007. Yet the generally slow pace of recovery did not increase as The Road Home expanded, and further counseling was provided. Applications from the zip code including the Ninth Ward rose from about 5,600 in February 2007 to over 7,000 in October 2007—still well below the 20,000 households living in the zip code before Katrina. About 20 percent of those applicants were unsure about whether they would rebuild in the neighbor-hood or take a relocation option—higher than the citywide average undecided rate of 13 percent. A year later, the U.S. Postal Service reported delivering mail to just over 9,200 addresses in the zip code—an increase of only 3,000 during 2007, the year that The Road Home grants were predicted to have major impact (pre-Katrina, USPS reported 20,000 active residential addresses, according to the Greater New Orleans Community Data Center).

The Road Home program grant process included two significant obstacles for homeowners in low- and moderate-income neighborhoods—again, largely African Americans. These issues—long-standing problems with property tax value assess-ments and the common practice of leaving properties in heirship rather than pro-cessing ownership in probate court—appear to have been largely unanticipated, and resolutions were slow and incomplete.

The first issue was the reliance on Orleans Parish tax assessments as the basis of home valuation. Property valuation in New Orleans has been a problem for some time, with multiple elected assessors significantly undervaluing property. A 2004 ar-ticle in the *Times-Picayune* by Gordon Russell (Russell 2004) and a report compiled by the Louisiana Tax Commission brought to light problems in the Orleans Parish assessment system. These studies found that the system's unequally sized districts, in-consistent assessment methods, and falsely inflated millage rates were underlying causes of unequal assessments across neighborhoods. While homeowners could ap-peal The Road Home's stated home value based on pre-storm tax assessments, this significantly lengthened the application process. Even with appeals, patterns of met-ropolitan segregation and disinvestment in African-American neighborhoods result-ing in lower values of black homes, compounded by assessment-quality issues, leave black New Orleans homeowners' Road Home grants limited by low valuations.

Second, many homeowners were delayed or prevented from completing The Road Home process by not having a clear title to their homes. As reported by Jarvis De-Berry, for many lower-income homeowners in Louisiana, when a property was passed down after a death, the family simply agreed on who would occupy and "own" the house but never completed succession in court (*Times-Picayune* March 25, 2008). When the occupying family member attempted to apply for The Road Home, it was discovered that, legally, the property was owned by multiple siblings or cousins. This status, called heirship, had to be cleared before receiving a Road Home grant or any loans on the property. In February 2007, the state Office of Community Development budgeted just over half a million dollars for legal aid attorneys to help applicants clear titles on their homes, but in two articles, David Hammer and Jarvis DeBerry noted that the large number of cases exceeded the budget as of December (*Times-Picayune* March 25, 2008 and March 28, 2008). The shortfall left 2,200 cases unprocessed as of March 2008, with additional applicants continuing to seek services from legal aid agencies. Mark Moreau, director of Southeast Louisiana Legal Services, told the *Times-Picayune* that additional low-income homeowners had been incorrectly told they needed to clear titles before applying to the program and missed The Road Home application cutoff entirely (*Times-Picayune* March 25, 2008).

Even when homeowners received award letters, getting to closing—when funds are actually disbursed—took longer. Statewide, The Road Home program moved extremely slowly, with about 1 percent of applications reaching completion during the first year to 18 months of the program. For the first 18 months of The Road Home program, fewer than 100 owners in the 70117 zip code area (which encompassed the Upper and Lower Ninth Ward) had closed on their grants, out of over 5,600 applicants for approximately 17,500 damaged units. According to The Road Home weekly reports, starting in May 2007, there was a dramatic increase in the number of The Road Home applications closing citywide. With this increased pace of processing, by October 2007, approximately 55 percent of New Orleans homeowners who chose their option to rebuild or relocate had closed on their grants, but in the 70117 zip code, only about 35 percent had done so, as shown in Figure 11.3. The gap between closure rates citywide and in the 70117 zip code has remained consistent, ranging from approximately 8 percent at its lowest point to over 20 percent at its greatest. As of April 2008, at the writing of this chapter, an approximate 15 percent gap remains between closure rates in the 70117 zip code and citywide.

For homeowners relying on The Road Home funds to make repairs, the delays in program administration meant delaying the return home. Furthermore, according to The Road Home's Web site, due to anticipated shortfalls in funds, the additional $30,000 FEMA home mitigation grants that could be used to fund foundation elevation were delayed until the spring of 2008. Owners had to apply separately during the spring of 2008 to request the additional funds. For owners whose properties had to be elevated, but who did not receive enough The Road Home funds to complete all repairs, their work was delayed until these funds became available. As of May

FIGURE 11.3—Percentage of Applications for The Road Home Grants Closed

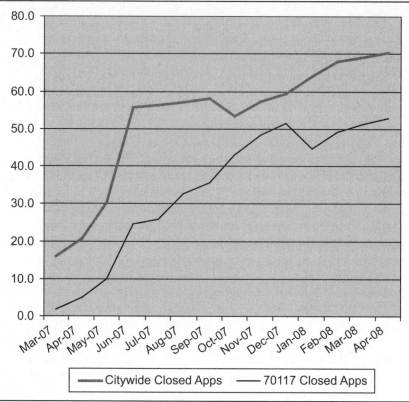

Note: The dip in closings in the 70117 zip code in January 2008 reflects a surge of application submittals at the end of 2007, the deadline for homeowners to choose to return or relocate.

Source: The Road Home Situation and Pipeline Reports.

2008, approximately 2,000 elevation grants had been disbursed out of over 25,000 applications, as reported in The Road Home Pipeline Report for Week 102.

FINANCIAL GAPS IN REBUILDING THE NINTH WARD

Examining data from the Greater New Orleans Community Data Center made available in April 2008 allows an assessment of how the interplay of home values and damage estimates in The Road Home grant calculation has left Lower Ninth Ward homeowners with a serious finance gap. Maximum grant awards are based on the lesser of the home's value and its cost to recover—calculated on a set construction cost of $130 per square foot, multiplied by the percent damage to the house's area.

For a house in a low-income neighborhood, The Road Home grant was capped by its lower pre-Katrina home value. For a house within a high-income neighborhood, where home values exceeded the maximum grant amount, the value of the grant received was based on estimated repair costs up to the maximum $150,000 grant limit. As reported by David Hammer of the *Times-Picayune,* this decision to use the lesser of the two values emerged from a compromise with HUD, the federal agency funding The Road Home, which then added the low-income grant of $50,000 to attempt to make up for the gap caused by using low house values (*Times-Picayune* May 26, 2008).

For upper-middle-income and wealthy homeowners, the inclusion of land prices in the home value calculation means that both pre-Katrina value and repair costs were well above the $150,000 maximum, and their grants are on the whole larger than those of low-income homeowners, even when damage levels were less. Regardless of the actual cost of rebuilding, for low- and moderate-income African-American homeowners, the grant was capped by lower home values. These home values were typically substantially less than the cost of replacement housing, reflecting decades of segregation, institutional disinvestment, biased assessments, and limited opportunities.

Based on The Road Home grant calculation guidelines, it was possible for the low-value homeowner with substantial damage to receive a grant less than the estimated repair costs. This can be illustrated by examining two areas of the city that were flooded due to levee failure—some of the predominantly black and low-to-moderate-income neighborhoods of the Ninth Ward, with average house values below $150,000; and the virtually all-white and traditionally high-income neighborhoods of the Lakeview District. Both areas received extensive flooding of up to 15 feet.

Yet owners in the Lower Ninth Ward neighborhood received substantially less funding for rebuilding, averaging $82,000, than residents in wealthier neighborhoods, where repair costs rather than pre-storm value dictated the maximum value of the grant (see Table 11.2). If a homeowner needs to completely rebuild—either due to extensive structural damage or a damage estimate above 50 percent and a foundation type that could not be elevated—costs were estimated to be approximately $150,000 for a moderately sized house constructed by area nonprofit builders. It was in these situations that the potential for funding gaps were greatest (NORA Board Meeting 2008).

With low levels of flood insurance in the Ninth Ward, The Road Home grant may be the only resource homeowners can draw on for rebuilding. Thus, even with higher assessed damage, Lower Ninth residents often wound up with fewer recovery resources. While the program does not consider the race of the applicant or the neighborhood per se, the consequences of policy choices are clear: Low-to-moderate-income African Americans, who tended to live in homes with depressed pre-Katrina values, to be displaced to distant cities, to be underinsured, and to have had more stringent damage assessments, receive grant amounts well below those of high-income, well-insured,

TABLE 11.2—The Road Home Grants and Damage Levels for Selected Neighborhoods in New Orleans

Neighborhood	% Black Population	Average Damage Level	Average Pre-Storm Value	Average Grant
Lower 9th	98.3%	51%	$89,000	$82,000
Holy Cross*	87.5%	41%	$111,900	$90,000
Florida**	98.4%	38%	$106,900	$74,000
Lakewood	1.7%	41%	$250,000	$96,000
Lakeview	0.7%	40%	$281,250	$109,000
Lakeshore	0.6%	25%	$221,000	$101,000

  * Historic neighborhood of the Lower Ninth Ward.
** Low-income black neighborhood in the Upper Ninth Ward.

Source: The Road Home Pipeline data/ ICF International, May 2008.

single-family homeowners, who are most likely white. When The Road Home program implementation problems created delays in disbursing grants, low- and moderate-income homeowners were most affected, having few other resources to begin rebuilding. With maximum grants capped by low home values, owners with extensive repair costs did not receive grants that would cover even the construction of modest replacement housing.

In May 2008, Kate Moran reported that mortgage industry actor Fannie Mae had developed a program offering loan refinancing and additional debt financing for homeowners whose grants did not cover repairs. This funding is available only to those whose original mortgage is held by Fannie Mae, which may include 3,000 Louisiana homeowners, and to those whose mortgage is not delinquent, which may limit its impact for low-income homeowners in the Ninth Ward (*Times-Picayune,* May 6, 2006). However limited the Fannie Mae program may be, it appears to be the only major assistance program for homeowners whose grants, insurance payments, and personal resources are not enough to repair their housing.

CONCLUSIONS

The disparity in the recovery of New Orleans' neighborhoods is hardly surprising. Experts observing a wide range of disasters in the United States have concluded that disaster housing policy works best for those with the most resources and that the co-incidence of low income and low asset status with race means that African Americans experience considerable obstacles in recovering from disasters. Life in New Orleans after Katrina and Rita demonstrates these findings again, albeit on a more catastrophic scale. Based on our analysis of housing policy post-Katrina, we re-emphasize some lessons learned from past disasters, lessons that should guide current and future policy adjustments.

Post-disaster recovery could be substantially improved to ensure full recovery and viability for African-American neighborhoods. First, we must plan for the reconstruction of housing, paying special attention to problems of affordability and housing quality before a disaster. Homeowners with limited means need assistance to prepare their homes for potential flooding and high winds, thereby reducing damage when hurricanes strike.

Pursuing strategies for sustainable low-to-moderate-income home ownership, even when not directly related to disasters—combating predatory lending and insurance redlining that disadvantage black households—can help owners with financial stability and reduce financial vulnerability to disasters. Second, prospects for homeowners with limited resources could be improved via technical assistance for challenging damage assessments and the involvement of community-based organizations in the resource allocation process. The studies commissioned by ACORN/ACORN Housing Corporation were used to challenge ideas about neighborhood viability and also could be used to help homeowners challenge their individual damage assessments.

Community-based organizations were vital in reaching out to New Orleanians in the diaspora with information and assistance on The Road Home program, although their potential was realized only belatedly by the Louisiana Recovery Authority. These organizations could have been involved from the program design stage, as they could have provided vital information about residents' problems and obstacles to help anticipate issues with The Road Home application process. Most importantly, to avoid re-creating the gross inequities of the pre-Katrina housing market, rebuilding assistance must be based on post-storm needs and capacity, not pre-storm value.

Creating grants calculated on house and land values skewed by long-standing segregation and institutional racism only reinforces the disparities in homeowner security and wealth. While The Road Home program did supplement low-income owners' grants, many moderate-income African-American households were left out of the program, and the supplement still did not offer the resources needed for modest rebuilding in many cases. Overall, program design and implementation decisions have maintained the bias towards well-insured homeowners with sufficient private resources, to the detriment of African-American homeowners in the Lower Ninth Ward.

NOTES

1. The Upper Ninth Ward is an upriver neighborhood that was divided from the Lower Ninth Ward by the construction of the Industrial Canal in the mid-1920s. The Upper Ninth Ward is divided between relatively prosperous and gentrified small neighborhoods along the riverfront and predominantly low-income black neighborhoods with a mix of owner-occupied and rental units.

2. A household survey of over 150 residents documented recovery plans and was led by Richard Kiely, Ken Reardon, and Pierre Clavel of Cornell University; a survey of four

major business arterials was conducted by students from the University of Illinois, Urbana-Champaign, led by Lisa Bates; and a parks damage survey was conducted by Michelle Thompson, affiliated with Cornell University. A survey of residential damage and recovery conditions was carried out by 45 planning, engineering, and architecture students from Cornell and Columbia University in teams of two. These students were overseen by graduate student coordinators and supervised by Michelle Thompson and Rebekah Green. Additional support was provided by Cornell-affiliated faculty, John Forester and Jeremy Foster, and Columbia-affiliated faculty, Andrew Smyth and George Deodatis. Further information regarding this multi-university collaboration can be found in the *People's Plan for Overcoming the Hurricane Katrina Blues: A Comprehensive Strategy for Building a More Vibrant, Sustainable, and Equitable 9th Ward* (AHUP 2007). A complete list of the many dedicated students, faculty, and staff—without whom the data collection, entry, and analysis effort could not have been possible—can also be found there.

3. Copies of survey forms can be found in the appendices of the People's Plan (AHUP 2007; more detail on the survey methodology and findings are in Green et al. 2008).

REFERENCES

AHUP (ACORN Housing/University Partnership). 2006. "Planning District 7 and 8 Assessment and Needs Analysis." 20 October. Washington, DC: ACORN Housing/University Partnership for Unified New Orleans Planning Process.

———. 2007. "A People's Plan for Overcoming the Hurricane Katrina Blues: A Comprehensive Strategy for Building a More Vibrant, Sustainable, and Equitable 9th Ward." Ithaca: ACORN Housing/University Partnership.

ATC (Applied Technology Council). 2004. *ATC-45 Field Manual: Safety Evaluation of Buildings After Wind Storms and Floods.* Redwood City, CA: Applied Technology Council.

Bates, L. K. 2006. "Post Katrina Housing: Problems, Policies, and Prospects for African-Americans in New Orleans." *The Black Scholar* 36 (4): 13–32.

Blanchard-Boehm, D. 1997. "Risk Communication in Southern California: Ethnic and Gender Response to 1995." Boulder: Earthquake Probabilities, Natural Hazards Research and Applications Information Center.

Bolin, R. 1986. "Disaster Impact and Recovery: A Comparison of Black and White Victims." *International Journal of Mass Emergencies and Disasters* 4 (1): 35–50.

Comerio, M. 1998. *Disaster Hits Home: New Policy for Urban Housing Recovery.* Berkeley: University of California Press.

Comerio, M. C. 1997. "Housing Issues After Disasters." *Journal of Contingencies and Crisis Management* 5 (3): 166–178.

Fothergill, A., E. G. M. Maestas, and J. DeRouen Darlington. 1999. "Race, Ethnicity and Disasters in the United States: A Review of the Literature." *Disasters* 23 (2): 156–173.

Girard, C., and W. G. Peacock. 1997. "Ethnicity and Segregation: Post-hurricane Relocation." In W. G. Peacock, B. H. Morrow, and H. Gladwin (eds). *Hurricane Andrew: Ethnicity, Gender, and the Sociology of Disasters.* New York: Routledge.

Greater New Orleans Community Data Center. 2006. "Neighborhood Snapshots." Available at http://www.gnocdc.org/impact.html (accessed August 1, 2008).

LRA (Louisiana Recovery Authority). 2007a. *The Road Home Homeowner Policies, Version 4.1.* Baton Rouge: Louisiana Road Home Program of the Louisiana Recovery

Authority. Available at http://www.road2la.org/Docs/TRH_Deliverable_00035
_Homeowner_Program_Policies_5-15-07.pdf.

Morrow, B. H. 1999. "Identifying and Mapping Community Vulnerability." *Disasters* 23
(1): 1–18.

National Flood Insurance Program, FEMA. 2002. "NFIP Program Description." Available at http://www.fema.gov/doc/library/nfipdescrip.doc (accessed August 1, 2008).

Peacock, W., B. H. Morrow, and H. Gladwin. 1997. *Hurricane Andrew: Ethnicity, Gender
and the Sociology of Disasters*. New York and London: Routledge.

Peacock, W. P., and C. Girard. 1997. "Ethnic and Racial Inequalities in Hurricane Damage and Insurance Settlements." In W. G. Peacock, B. H. Morrow, and H. Gladwin
(eds.). *Hurricane Andrew: Ethnicity, Gender, and the Sociology of Disasters*. New York:
Routledge.

Phillips, B. D., and B. H. Morrow (eds.). 2008. *Women and Disasters: From Theory to
Practice*. International Research Committee on Disasters.

Quarantelli, E. L. n.d. "The Disaster Recovery Process: What We Know and Do Not
Know from Research." University of Delaware Disaster Research Center.

Quarantelli, E. L. 1991. "Patterns of Sheltering and Housing in American Disasters."
University of Delaware Disaster Research Center, Paper #170.

Russell, G. 2004. "Dubious Value." *Times-Picayune*. April 4.

PART IV

POLICY CHOICES FOR SOCIAL CHANGE

CHAPTER 12

UNNATURAL DISASTER

Social Impacts and Policy Choices After Katrina

John R. Logan

Early media reports about the wind damage and flooding caused by Hurricane Katrina focused on New Orleans, and especially on the people who had been unable to escape the city before it flooded. Images of poor and predominantly black people crowded into the Superdome and Convention Center created indelible impressions about who was affected most strongly. We now know that most residents had evacuated safely and that even some mostly white and predominantly middle-class neighborhoods were decimated by the flooding. And yet the initial impression is true: Katrina disproportionately affected poor, black neighborhoods. Because these are the residents with the least market resources, policy choices affecting who can return, to which neighborhoods, and with what forms of public and private assistance will greatly affect the future character of the city.

One year after the hurricane, what stands out is the failure to formulate a coherent policy. But what is visible so far is disturbing. It now appears that the recovery of New Orleans will be unusually slow. A reliable estimate of the city's population prepared by the Louisiana Department of Health and Hospitals (2006) estimated a total of 201,000 persons a year after the storm. The white population in the period June–October 2006 was about two-thirds of its former size, while the black population was down by nearly three-quarters. Three years after the storm, the Brookings Institution and the Greater New Orleans Data Center place the city at 72 percent of its pre-Katrina population of 450,000 (Liu and Plyer 2008).

Several questions will be addressed here to understand the impact of Katrina and interpret its future implications: (1) who was displaced by Katrina, (2) how does the pattern of displacement affect people's chances of returning, (3) how are public policy decisions affecting the recovery process, and (4) what do shifts in local political influence portend for the future?

DISPLACEMENT FROM NEW ORLEANS

The best information about displacement, including the neighborhood location and social composition of affected people, is based on counts of the population living in areas that were flooded. My estimate is that nearly 650,000 persons lived in heavily damaged areas in the New Orleans metropolitan region and Mississippi Coast (Logan 2006a). More than half of these, 354,000, lived in the city proper, Orleans Parish (for a similar conclusion, see the report by the Congressional Research Service: Gabe et al. 2005).

Figure 12.1 shows flooded and non-flooded areas of Orleans Parish along with the racial composition (percent black) of census tracts. This map shows that the undamaged areas of the city were mainly in two areas. One is just north of the Mississippi River in a zone extending westward from downtown. The other is across the river on the West Bank, in a district known as Algiers. The map shows that some predominantly white neighborhoods in the northwest part of the city were entirely flooded. However, almost all of the neighborhoods that were in the range of 75 percent to 100 percent black at the time of Census 2000 were flooded. I estimate that about 265,000 of the city's Census 2000 black population of 325,000 lived in flooded zones. This compares to about 68,000 of 129,000 non-blacks.

Separate analyses demonstrate that damaged areas were also disproportionately composed of renters and lower-income residents. However, it is the division by race that stands out most strongly, because the most damaged black neighborhoods had varying class composition, ranging from predominantly middle-class New Orleans East to the much less affluent Lower Ninth Ward, to neighborhoods with public housing projects where a majority of residents were below the poverty line.

Discussions of the racially differential impact of Katrina have often emphasized the Lower Ninth Ward (where many homes were entirely demolished by the breach in the levee of the Industrial Canal) and New Orleans East. Most neighborhoods in these planning districts were more than 85 percent black, and most residences were damaged. A majority of residents of both of these planning districts were homeowners, though there were clear class distinctions between the two areas. More than a third of Lower Ninth Ward residents were below the poverty line, and nearly 14 percent were unemployed. New Orleans East had a considerably larger middle-class component, though it was not among the city's most affluent sections.

Many of the most segregated neighborhoods with the highest poverty rates are those identified as projects, a reference to the prominence of public housing within their borders. The project neighborhoods typically had poverty rates in the range of 60–80 percent of the population, unemployment was above 20 percent, they were all predominantly black (with African Americans accounting for 90 percent or more of their residents), and 80 percent or more of residents were renters. There are six such neighborhoods in New Orleans (though there are concentrations of public

FIGURE 12.1—Race and Flooding in New Orleans

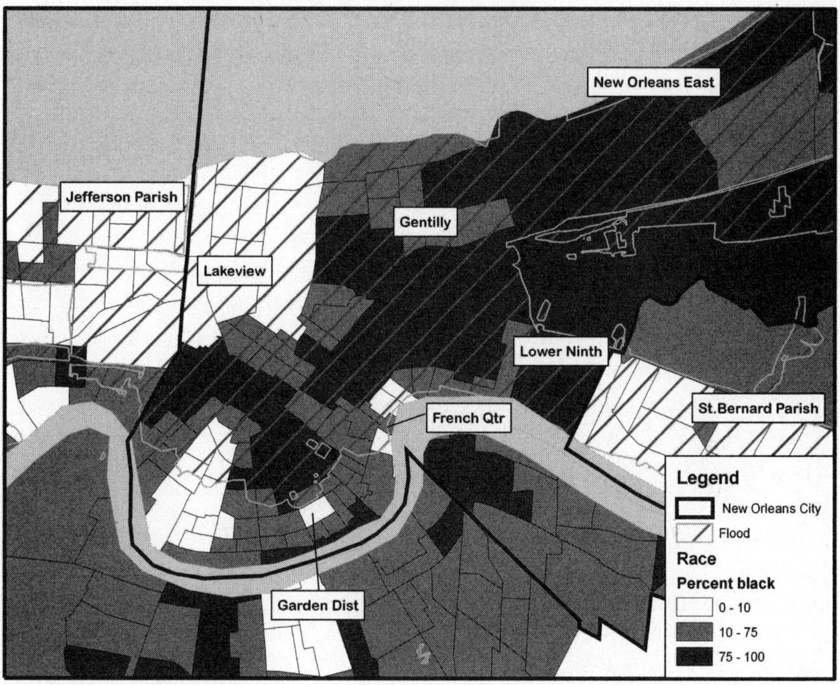

Source: Developed by the author.

housing or Section 8 housing in other parts of the city). In five of them with a combined 2000 population of over 15,000 persons (Calliope, Iberville, St. Bernard Area, Desire, and Florida), the entire territory was damaged.

At the other end of the class spectrum are a number of more advantaged neighborhoods with poverty rates below 10 percent or unemployment rates below 5 percent. In the most heavily impacted planning districts, only a few neighborhoods meet either criterion. These include the Lake-Terrace/Lake Oaks neighborhood in Gentilly and the Read Boulevard East neighborhood in New Orleans East. Most such neighborhoods are in the Lakeview Planning District, which is an area with a small black population, mostly homeowners, and very low rates of poverty and unemployment. Here only the Lakeshore/Lake Vista neighborhood, adjacent to Lake Pontchartrain, was partly spared.

Few residents in the French Quarter, a predominantly white neighborhood with a poverty rate of about 11 percent and unemployment below 5 percent, lived in tracts that were flooded. Among other neighborhoods with a national reputation for affluence, the Garden District neighborhood was not flooded, and only 40 percent of the Audubon/University neighborhood (home of Tulane University and Loyola University) was damaged.

WHERE PEOPLE WENT

The census data represent the numbers of persons who were at greatest risk of being displaced for more than a few weeks. What is known about the actual long-term displacement of population? Evidence is given here from three different sources. Each source has its own limitations, but taken together these sources offer a consistent picture: The majority of the city's population is still living elsewhere, of these the largest share is living outside the state, and black residents (especially poor black residents) are disproportionately found at the greatest distance from their prior homes.

One source is postal change of address data in the post-Katrina period, tabulated by the U.S. Postal Service (Russell 2006). These data identify the original pre-Katrina three-digit zip code (origin) and current three-digit zip code (destination) of households that filed changes of address. At the end of March 2006, more than 160,000 households were relocated from their original address in Orleans Parish. Of these, about 17,000 were at a new address within Orleans Parish. About 21,000 were elsewhere in the metropolitan region, plus 15,000 in Baton Rouge and 12,000 in other parts of Louisiana. Close to two-thirds were out-of-state, most prominently in Texas (52,000). The most common out-of-state destinations were Houston (27,000), Dallas (14,000), and Atlanta (8,000).

Another source is FEMA's tally of the reported addresses of area residents who had applied for assistance. This information was prepared in mid-February 2006 and made available in the federal court case that challenged election procedures *(Wallace v. Blanco)*. An astounding total of nearly 400,000 persons initially living in Orleans Parish had applied for assistance. Of these, 154,000 were living within Louisiana, including a number of persons who had suffered relatively minor damage and returned to their original homes. But over 100,000 reported addresses in Texas and an even larger number were living in other states. These numbers reinforce the conclusion above about the significance of displacement outside of Louisiana, especially to Texas.

The impacts of displacement depend not only on its volume but also its location—and the farthest away turn out to be African Americans, especially those with the lowest incomes. The only public source of information about the racial composition and income levels of displaced persons is the Current Population Survey (CPS), conducted by the U.S. Department of Commerce. CPS is collected monthly for a national sample of 60,000 households. It is designed to be representative of the civilian non-institutional population aged 16 and above.

Beginning in November 2005, CPS included a question to identify persons who were evacuated as a result of Hurricanes Katrina and Rita. Its principal limitations are its relatively small sample size and its exclusion of persons living in shelters, hotels, or other forms of group quarters. The sample weights provided by the Bureau of Labor Statistics allow the sample to be used to produce population estimates, and I have used the sample data from December 2005 to evaluate the racial composition and income levels of displaced persons (Logan 2006b). I selected only persons whose original pre-Katrina residence was in the state of Louisiana. I focused on non-Hispanic whites and non-Hispanic blacks. The number of evacuees identified as Hispanic, Asian, or other race is too small to permit analysis.

In December 2005, evacuees identified in CPS-sampled households represented about 1.1 million persons aged 16 and over who had evacuated from where they were living in August. Just over half of these persons had returned to the home from which they had evacuated. According to this source, more than 400,000 whites were evacuated, of whom 67 percent had returned home. Among blacks, more than 200,000 were evacuated, of whom less than 40 percent had returned home. Of those who were still displaced, nearly two-thirds of whites were in Louisiana, while three-quarters of blacks were out of state.

It is also relevant to compare the income levels of white and black evacuees. White evacuees had similar income levels regardless of their current location, with a median just under $50,000 and less than 15 percent in households with income under $20,000. Black evacuees who had returned home had somewhat lower incomes than whites. Blacks who remained displaced had much lower incomes, with a median of under $15,000 and more than 60 percent below $20,000. It is clear, therefore, that blacks—because they were farther away and had fewer personal resources—faced great obstacles to their return to New Orleans.

POLICY CHOICES

The sheer number of people who lived in heavily damaged areas is a reminder of the scale of Katrina's impact. Because the storm hit large numbers of people of every race and class, it is not surprising that initial public support for policies to assist these people also cut across race and class lines. However, there was also a substantial disproportionate impact on African Americans and people with fewer resources. These disparities stem from within the city of New Orleans itself, and more specifically from vulnerability to flooding. This is a pattern with deep roots, and although Katrina caused the most extensive flooding in memory, prior studies by historians (such as Colten 2005) have demonstrated that both high ground and public investments in drainage and pumping systems consistently worked to the advantage of certain neighborhoods in past storms.

There are major variations across the region that are likely to affect the process of recovery. Damage was extensive on the Mississippi Coast, and the area's largest single source of employment—casino gambling—was knocked out of operation. In comparison to New Orleans, however, the number of people living in areas of moderate or greater damage was small, only about 50,000. And also in contrast to New Orleans, only a small share of these people were black and a majority were homeowners. It is difficult to assess the importance of race in recovery policy in Mississippi, but in a politically conservative state it could make a big difference that white homeowners constitute the bulk of claimants for state assistance. Further, these people are easier to serve for several reasons.

1. First, they are identifiable and—because they retain an ownership interest in their properties—they should prove easier for authorities to contact.
2. Second, since much of the damage wrought by Katrina in this area was by wind and rain damage, standard homeowner policies offer substantial private-sector coverage of damage losses. For those with uninsured flood damage, Mississippi state government expects federal aid to be sufficient to fund payments of $150,000 to individual homeowners.
3. Third, the low density of housing in this area means that typically even when one's home was uninhabitable, there was space for a trailer in the driveway. Since in addition the loss of electrical power was relatively short-term in Mississippi, and basic public services could be restored within a reasonable time, homeowners in this region more readily met the requirements for a FEMA-provided trailer space and confirmed utility hookups.

In contrast, consider the situation in New Orleans. Six months after Katrina, observers were beginning to see signs of progress (Russell 2006b). But more than half the persons in damaged areas were renters, unlikely to be protected in any way by property insurance, and 30 percent fell below the poverty line and were therefore unlikely to have their own funds to return to the city. By the end of 2005, power was still unavailable to much of the city, and actual connections to electric power required residents to present evidence of inspection by a licensed electrician before power would be restored to an individual home.

The utility company (a subsidiary of the Entergy Corporation) had filed for bankruptcy protection in September. Large areas of the city remain vacant even at the beginning of 2007. Though most debris has been removed and many homes have been gutted, reconstruction work had not begun on most homes. Basic public services had not been restored in many neighborhoods. For example, only 54 public schools reopened in the fall of 2006, compared to 128 before Katrina. As shown in Figure 12.2, these schools were concentrated in high-ground neighborhoods close to the Mississippi River, with almost none in New Orleans East, the Lower Ninth Ward, Gentilly, and Lakeview.

Among the key policy choices confronted by the city, three stand out as especially significant (more generally see Popkin, Turner, and Burt 2006; Nossiter 2006). These are the questions of how to allocate housing assistance funds to residents, how to restructure public housing, and where to concentrate support for neighborhood rebuilding. Initial steps do little to support the most disadvantaged and favor people and neighborhoods that have more market resources.

Housing Assistance

The principal public source of funding for housing reconstruction is the federal government, with $10.4 billion in Community Development Block Grant support authorized in June 2006 for Louisiana (Maggi 2006). The state's plan for using these

FIGURE 12.2—The State of Schools in New Orleans, Fall 2006

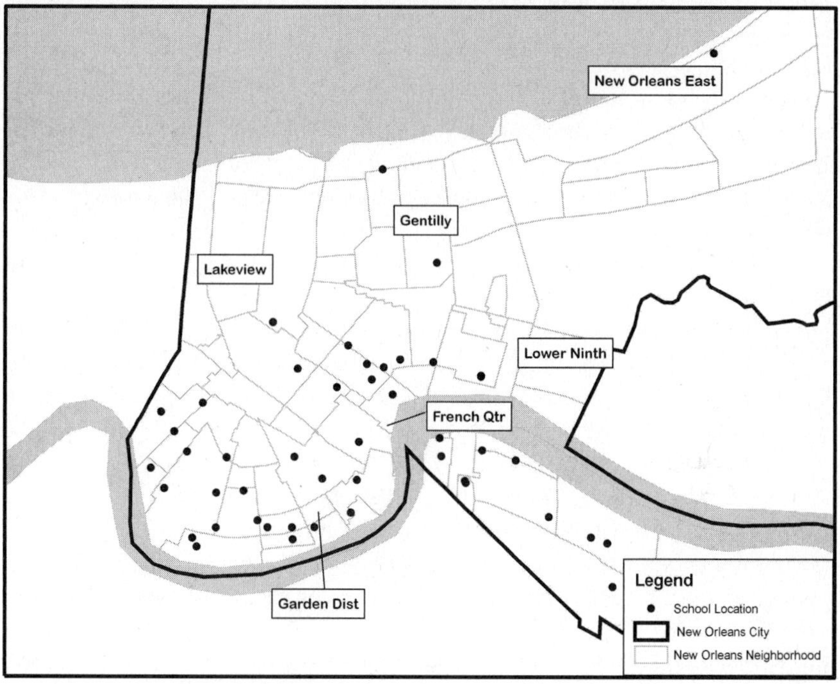

New Orleans East

Gentilly

Lakeview

Lower Ninth

French Qtr

Garden Dist

Legend
● School Location
▭ New Orleans City
▭ New Orleans Neighborhood

Source: Developed by the author.

funds is called The Road Home (Louisiana Office of Community Development 2006). It targets about $8 billion for assistance to homeowners. Only $1.5 billion is allocated to a program to redevelop rental housing.

According to estimates by the U.S. Department of Housing and Urban Development (2006a), there were a total of almost 100,000 housing units in New Orleans that suffered major or severe damage or were destroyed. Of these, 52 percent were owner occupied and 48 percent occupied by renters. By this measure alone, the policy of allocating most funds to homeowners is not proportionate to the damage. Given that rents have risen by as much as 30–40 percent and the vacancy rate for rental housing is near zero (U.S. Department of Housing and Urban Development 2006b), it seems clear that a more focused effort to build or rehabilitate rental housing would be needed in order to allow many rental households to return to the city.

Public Housing

A special category of housing is public housing controlled by the Housing Authority of New Orleans. Prior to Katrina, there were about 8,000 units, although due to poor maintenance (and consistent with a general plan of reducing this segment of the housing stock), only 5,100 were occupied at the time of Katrina. As was also true nationally, efforts were underway to restructure the system by demolishing existing units and replacing them with new mixed-income developments. This had already been done with one complex, the St. Thomas Project in the Central City/Garden District, which was demolished in 2002 and replaced by a Wal-Mart and new predominantly market-rate condominiums. Originally built for 1,500 low-income families, the new development so far accommodates only 200. Most public housing complexes were sealed after the hurricane (with metal barriers bolted over the doorways) to prevent tenants from returning.

Confirming speculation during the preceding year, including comments by public officials that only "people who are willing to work" should be allowed to return to public housing, specific plans were announced in June 2006 by HUD Secretary Alphonso Jackson to demolish 5,000 more units (Saulny 2006). The St. Bernard, C. J. Peete, B. W. Cooper, and Lafitte housing developments would be entirely removed. They would be replaced by mixed-income developments following the St. Thomas model.

At the same time, HUD increased by 35 percent the amount that it would pay as the "fair market rent" through housing vouchers. If there were vacancies at this rate ($976 for a two-bedroom unit as of October 2006), a system of housing vouchers for low- and moderate-income people could be evaluated as a reasonable alternative to public housing. But in the context of a zero-vacancy rental market at any price, the decision to press ahead with public housing demolition means that few displaced low-income families will have any opportunity to live in New Orleans in the future.

Neighborhood Triage

Although public officials have assiduously avoided saying so, there is a high probability that redevelopment in some neighborhoods will be discouraged by public policy. If this is not done by an overt designation of areas as off-limits for building permits, the same outcome may be achieved passively by choosing not to make the public investments that are required for livable communities. These include repair of infrastructure damage and reopening of facilities such as schools and police and fire stations.

The notion of neighborhood triage was implicit in the proposals made by the Bring New Orleans Back Commission (2006) in the public report of its Urban Planning Committee in January 2006. Some zones of the city were designated as "immediate opportunity areas" where the city should identify vacant and underutilized property for new construction, expedite permits for repairs and construction of new housing, provide/support community and cultural facilities and services, assist educational/ health institutions to address immediate needs, and begin repair/reconstruction using current rules and regulations. Others were proposed to be neighborhood planning areas, where the city should conduct a neighborhood planning process to determine the appropriate future. In these areas, the city was advised not to issue any permits to build or rebuild.

Although this report was not adopted, and indeed was widely criticized, it sets forth the key planning question: Given that there are insufficient public resources to support fully the rebuilding of all neighborhoods, by what criteria should choices among neighborhoods be made? Mayor Nagin has repeatedly suggested one approach, to let the decisions be guided by residents who "vote with their feet" to return. Neighborhoods where a will to recover is demonstrated by individual investments and collective action should be supported; in other areas, individuals should be counseled against trying to rebuild. This is essentially a proposal to let the market decide the future of the city.

For many of the same reasons that rebuilding will be facilitated on the Mississippi Coast, white residents of New Orleans are more likely than black residents to be able to return to their neighborhoods, even if the neighborhood is reopened. Whites are more likely to be homeowners (55 percent compared to 42 percent among African-American households), but more important, they are much more likely to have the personal resources to reinvest in their homes or to find a new residence in a difficult housing market. In the pre-Katrina black population, 35 percent were below the poverty line and the median household income was only $25,000. Among whites, only 11 percent were poor, and the median income was more than twice as high—$61,000. Therefore even among homeowners, blacks are less likely to have the means to rebuild than are whites.

In conjunction with public support for homeowners over tenants and the plan to demolish most public housing, market-based policies point toward a future in which New Orleans—though it may be much smaller than before—will also have a smaller share of black residents, tenants, and poor and working-class families. To the extent that the city's labor force continues to require a certain share of persons with low skills and low wages, which is typical of a tourist economy, this means that these workers will mostly live elsewhere.

THE FUTURE IN THE BALANCE: SHIFTING ELECTORAL POLITICS

Although there appears to be an emerging direction in local recovery policy, final decisions have not been made. The provisions of Louisiana's Road to Recovery and the demolition of public housing are being contested in court, and the election of Democratic majorities in the U.S. House and Senate may have some influence on how federal resources will be used. There is also a formal neighborhood planning process put in place in the fall of 2006, supported by a large grant from the Rockefeller Foundation, through which neighborhood organizations have been encouraged to make their voices heard. Another factor that may make a difference is the shifting constituencies in local politics.

There has been a potential for political coalitions that cut across the racial and class divisions that have helped structure city politics over the decades. Residents of such very different neighborhoods as Lakeview and the Lower Ninth Ward have a shared interest in short-term assistance programs such as subsidies for temporary housing outside the city. Yet variations across neighborhoods—and across race and class—are likely to support the emergence of a sense of conflicting interests.

In December 2005, conflict took the form of opposition to proposals to locate FEMA trailers in public spaces within neighborhoods that sustained less damage. In this case the interests of advantaged neighborhoods (advantaged by protection from flooding and by having residents in place to express their views) were in conflict with the interests of absent residents who have no place to return. Not surprisingly the City Council gave its members veto power over new trailer parks in the areas that they represent.

The mayoral election in spring 2006 offers evidence that conflicting interests are likely to overcome consensus (Logan 2006b), and it is not obvious whose interests will predominate. On the one hand, there was a substantial change in the composition of the electorate, reflecting the disproportionate displacement of lower-income black voters. On the other, there was a surprising shift in the source of Mayor Ray Nagin's electoral support that could make him more responsive to that same constituency.

The first indicator of change is turnout. In the previous municipal election (2002), when the current mayor, Ray Nagin, defeated Richard Pennington, there was a modest turnout of 130,000 voters (out of a total pool of registered voters that has remained close to 300,000 for the last several years). In the more recent presidential election of 2004, when few local positions were at stake but there was considerable interest in the contest between President George Bush and challenger John Kerry, turnout was over 197,000. Compared to either standard, participation in 2006 was depressed, with a total of under 115,000 votes cast.

Of course, a lower turnout was inevitable. More interesting is how turnout varied across neighborhoods. From the perspective of future urban policy, neighborhoods with the highest electoral participation have likely strengthened their hands in the battles over public investment and development planning that are sure to be a major feature of local politics in the next several years. Figure 12.3 displays turnout levels in 2006 as a proportion of the 2002 level. This map can be compared to the map of racial composition and flood damage presented above.

The neighborhoods with the largest declines in turnout are in the Lower Ninth Ward, New Orleans East, and parts of Mid-City and Bywater. These are all predominantly black neighborhoods, but they have widely varying class composition. In Mid-City and Bywater, it is especially the public housing projects whose former residents have been barred from returning to the city up to now. The Lower Ninth Ward is a mixed-income area with many working-class homeowners. These are areas where the loss of public infrastructure and government restrictions on entry have seriously delayed recovery efforts. New Orleans East, in contrast, has been an important base for the black middle class. All these areas suffered close to 100 percent flooding, and displacement is the most obvious explanation for low turnout.

Among white neighborhoods there is generally a positive correlation between voter turnout and extent of flood damage. For example, the Uptown/Carrollton and Central City/Garden Districts include some neighborhoods with very little flood damage

FIGURE 12.3—Voter Turnout, 2006 Compared to 2002

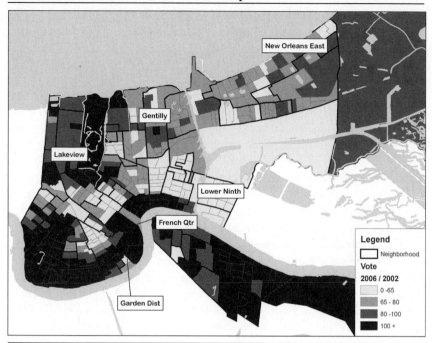

Source: Developed by the author.

and others that were hard hit. Neighborhoods with no flooding like Uptown and Garden District had considerably higher participation than in 2002, while those with more damage like Broadmoor and Milan suffered a loss. But there are two other significant patterns to point out.

First, several planning districts show little impact of Katrina. The French Quarter and central business district actually had higher turnout than in 2002, as did New Aurora and Algiers on the West Bank. These are among the areas of the city with the least flood damage. The surprise here is how much participation declined in comparison to the 2004 presidential election, with a fall of 25–30 percent that seems unlikely to be due to population loss. In what may have been the most important election in the history of the city, why was turnout in these areas no more than the usual local standard? There may be evidence here of forces beyond displacement, evidence of surprising apathy, alienation, and disaffection from the political process by the residents of these relatively advantaged communities.

Second, despite its devastation, Lakeview shows an exceptional turnout. The number of Lakeview voters was nearly (94 percent) as high in 2006 as in 2002. Even more, there are only modest variations within the district between Lake Shore/Lake Vista, which was only partly flooded, and areas like Navarre that were heavily damaged. Lakeview's participation may have been influenced by a special tax measure on the ballot that would increase property taxes in this district for the purpose of improved policing. A greater factor probably was extensive voter mobilization by local civic groups. Lakeview is known to have a strong civic association that has built upon the many smaller neighborhood associations that used to operate in the area, and in this election it translated its affluence and high levels of home ownership into political clout.

Another planning district with a relatively high turnout despite considerable damage is Gentilly, especially the racially mixed neighborhoods of Fillmore (94 percent as high as 2002) and Gentilly Terrace (88 percent as high). The Gentilly neighborhood was severely damaged following Hurricane Katrina when the London Avenue Canal levees breached in two places. Some sections of the neighborhood did not receive flooding because they had been developed along the Gentilly Ridge, a long stretch of high ground along the former banks of Bayou Gentilly. The Gentilly's population has slowly returned, with most homes requiring major gutting and repair work before they could be reoccupied. Beginning in the early part of 2007, the area is moderately populated with something less than half of residents and businesses returned.

Gentilly is also home to historically black Dillard University, founded in 1869, which received extensive flood damage. The present 55-acre campus near Gentilly Boulevard and the London Avenue Canal was established in the 1930s. In spring 2006, for seven months, the New Orleans Hilton Riverside Hotel became the home away from home for Dillard's 1,100 students. The Hilton became known as Hotel Dillard (Collette 2006). Dillard students took their normal classes at the New Orleans World Trade Center and the New Orleans Hilton Riverside Hotel. On September 5, 2006, Dillard's home on the Avenue of the Oaks finally reopened after being closed for 12 months. The fall 2007 enrollment at Dillard was only 44 percent of its pre-Katrina total, compared to 90 percent for Our Lady of Holy Cross, 80 percent for Loyola University and Tulane University, 79 percent for Delgado Community College, 75 percent for Xavier University, 72 percent for Southern University of New Orleans, and 65 percent for the University of New Orleans (Liu and Plyer 2008, 9).

Although Hurricane Katrina reshaped the political map of the city by suppressing the vote in the poorest and blackest neighborhoods, the dynamics of the mayoral campaign also represent a more remarkable shift in the composition of support for the winning candidate, Mayor Ray Nagin. Having been elected in 2002 on the basis of his strong showing in white and more affluent neighborhoods, the mayor was reelected with his main edge among neighborhoods with predominantly black and low- and middle-income residents.

Figures 12.4 and 12.5 illustrate the shift with maps showing the extent of support for Nagin in his first race in 2002 and in the 2006 primary by precinct. Comparing these maps to the map of racial composition presented above, in 2002 it is clear that Nagin ran strongest in the neighborhoods with smaller black populations. Reports from the period suggested that in fact his election depended on support from white neighborhoods (and financial backing from people described as the "Uptown white establishment").

FIGURE 12.4—Nagin Support in 2002

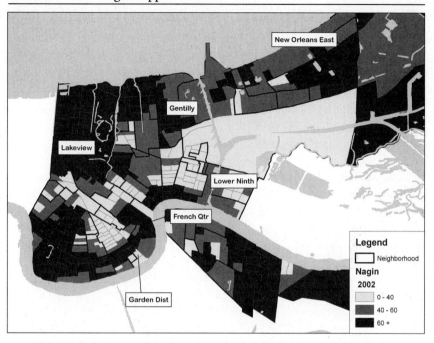

FIGURE 12.5—Nagin Support in 2006

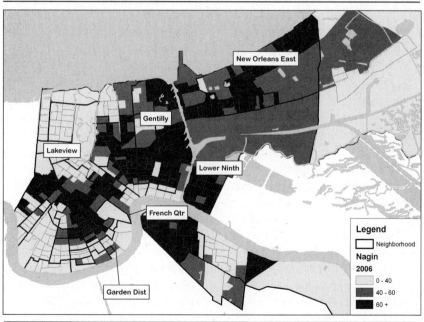

Source: Developed by the author.

In a surprising remaking of the electoral map, Nagin's support in 2006 shifted almost 180 degrees—neighborhoods that had supported him now supported his opponents, and areas where he had found the least votes now constituted his core constituency. The planning districts with the highest levels of support for Nagin are the Lower Ninth Ward (83 percent in 2006 compared to only 40 percent in 2002) and New Orleans East (71 percent, up from 55 percent). The individual neighborhoods with the highest shares of Nagin votes are project neighborhoods: above 90 percent in Calliope Project, Desire Project, and Fischer Project, all areas where he previously received at most a third of votes.

In contrast, Nagin lost heavily in predominantly white areas. In the Garden District, for example, which is only 2 percent black, he had gained 85 percent of the votes in 2002 but only 22 percent in 2006. Lakeview, also 2 percent black, voted overwhelmingly for Nagin in 2002 (87 percent) but against him in 2006 (22 percent).

THE ROAD AHEAD:
A NEW POLITICAL GEOGRAPHY

The new political geography of New Orleans certainly will be a factor as policy decisions are made in the coming months and years. Where will schools reopen, where will policing and other public services be brought back on line soonest, where will rebuilding be encouraged by city officials and what neighborhoods will have a lower priority? Areas like the Lower Ninth Ward, New Orleans East, and the less affluent and predominantly black sections of Bywater and Mid-City have experienced sharp declines in their participation in the political process. Historically, these were strong voting blocs. In contrast, Lakeview nearly matched its 2002 vote total despite dislocation of most of its residents, and areas like Algiers, Uptown-Carrollton, the French Quarter, and Garden District see their political influence on the rise in this respect.

But there is also a countervailing force, an unexpected consolidation of voting patterns along racial lines in which a politically conservative black mayor turned successfully to a black and low-income constituency that previously had denied him their support. This outcome potentially diminishes the political losses that this part of the electorate, and the neighborhoods where they are concentrated, seemed sure to suffer. Much now depends on how well groups play their cards and what role the backroom players (the investors and real estate entrepreneurs who eventually once again contributed to Nagin's campaign war chest) have in the process.

Support from areas like the projects, Lower Ninth Ward, and New Orleans East was critical, but their voices will have to be heard from a distance. White Republican neighborhoods backed the losing candidate, but the 20 percent or more of their votes that went to Nagin were indispensable to his victory. This is a situation where a public official will face conflicting pressures but may also find considerable room to maneuver and provide leadership for a city that has put key decisions on hold for too long.

REFERENCES

Bring New Orleans Back Commission, Urban Planning Committee. 2005. "Action Plan for New Orleans: The New American City." Available at http://www.bringnew orleansback.org/Portals/BringNewOrleansBack/Resources/Urban%20Planning%2 0Final%20Report.pdf (accessed August 8, 2008).

Collette, S. 2006. "New Orleans Hilton Becomes 'Hotel Dillard.'" *The Black Collegian.* January 13. Available at http://www.imdiversity.com/special/bcwire_hilton_hotel.asp (accessed July 2, 2007).

Colten, C. 2005. *An Unnatural Metropolis: Wresting New Orleans from Nature.* Baton Rouge: Louisiana State University Press.

Gabe, T., G. Falk, M. McCarty, and V. W. Mason. 2005. "Hurricane Katrina: Social-Demographic Characteristics of Impacted Areas." Washington, DC: Congressional Research Service, Library of Congress. Available at http://www.gnocdc.org/reports/crsrept.pdf (accessed August 8, 2008).

Liu, A. and A. Plyer. 2008. *The New Orleans Index. Tracking Recovery of the New Orleans Metro Area: Anniversary Edition Three Years After Katrina.* The Brookings Institution and Greater New Orleans Community Data Center. August.

Logan, J. R. 2006a. "The Impact of Katrina: Race and Class in Storm-Damaged Neighborhoods." Report by the American Communities Project, Brown University. January 25. Available at www.s4.brown.edu/Katrina/report.pdf (accessed August 8, 2008).

———. 2006b. "Population Displacement and Post-Katrina Politics: The New Orleans Mayoral Race, 2006." Report by the American Communities Project, Brown University. June 1. Available at www.s4.brown.edu/Katrina/report2.pdf (accessed August 8, 2008).

Louisiana Department of Health and Hospitals. 2006. "Louisiana Health and Population Survey Report, November 29, 2006: Orleans Parish." Available at http://popest.org/popestla2006/files/PopEst_Orleans_SurveyReport.pdf (accessed August 8, 2008).

Louisiana Office of Community Development. 2006. "Action Plan for the Use of Disaster Recovery Funds." Available at http://www.doa.la.gov/cdbg/dr/plans/ActionPlan -Approved_06_04_11.pdf (accessed August 8, 2008).

Maggi, L. 2006. "Housing Aid Plan Challenged; Renters Neglected, Nonprofit Groups Say." *Times-Picayune.* June 21, p. 2.

Nossiter, A. 2006. "In New Orleans, Money Is Ready but a Plan Isn't." *New York Times.* June 18, p. 1.

Popkin, S., M. A. Turner, and M. Burt. 2006. "Rebuilding Affordable Housing in New Orleans: The Challenge of Creating Inclusive Communities." Washington, DC: The Urban Institute. Available at http://www.urban.org/UploadedPDF/900914 _affordable_housing.pdf (accessed August 8, 2008).

Russell, G. 2006a. "Address Changes Offer Insight Into City." *Times-Picayune.* February 5, p. 1.

———. 2006b. "Six Months Later, Recovery Gaining Focus; City May Be Near Turning Point." *Times-Picayune.* February 26, p. 1.

Saulny, S. 2006. "5,000 Public Housing Units in New Orleans Are to Be Razed." *New York Times.* June 15.

U.S. Department of Housing and Urban Development, Office of Policy Development and Research. 2006a. "Current Housing Unit Damage Estimates Hurricanes Katrina,

Rita, and Wilma." February 12, 2006. Revised April 7, 2006. Available at http://www
.gnocdc.org/reports/Katrina_Rita_Wilma_Damage_2_12_06_revised.pdf (accessed
August 8, 2008).

———. 2006b. "Economic and Housing Market Conditions of the New Orleans-Metairie-
Kenner, Louisiana Metropolitan Statistical Area as of September 1, 2005, with Up-
dates to February 1, 2006." Available at http://www.huduser.org/publications/pdf/
CMAR_NewOrleansLA.pdf (accessed August 8, 2008).

AFTERWORD

Looking Back to Move Forward

Beverly Wright and Robert D. Bullard

August 29, 2008, marked the third anniversary of Hurricane Katrina. Recovery and reconstruction over the tumultuous three years have been mixed and uneven. There has been a slow but steady return of individuals and families to the city. Repopulation of New Orleans is tied more to who has resources, including financial settlements of housing and insurance claims, transportation, and employment. Thousands of native New Orleanians who were displaced by Hurricane Katrina, most of whom are black and poor, still have a desire to return home but lack the resources. The shortage of low-income and affordable rental housing will keep most of these evacuees from returning (Bullard 2007).

Many of the families fall into the category of internally displaced persons—not refugees (Kromm and Sturgis 2008). For some, the evacuation via bus, plane, and train set in motion their permanent displacement. To ensure that this "black diaspora" is complete, numerous obstacles have been erected in their way, such as the demolition of public housing, failure to rebuild working-class housing that was destroyed by the storm and flood, loss of small minority businesses, lack of clean-up of contamination and toxic hot spots left by receding floodwaters, and spotty efforts to target federal rebuilding funds to hard-hit mostly black areas of the city.

Some policy analysts and elected officials have presented the plight of the city's displaced citizens as a "silver lining" in dispersing New Orleans' poor in Houston, Dallas, San Antonio, Memphis, and Jackson. They spin it as an unintended positive effect of the storm—breaking up concentrated poverty—something that government officials had been trying to achieve for decades. However, the best way to break up concentrated poverty is not displacement but concentrated employment at a livable wage. Many Katrina evacuees had worked two minimum-wage jobs just to get by before the storm. Louisiana is a right-to-work state. Some critics would argue that it's a "right to work for nothing" state, making low-wage, non-union service workers vulnerable. The same jobs performed by hotel, restaurant, casino, entertainment, taxi, and tourist workers in Las Vegas or Atlantic City pay a livable wage, but not in New Orleans. Many of these service jobs are performed by the working poor.

Katrina allowed "disaster capitalism" to shift into high gear (Klein 2008). Let's face it. There are big bucks in disaster. Immediately after the flood, billions of no-bid contracts were awarded to a handful of politically connected national contractors; the federal Davis-Bacon Act, which mandates workers be paid the prevailing wage, was suspended; and a host of environmental waivers were granted.

Hurricane Katrina made clear the links between race, place, and vulnerability. What people often term natural disasters or acts of God are in fact acts of social injustice perpetuated by government and business on the poor, people of color, the most vulnerable of our society—groups least able to withstand such disasters (Squires and Hartman 2006). Decades of government neglect, denial, and old-fashioned greed created a nightmare in the aftermath of the storm.

For decades, budget cuts to the Army Corps of Engineers, the federal agency charged with oversight of the levee system, allowed New Orleans to be underprotected. It does not take a rocket scientist to figure out which communities were least protected and most vulnerable or which communities will reap the lion's share of benefits—who is left "high and dry" once the multi-billion-dollar levee and coastal restoration plans are completed. Residents in New Orleans were told, "You're on your own" (Nolan 2005). One need only overlay race and class characteristics atop an Army Corps flood-protection map to see what color communities received the sharpest increase in protection. Some would label this a not so subtle form of "levee redlining," with people-of-color communities receiving the least amount of flood protection.

An entire movement was founded some three decades ago to address environmental injustice. This movement defines environment as where we live, work, play, worship, attend school, as well as the physical and natural world. Environmental justice embraces the principle that all communities have a right to equal protection under our nation's environmental, health, housing, transportation, energy, land use, and civil rights laws (Bullard 2005).

The Environmental Justice Movement was even able to get a president, Bill Clinton, to sign an Executive Order on Environmental Justice—an order that requires federal agencies such as the Federal Emergency Management Agency (FEMA), the Army Corps, the U.S. Department of Housing and Urban Development (HUD), the Centers for Disease Control (CDC), and others to examine their policies and practices to see if they have an adverse and disproportionate impact on low-income and minority populations. Katrina tested the limits of the EJ Executive Order 12898 and the agencies it covers. Government policies and practices before, during, and after Katrina allowed thousands of low-income and minority populations, the two protected classes covered by the order, to be disproportionately and adversely affected. The Environmental Protection Agency (EPA) failed to order clean-up of toxic contamination; FEMA subjected storm victims to toxic travel trailers; the CDC delayed in testing toxic FEMA trailers; HUD allowing public housing to be demolished during a housing shortage; and the Army Corps provided unequal flood protection after the levee repair.

How can these environmental disparities be explained? Don't all communities have a right to "equal protection under the law"? Should your race determine whether or not the government protects you? The historical legacy of segregation and housing discrimination quite often dictated where African Americans could live, rent, buy homes, play, and shop. It is no accident or chance happening where African Americans live in New Orleans. The same holds true for whites in the city.

Historically, affluent whites generally take the high ground, leaving to the poor, working-class, and African Americans the more vulnerable low-lying land. However, even when whites occupy low-lying areas, they get special privileges for being white, as in the case of New Orleans' affluent and mostly white Lakeview neighborhood, which received more than five feet of increased flood protection, compared to low-lying black neighborhoods that received significantly less or no increase in flood protection. Despite decades of anti-discrimination laws, "white privilege" still provides an edge for white disaster victims, while penalizing people-of-color disaster victims (Bullard and Wright 2006).

Hurricane Katrina personalized how "racialized place" operates to disenfranchise African Americans and other people of color in their attempt to evacuate, return, rebuild, and reclaim their lives, neighborhoods, and institutions. The slow government response to evacuate individuals who were left in squalid conditions in the Superdome and Convention Center mirrors the differential treatment in providing environmental clean-up of contamination, health care, including mental health, and transportation that were devastated by the flood.

New Orleans' African-American neighborhoods were redlined before Katrina. Redlining by banks, insurance, and commercial businesses has accelerated since the storm—killing black areas. Although it is illegal, it is still practiced. Large swaths of neighborhood have been racially redlined—with little commercial or business activity—even though many of the former residents have returned.

Katrina increased competition for housing—placing a special burden on black renters and black home buyers seeking replacement housing—exposing them to housing discrimination. Black New Orleanians have always faced housing discrimination. This is a fact of life in the South, but the housing shortages in post-Katrina New Orleans have allowed housing discrimination to run rampant—causing African-American Katrina survivors to spend more time, more effort, and more money than whites in their search for replacement housing.

Hurricanes and floods marginalize already marginalized populations. In the post-Katrina rebuilding stage, storm survivors who are lucky enough to make it back home are exposed to price gouging, home repair scams, banking and insurance redlining, and predatory lending practices. These unfair practices are not limited to fly-by-night business operations. They also include well-established large banking, mortgage, and insurance companies. Homeowners are forced into a tug-of-war with insurance companies that use the wind-or-water argument to unfairly deny legitimate claims. Homeowners with limited means often agree to low settlement claims offered by insurance companies, while more affluent homeowners hire lawyers. Having resources in a time of crisis can make a difference in evacuation, and it also make a difference in disaster recovery—including rebuilding one's home, churches, schools, and other valued institutions.

Katrina closed a number of colleges and universities in New Orleans—displacing over 75,000 college students. The storm severely damaged three historically black universities in New Orleans (Dillard University, Southern University in New Orleans, and Xavier University). These three universities were home to more than 10,500 African-American college students before the storm (Liu and Plyer 2008). New Orleans holds the distinction as the only U.S. city, besides Atlanta and Nashville, that has three or more historically black colleges and universities (HBCUs). Atlanta has five and Nashville has three.

There is little doubt that New Orleans' predominately white public and private universities will be rebuilt. Three years after the storm, most New Orleans white college students are back on campus, while the black colleges struggle. New Orleans–based HBCUs struggled before Katrina. Clearly, special initiatives are needed to rebuild these institutions and support the return of their students.

Race matters. It mattered in the evacuation, and it matters in the rebuilding and reconstruction phase. New Orleans' white population has returned, while nearly half of the city's black population remains scattered. White and affluent neighborhoods are back. Many have been rebuilt and some have actually seen an increase in population. It is not just the low-income black areas that are struggling to recover, even New Orleans East's middle-income black neighborhoods find themselves on the short end of the recovery when it comes to housing, insurance coverage, banking services, shopping, and food service.

A service desert, an area with limited health services and full-service supermarkets, existed in black New Orleans before the storm. Residents who have returned to the homes in the East are forced to drive long distances for basic services that most Uptown and Lakeview residents take for granted. This is not an insignificant point with gasoline at $4 a gallon. New Orleans is a nightmare for those without personal automobiles. Having a car was important in evacuation before Katrina. It is equally important in the city where transit is only a fraction of the pre-Katrina operation. The New Orleans Rapid Transit Authority (NORTA) operates less than half the buses it ran before the storm. The cutback in service makes it difficult for many transit-dependent riders to get around.

Suffering in post-Katrina is not uniformly spread across the city. The New Orleans downtown is displaying the same charm as before Katrina. Tourism is increasing, and large conferences, sports events, and festivals have returned. The streets are clean, the streetlights are working, and it appears that the city is on track for a slow but steady and full recovery. Some impacted New Orleanians have made progress in rebuilding their lives and retaining stability, while others continue to face barriers to recovery. But how do we measure the progress of the city's recovery? Recovery is certainly in the eye of the beholder. Where you lived before the storm may well determine how you live after the storm.

Where one was employed before the storm affects post-Katrina recovery. Just 50 percent of African-American households are currently working for their pre-storm employer compared to 70 percent of white households. Many African-American Katrina survivors began their road to recovery not by returning to a job but by looking for a job. Given these dismal statistics, it is no wonder that nearly half of the city's African-American population is still displaced.

The desirability of a city is often determined by its amenities, which require a functioning infrastructure. The city of New Orleans is a very old city; in fact, it is older than the United States. Consequently, it has a very old infrastructure. Compounding the situation is the fact that the already stressed infrastructure of this old city was decimated by Katrina. The immediate challenges after Katrina were the rebuilding or repairing of the structures and systems supplying electricity and water.

Provision of electricity, gas, and telephone service, although functional for most of the city, was also a challenge. Entergy Corporation, the local electric and gas service provider, was bankrupt. The city brokered a deal that allowed the company to survive and the city is now "powered up." However, the connection of electrical services for persons returning to the city can take some time due to the amount of damage to the equipment.

Racial geography plays out in service recovery. Those areas least flooded received service more quickly than flooded areas. It should be no surprise that black areas were more flooded than white areas. While the Lower Ninth was one of heaviest damaged areas from floodwaters, it was the last neighborhood whose tap water was given a clean bill of health. Telephone service is still a challenge, requiring residents to expend more time and resources to get reconnected. On the average, connection of nondigital phone service takes 30 days. Compare this to an approximately three-day wait before Katrina.

The problems of the city's Sewerage and Water Board, with its crumbling infrastructure, are serious. The underground system of pipes is very old and riddled with holes. Before Katrina, it was not unusual to see broken water lines with water gushing out into the streets. Three years after the storm, the city loses millions of gallons of water daily. It will take billions of dollars to repair the system. While New Orleans residents presently have clean running water and flushing toilets, plumbing is a very lucrative business in the city these days—making unsuspecting homeowners easy prey to scams and rip-off artists disguised as plumbers, electricians, and contractors.

The word in the city is, "There are only two types of houses in New Orleans; houses with plumbing problems and houses that will have plumbing problems." The city's drainage system, in many areas, is still clogged with debris from Katrina, causing street flooding during heavy rainfall in areas that were not problematic before the storm. But, we have still made tremendous progress.

The hospital system and the availability of private physician's offices is another challenge for city residents, especially the poor. New Orleans' Charity Hospital, the major medical service provider for the poor in New Orleans and surrounding parishes, was shut down after Katrina. Today, we have only two hospitals with a limited number of beds available. Methodist Hospital, located in the largely black community of New Orleans East, has been closed with no date for reopening slated. We all remember the scenes in New Orleans after Katrina when doctors were working under tents, providing medical services to patients. At that time, many residents had not seen a doctor in over a year.

Many doctors did not return to the city. This was especially true of African-American doctors, who lost nearly all of their service population. Since Katrina, a small number of African-American doctors have returned. One has to question whether this can be considered progress.

Hurricane Katrina damaged or destroyed more than 100 of the New Orleans Public Schools (NOPS) district's 128 school buildings. NOPS served approximately 65,000 students pre-Katrina. As a result of legislation passed in November 2005 by the state, 102 of the city's worst-performing public schools were transferred to the Recovery School District (RSD), which is operated by the Louisiana Department of Education. The RSD was created in 2003 to allow the state to take over failing schools.

Charter schools now predominate in New Orleans and comprise 53 percent of the post-Katrina enrollment of 33,200 students. Before the hurricane, charters had about 2 percent of the city's 67,000 public students. After Katrina, charters snapped up rent-free school buildings, recruited students they wanted, and shut their doors to other applicants (Mathews 2008, A01). In several cases, black families have had to resort to lawsuits to get their children enrolled in some charter schools. This over-reliance on charter schools has left the city's regular schools struggling to serve a disproportionate number of students with special needs (Dingerson et al. 2008).

The city has experienced a decrease in the number of supermarkets, and consequently, smaller grocery stores in many areas are filling the gap. Before Katrina, the predominantly black New Orleans East area saw a decline in essential service businesses, including supermarkets, and since the storm, only one supermarket has returned there to serve 60,000 community residents. There has been an enormous increase in undesirable fast-food and liquor stores in the area. The fact that there is one Winn-Dixie supermarket is a sign of progress. Ironically, drug stores have returned in almost full force to New Orleans East.

In pondering the question of how to measure the recovery of a city further, we realize that one's response depends upon one's perspective. It is clear that race and place greatly determine personal ability to recover from Katrina and color a personal view of recovery. Communities least affected by the storm tend to have larger percentages of white residents. These communities are also more likely to describe the recovery as satisfactory. While these areas received less damage, they have also benefited the most from federal dollars for recovery. Flood insurance claims were larger, leading to a large concentration of hazardous mitigation dollars flowing into these areas. Because of this, these areas are well on the way to a full recovery.

The Lower Ninth Ward and New Orleans East are further behind. Streetlights are not in service in all areas, and lights on Interstate 10 in some areas of these communities function only sporadically. Most schools remain closed three years after the storm, and supermarkets have not returned in adequate numbers to service these predominantly African-American areas.

The New Orleans East community, however, is vibrant and hopeful. Community and neighborhood meetings and meetings with state and federal officials are well attended. The number of returning residents increases daily. There are signs of work being done on increasing numbers of homes.

New Orleans East is home to seven exclusive subdivisions built on man-made lakes, two of which are gated communities—Eastover and McKendal Estates. There are playgrounds and green spaces as well as a very large park housing a wildlife preserve that were centers of community recreation and family activity before Katrina. Neighbors can now be seen once again walking in the mornings and evenings, tending their lawns and gardens. Children are playing more outdoors, and once again, family pets can be seen and heard throughout the neighborhoods.

Affluent black homeowners, including doctors, lawyers, insurance executives, and a few professional athletes and entertainers understand too well that that they are not immune to the slow pace of services returning to their exclusive neighborhoods. Black professionals in the East, like individuals in Section 8 rental units in the neighborhood, are forced to drive long distances to shop, eat at a sit-down restaurant, and take in a first-run movie. This reality cannot be reduced to a "poverty thing."

While the government and its responses to Katrina related to rebuilding can and do determine the speed of recovery, what we have learned is that it is the people who will determine the city's recovery. We know that race and place can influence how you live. We also know that people of color and residents of low-income communities are more affected by negative environmental factors and community disparities that impact health.

The neighborhoods in New Orleans most affected by the storm are segregated by race and income. Like other communities of color and low-income communities across the country, they were plagued with overwhelmingly high crime rates, underfunded and ineffective schools, insufficient essential services, poor transportation and housing options, as well as other factors that challenge individual and community health. Many residents have had little, if any, help from government. Some residents no longer even expect it. But they are determined to return home. Citizens in communities are leading all kinds of rebuilding projects. They are building eco-friendly houses, steel houses, and concrete houses instead of the traditional wood-frame houses we are used to seeing built in the city. There are communities that have decided to be carbon free and are installing solar panels and solar hot water heaters, in addition to using the latest in eco-friendly weatherization techniques and materials.

There are neighborhoods fighting *against* the opening and locating of landfills and other disamenities in their communities and fighting *for* a fair share of the new green economy and green jobs that are beginning to take hold in the city (Bullard and Harden 2005; Bullard and Wright 2006).

There is no question that rebuilding New Orleans and the Gulf Coast region should employ the best green and sustainable technology. However, it is imperative that rebuilding, green or otherwise, is fair, just, equitable, inclusive, and carried out in a nondiscriminatory way. Greenbuilding combats the use of environmentally unsustainable building materials. The rebuilding of New Orleans and the Gulf Coast should include a concerted effort to bring together the predominantly white green-building adherents and displaced African-American residents.

In moving New Orleans toward a greener, healthier, more sustainable, and more just reconstruction of New Orleans that protects the environment while respecting the city's culture and the well-being of its residents, BuildingGreen (2005) offered a ten-point plan, which was developed with the help of experts in sustainable planning and design. The plan is summarized below:

1. Institute a *Sustainable New Orleans* planning task force. This task force, comprised of leading national experts in sustainable development and community leaders from the New Orleans area, should develop a series of neighborhood, community, city, and regional plans over the next six to twelve months.
2. Pursue coastal and floodplain restoration as the number-one priority in rebuilding New Orleans. Rebuilding without addressing the fundamental hydrologic forces that influence this region would be folly.
3. Immediately establish *Sustainable New Orleans* enterprise-zone businesses to salvage and warehouse building materials. Even as the planning gets underway for rebuilding New Orleans, locally owned businesses that employ residents should be set up to deconstruct damaged buildings and recover materials that can be used in rebuilding.
4. Rebuild a levee system around the city that is second to none. If New Orleans is to be maintained in its present location, a levee system able to withstand Category 5 hurricanes and storm surges is critical. Where possible, the levees should be integrated into a perimeter park, providing a new recreational amenity to the city.
5. Create *Sustainable New Orleans* overlay zoning for the city to ensure that the goals of sustainability, safety, and urban vitality will be followed in the city's redevelopment. Emerging from the planning process outlined above, the zoning should provide for mixed uses, pedestrian access, energy efficiency, renewable energy systems that can help residents weather extended power outages, and a strong platform of building science for all construction.
6. Retain and restore those buildings that can be salvaged. While many of the buildings not leveled by the flooding will have to be demolished due to mois-

ture, mold, and structural damage, those buildings that can be detoxified and renovated should be salvaged.

7. Mandate or incentivize greenbuilding. The city, state, and federal governments, as well as insurance companies and banks, should encourage going well beyond minimum standards in the reconstruction of the city. Affordable housing should be built at least to Enterprise Foundation Green Communities standards, and public buildings should be required to meet LEED(R) Gold standards.

8. Work with ecologists and fisheries biologists to create more sustainable fisheries for the Gulf Coast. Because seafood is such an important element of New Orleans' economy and culture, and because local fisheries have suffered from heavy pollutant loadings, protecting and rebuilding those fisheries should be a high priority.

9. Clean up the new brownfields of New Orleans. The most ecologically responsible means, including bioremediation, phytoremediation, and ecological restoration, should be used to detoxify the pollutant-laden sediments left by the flooding.

10. Work with industry to clean up the factories along the Gulf Coast. As part of rebuilding efforts in the New Orleans region, partnerships should be forged among industry, government agencies, environmental organizations, and affected residents to find long-term solutions for greening the industries in this area, which is known as Cancer Alley.

New Orleans residents are engaged in collaboration with national organizations to green their public schools, universities, parks, hospitals, supermarkets, and churches. From our perspective in measuring the recovery of this city, significant progress is due in large measure not to government intervention but to the heart and soul of the city, its people, volunteers, and nongovernmental organizations that want to make a difference.

REFERENCES

BuildingGreen. 2005. *Environmental Building News Offers Ten-Point Plan for Rebuilding New Orleans.* October 4. Available at http://www.buildinggreen.com/press/new -orleans.cfm (accessed July 30, 2008).

Bullard, R. D. (ed.). 2005. *The Quest for Environmental Justice: Human Rights and the Politics of Pollution.* San Francisco: Sierra Club Books.

_____. 2007. *The Black Metropolis in the Twenty-First Century: Race, Power, and the Politics of Place.* New York: Rowman and Littlefield.

Bullard, R. D., and M. Harden. 2005. "Will 'Greening' the Gulf Coast After Katrina Help or Hurt Blacks?" November 10. Published by the Environmental Justice Resource Center at Clark Atlanta University. Available at http://www.ejrc.cau.edu/ greeningafterkatrina.html.

Bullard, R. D., and B. Wright. 2006. "Cleaning Up Toxic 'Time Bombs' Left Behind by Katrina." *Focus Magazine. Special Issue on Hurricane Katrina: Health Impacts in Louisiana, Joint Center for Political Studies* 34, no. 10 (February).

Dingerson, L., B. Miner, B. Peterson, and S. Walters. 2008. *Keeping the Promise?: The Debate Over Charter Schools.* Milwaukee: Rethinking Schools Ltd.

Hartman, C., and G. Squires. 2006. *There Is No Such Thing as a Natural Disaster: Race, Class and Hurricane Katrina.* New York: Routledge.

Klein, N. 2008. *The Shock Doctrine: The Rise of Disaster Capitalism.* New York: Picador.

Kromm, C., and S. Sturgis. 2008. *Hurricane Katrina and the Guiding Principles of Internal Displacement: A Global Human Rights Perspective on a National Disaster.* Durham, NC: Institute for Southern Studies. January.

Mathews, J. 2008. "Charter Schools' Big Experiment." *Washington Post.* June 9.

Nolan, B. 2005. "In Storm, N.O. Wants No One Left Behind." *Times-Picayune.* July 24.

ABOUT THE AUTHORS

Debra Lyn Bassett is Professor of Law and Judge Frank M. Johnson, Jr., Scholar at the University of Alabama School of Law. Author of four books and more than twenty law review articles, Professor Bassett's scholarship addresses two primary areas—issues of the federal courts, and the significance of place. Before teaching, she clerked for the Honorable Mary Schroeder, Chief Judge of the Ninth Circuit Court of Appeals, and practiced law with Morrison and Foerster in San Francisco.

Lisa K. Bates, Ph.D., is an Assistant Professor at the University of Illinois. Her research examines housing and neighborhood investment strategies in distressed urban areas, and includes following housing market recovery in New Orleans.

Robert D. Bullard, Ph.D., is the Edmund Asa Ware Distinguished Professor of Sociology and founding Director of the Environmental Justice Resource Center at Clark Atlanta University. His most recent books include *The Quest for Environmental Justice: Human Rights and the Politics of Pollution* (Sierra Club Books, 2005), *Growing Smarter: Achieving Livable Communities, Environmental Justice, and Regional Equity* (MIT Press, 2007), and *The Black Metropolis in the Twenty-First Century: Race, Power, and the Politics of Place* (Rowman & Littlefield, 2007).

Rachel Godsil teaches Equality Under American Law, Property, and Zoning and Land Use Policy at Seton Hall University School of Law. Professor Godsil has been involved in environmental justice law and policy, and has recently been working with attorneys representing the South Camden Citizens in Action. Professor Godsil has written extensively on the convergence of race, poverty, and the environment.

Rebekah A. Green, Ph.D., is a research associate at the Institute for Global and Community Resilience at Western Washington University, where she works on disaster resilience. She received her Ph.D. from Cornell University, studying earthquake vulnerability and risk perceptions in Istanbul, Turkey. During a post-doctoral fellowship at Columbia University, she worked with low-income survivors of Hurricane Katrina to develop recovery plans.

Albert Huang is an environmental justice attorney with the New York office of the Natural Resources Defense Council (NRDC). In addition to litigation, his work focuses on regional and national environmental justice policy advocacy and development. Prior to joining NRDC, Mr. Huang was a policy advocate at the Environmental Health Coalition, a community-based grassroots organization located in California, where he worked on water quality, environmental justice, and energy issues.

Glenn S. Johnson is a research associate in the Environmental Justice Resource Center and associate professor in the Department of Sociology and Criminal Justice at Clark Atlanta University. He is co-editor of *Just Transportation: Dismantling Race and Class Barriers to Mobility* (New Society Publishers, 1997), *Sprawl City: Race, Politics, and Planning in Atlanta* (Island Press, 2000), and *Highway Robbery: Transportation Racism & New Routes to Equity* (South End Press, 2004).

Rita J. King is an award-winning investigative reporter and the author of *Big, Easy Money: Disaster Profiteering on the American Gulf Coast,* a report that exposed widespread corruption after Hurricane Katrina. She is currently a Senior Fellow at the Carnegie Council for Ethics in International Affairs and the CEO and Creative Director of Dancing Ink Productions, a company that fosters the evolution of a new global culture in the Imagination Age.

Mafruza Khan is an independent consultant based in New York City and former Deputy Director of the Center for Social Inclusion, an applied research organization working to build a fair and just society by dismantling structural racism.

John R. Logan is Professor of Sociology at Brown University. He is co-author or editor of many books, including *Urban Fortunes: The Political Economy of Place* (University of California Press, 1987), *Beyond the City Limits: Urban Policy and Economic Restructuring in Comparative Perspective* (Temple University Press, 1990), *Family Ties: Enduring Relations Between Parents and Their Grown Children* (Temple University Press, 1996), *The New Chinese City: Globalization and Market Reform* (Blackwell, 2002), and *Urban China in Transition* (Blackwell, 2007).

Marc H. Morial is a former mayor of New Orleans and the current President and CEO of the National Urban League, the nation's largest and oldest civil rights and direct services organization empowering African Americans and other ethnic communities. Morial has helped thrust the League into the forefront of major public policy issues, research, and effective community-based solutions.

Earthea Nance, Ph.D., is an environmental engineer and scholar of urban environmental studies. She is currently the Director of Infrastructure and Environmental Planning for the Mayor's Office of Recovery Management, City of New Orleans.

Mtangulizi Sanyika, Ph.D., is on the faculty at Dillard University in New Orleans, where he teaches courses in African World Studies, Global Encounters, and Research and Writing. He has previously taught at Harvard, Massachusetts Institute of Technology, Brown, University of Massachusetts, University of California, Berkeley, and the OUT in Tanzania, and East Africa.

Gina Solomon, M.D., is a senior scientist at Natural Resources Defense Council and a physician with dual specialties in internal medicine and occupational/environmental medicine.

Denise Strong is Assistant Professor in the Department of Political Science at the University of New Orleans. Her research interests include public/partnerships and workforce development.

Angel O. Torres is a GIS Training Specialist with the Environmental Justice Resource Center at Clark Atlanta University. He has a Master's Degree in City Planning from Georgia Institute of Technology, with a concentration in GIS. He co-edited *Sprawl City: Race, Politics, and Planning in Atlanta* (Island Press, 2000) and *Highway Robbery: Transportation Racism & New Routes to Equity* (South End Press, 2004).

Sheila J. Webb, Ph.D., R.N., CNS, serves as Director of the Center for Empowered Decision Making and Associate Clinical Director at EXCELth, Inc. Dr. Webb is a Clinical Nurse Specialist. She holds a Bachelor of Science Degree in Nursing from Dillard University, a Master of Science Degree in Nursing from the University of Southern Mississippi at Hattiesburg, and the Doctor of Philosophy Degree in Nursing from Southern University and A & M College in Baton Rouge, Louisiana.

Robert K. Whelan is Visiting Professor, University of Texas–Arlington, and Professor Emeritus, University of New Orleans, Urban and Public Affairs.

Beverly Wright, Ph.D., is a sociologist and the founding director of the Deep South Center for Environmental Justice (DSCEJ) at Dillard University New Orleans. She is co-chair of the National Black Environmental Justice Network and the Environmental Justice Climate Change (EJCC) Initiative. Her most recent publications include *In the Wake of the Storm: Environment, Disaster, and Race After Katrina* (Russell Sage Foundation, 2006) and *Toxic Wastes and Race at Twenty: 1987–2007* (United Church of Christ, 2007). She is a native of New Orleans and a survivor of Hurricane Katrina.

INDEX

AAA (African American Agenda), 91
AALP (African-American Leadership Project), 91–92, 95–100, 102, 103, 110n8, 111n9
ACORN (Association of Community Organizations for Reform Now), 198, 234
ACORN Housing Corporation (AHC), 198–199, 234, 238, 243
Acquisition Solutions Inc., 175–176
"Active status" contractors, 172
Advancement Project, 107–108, 178–179
AFL-CIO job training program, 197
African American Agenda (AAA), 91
African American middle-class community, xxi, 7, 22, 38–40, 119. *See also* New Orleans East
African Americans, 87, 108–110
  demographics from 2000 census, 186
  disadvantaged business enterprises of, 99–100
  exclusion from rebuilding plans, 94, 95
  and Jim Crow laws, 117
  loss of HBCUs, 268
  physical isolation from jobs, 65–66
  result of Road Home policies, 241–242
  risk of storm-related damage and losses, 2, 145–147
  See also Racial injustice
African-American Leadership Project (AALP), 91–92, 95–100, 102, 103, 110n8, 111n9
Agriculture Street Landfill, 23–25, 118, 120, 126, 154
AHC (ACORN Housing Corporation), 198–199, 234, 238, 243
Air quality, 42, 126–127
Allbaugh, Joseph, 171

America Speaks, 183, 184, 216
Americold Logistics of Atlanta, 172–173
Annie E. Casey Foundation, 187
Appropriate technology principle, 159–160
Army Corps of Engineers, 6, 38–39, 40–41, 155, 191, 266
Arsenic levels in soil, 34, 123
Asbestos monitoring, 34, 42
AshBritt company, 171–172, 175
Ashdown, Keith, 172–173
Association of Community Organizations for Reform Now (ACORN), 198, 234
Automobile ownership statistics, 66–69

Baker, Richard, 29, 197, 224n12
Baker bill, 197–198
Bankruptcy laws, 58
Barthelemy, Sidney, 89, 184–185
Baton Rouge, 5, 71, 146–147
Bechtel, 176, 180
Bioremediation, 273
Black Enterprise Magazine, 7
Black Social Scientists, 224–225n14
Black Sunday, xxii
Blakely, Edward, 107, 185, 200
Blanco, Kathleen, 196
Bond, Mississippi, 52
Breast cancer diagnoses, 140–141, 142, 143
Bring New Orleans Back (BNOB) Commission, 95, 99, 110n7, 147, 184, 214–215, 217–219, 256–257
Brookings Institution, 30, 189, 198, 199, 226n17, 249
Brown, Michael, 74, 93, 173, 176, 181
BuildingGreen, 272–273
Burns, Peter, 187–188